BASEBALL
DYNASTIES

BASEBALL
DYNASTIES

THE GREATEST TEAMS OF ALL TIME

Rob Neyer and Eddie Epstein

W. W. Norton & Company   New York • London

Excerpt from *The October Heroes: Great World Series Games Remembered By the Men Who Played Them* by Donald Honig reprinted by permission of the University of Nebraska Press. Copyright © 1979 by Donald Honig.

For information about permission to reproduce selections from this book, write to Permissions, W. W. Norton and Company, Inc., 500 Fifth Avenue, New York, NY 10110

The text of this book is composed in Weiss
with the display set in Copperplate and Trade Gothic
Composition by Allentown Digital Services Division of R.R. Donnelley & Sons Company
Manufacturing by Haddon Craftsmen
Book design by Chris Welch

Library of Congress Cataloging-in-Publication Data

Neyer, Rob.
Baseball dynasties: the greatest teams of all time / Rob Neyer and Eddie Epstein.
p. cm.
ISBN 0-393-04894-2—ISBN 0-393-32008-1 (pbk.)
1. Major League Baseball (Organization)   2. Baseball teams—United States—Statistics.
I. Epstein, Eddie.   II. Title.

GV875.A1 N49 2000
796.357'164'0973—dc21   99-056940

W. W. Norton & Company, Inc., 500 Fifth Avenue, New York, N.Y. 10110
www.wwnorton.com

W. W. Norton & Company Ltd., 10 Coptic Street, London WC1A 1PU

1 2 3 4 5 6 7 8 9 0

ACKNOWLEDGMENTS

We are grateful to the many people who assisted in the making of this book. Our thanks to:

The staff at the National Baseball Library in Cooperstown, New York, especially Bill Francis and Bruce Markusen. Bill Burdick assisted in the acquisition of photos from the Hall of Fame's archives;

Bill Deane, who read every page of the manuscript and found errors on nearly all of them. If you're writing a baseball book and you haven't talked to Bill, then you need to;

Dave Smith, who was, as usual, generous with his time while sharing with us the vast resources of Retrosheet, one of the last bastions of nonprofit baseball research around (not to mention the best);

Pete Palmer, a kind and generous man who has, to our knowledge, never failed to assist a baseball researcher in need. Pete has helped both of us in many ways great and small over the years, and for this book he provided the sacrifice-hit data that appear in the chapter on the 1970 Orioles;

Bill James, Davey Johnson, and George Will, all of whom took the time to read portions of the manuscript, and had nice things to say about it;

our agent, Jay Mandel, without whom this book would not exist;

and our wonderful editor, Patricia Chui, whose early interest in the project kept us going and whose continuing interest in the project got the book in the stores before Opening Day.

Eddie Epstein extends a heartfelt thanks to Brad Adler, Lon Babby, Bob Flanagan, Calvin Hill, Gary Lazarus, Ken Nigro, Alan Ostfield, and Ross Salawitch.

Rob Neyer is particularly grateful to have friends and colleagues like Jim Baker, Jan Boyd, Kathleen Kinder, John Marvel, Pat Quinn, Geoff Reiss, Lisa Roullard, David Schoenfield, and Bob Valvano, all of whom were exceptionally patient and supportive through the many months during which this book was put together.

Contents

Order Out of Chaos

The Greatest Team of All Time. For baseball fans, those six words carry a wonderful resonance, right up there with *World Series* and *Babe Ruth.*

The question—*Which team was the greatest ever?*—is perhaps with us more now than ever before, thanks to both the 1998 New York Yankees and the impending end of the century. These days, it seems, "greatest ever" lists are nearly as common as millennium alarmists.

But why? Why do we debate this topic endlessly; why do so many of us care so much; why do fans, writers, and ex-players alike become so passionate about the subject? One reason is that sports fans generally admire great achievement. Following a great team or, for that matter, a great golfer or a great racehorse, appeals to us because it relates to the striving for perfection that exists in almost all of us. Too, most sports fans are by nature opinionated, and since no one can "prove" who is the best, that leaves room for debate, and debate is something to occupy those long winter months between the World Series and spring training (or, for that matter, those long hours between the last out of yesterday's game and the first pitch of tonight's).

Finally, people like to rank things to make order out of disorder. Baseball history, particularly the details, is long and incomprehensible to almost everybody. Compiling and ranking the greatest teams of all time is simply another way to reduce the level of chaos.

Speaking of creating chaos, this certainly isn't the first book purporting to list and rank the greatest teams. So what makes this one different? Well, we hope we've brought a more enlightened approach to the subject. Most of those other books are either based solely on the writer's subjective opinion, or they're based on arbitrary and simplistic statistical analysis. Also, they all come to the same conclusion—that the 1927 New York Yankees were the Greatest of Them All.

Although it might be nice to somehow guarantee a different answer, thus separating us from our predecessors, we are making no such guarantees. In fact, any discussion of the greatest baseball team of all time probably *should* start with the 1927 Yankees. The problem is that the '27 Yankees have never really been held up to a rigorous examination. If, after such an examination, the Bronx Bombers come out on top, so be it. (We're withholding our conclusion until the end of the book.) But they've got some pretty stiff competition, that's for sure.

What do we look for in a great team? First, let's discard the popular myth that holds that the truly good teams are the ones that win the close games. That's complete bullshit. Since 1900, teams playing .600 or better in a season have an aggregate winning percentage of .633. What was their winning percentage in one-run games? The myth would say higher than .633; the truth is .580. In games decided by four or more runs, this same group of teams has a winning percentage of .686. Truly great teams win their fair share of close games, sure, but what they *really* do is blow away their competition. So when you're looking for a great team, you look for a club with a great record *and* a run differential consistent with that record.

Another criterion, although not a major one, is that the teams have some true star(s) and league leaders. And, of course, postseason performance must be considered. It's also important that a team be something more than a one-year wonder. Those teams, even if they have great numbers all the way around, are more likely to have been the beneficiary of some out-of-context seasons by some of their players and thus are not fundamentally as excellent as their one-season record might suggest. Probably the best example is the 1984 Tigers, who truly dominated the American League, then cruised through the postseason. But how good were they, deep down, given their failure to win even a division title in 1983 or 1985? Or, for that matter, in 1982 or 1986? So although we've focused on single seasons, you'll also see records and stats for two- and three-season periods, and references to even longer spans, within the team chapters.

We'll get a bit more specific about our methods later in this introduction and later in the book, but first we'd like to point out another approach that makes this book different, and we hope better, than those that have come before. Most of the other books on the greatest teams look at the clubs in something of a vacuum. You know, here are the 1927 Yankees, here's the lineup, here's how many runs they scored, here's how many games they won, yada yada yada. But baseball teams don't exist in vacuums. They must be examined within the context of their individual seasons, within the context of their eras, and within the context of baseball's entire history. This brings to mind James Burke and his television show, *Connections*. Burke is probably not a baseball fan, but he might appreciate all the connections in baseball, which is one of the best things about the sport. Just as an example, in Chapter 6, which discusses the great Philadelphia Athletics teams of the late 1920s and early 1930s, we've included an article on the great Baltimore Orioles teams of the early 1920s, which were eventually a source for much of the Athletics' talent. Even though we're only writing extensively about fifteen or so teams, we'll touch on enough peripheral but related subjects to give you a decent flavor of a large portion of the game's history.

As for the methods we've used, it's important to note that comparing teams from different eras is not as easy as you might think. For relatively modern times, of course, we can use a simple ratio of performance—for example, a player's OPS (on-base percentage plus slugging percentage) divided by the league average. However, as we have moved through time, something has happened that can skew such ratios if you're trying to make historical comparisons. Without getting too technical about it, the dispersion, or distribution, of performance for players and teams has gotten smaller.

This is an extraordinarily important point. If we take the performance of two players seventy years apart and notice (for example) that they're both 20 percent more productive than the league average, does that mean their performances were identical? No, it doesn't. Not even considering the numerous qualitative changes that have taken place in baseball, the fact that there is less dispersion in modern times makes such a direct, unadjusted comparison something less than valid.

The best measure of dispersion, or spread, is something called *standard deviation*. Let's say we have two groups of numbers: the first is 1,2,3,4,5; the second is 1,3,3,4,4. The mean, or average, of both groups is 3.0. However, the second group is bunched closer together than the first group. In the same way, modern performance, both team and individual, tends to be more closely bunched together in a given modern season than it was earlier in the century.

Standard deviation simply puts a number on the bunching. The smaller the deviation, the more bunched the numbers. For example, the standard deviation of our first group of numbers is 1.4, but for the second group it's 1.1. (If you really want to know how that's calculated, see the Glossary of Statistical Terms.) Two players from two different eras could both be 20 percent better than their league, but could and probably will not have the same distance from the average if measured by how many standard deviations they are from the average.

Let's look at a team example. If one team scored 800 runs in a season with a league mean of 700, then they were about 14 percent above average. If the standard deviation of runs scored for that league in that season was 100 runs, then that team was 1 standard deviation above average.

Suppose another team sixty years later also scored 800 runs in a season with a league average of 700. They would be 14 percent above average, just like the first team, but what you would almost certainly find is that the standard deviation would be smaller than 100 runs, probably closer to 70. So, instead of being just 1 standard deviation better than average, this team would actually be 1.4 standard deviations better than average, which is obviously more impressive.

What we do in this book is use *standard deviation from the league mean* as the primary statistical method for evaluating teams. Of course, we're not going to rate teams solely on the basis of standard deviations because they're not the last word in winning ballgames. Standard deviations are always in the forefront of the discussion, though.

Before we get started, we should probably mention our immense debt to Bill James. The ways in which we think about baseball are largely a result of Bill's writings, and anyone familiar with his work will also notice some similarities in format and, to a lesser extent, methods between this book and some of Bill's books.

We're eager to jump right into our 15 teams, but we'll all be better off if you can spend a few minutes with the glossary that follows this introduction. It won't take long, and it will lay the groundwork for the statistics described throughout the book.

GLOSSARY OF
STATISTICAL TERMS

For the most part, the statistics and terms used in this book will be familiar to even casual baseball fans. However, a few might be unfamiliar, and it doesn't hurt to supply the actual formulae even for the ones with which readers may be familiar.

This might also be a good time to suggest that anyone reading this book keep a good baseball encyclopedia close at hand. *Total Baseball*, the *STATS All-Time Major League Handbook*, and the *STATS All-Time Baseball Sourcebook* were all prime sources for the statistics used throughout this book, and we heartily recommend all three.

Standard Deviation (SD)
SD (in statistics textbooks, abbreviated simply as S) is the most commonly used measure of the dispersion of a group of numbers. Using the example given in the Introduction, if group A is 1,2,3,4,5 and group B is 1,3,3,4,4, then both groups have an average, or mean, of 3.0, but group A has an SD of 1.4 whereas group B has an SD of 1.1. Group A is more widely dispersed than group B.

The concept of SD is important when making historical comparisons in baseball because, through time, the SD of performance for players and teams has tended to get smaller.

Standard Deviation Score

A measure of a team's performance in a given season, relative to its league, uses its runs scored and runs allowed totals and how many SDs from the mean (or average) those totals were.

Let's work through the 1927 Yankees. The '27 Yankees scored 975 runs, the league mean was about 762, and the SD of team runs scored in the 1927 American League was about 115 runs. Taking the Yankees' difference from the league average (975 minus 762 equals 213) and dividing by the SD (115), the 1927 Yankees were 1.85 SD above the league mean in runs scored. The '27 Yankees allowed 599 runs, and the SD in runs allowed in the American League that year was about 88.5 runs. The Yankees allowed 163 runs fewer (better) than the league average, and dividing that by the SD (88.5) tells us that they were 1.84 SD above the league mean in runs allowed. Adding 1.85 to 1.84 gives us a +3.69 SD score for the 1927 Yankees, which is outstanding. (If you've got a computer, a baseball encyclopedia, and some time on your hands, it's easy to figure SD scores.)

An SD score of +3.00 or higher for a season is very good. Through 1998, just 37 teams had reached +3.00 for a single season. The 78 teams in this century that won 100 or more games averaged a +2.77 SD score. An SD score of 0.00 would represent an average team. Negative SD scores represent below-average teams. Get used to SD scores; you're going to see a lot of them in this book.

Why don't we just depend on team winning percentage, a simpler statistic? Because if you make a list of the teams with the best winning percentages, for the most part they're all from the first third of the twentieth century. SD scores, on the other hand, result in a nice mix of teams from all years. If you don't believe us, take a look at the Appendix, where we list the top 50 and bottom 50 SD scores for one-, two-, three-, four-, and five-season spans.

Pythagorean Method

The Pythagorean method is used to figure how many games a team typically would have won, given its runs scored and allowed. Most teams finish within four wins of their Pythagorean projection. Here's the formula:

$$\text{Pythagorean winning percentage} = \frac{(\text{runs scored}^{1.83})}{(\text{runs scored}^{1.83} + \text{runs allowed}^{1.83})}$$

Note that runs scored and runs allowed are weighted equally. (So much for the notion that "baseball is 75 percent pitching.") So when we write that a team has "outperformed" or "under-performed" its Pythagorean projection, we mean that it won or lost more games than predicted by its runs scored and allowed. In 1998, for example, the New York Yankees scored 965 runs and allowed 656. Plugging those numbers into this formula yields a projected winning percentage of .670 and projected record of 108-54. The Yankees' actual record was 114-48, meaning that they outperformed their Pythagorean projection by six games.

Offensive Winning Percentage (OW%)
OW% is an estimate of what a team's winning percentage would be if all of its players hit like this player and the team allowed an average number of runs. This puts the player's performance in the context of his home ballpark and league. For example, Frank Chance had an ROV (see explanation of Real Offensive Value) of .338 in 1906. That number is adjusted for ballpark. His OW% was .825. In 1939, Joe DiMaggio's ROV was .406, but a very comparable .830 OW%. Obviously, in terms of run production, the 1939 American League was worlds apart from the 1906 National League.

The comparison to the league average includes pitcher batting, where applicable, so some people might say that all of these OW% numbers are too high because the offensive performance of position players is being compared, in part, to the offensive performance of pitchers. However, it is true that if all nine players produced runs at the rate of eight per game in a four-runs-per-game league, then the team's winning percentage would most likely be .780.

On-Base Percentage (OBP)
OBP is one of the two most important offensive statistics, along with slugging percentage, and correlates much better with both run production and winning than does batting average.

On-base percentage = $(H + W + HBP)/(AB + W + HBP + SF)$,

where H is hits, W is walks, HBP is hit by pitch, AB is at-bats, and SF is sacrifice flies.

On-Base plus Slugging (OPS)

OPS is simply short for "on-base percentage plus slugging percentage," which combines the two most important offensive statistics.

Real Offensive Value (ROV)

ROV is the expression of a player's batting line in a number that looks like and has the same standards as batting average but is a number that correlates far better with scoring runs and winning games than batting average.

Except for players with very low values of runs created per 27 outs (RC/27), $ROV = .0345 + .1054\sqrt{(RC/27)}$. ROV is adjusted for ballpark context by adjusting the RC/27 value for the player's home ballpark. Not that it matters very much, but the "real" ROV uses a different method for getting to the RC/27 step, but because the RC/27 values are available for every player in the *STATS All-Time Major League Handbook*, we decided to use those values and save us oodles of time.

Runs Created (RC)

Invented by Bill James, RC is an attempt to summarize all statistical contributions made by a hitter. The formula, including all data available in the 1990s, is:

$$(H + BB + HBP–CS–GIDP) \times [\text{total bases} + .26(TBB–IBB + HBP) + .52(SH + SF + SB)] / (AB + TBB + HBP + SH + SF),$$

where H is hits, BB is bases on balls, CS is caught stealing, GIDP is grounded into double plays, TBB is total bases on balls, IBB is intentional bases on balls, HBP is hit by pitch, SH is sacrifice hits, SF is sacrifice flies, SB is stolen bases, and AB is at-bats. The all-time leaders in RC are Babe Ruth (2,847), Ty Cobb (2,810), Stan Musial (2,625), Henry Aaron (2,550), and Ted Williams (2,538).

Slugging Percentage

Slugging percentage is a measure of power, though a player with a high batting average and not much power can sport a respectable slugging percentage. Essentially, slugging percentage is simply total bases divided by at-bats, but if you don't have total bases you can figure slugging percentage like this:

$$(\text{Hits} + \text{doubles} + 2 \times \text{triples} + 3 \times \text{home runs}) / (\text{at-bats})$$

Just as .300 is traditionally the benchmark for batting average, .500 is the benchmark for slugging percentage, though of course you have to consider the context of the era. For example, in 1906 Harry Lumley led the National League with a .477 slugging percentage, and in 1998 Mark McGwire led the National League with a .752 slugging percentage. So again, .500 is just a loose guideline.

Save

There have been three different definitions of the save over the years, but only two matter for the purposes of this book. The save first became an official statistic in 1969 and was credited to any relief pitcher who finished a game his team won. That's still the definition used for all pitchers prior to 1970. From 1970 on, the qualifications are a bit tougher and can be found in any current rulebook. A pitcher is credited with a save when he is the finishing, but not winning, pitcher and he has pitched at least one inning with no more than a three-run lead; or, when entering the game, the potential tying run is at-bat, on base, or on deck; or he pitches effectively for at least three innings.

Total Player Rating (TPR)

TPR is defined in *Total Baseball* as "the sum of a player's Adjusted Batting Runs, Fielding Runs, and Base Stealing Runs, minus his positional adjustment, all divided by the Runs per Win factor for that year." Essentially, TPR attempts to summarize all of a player's statistics and arrive at a number of games he was better (or worse) than an average player at the same position. Through the 1996 season, 104 players had posted single-season TPRs of 6.6 or better.

Total Pitcher Index (TPI)

TPI is defined in *Total Baseball* as "the sum of a pitcher's Pitching Runs . . . Batting Runs (in the A.L. since 1973, zero), and Fielding Runs, all divided by the Runs Per Win factor for that year; abbreviated as TPI." Much like TPR, TPI summarizes a pitcher's statistical contributions in one number, describing that pitcher's contribution in victories relative to an average pitcher in the league. In the modern era, the top TPI typically ranges between 4.0 and 7.0. Through the 1996 season, only 20 pitchers had posted an 8.0-plus TPI, all of them coming before 1945, and 10 of them coming in the nineteenth century.

BASEBALL
DYNASTIES

CHAPTER 1

1906 Chicago Cubs

Chicago has had some great baseball aggregations. It would be a safe bet that if a vote were taken among the fans of Chicago as to which team was the greatest that represented the city, the vote would favor the Frank Chance team of two decades ago. There are thousands of fans outside of Chicago who think the same way, who believe the Chicago Cubs from 1905 until 1910 were about as powerful and successful a team as the game ever had.

—MacLean Kennedy in *The Greatest Teams of Baseball*

Record: 116-36, .763 (1st)*
Two-Year (1906–07): 223-81, .734 (1st)
Three-Year (1906–08): 322-136, .703
  (1st)

SD Score: 3.73 (2d)*
Two-Year: 6.29 (7th)
Three-Year: 8.20 (11th)

Results:
1906 National League Champions
1907 World Champions
1908 World Champions

Days in First Place: 147 of 179;
  clinched on September 19

Longest Winning Streak: 14 games
Longest Losing Streak: 3 games

*Throughout the book, win-loss record and SD score rankings are for all teams in the twentieth century.

1906 Chicago Cubs *(National Baseball Hall of Fame Library, Cooperstown, NY)*

The Pennant Race: On the evening of July 29, 1906, the Cubs sat atop the National League standings with a brilliant 61-26 record, but that was good for just a five-game lead over the Pittsburgh Pirates. No matter. The Cubs went 55-10 the rest of the way and finished with a 20-game edge over the second-place New York Giants.

Against the Contenders: There were really only three contenders, not only in 1906 but in the entire decade. From 1901 through 1910 nine pennants were available, and the Cubs (four times), Pirates (four times), and Giants (twice) won all of them. That domination continued into the next decade because it wasn't until 1914 that another N.L. club (the Braves) broke the Big Three's collective headlock on the flag.

In 1905 the Cubs finished in third place, 13 games behind the Giants and four games behind Pittsburgh.

In 1906 the Cubs took 15 of 22 from the Giants and 16 of 21 from the Bucs, who finished second and third, respectively. That's what you call "making a statement."

Runs Scored: 705 (1st)*

The Giants ranked second, with 625 runs scored.

Runs Allowed: 381 (1st)*

Those 381 runs are the fewest allowed by a team in the twentieth century. The third-place Pittsburgh Pirates ranked second, allowing 470 runs. It's astounding not that the Cubs led the National League in both runs scored and allowed, but that they did it by such hefty margins.

Pythagorean Record: 115-37

This number is perhaps even more incredible than the Cubs' actual record because most teams with stupendous records over-achieve somewhat, relative to their runs scored and allowed. But the Cubs won almost exactly as many games as they "should have."

Manager: Frank Chance

A fine hitter, baserunner, and defensive first baseman, Chance was most famous for his leadership. His nickname, "The Peerless Leader," became so ingrained that newspaper writers eventually just started referring to him as "the P.L."

Regular Lineup:

Player	Position	ROV	OW%
Jimmy Slagle	CF	.246	.555
Jimmy Sheckard	LF	.266	.635
Wildfire Schulte	RF	.266	.634
Frank Chance	1B	.338	.825
Harry Steinfeldt	3B	.312	.770
Joe Tinker	SS	.224	.456
Johnny Evers	2B	.246	.555

*Throughout the book, rankings for runs scored and runs allowed are for the single season.

Pitching Twins

Cubs righthanders Orvie Overall and Jack Taylor were the same pitcher in 1906. As we've noted elsewhere in this chapter, both came to the Cubs in summer trades. Once in Chicago, Overall went 12-3. So did Taylor. Overall pitched 18 games, 144 innings. Taylor pitched 17 games, 147 innings. Overall posted a 1.88 ERA; Taylor's was 1.84. Overall allowed 116 hits. So did Taylor. Overall tossed two shutouts. So did Taylor. Overall allowed 30 runs. So did Taylor. The only real differences between the two? Overall was seven years younger than Taylor, and he struck out 60 more hitters (94 versus 34).—*Rob*

Player	Position	ROV	OW%
Johnny Kling	C	.295	.728
Miner Brown	P		

Top to bottom, a solid lineup, with all but one regular posting a .500+ OW%, and three were over .700.

Bench: Pat Moran backed up Johnny Kling, who was generally regarded as one of the top two catchers in the National League (along with New York's Roger Bresnahan). Solly Hofman played 23 games in the outfield plus every infield position, and in the World Series he took over in center field for Jimmy Slagle, who was suffering from a bruised chest and something called "intercostal neuralgia."

Scouting the Pitchers: Mordecai Peter Centennial Brown (26-6, 1.04), better known as "Three Finger" Brown ranked as one of the game's great hurlers. Despite missing half of his index finger, which is, for most pitchers, a vitally important digit, Brown thrived on the mound. In fact, most observers credited his "handicap" with making Brown the pitcher that he was. His overhand curveball, which broke sharply down and away from right-handed batters, was practically unhittable.

Jack Pfiester (20-8, 1.56) didn't feature a big repertoire, mostly fastballs and curves, but he delivered his pitches from a bewildering array of angles, submarine to overhand and everything in between.

Johnny Evers once described Ed Reulbach (19-4, 1.65) as "near a physically perfect man as possible," and Reulbach often dazzled hitters with his hard curve. (In 1908 Reulbach set a record that has never been equaled, tossing two shutouts in one day.)

How Were They Built? Frank Chance would attain fame as the first baseman and manager of the Cubs, but when he joined the club in 1898 he was a twenty-year-old catcher. In 1901, Johnny Kling—regarded by some as the top defensive backstop of the decade—took over behind the plate, and Chance shifted to the outfield.

Frank Selee was hired as manager for the 1902 season, and he suggested that Chance move once again, this time to first base. According to Johnny Evers, Chance threatened to retire rather than play first, but finally agreed after being granted a pay raise.

Joe Tinker was purchased from the Portland (Pacific Northwest League) club after the 1901 season. He'd played both shortstop and third base, but Selee immediately installed Tinker at shortstop.

Mordecai Brown came to the Cubs after the 1903 season in a trade that sent Jack Taylor and Larry McLean to the Cardinals. Brown had gone just 9-13 in his first and only season with St. Louis, but his 2.60 ERA wasn't far from the league leaders. (Interestingly, Taylor—who would return to Chicago in 1906—had been the Cubs' top winner in 1903 and was available only because then-owner Jim Hart suspected him of throwing a game in a 1903 postseason exhibition series against the White Sox.)

Scout George Huff signed Notre Dame prospect Ed Reulbach, who would win 136 games and lose only 65 as a Cub. Huff also recommended outfielder Wildfire Schulte and utility man Solly Hofman.

In the middle of the 1905 season, Selee's tuberculosis, one symptom of which was violent coughing fits, made it impossible for him to continue managing the club. According to Johnny Evers, Selee let the players vote on who should captain the Cubs on the field. Catcher Johnny Kling garnered two votes, third baseman Doc Casey four, and Frank Chance won going away with eleven votes. (Selee moved to Colorado in August, and owner Jim Hart officially named Chance manager.)

After that season, Chance got rid of Casey and speedy right fielder Billy Maloney, and replaced them with Harry Steinfeldt (from Cincinnati) and Jimmy Sheckard (from Brooklyn). Both played regularly and well in 1906.

Once Steinfeldt was on board, Chance reportedly remarked that if he could just add a little pitching strength the team would win the pennant. So Scott Huff recommended Jack Pfiester, who was promptly purchased for $2,500.

As if they weren't doing well enough once the 1906 season got going, Chance made a couple of fine midseason trades. First, on June 2 he picked up righthander Orval Overall from the Reds in exchange for Bob Wicker and two thousand dollars. Overall had gone just 3-5 with Cincinnati, but he went 12-3 for the Cubs, and then from 1907 through 1910 he went 70-36. A month after acquiring Overall, Chance re-acquired Jack Taylor from the Cardinals. Taylor also went 12-3 after returning to Chicago.

What Brought Them Down? Nothing, really. They finished second in 1909, but it was a brilliant second, as the Cubbies won 104 games and simply couldn't match the awesome Pittsburgh Pirates, winners of 110.

The Cubs were back on top in 1910, but fell to the Philadelphia Athletics in a quick five-game World Series. Then began a slow decline, as the stars of the "aughts" grew old and no replacements were available.

Most Valuable Cub: Three Finger Brown was arguably the best pitcher of the decade, and 1906 marked his best season. Brown's 1.04 ERA still stands as the third-lowest in major league history.

Worst Regular: Center fielder Jimmy "Rabbit" Slagle was once described by Johnny Evers (or Hugh Fullerton, Evers' ghostwriter) as "one of the greatest judges of batters and the direction of their hits," but by 1906 (he turned thirty-three that July) Slagle was only a decent hitter. He remained more or less the regular through the 1908 campaign, yet didn't manage even a .300 slugging percentage in any of the Cubs' pennant-winning seasons.

Hall of Famers: Three Finger Brown was elected by the so-called old-timers committee in 1949, three years *after* Frank Chance, Johnny Evers, and Joe Tinker were elected by the same committee *en masse*. Go figure. On a happier note, in 1999 the Veterans Committee elected Frank Selee, some ninety years after his death.

Our Hall of Famers: Brown is clearly a Hall of Famer, and Selee was a brilliant manager who won five pennants in Boston before building the powerhouse in Chicago. But as for Chance, Evers, and Tinker . . . well, you gotta do some real manipulatin' to justify their enshrinements.

Still, it's not as though the 1906 Cubs were just a bunch of good players having great years. We're talking about a team that won four pennants in five years and posted the best five-year record (530-235) of any team this century. There's just no way that's luck.

The 1906 Cubs were, we believe, a club with a number of fine players who, for whatever reasons, simply didn't enjoy long enough careers to merit inclusion in the Hall of Fame. When healthy, Johnny

Kling was as good a catcher as there was. Jimmy Sheckard was a wonderful player when he wanted to be. Harry Steinfeldt and Wildfire Schulte were both talented fellows. Tinker and Evers and Chance were good and sometimes great, though they didn't prove particularly durable.

Essentially, the secret to the Cubs' success was that they had *zero* weak links, and that's something you can say about very few teams, even the ones in this book.

The Pennant Race: Believe it or not, the National League wasn't a foregone conclusion early on. On June 2, only three games separated the first-place Cubs from the fourth-place Phillies. And although the Cubs boasted a 61-26 record at the close of play on July 29, that was only good for a moderate lead over the Pirates (5½ games) and Giants (6 games).

And then they left everyone in the dust, with an amazing 55-10 record from July 30 through the end of the regular season. It's quite likely the best two months any team has ever had, or ever will have. The Cubs clinched on September 19, but by the end of August nobody else had a chance of winning anything but second place.

The 1906 World Series: See separate article, "The Big Shocker."

The Ballpark: The Cubs played their home games at West Side Park, a.k.a. West Side Grounds, at the corner of Polk and Lincoln (now Wolcott, if you're planning on taking a look). It was 340 feet down the left-field line and 316 down the right-field line, but a whopping 560 feet to straightaway center field.

The Cubs played at West Side Park from 1893 through 1915, at which time they moved to their current home, Wrigley Field. The Illinois State Hospital and Medical School now stands on the site of the old ballpark.

Books about the 1906 Cubs: Aside from the New York teams and perhaps the Red Sox, the Cubs are probably the most written-about team around. There are two primary sources for information about the dynastic Cubs: *Touching Second* (Chicago: Reilly & Britton, 1910), by Johnny Evers and Hugh Fullerton; and the Cubs entry in the Putnam series of team histories, written by Warren Brown.

Touching Second, which was probably written solely by Fullerton—perhaps the most perceptive sportswriter of his generation—is full of "inside dope" on the Cubs and other teams of the time (it was published after the 1909 season). The book compares favorably to Christy Mathewson's *Pitching in a Pinch* (New York: G. P. Putnam's and Sons, 1912), but for some reason doesn't have the same reputation. An original copy is prohibitively expensive, but one of these years some university press will reprint the book, and then you can have your very own.

Brown's book, *The Chicago Cubs* (New York: G. P. Putnam's Sons, 1946), is competently written, yet he somehow devotes just 17 of 248 pages to the 1906–08 Cubs.

Peter Golenbock's *Wrigleyville: A Magical History Tour of the Chicago Cubs* (New York: St. Martin's Press, 1996) has some good material and devotes fifty-odd pages to this club. However, much of the best stuff is simply lifted from (and attributed to) *Touching Second.*

The Hitless Wonders

The nickname "Hitless Wonders" was technically accurate, but misleading to a fault. True, the White Sox finished the 1906 campaign with a .230 batting average, the lowest in the American League. However, they also scored 570 runs, good for third-best in the loop, and ranked second in the league in road scoring.

How did they do it? Well, they led the league (by a wide margin) with 453 walks.

The Big Shocker

The World Series pitted the Chicago Cubs, dubbed "The Wonder Team," against the Chicago White Sox, the "Hitless Wonders" (see sidebar).

The Cubs, having won 23 more games than the Sox during the regular season, were of course installed as prohibitive favorites, perhaps three to one. The American Leaguers' chances were dimmed even further when their star shortstop, George Davis, began suffering from a sore back a few days before the Series and wasn't expected to play in the opener, if at all.

There was at least one dissenting voice, however. Hugh Fullerton, baseball scribe for the *Chicago Tribune,* forecast a White Sox victory. According to Fred Lieb in *The Story of the World Series,*

His city editor, Jim Keeley, thought Hughie was so screwy in picking the White Sox to win that he hesitated to print it. He did so only after Hughie predicted a day of rain after the third game, so people wouldn't take his prediction too seriously. There is a popular legend that Hughie even went right on the day of rain, but this is a bit of an exaggeration as the Series was played through six successive days, most of it in near-freezing weather with occasional snow flurries, but with no break in the schedule.

Mother Nature can be fickle in Chicago, and the World Series opened on October 9 under cold, gray, coal-polluted skies that occasionally spit out snow flurries.

With the Sox's George Davis out of the lineup, regular third baseman Lee Tannehill shifted to shortstop, with utility man George "Whitey" Rohe moving to third. And with the game still scoreless, Rohe led off the fifth inning with a triple to deep left field off Three Finger Brown. After a strikeout, Rohe slid home with the game's first run when Brown fielded a grounder but Johnny Kling dropped his throw to the plate. The Sox scored once more in the sixth, and that was enough as the Cubs were only able to muster a single run for themselves, also in the sixth. Brown and White Sox starter Nick Altrock both permitted only four hits, but Altrock earned the 2–1 victory, and the underdogs were on top, at least for a day.

Normalcy returned in game 2, as Ed Reulbach fired a one-hitter and the Cubs scored five unearned runs to beat the Sox, 7–1.

Game 3 belonged to Whitey Rohe and spitball pitcher Big Ed Walsh, as the latter allowed just two hits and struck out twelve Cubs, whereas the former accounted for all the scoring with a bases-loaded triple down the left-field line in the sixth inning. The Sox won 3–0.

The Cubs evened the series with a game 4 victory that featured a rematch of game 1 starters Brown and Altrock. Brown was at the top of his game, and he had to be because Altrock permitted only a single run, when Johnny Evers singled home Frank Chance in the top of the seventh. Through four games, "The Hitless Wonders" were almost literally so, having played the Cubs to a standstill despite an .097 team batting average (11-for-113).

Those four games had seen relatively sparse crowds, thanks to miserable weather. But with game 5 scheduled for the N.L. club's West Side Grounds, the temperature and attendance both rose significantly. Though the ballpark's official seating capacity was approximately 16,000 fans, the paid attendance for game 5 was 23,257. How? Well, in the early days of the century, when there were more paying customers than bleacher perches, the overflow would be directed to the perimeter of the playing field. Balls hit into such over-

With 83 walks, Fielder Jones ranked second in the league, and Ed Hahn was third with 72 (3 with the New York Highlanders, then 69 more after coming to the Sox). But it was more than just the walks. After all, even with all those free passes Chicago ranked fifth in the American League with a .301 on-base percentage, and their .286 slugging percentage was last. Those added up to a .587 OPS, also the worst in the league.

So again we ask, how did they do it? Well, the available evidence suggests that they hit exceptionally well with men on base. Given their statistics, the White Sox could have been expected to score 531 runs. But as we noted, they actually scored 570, and that difference of 39 must be partly explained by good clutch hitting.

The best example is George Davis, who is listed in *Total Baseball* as the major league leader in something called *clutch hitting index*, at 154, which means that Davis drove in 54 percent more runs than you'd expect from his hitting stats. Indeed, he finished third in the American League with 80 RBI, not bad for a thirty-five-year-old shortstop.—*Rob*

Wildfire's Arm

In the first edition of his *Historical Baseball Abstract,* Bill James wrote that Cubs right fielder Wildfire Schulte boasted the best throwing arm of the decade. Well, Schulte may well have had a great arm, but you sure can't tell from the stats. We made a list of all the men who played at least 400 games in the outfield from 1901 through 1909 and also noted their assists. Fifty-two outfielders qualified for the study, and they averaged 18.2 assists per 150 games. Schulte averaged 16.4 assists per 150 games, thirty-fifth best in the group.

Although Schulte might not have been the best-throwing right fielder around, he was nevertheless a hell of a player. Nobody hit many home runs in his day, but Schulte finished fourth in the National League in homers in

flow crowds were ground-rule doubles, and many important games were settled by such hits.

For example, the record books will tell you that in game 5, the two teams combined for eleven doubles (eight for the White Sox and three for the Cubs), and Sox second baseman Frank Isbell hit four all by himself, both of which still represent all-time World Series records. What the record books won't tell you is that at least three of those eleven doubles went into the crowd and might or might not have been doubles if not for the fans.

George Davis, who went 0-for-3 in his return to the lineup in game 4, came through with two doubles and three RBI in game 5. Whitey Rohe remained at third base and went 3-for-4 with an RBI. In addition to his four doubles, Isbell scored three runs. And with White Sox hurler Doc White tossing three scoreless innings in relief, the American Leaguers captured an 8–6 triumph.

For game 6, the Series returned to South Side Park, home of the White Sox, where, according to historian Lee Allen, "The crowd was huge and even more disorderly than on the day before. The paid attendance was 19,249, but there must have been at least 25,000 in the park. Hidden by the mob in the outfield, police tore boards off the fences and let fans in at one dollar a head. Ushers slipped hundreds more through side gates for a similar consideration."

On the brink of elimination, Frank Chance once again called on Brown, who had thrown so brilliantly just two days earlier. Another overflow crowd contributed to the result. In the first inning, after a hit by Davis had dropped into the edge of the crowd for a double, Wildfire Schulte, who had been waiting there for the ball, pointed his finger into a policeman's face and screamed, "He shoved me!"

Schulte's protestations aside, Brown simply didn't have anything. After two innings the Sox were up 7–1, and from there they coasted to an easy 8–3 victory to clinch their unlikely championship. Orvie Overall pitched effectively in relief for 6⅓ innings for the Cubs, so Chance was second-guessed for not starting Overall instead of Brown, but Overall had just tossed 5⅔ the day before.

Many had expected an easy time for the Cubs, and the White Sox dashed those plans early on. Still, with the Series tied at two games apiece, the Cubs had been in fine shape. But then the pitching fell apart. After allowing eight or more runs in only five games all season (and not at all since July 24), Cub pitchers permitted eight runs in both games 5 *and* 6, losing them both and thus the Series. In their defense, it's quite likely that the overflow crowds in both games inflated the scores, but of course the rules were the same for both teams.

In retrospect, Chance's selection of Miner Brown to start game 6, on just one day of rest, looks like the key tactical blunder of the Series. Although it's true that Brown permitted only six hits in his first 18 innings of Series work, it's also true that he'd been complaining of a tired arm for most of September, and he had not started a game on one day's rest even once during the regular season.

It's an old cliché, "Anything can happen in a short series," but it's nonetheless true. And perhaps it was even more true in the dead-ball era, when the scarcity of runs meant a game could quite easily turn on a single well-placed ground ball, a single mental mistake, and so on.

On the other hand, the 1906 Series wasn't simply a matter of the Sox squeaking by in the close games. They won game 1 by one run, game 3 by three, game 5 by two, and game 6 by five. Overall, the Sox outscored the Cubs 22–18 (and 21–11 if you ignore the game 2 blowout).

And what of Whitey Rohe, who smashed two triples in the Series after hitting only one during the regular season? In large part because of his performance against the Cubs, Rohe was installed as starting third baseman for the Sox in 1907. He batted .213 with two triples in 144 games and never played in the majors again. Hughie Fullerton? He parlayed his amazing prediction into a long-running arrangement whereby he provided World Series previews to newspapers all over the country. As for the Cubs, they didn't let this little setback bother them much, and they trounced the Detroit Tigers in each of the next two World Series.—Rob

Tinker to Evers to Chance (A Primer)

Before we even start, let's all be clear on the pronunciation of Johnny Evers' name—it's EE-vers, as in "Evers rhymes with beavers." (Please continue to pronounce "Tinker" and "Chance" as you always have.) Now, a couple of things about the "poem" published in the *New York Evening Mail* on July 10, 1910. First of all, the title is *not*

1906 (with 7), tied for first in 1910 (10), was first in 1911 (21!), and was second in 1912 (12). He could run, too.

Schulte's 1911 campaign was his finest, as he totaled more than 20 doubles (30), triples (21), and home runs (the aforementioned 21!). Schulte remains one of only five players in major league history to top 20 in all three categories. He also led the National League that season in RBI and slugging percentage, stole 23 bases, and won the league's first Chalmers Award, forerunner of the MVP.—*Rob and Eddie*

Stats 'n' Stuff

◆ On June 19, the Cubs exploded for 11 runs in the first inning against Giants aces Christy Mathewson and Joe McGinnity, on their way to a 19–0 laugher.

◆ Speaking of Jack Taylor, an impressive streak of his ended on August 13, when Brooklyn drove him from the mound in the third inning. That ended a record run that saw him finish 202 straight games, including

187 starts and 15 relief appearances. Over his ten-year career, Taylor would complete 278 of 286 starts.

◆ On August 7, the Cubs were awarded a forfeit victory over the Giants when New York manager John McGraw refused to allow umpire James Johnstone inside the ballpark. The day before, McGraw had been suspended indefinitely for abusing Johnstone during a game.

◆ Frank Chance led the National League with 57 stolen bases in 1906, and he remains one of only three first basemen this century to lead a major league in steals. (The others were Frank Isbell in 1901 and George Sisler in 1921, 1922, and 1927.)—*Rob*

Around the Majors

May 8 With his club thinned by injuries, Philadelphia Athletics manager Connie Mack sends pitcher Chief Bender to left field in the sixth inning. Bender hits two home runs,

"Give this to Evers and see that he passes it on to Chance when he's finished."

"Tinker to Evers to Chance." Here's the verse as it originally appeared, along with its original title:

Baseball's Sad Lexicon

These are the saddest of possible words,
"Tinker-to-Evers-to-Chance."
Trio of Bear Cubs fleeter than birds,
Tinker and Evers and Chance.
Ruthlessly pricking our gonfalon bubble,
Making a Giant hit into a double,
Words that are weighty with nothing but
  Trouble.
"Tinker-to-Evers-to-Chance."
                    —*Franklin P. Adams*

For Frank Adams it was a "sad lexicon" because he was a fan of the New York Giants. In fact, Adams wrote the verse because he was in such a hurry to get to the ballpark. As he later remembered, "I wrote the piece because I wanted to get to the game, and the foreman of the composing room . . . said I needed eight lines to fill."

What exactly is a "gonfalon"? According to my dictionary, it's "a banner suspended from a crosspiece," so apparently Adams was saying that Tinker and pals were hurting the Giants' pennant chances with their double-play antics.

It's been fashionable in recent years to question the double-play skills of Tinker and Evers. Is it possible that the two weren't really all that proficient, but were merely by-standing beneficiaries of Adams' verse? To be sure, it's quite possible, perhaps even likely, that one or both (and Chance, too) might not be in the Hall of Fame if not for the poem. Their career stats simply are not typical of Hall of Fame players, even middle infielders. It's also true, as various pundits have pointed out, that from 1906 through 1911 the Cubs never led the National League in double plays. Individually, Evers never led N.L. second basemen in double plays, and Tinker topped N.L. shortstops in double plays only once.

Some revisionists have even suggested that the double-play skills of Tinker and Evers have been greatly overrated. In his wonderful book, *The Cultural Encyclopedia of Baseball*, Jonathan Fraser Light opines, "The trio was not a top double play threat or the best infield unit of the era." Writing negatively of their Hall of Fame qualifications in 1999, *USA Today*'s Tom Weir noted, "Despite the poetry, the three ranked as the National League's best double-play combo only once."

Well, there's more to playing the infield than raw numbers of double plays. The Cubs featured an outstanding pitching staff, a pitching staff that permitted relatively few baserunners. In turn, that limited the number of double-play opportunities available to the Cub infielders.

So is there an easy way to evaluate the Cubs' double-play abilities given the statistics at our disposal? Yes, there is. Bill James has come up with a system to measure what he calls *expected double plays* for a team, based on (essentially) the number of runners the opposition has on first base and the estimated number of ground balls hit by the opposition. In case you're really interested, the formula for expected double plays is: [(league double-play average × opposition runners on first base) / (league average of runners on first base × team assist total)] / league average assist total.

The chart below lists, for the Cubs' five-year period of dominance,

both of them inside the park, which will represent one-third of his lifetime output.

May 25 Boston Pilgrims ace Jesse Tannehill beats the White Sox 3–0, thus ending Boston's 20-game losing streak.

July 5 In his first major league appearance, Athletics righthander Jack Coombs shuts out the Washington Senators, 3–0.

August 31 The injury-riddled Detroit Tigers sign future Hall of Fame outfielder Sam Thompson, now forty-six years old, and he drives in two runs in his first game since 1898.

September 1 Philadelphia rookie Jack Coombs and Boston's Joe Harris both pitch complete games as the Athletics top the Pilgrims in 24 innings, 4–1. The same day, the New York Highlanders sweep a doubleheader from Washington for the third straight day.

September 3 After a six-week absence, nineteen-year-old Ty Cobb returns to the Detroit Tigers lineup. Cobb ended up hitting .318 in 1906, his rookie season in the majors. However, he did not play from July 18 until September 3 due to an undisclosed condition. Cobb had surgery in early August, but the reason for the surgery was never reported, and all the research in the years since hasn't cleared up the mystery.

That Toddlin' (Baseball) Town

In 1906, both the Cubs and White Sox led their respective leagues in attendance by healthy margins. At 654,300 fans, the Cubs were 88 percent better than the N.L. average. And at 585,202, the Sox were 59 percent above the A.L. average. This season was the only time in the decade that both Chicago teams led their leagues in attendance and, in fact, it's the only time in the twentieth century that they did so. However, there's no doubt that Chicago was a great baseball city in the early years of the century.

their actual double plays turned, their expected double plays, and the difference between actual double plays and expected double plays. Keep in mind that a positive differential means the Cubs (or any team) has turned more double plays than might reasonably be expected.

Cubs	Double Plays (N.L. Rank)	Expected Double Plays	Differential (Rank)
1906	100 (3)	82	+18 (2)
1907	110 (4)	96	+14 (2)
1908	76 (3)	75	+ 1 (4)
1909	95 (6)	86	+ 9 (3)
1910	110 (5)	102	+ 8 (3)
Totals	491 (3 [tied])	441	+50 (1)

It's an impressive performance, certainly. Yes, the Cubs only tied for third in total double plays over these five seasons, which is nothing special in an eight-team league. But going a little deeper, the Cubs turned 50 more double plays than expected, easily the most in the National League (the Phillies are next at +28). So while Tinker and Evers never really dominated the National League in a single season, nobody could match their consistency. Without running the numbers for every team in history, it's probably safe to say that Tinker and Evers weren't the greatest keystone combination of all time (1960s Pirates Gene Alley and Bill Mazeroski come to mind). However, it also seems safe to say that they were probably the best of their era and an important factor in the Cubs' amazing run.

It's too bad that they couldn't have enjoyed each other a little more. It seems that Joe Tinker and Johnny Evers, paragons of keystone teamwork, once went upwards of two years without speaking to each other. In 1936, New York *World-Telegram* columnist Joe Williams got to talking with Evers about the old-time Cubs, and Williams asked if all the stories about the feud were true.

"That's right," admitted Mr. Evers. "We didn't even say hello for at least two years. We went through two World Series without a single word. And I'll tell you why. I'm 55 years old now and Joe is 56. Poor fellow, they tell me he is dying down in Florida. A great fellow and a great ballplayer.

"But one day—it was early in 1907—he threw me a hardball. It wasn't any further than from here to there (Mr. Evers pointed to a bridge lamp about 10 feet away). It was a real hardball. Like a catcher throwing to second. And the ball broke my finger. This finger here (he showed a gnarled finger on his right hand). I yelled at him, 'You so and so!' He laughed. That's the last word we had for—well, I just don't know how long."

Other sources have reported that the feud actually began in 1905, when there was a mix-up over a cab the two were supposed to share. By all accounts, though, Evers was an incredibly high-strung fellow. According to Christy Mathewson, "Evers cannot keep a watch going because his body is so full of electricity. This may sound ridiculous on the face of it, but it is absolutely true. Evers has been presented with several fine watches and they will not keep accurate time when he carries them because of something in his physical makeup which prevents every timepiece from doing its job properly."

Frank Chance got so sick of listening to his irascible second baseman that he considered shifting Evers to the outfield. These days, I suppose you'd call Evers an extreme type-A personality, and he didn't really get along with anybody, which is probably why everyone called him "The Crab." Evers missed most of the 1911 season after suffering a nervous breakdown. Nevertheless, he succeeded Chance as player-manager in 1913, leading a disgusted Tinker to demand a trade. After the season, Evers himself was traded to the Boston Braves, for whom he played a major role in their miraculous, World Series–winning 1914 campaign. Evers managed the Cubs (again) in 1921 and the White Sox in 1924, but he didn't last the entire season either time.

Table: Ballpark Attendance

Two-Team City	Population 1910	Attendance 1903–1910
Chicago	2,185,283	8,686,826
New York	4,766,883	7,796,345
Philadelphia	1,549,008	6,589,697
Boston	670,585	5,598,390
St. Louis	687,029	5,316,931

For comparison's sake, we can look at the five cities that supported two major league teams: Chicago, Philadelphia, Boston, St. Louis, and New York. (See table on ballpark attendance, below. For our purposes, Brooklyn is separate from New York. The American League began life as a major circuit in 1901, but New York didn't have two teams until 1903 when the Baltimore franchise relocated there, so we'll start with that season.)

Obviously, there are mitigating factors here. Chicago was the second-most populous of the five cities, and the Cubs were the National League's best team in the same decade that the White Sox were generally competitive.

On the other hand, the New York teams were also competitive, yet the Chicago teams outdrew them despite being at a significant disadvantage population-wise. The evidence suggests that Chicago truly was a great baseball town.
—*Rob and Eddie*

More Than an Answer

For a lot of baseball fans, Harry Steinfeldt is nothing but the answer to the trivia question, "Who was the third baseman in the Tinker to Evers to Chance infield?" But he was more than that. The fact is, Steinfeldt was a fine player in his own right and probably the third-best player on the 1906 Cubs, behind only Miner Brown and Frank Chance.

Steinfeldt was born in St. Louis in 1877 and, according to legend, as a young man in Texas he deserted his musical troupe (Al Field's Minstrels) to help a ball club in need and never returned to the stage. Steinfeldt made his major league debut with Cincinnati in 1898, and in March of 1906 he was traded to the Cubs for third baseman Hans Lobert and pitcher "Tornado Jake" Weimer.

According to Johnny Evers, "Chance realized that third base must be filled or his pennant hopes would filter away at that corner. He knew the man he wanted, Harry

As for Frank Adams, he reportedly thought his famous lines "weren't much good." Adams later became a member of the famed intellectual group the Round Table of the Algonquin, and for years he was associated with the *Information Please* radio program.

Before we leave this subject, here's one more bit of verse, a follow-up to "Baseball's Sad Lexicon" from Ogden Nash's "Line-up for Yesterday: An ABC of Baseball Immortals."

> *E is for Evers,*
> *His jaw in advance;*
> *Never afraid*
> *To Tinker with Chance.*
> —Rob

T. F. Brown

Once, when Mordecai "Three Finger" Brown was asked if his unusually effective curveball was the result of his "unusual" hand, he replied that he didn't know because he had never thrown with a normal hand. Ty Cobb said of Brown's famous bender, "It was a great ball, that down-curve of his. I can't talk about all of baseball, but I can say this: It was the most deceiving, the most devastating pitch I ever faced." Brown was the undisputed ace of the pitching staff of the Cubs team that virtually ruled the National League from 1906 through 1910.

I guess I'm obliged to repeat for the umpteenth time how Brown's hand ended up as it did. When he was seven, his index finger got caught in his uncle's corn shredder and was amputated above the knuckle. Just a few weeks later, Brown broke the third and fourth fingers on his right hand while chasing a pig (no rest for the weary or, apparently, the maimed) and the fingers didn't heal properly, leaving them forever misshapen.

Brown's big league career started in 1903 at the age of twenty-six with the St. Louis Cardinals. Though he's remembered now as "Three Finger" Brown, during his playing career he was more popularly known by the nickname "Miner" because he had been a coal miner before he started playing professional ball. In December 1903, Brown was traded to the Cubs along with catcher Jack O'Neill for pitcher Jack Taylor and catcher Larry McLean. (As we noted earlier, Taylor would rejoin the Cubs in 1906.)

Brown's performance from 1904 through 1910 was truly amazing, as he finished in the top five in the league in ERA in each of those seasons without help from his home park, which was fairly neutral. In addition, his ERAs were consistent with his overall numbers. Here are Brown's ERAs, along with his virtual ERAs (VERA; a number I developed in the mid-1980s that factors out the luck component in a pitcher's ERA), his league ranks, and the park run index for that period:

Year	ERA (Rank)	VERA (Rank)	Park Run Index
1904	1.86 (3)	1.61 (1)	96
1905	2.17 (5)	2.21 (6)	102
1906	1.04 (1)	1.49 (1)	103
1907	1.39 (3)	1.67 (2)	108
1908	1.47 (2)	1.18 (1)	106
1909	1.31 (2)	1.32 (2)	89
1910	1.86 (2)	2.24 (1)	93
Totals	1.56 (1)	1.65 (1)	100

For the rankings in the 1904–10 totals, we considered all N.L. pitchers who threw at least 1,000 innings. The park run index of 100 means that, over these seven seasons, almost exactly the same number of runs were scored in Cubs home games and Cubs road games. Which is to say that if Brown was helped at all by West Side Park, it's not at all apparent from the record.

That is a remarkable stretch of championship-caliber pitching, and one is drawn to conclude that Brown was the best pitcher in the National League over that stretch, or at worst second behind Christy Mathewson (who ranks second in both ERA and VERA but did total about 350 more innings over the period in question).

What's more, Brown also doubled as the team's "closer," though of course no one used that word in his day. He led or tied for the league lead in saves in four straight seasons (1908–11). Although no one knew it at the time, Brown was the first pitcher to reach double fig-

Steinfeldt, who was playing indifferent ball with Cincinnati. He was slow, a heavy hitter, a good fielder, and a wonderful thrower."

There were unflattering rumors floating around about Steinfeldt, and Chance spent a fair amount of time convincing Cubs owner Charlie Murphy to make a move. Murphy finally relented, however, and the last piece of the puzzle was in place. The Cubs, who had been a good team but still finished double-digit games out of first place in 1904 and 1905, turned into a team that won four pennants and posted a 530-235 record from 1906 through 1910. And when Steinfeldt left, the Cubs stopped winning pennants.

Though some sources say that Steinfeldt was sold to the Boston Rustlers in March 1911, he was actually sold to St. Paul of the American Association on April 5. However, Steinfeldt refused to report, saying he'd play for only the Cubs or the Cincinnati Reds, his old club. Given a chance to return to the National League with the Rustlers, however, Steinfeldt relented, accepting a trade that sent him from the St. Paul club to Boston. He played in only 19 games for the Beaneaters due to a leg injury and, in the settlement of a nasty dispute between him and Boston, Steinfeldt was granted his release by the National Commission in December of 1911. (There is some evidence, by the way, that Steinfeldt suffered a nervous breakdown in 1911.) In 1912, he agreed to manage the Cincinnati team in the new United States League, but the league folded in late May.

Steinfeldt died in August 1914. Many of the newspaper stories reported that he had been "ailing for several years," and had been in critical condition for weeks before he died. The exact nature of the illness was not disclosed, but his death certificate lists "cerebral hemorrhage" as the cause of death. Harry Steinfeldt's "window" wasn't very long; eight and a half years after he joined the Cubs, he was dead.

—*Eddie and Rob*

ures in saves for a single season, with 13 in 1911. That season, he pitched in almost as many games out of the pen (26) as he did as a starter (27). Perhaps that workload, combined with Brown's advancing age, led to his decline. Also in 1911, Brown completed 20-plus games as a starter *and* finished 20-plus games as a reliever. I can't say this for sure, but I seriously doubt that any other pitcher in major league history has ever done that.

Brown had much to do with the outcome of the amazing 1908 National League pennant race. He played a major role in the Cubs doubleheader sweep of the Giants on September 22, the day before *the* game, saving the first game in relief of Orval Overall, then pitching a complete-game victory in game 2. Of the effort, the *New York World* wrote, "The team was overcome by 'Three-Fingered' Brown. . . . The only thing for McGraw to do to beat Chicago is to dig up a pitcher with only two fingers." (Somehow, I can't imagine any newspaper printing anything like that today.)

In the October 8 game that decided the 1908 pennant, Brown relieved Jack Pfiester in the first inning (supposedly without warming up) after four of the first five Giants batters reached. Brown escaped the inning with just one run scored. He later wriggled out of a bases-loaded jam in the seventh, and the Cubs wound up beating the Christy Mathewson and the hated Giants, 4–2. Shortly thereafter, of course, the Cubs captured their second straight World Series title with a five-game victory over Ty Cobb's Detroit Tigers.

Brown was a major contributor in 1906, too. His 1.04 ERA led the league by nearly a half-run per game. He recorded 26 wins (second in the league), an .813 winning percentage (also second), 9 shutouts (first), and ranked near the top of the National League in various other pitching categories.

Many players have a "hook" by which they're remembered; unfortunately for many players, the hook is a less-than-three-dimensional representation of their career and very often shortchanges the contribution that player made. This could indeed be said about Mordecai Peter Centennial Brown. Many fans know him for his three fingers, but very few know how great a pitcher he was.—Eddie

TEAM STATISTICS

Hitting

	Games by Position	Age	G	AB	R	H	2B	3B	HR	RBI	BB	SB	Avg	OBP	Slug
Johnny Kling	C,96; OF,3	31	107	343	45	107	15	8	2	46	23	14	.312	.357	.420
Frank Chance	1B,136	26	136	474	**103**	151	24	10	3	71	70	57	.319	.419	.430
Johnny Evers	2B,153; 3B,1	24	154	533	65	136	17	6	1	51	36	49	.255	.305	.315
Joe Tinker	SS,147; 3B,1	25	148	523	75	122	18	4	1	64	43	30	.233	.293	.289
Harry Steinfeldt	3B,150; 2B,1	28	151	539	81	**176**	27	10	3	83	47	29	.327	.395	.430
Jimmy Sheckard	OF,149	27	149	549	90	144	27	10	1	45	67	30	.262	.349	.353
Jimmy Slagle	OF,127	32	127	498	71	119	8	6	0	33	63	25	.239	.324	.279
Wildfire Schulte	OF,146	23	146	563	77	158	18	**13**	7	60	31	25	.281	.324	.396
Pat Moran	C,61	30	70	226	22	57	13	1	0	35	7	6	.252	.281	.319
Solly Hofman	OF,23; IF,38	23	64	195	30	50	2	3	2	20	20	13	.256	.326	.328
Ed Reulbach	P,33; OF,1	23	34	83	4	13	0	0	0	4	2	0	.157	.176	.157
Doc Gessler*	OF,21; 1B,1	25	34	83	8	21	3	0	0	10	12	4	.253	.354	.289
Carl Lundgren	P,27; 2B,1	26	28	67	4	12	3	0	0	2	9	0	.179	.276	.224
Pete Noonan*	1B,1	24	5	3	0	1	0	0	0	0	0	0	.333	.333	.333
Tom Walsh	C,2	21	2	1	0	0	0	0	0	0	0	0	.000	.000	.000
Bull Smith		25	1	1	0	0	0	0	0	0	0	0	.000	.000	.000
Totals		27		5,018	**705**	**1,316**	181	**71**	20	**539**	448	283	**.262**	.328	**.339**

*Played for another team during season. Statistics are those compiled with 1906 Chicago Cubs only.

Pitching

	Threw	Age	Games	GS	CG	ShO	IP	H	HR	BB	SO	W	L	Pct	Sv	ERA
Miner Brown	Right	29	36	32	27	**9**	277	198	1	61	144	26	6	.813	3	**1.04**
Jack Pfiester	Left	28	31	29	20	4	251	173	3	63	153	20	8	.714	0	1.51
Ed Reulbach	Right	23	33	24	20	6	218	129	2	92	94	19	4	**.826**	3	1.65
Carl Lundgren	Right	26	27	24	21	5	208	160	3	89	103	17	6	.739	2	2.21
Jack Taylor*	Right	32	17	16	15	2	147	116	0	39	34	12	3	.800	0	1.83
Orval Overall*	Right	25	18	14	13	2	144	116	1	51	94	12	3	.800	1	1.88
Bob Wicker*	Right	28	10	8	5	0	72	70	0	19	25	3	5	.375	0	2.99
Fred Beebe*	Right	25	14	6	4	0	70	56	1	32	55	7	1	.875	1	2.70
Jack Harper*	Right	28	1	1	0	0	1	0	0	0	0	0	0	—	0	0.00
Totals		27	187	155	125	**30**	**1,388**	**1,018**	**12**	446	**702**	**116**	**36**	**.763**	10	**1.75**

*Played for another team during season. Statistics are those compiled with 1906 Chicago Cubs only.

CHAPTER 2

1911 Philadelphia Athletics

Of all the teams that Connie managed, it has been reported that the 1911 edition was his favorite. If true, then not a bad choice, since this was the first truly great ball club in American League history and one of the greatest ever.
—Donald Honig in *Baseball's 10 Greatest Teams*

Record: 101-50, .669 (tied for 29th)
Two-Year (1910–11): 203-98, .674 (14th)
Three-Year 1909–11): 298-156, .656
  (19th)

SD Score: 3.15 (22d)
Two-Year: 5.77 (18th)
Three-Year: 8.28 (9th)

Results:
1909, second place in American League
1910 World Champions
1911 World Champions

Days in First Place: 66 of 180;
  clinched on September 26

Longest Winning Streak: 10 games
Longest Losing Streak: 6 games

The Lucky Hunchback, Part I

Everyone knows that the ballplayers of our time are a superstitious lot, but today's athletes are pikers compared to their baseball ancestors. For many years, ballplayers were always on the lookout for a midget or hunchback who might serve as a combination batboy and good-luck charm. A case in point is Louis Van Zelst, who was diminutive *and* hunchbacked. Van Zelst was with the Athletics from 1910 through 1914, during which time the club won four pennants and three World Series.—*Rob*

Around the Majors

March 17 The American League Base Ball Park in Washington, D.C., is destroyed by fire. Rudimentary stands are hastily constructed in time for Opening Day (April 14), but work on the new park is

The Pennant Race: See separate article, "The Pennant Race."

Against the Contenders: It was a two-team race, and team number two (the Tigers) actually took 12 of 22 from team number one (the Athletics).

Runs Scored: 861 (1st)

Runs Allowed: 601 (1st)

Pythagorean Record: 99-52

Manager: Connie Mack

Regular Lineup:

Player	Position	ROV	OW%
Bris Lord	LF	.300	.641
Rube Oldring	CF	.278	.566
Eddie Collins	2B	.367	.803
Frank Baker	3B	.333	.734
Stuffy McInnis	1B	.302	.649
Danny Murphy	RF	.325	.714
Jack Barry	SS	.266	.520
Ira Thomas	C	.265	.517
Jack Coombs	P		

Not many second basemen have ever posted an .800-plus offensive winning percentage in a season, but then Collins was one of the five or six greatest second basemen of all time.

Bench: Harry Davis, team captain and veteran first baseman, was a backup during the regular season but started every game in the World Series after the rookie Stuffy McInnis was laid low with a broken finger. Amos Strunk served as the club's fourth outfielder, contributing little with the bat in 74 games. Jack Lapp, the backup catcher, batted a robust .353 and scored 35 runs in 68 games.

Scouting the Pitchers: Jack Coombs (28-12, 3.53) topped the American League in victories, though his 3.53 ERA represented a huge increase over his 1.30 mark in 1910. Coombs might have been the most famous Athletics pitcher at the time, but it was his staff-mates Eddie Plank (23-8, 2.10) and Chief Bender (17-5, 2.16) who would eventually go into the Hall of Fame.

Plank, arguably baseball's greatest lefthander before Lefty Grove, was famous for his time-consuming mound mannerisms, as he lulled hitters to sleep by pulling on his belt and his cap, moving his feet around, and delaying his pitching motion. Plank generally threw three-quarters, but he would occasionally drop to sidearm. He threw a brilliant change-up, along with solid fastballs and curves, and possessed a great pick-off move.

Ty Cobb maintained that Bender had the best stuff among Philadelphia's starters, noting that although Plank "had a nice crossfire style . . . Bender had more stuff—a wicked curve, and a fastball second only to [Walter] Johnson's."

How Were They Built? Connie Mack liked intelligent players, and half of the famed "$100,000 Infield" were college men: Eddie Collins came out of Columbia University and Jack Barry graduated from Holy Cross. As for the pitchers, Jack Coombs spent four years at Colby College, Harry Krause graduated from St. Mary's (Oakland, California), and Dave Danforth went to Baylor for two years.

The signing of Collins was handled, shall we say, a tad clumsily. For many years Mack depended on a vast network of friends who also functioned as scouts. When Collins was still at Columbia, he played semi-pro ball in the summers for a number of teams, including one managed by former big leaguer Billy Lush. Lush tipped off Mack, who sent scout Jim Byrnes for a look. Byrnes agreed with Lush, so Mack signed Collins to a professional contract after Eddie's sophomore season.

Collins went back to Columbia for his junior year and again played semi-pro ball that summer. Because classes didn't start until October, Mack invited Collins along for the Athletics' last road trip of 1906, and he got into six A.L. games. However, then as now, college players weren't supposed to play professional ball. So in the box scores of those six games, Collins is "Sullivan." As Mack casually explained years later, "This was not uncommon at the time."

not completed until the middle of the season.

April 14 A good portion of the Polo Grounds, home of the New York Giants, burns to the ground. The Giants accept the Yankees' invitation to play their home games at Hilltop Park before moving into the new Polo Grounds in September.

May 10 Nearly a month into the season, the Detroit Tigers finally lose a home game.

June 18 The Tigers stage the biggest comeback in major league history, overcoming a 13–1 deficit in the fifth inning to defeat the White Sox, 16–15.

July 11 A baseball disaster is narrowly avoided early in the morning, when a train carrying the St. Louis Cardinals derails. The wreck leaves fourteen passengers dead and forty-seven injured, but the baseball players are unhurt, only because their car had been moved from the front to the rear of the train the evening before.

July 24 The first all-star game is played, in which a squad of American Leaguers faces the Cleveland Indians in a benefit that raises $12,914 for the widow of Addie Joss.

August 16 Cubs right fielder Wildfire Schulte hits his fourth grand slam of the season, setting a National League record that stands for forty-four years. These four are the only grand slams of Schulte's eleven-year career.

September 22 Cy Young records the 511th and final victory of his career, shutting out Pittsburgh 1–0.

Double Trouble

The Athletics played eighteen doubleheaders, and lost only one of them (to Boston). They swept ten twin bills, split six, and in another they won the first game and tied the second. According to the 1912 Reach guide, "The Athletics' wonderful success in double-headers was a large factor in their capture of the pennant, inasmuch as

The subterfuge did not work. Someone at Columbia discovered the secret and, as Fred Lieb noted, "They could wink at Plattsburg and Rutland, but playing with the Philadelphia A's was too much. Eddie was declared ineligible for further participation in Columbia's athletics, and in the Blue and White's 1907 baseball season he was the team's nonplaying captain."

Aside from Collins, the other Hall of Famer in the everyday lineup was Frank Baker. He came up in 1908 from the Reading club in the Tri-State League, of which the Athletics owned a large part.

What Brought Them Down? The demise of this dynasty is one of the most famous, and certainly the most precipitous, in the game's long history. The Athletics finished third in 1912 behind the Red Sox and Senators, but rebounded in 1913 with another American League pennant and another World Series victory over the New York Giants.

The Federal League, aspiring to "major league" status, started signing American and National Leaguers after the 1914 season. This, of course, drove up the salaries of all the players, and Mack wasn't having any of it. Rather than pay his stars their new market value, he chose instead to simply give up on playing a competitive brand of baseball.

The question, of course, is "Why?" The Athletics played in a fine ballpark, attendance was passable (even after an inexplicable sharp decline from 1913 to 1914), and of course the club had been quite successful in recent seasons. In Mack's book, *My 66 Years in the Big Leagues,* he writes,

> After giving the crisis much careful thought, I decided that the war had gone too far to stop it by trying to outbid the Federal moneybags. Nothing could be more disastrous at this time than a salary war.
>
> There was but one thing to do: to refuse to be drawn into this bitter conflict, and to let those who wanted to risk their fate with the Federals go with the Federals.
>
> The first to go were Bender and Plank. I didn't get a nickel for them. This was like being struck by a hurricane. Others followed. There was only one way to get out from under the catastrophe. I decided to sell out and start over again. When it became known that my players were for sale, the offers rolled into me.

If the players were going to "cash in" and leave me to hold the bag, there was nothing for me to do but to cash in too. So I sold the great Eddie Collins to the White Sox for $50,000 cash. I sold Home Run Baker to the Yankees. My shortstop, Jack Barry, told me he wanted to go to Boston, so I sold him to the Bostons for a song.

"Why didn't you hang on to the half of your team that was loyal and start to build up again?" This question has often been asked me.

My answer is that when a team starts to disintegrate it is like trying to plug up the hole in the dam to stop the flood. The boys who are left have lost their high spirits, and they want to go where they think the future looks brighter. It is only human for everyone to try to improve his opportunities.

Whatever. If it was so hard to pay the new salaries, why were the other, less successful teams in the league able to keep most of their stars?

After finishing in first place with 99 victories in 1914 (but losing to the Miracle Braves in the World Series), in 1915 the Athletics finished *last* with 43 victories (and 109 losses!). Attendance dropped from 346,641 to 146,233. It was the first of seven straight last-places finishes for Mack's team.

Most Valuable Athletic: Jack Coombs paced the American League with 28 wins, but his 3.53 ERA wasn't anywhere near the league leaders, as his teammates Eddie Plank (2.10) and Chief Bender (2.16) finished fourth and fifth.

As good as Bender was, he won only 17 games due to a slow start, which narrows the competition down to third baseman Frank Baker and second baseman Eddie Collins.

Baker ranked fourth in the league in hits (198), *first* in home runs (11), fourth in total bases (301), second in RBI (115) and fifth in slugging percentage (.508). He was generally regarded as a solid defender and led A.L. third basemen with a .942 fielding percentage.

Collins didn't lead the American League in any category, but he was excellent across the board, and his 932 OPS ranked fourth in the league. He played only 132 games.

So it's close, this battle between two evenly matched Hall of Famers, but we'll give it to Baker, the guy who played nearly every day.

they would probably have lost a large percentage of the games postponed early in the season than they won later in the season, owing to the fact that the Athletic team was way below form in the first two months of the campaign, their pitchers especially going badly."
—Rob

Call him "Sneaky" McInnis

In 1911, the American League instituted a rule, apparently designed to speed up the games, that prohibited pitchers from taking "free" warm-up tosses between innings. On June 27 in Boston, Athletics first baseman Stuffy McInnis took full advantage of the new rule.

Just before the bottom of the eighth, with Red Sox hurler Ed "Loose" Karger tossing a few warm-ups to rookie catcher Les Nunamaker, McInnis jumped in and took a cut. The ball flew into center field and started rolling because

Boston's outfielders had yet to take their positions; McInnis circled the bases for an inside-the-park home run. (By the way, if you're wondering why the A's were batting in the bottom of the eighth when the game was in Boston, until 1950 the home team was given the choice of batting first or last. In the early part of the twentieth century, teams would occasionally take the former option.)

Philadelphia already led Boston 6–3 at the time of McInnis' homer, and the game ended 7–3. Nevertheless, the Red Sox protested McInnis's home run to A.L. President Ban Johnson on the grounds that two Philadelphia players were still leaving the field and in fair territory when McInnis struck his blow. Johnson denied the protest.—*Rob*

Meanwhile, Over at the Baker Bowl . . .

Things weren't going quite so well at the Baker Bowl,

Worst Regular: It's a competition between outfielders Bris Lord and Rube Oldring. Lord had a better year with the bat (784 OPS) than Oldring (726), and Lord also played 13 more games than Oldring. On the other hand, Oldring was considered a fine defensive center fielder, whereas Lord played left. What's more, Oldring played 1,238 games in the major leagues, as opposed to only 742 for Lord. Tough choice, then, but Bris Lord "wins" by a nose. (Incidentally, Lord's nickname was "The Human Eyeball" and, to date, the best efforts of researchers have failed to discover why.)

Hall of Famers: Eddie Collins, Frank Baker, Chief Bender, and Eddie Plank are all in the Hall of Fame, along with Connie Mack.

Our Hall of Famers: Collins, Baker, Plank, and Mack are all legit. Bender is somewhat marginal, given that he won only 212 games in his career, and he won 20 or more games in only two seasons. By the standards of his era, Bender simply wasn't very durable, and he was essentially washed up at the age of thirty-one.

The 1911 World Series: See article, "Frank Gets a Nickname."

The Ballpark: The Athletics played in Shibe Park, the first modern, steel and concrete ballpark, which opened for business in 1909. Shibe—renamed Connie Mack Stadium in 1953—served as the club's home until 1955, when the A's moved to Kansas City. The Phillies also played at Shibe from 1938 through 1970. The ballpark, at the corner of Twenty-first Street and Lehigh Avenue, was demolished in 1976.

Books about the 1911 Athletics: Well, the teens weren't exactly the golden age of baseball books. However, Christy Mathewson devotes a fair portion of his *Pitching in a Pinch* (New York: G. P. Putnam's Sons, 1912) to the 1911 World Series. Someday soon, someone will write a book about Home Run Baker or Eddie Collins, and there has been talk about a new biography of Connie Mack for years. Fred Lieb's *Connie Mack: Grand Old Man of Baseball* (New York: G. P. Putnam's Sons, 1945), the Athletics entry in the Putnam series of team histories, is probably the single best source on this team. In 1999, David Jordan's well-researched and competently written *The Athletics* *of Philadelphia: Connie Mack's White Elephants, 1901–1954* (Jefferson, NC: McFarland) was published.

Connie's Boy

Earle Mack, who played two games at third base in 1911, was the first major leaguer to play for his father. There haven't been many such combinations since then:

Family	Manager	Son	Years Together
Mack	Connie	Earle	1910–11, 1914
Berra	Yogi	Dale	1985
McRae	Hal	Brian	1991–94
Ripken	Cal, Sr.	Cal, Jr.	1987–88
Ripken	Cal, Sr.	Billy	1987–88
Alou	Felipe	Moises	1992–96

Few of these unions proved particularly fruitful. Earle Mack, though he saw action with three American League pennant winners, wasn't really a player. In his three seasons, he played in five games and went 2-for-16. It would be nearly seventy-five years before another son played for his father, but we've seen a number of such combinations since. After a few years with the Pittsburgh Pirates, shortstop Dale Berra joined the Yankees for the 1985 season. Unfortunately, manager Yogi Berra got fired 16 games into the regular season, making for a short family reunion. Brian McRae was the first full-time player to serve under his father, which he did for four seasons with the Kansas City Royals. The elder Cal Ripken managed the Orioles to a 67-95 record in 1987, then was fired when the O's opened the '88 campaign with six straight losses (the streak would eventually reach 21). Expos skipper Felipe Alou got paid to watch his son reach All-Star status, but even that was bittersweet, as Moises eventually left for greener (i.e., richer) pastures than Montreal. One thing we still haven't seen is a manager with a son/pitcher. That would make for some interesting mound conversations, one would think.

Earle Mack, by the way, also served under his old man as a coach

home of the Philadelphia Phillies and only six blocks from Shibe Park. The year 1911 marked the Phillies' twenty-ninth season in the National League, and they had never won the pennant. In fact, they'd finished second just twice. After going 52-100 in 1905, the Phils were respectable for the rest of the decade, and in 1911 they finished a distant fourth, at 79-73. Of those 79 victories, 28 were credited to rookie pitcher Grover Cleveland Alexander. Four years later, with the Athletics dropping to last place in the American League, Alexander and the Phillies took up the slack in Philadelphia with their first-ever pennant.—*Rob*

Stats 'n' Stuff

◆ How dominant were the Athletics? Four of Philadelphia's starters finished among the top five in the league in winning percentage, with only Cleveland's Vean Gregg in second place (at .767) to spoil the A's hegemony.

◆ With six shutouts, Eddie Plank tied Walter Johnson for the league lead. Cy Morgan topped the American League by hitting 21 batters with pitches.

◆ A's fielders committed only 224 errors, easily the fewest in the American League, and 76 fewer than the league average.

We've Got Your Number

The 1911 Athletics were the first American League team to beat another team 20 or more times in the same season. The A's victims were the St. Louis Browns; the season series was 20-2 in favor of Philadelphia. (The Browns, as we'll see, were on the short end of another season series like this, losing 21 of 22 to the Yankees in 1927.)

One team winning 20 or more games in a season against another team has happened fourteen times. And for no apparent reason, eleven of those were in the National League. The 1909 Boston Beaneaters have the

for twenty-seven seasons, 1924 through 1950. Earle officially managed the Athletics twice, for 34 games in 1937 and 91 games in 1939, when Connie wasn't up to the job. It was widely believed that Earle would become manager when the Old Man finally retired, but the son was demoted to head scout early in the 1950 season.—Rob

Frank Gets a Nickname

Frank Baker led the American League with 11 home runs in 1911, but he wouldn't come by his famous nickname, "Home Run," until the World Series.

Even before it started, the 1911 Series was strange in a couple of ways. The regular season had run until October 12, so the Series didn't begin until October 14. What's more, the Series alternated cities with each game. The 1911 Series was a rematch of the 1905 Series, which the New York Giants won thanks largely to Christy Mathewson, who tossed *three* shutouts against the Athletics.

In game 1, Matty made it four straight over the A's, spinning a six-hitter to capture a slim 2–1 decision over Chief Bender.

Game 2 was tied 1–1 until the bottom of the sixth, when Baker drove a Rube Marquard pitch over the right-field wall for a two-run homer. The contest ended 3–1, Eddie Plank going the distance to earn the victory for the A's. According to Giants manager John McGraw, before game 2 he "instructed Marquard not to pitch a high, fast ball to Baker, but he forgot. He put one just in that spot and Baker 'whammed' it into the stands."

Mathewson and Marquard were both lending their names during the Series to syndicated newspaper columns (ghosted, of course, by newspaper writers). The morning after game 2, the headline on Mathewson's column read, "Marquard Made the Wrong Pitch." Matty hadn't actually written the column, nor even approved it for publication. Nevertheless, Rube wasn't thrilled when he saw that headline.

In game 3, Athletics starter Jack Coombs permitted just three hits, but two of them came in the third inning, and the A's trailed the Giants (and columnist/pitcher Mathewson) 1–0 after eight innings. Here's what happened next, as described by Mathewson in *Pitching in a Pinch:*

The roughest deal that I got from Baker in the 1911 series was in the third game, which was the second in New York. We had made one run and the ninth inning rolled around with the Giants still leading, 1 to 0. The first man at the bat grounded out and then Baker came up. I realized by this time that he was a hard proposition, but figured that he could not hit a low curve over the outside corner, as he is naturally a right-field hitter. I got one ball and one strike on him and then delivered a ball that was aimed to be a low curve over the outside corner. Baker refused to swing at it, and Brennan, the umpire, called it a ball.

I thought that it caught the outside corner of the plate, and that Brennan missed the strike. It put me in the hole with the count two balls and one strike, and I had to lay the next one over very near the middle to keep the count from being three and one. I pitched a curve ball that was meant for the outside corner, but cut the plate better than I intended. Baker stepped up into it and smashed it into the grand-stand in right field for a home run, and there is the history of that famous wallop. This tied the score.

In the top of the eleventh, the A's untied the game with pair of un-earned runs off Mathewson. The Giants did make it close, thanks to their third hit of the game (finally) and an A's error, but it wasn't quite enough and the end result was 3–2 Athletics, with Coombs going all the way. The Giants had set a N.L. record that season with 347 stolen bases, but in game 3 they were 0-for-5 trying to steal against Coombs and A's catcher Jack Lapp.

Game 4 was delayed six days by rain (the longest delay in Series history), allowing the Giants to start Mathewson again. He wasn't at his best, though, and took a 4–2 loss, while Chief Bender picked up his second victory of the Series.

It was finally the Giants' turn for late-inning heroics in game 5. Trailing 3–0, they scored a run in the seventh, two more in the ninth, and another in the tenth for a 4–3 triumph. The game-ending run came on Fred Merkle's sacrifice fly to deep right field, which plated second baseman Larry Doyle . . . well, sort of. Doyle never actually touched home plate, so umpire Bill Klem never called Doyle safe. But both clubs left the field without doing anything about it, so the run, and New York's victory, stood.

Game 6 was no contest, however. Bender won his second straight

dubious distinction of being on the short end of such a season series twice in the same year, losing 20 of 21 games to Pittsburgh and 21 of 22 to Chicago.

Contrary to what you might think, only five of the fourteen instances involved the pennant winner against the last-place team. For example, the last time this happened was in 1954, when the Indians beat the Red Sox 20 of 22; the Red Sox finished fourth (albeit 42 games out) with a 69-85 record.

The average record of the "dominator" team was 100-53 (.653); the average record of the "dominated" was 52-102 (.338). Of course, such an occurrence is impossible today because teams don't play each other anywhere near twenty times in a season. Some people argue that it would be better if teams played many more games against their divisional opponents than they do. Maybe that would be better than the current arrangement, but can you imagine being the Devil Rays in your first season (1998) and having to play the Yankees twenty-two times?—*Eddie*

The Chief's Brother

Although Home Run Baker ranked as the big star of the 1911 World Series, just as important was the performance of Athletics pitcher Albert "Chief" Bender, who went 2-1 with a 1.04 ERA. Albert's brother John also pitched professional ball, though he never reached the heights of his older sibling. Here's how the 1912 Reach guide summed up John's career:

Bender has played with the Fargo team of the Northern League, and with the Charleston, Augusta and Columbia teams, of the South Atlanta League. While a member of the Columbia team in 1908 he stabbed manager Win Clark with a knife. For this he was placed on the

Series start, and the Philadelphia hitters pounded Giants starter Red Ames and replacement Hooks Wiltse on their way to an easy 13–2, Series-clinching blowout.

And Baker, thanks solely to his two homers in the 1911 World Series—his career high during the regular season was twelve—would forever after be known as "Home Run."—Rob

They're Using a Corked Ball

A lot of fuss is made when a player is suspected of using a corked bat, and much more is made when he is actually caught using one. I don't really know if a corked bat makes that much difference, but I can tell you that a corked ball did. In 1911, both leagues began using cork-center baseballs (the two leagues used slightly different balls, with the American League favoring one manufactured by the A. J. Reach Co.), and run production skyrocketed:

Runs Scored per Game

Year	American League	National League
1910	7.28	8.06
1911	9.21	8.84
Percent Change	+26.5%	+9.6%

This radical one-year change didn't really affect the balance of power. Take a look at each league's standings for 1910 and 1911:

American League		National League	
1910	**1911**	**1910**	**1911**
Philadelphia	Philadelphia	Chicago	New York
New York	Detroit	New York	Chicago
Detroit	Cleveland	Pittsburgh	Pittsburgh
Boston	Chicago	Philadelphia	Philadelphia
Cleveland	Boston	Cincinnati	St. Louis
Chicago	New York	Brooklyn	Cincinnati

American League		National League	
1910	**1911**	**1910**	**1911**
Washington	Washington	St. Louis	Brooklyn
St. Louis	St. Louis	Boston	Boston

In the National League, the same four teams finished in the "first division" in each year (by definition, the "second division" also remained the same) with just the first and second teams flip-flopping. In the 1911 American League, five of the eight teams finished no more than one place removed from their 1910 standing.

Run production remained high in 1912, but for some reason it began to drop in 1913 and wouldn't really rise significantly until after World War I.

Runs Scored per Game

Year	American League	National League
1912	8.88	9.23
1913	7.86	8.29
1914	7.31	7.68
1915	7.93	7.25
1916	7.36	6.90
1917	7.30	7.05
1918	7.29	7.25
1919	8.19	7.30
1920	9.51	7.93

As far as anyone knows, there was no intentional change to the ball after the 1912 season. After World War I, a better quality of yarn became available, which may have unintentionally increased the liveliness of baseballs. This probably helps explain the increase in run production, especially in the American League, that began in 1919.—Eddie

ineligible list, the ban not being raised until the season of 1910. He started the 1911 season with the Charleston team and finished it with the Edmonton team of the Western Canada League.

And when they say "finished," they mean *finished*. On September 25, about three weeks before the Series opened, John died suddenly of heart failure while on the pitcher's mound. It was an early end to a rough life. Happily, the media in 1911 generally didn't engage in the feeding frenzies to which we're accustomed. Can you imagine what Fox Sports would do with something like this?—*Rob*

The Pennant Race

At first glance, it might not seem possible that the 1911 American League pennant was ever in doubt. Philadelphia won the pennant by 13½ games over second-place Detroit, and third-place Cleveland finished 22 games back. Statistically, there was really no comparison between the Athletics and the Tigers:

Team	Runs Scored	Runs Allowed	SD Score
Philadelphia	861	601	+3.15
Detroit	831	776	+0.40

However, it was Detroit that got off to a hot start, 31-9, and held the lead for most of the season. At the end of May, the Tigers were seven games ahead of Philadelphia:

Detroit	32-11	.744	—
Philadelphia	23-16	.590	7

At one point in May, Detroit actually boasted a 12-game lead over the Athletics.

The A's had a great June (19-6), closing the gap to one game by the end of the month, but the two teams were neck and neck through July. At the end of July, here's where they stood:

Detroit	62-32	.660	—
Philadelphia	60-33	.645	1½

At that point however, the Tigers' suspect pitching began to falter, whereas the A's never broke stride. Ty Cobb's respiratory illness in July and August didn't help Detroit's chances, either. Philadelphia passed Detroit on August 4 and kept on rolling, although they didn't clinch the pennant until September 26, when they beat the Tigers 11–5 at Shibe Park behind two homers and two doubles by Frank Baker. The Athletics were 42-17 from August 1 on (the Tigers were 27-33) and were 95-43 from May 1. Philadelphia also had an enormous advantage on the road, posting a 47-30 record away from Philadelphia, whereas the Tigers were only 38-40 in away games.

The Tigers spent 112 days in first place compared to the Athletics' 66 days, but of course it's where you are at the end that counts. For a good part of the summer, though, the two teams gave the fans a hell of a pennant race.—Eddie

Jack Coombs (*National Baseball Hall of Fame Library, Cooperstown, NY*)

Jack Coombs: World Series Hero, Philanthropist, and Author

By 1911, when he topped the American League with 28 victories, Jack Coombs already ranked as one the most famous baseball pitchers in the country.

A graduate of Colby College in Maine, Coombs signed with the Philadelphia Athletics in 1906. Without benefit of any minor league experience, Coombs made his professional debut on July 5 in which he tossed a complete-game shutout against the Washington Senators. On September 1 of that season, Coombs made an even bigger splash, pitching 24 innings to beat the Boston Red Sox, 4–1.

Coincidentally or not, Coombs came up with a sore arm in 1907 and went just 6-9 that season. (One old newspaper clipping says "he wrenched the ligaments of his pitching arm" in a game at Boston.) In fact, he was so ineffective that Connie Mack toyed with the idea of making an outfielder out of Coombs, who actually played 47 games out there in 1908. That didn't work so well because Coombs didn't hit much, but fortunately his pitching arm was rounding back into shape. Coombs started only 18 games that season, but he went 7-5 with a fine 2.00 ERA.

Years later Mack remembered the day on which Coombs' career turned around (or at least, the day that Mack *thought* turned Coombs' career turned around). "In the middle of the 1909 season, I had Jack finish a game," Mack remembered. "He worked six beautiful innings, and showed a little curve. It didn't break much, but I saw it could be developed into a baffling delivery. I called him aside after the game, and said, 'Jack, if you'll pitch that curve and practice it on every occasion, I'll promise you will be a great pitcher.'"

Coombs finished the 1909 campaign with a 12-11 mark and a 2.32 ERA in 30 games. That earned Coombs a raise for 1910, but he declined it, saying he didn't think his 1909 performance merited a pay increase. Club president Ben Shibe insisted, however, so Coombs took the money. Thus financially fortified, in 1910 Coombs went out and enjoyed one of the greatest seasons any pitcher ever had. He led the American League with 31 victories, recorded 13 complete-game shutouts (which is still the A.L. record), and started three games in the World Series—winning all three to lead the A's past the Chicago Cubs for their first-ever World Championship.

You don't top a season like that, but in 1911 Coombs again led the American League in victories, this time with 28. In 1912, he ran his three-year record to 80-31 (though for the second straight season his ERA was mediocre).

In the spring of 1913 at the Athletics' training camp, Coombs contracted typhoid fever. Apparently recovered early that summer, he joined the club for a road trip, but quickly decided to return home to Maine for more recuperation. Not long after, Coombs was diagnosed with spinal typhoid, a condition that generally proved fatal. For months, Coombs was confined to the hospital with weights strapped to his head and legs. He did recover, though, and eventually pitched a couple of games for the 1914 A's, who were on their way to yet another pennant. As we've seen, Mack dismantled his club after that season, and Coombs was granted his release. He signed with the Dodgers and pitched fairly well for a couple of years before sinking into ineffectiveness in 1917.

Coombs was an exceedingly intelligent man who studied chemistry in college and often entertained aspirations of making chemistry his profession. But once he became a professional baseball player, Coombs devoted his attentions to his new vocation. With his pitching career over after the 1920 season—he had also managed the Phillies for two months in 1919—Coombs turned his efforts toward teaching the game to young players. He coached baseball briefly at Williams College and then Princeton before settling in at Duke University for twenty-six seasons. His real legacy, though, would be a book—*Baseball: Individual Play and Team Strategy*—that first appeared in 1938 and remained the standard work on the subject for nearly two decades.—Rob

Missing Shoeless Joe

This is not a piece about whether or not Joe Jackson should be in the Hall of Fame, though the subject might pop up later in the book. What some of you may know is that Jackson was originally signed by Connie Mack and made his major league debut (five games' worth) with the Athletics in 1908 at the age of nineteen. He also played in five games with Philadelphia in 1909.

Jackson was traded to Cleveland in July of 1910 for outfielder Bris Lord. Although Connie Mack had an affinity for intelligent players, he would make exceptions for players with exceptional talent. Jackson, while illiterate, was a gifted player; but in the end Mack traded him anyway. Jackson was homesick and uncomfortable in the big city of Philadelphia, and the other Athletics played pranks on him.

Would Joe Jackson's life have turned out differently if he had stayed with the A's? Would he have survived the Mack purge of the winter of 1914–15? In answering the first question, although Mack and the White Sox's Charles Comiskey were both tough with the dollar, Mack had a gentlemanly way about him that makes it difficult to imagine his players "getting back" at him for being cheap by throwing a World Series. Maybe I'm being too naïve about that and too simplistic about the motives of the Black Sox, but Mack also cared more for his players than Comiskey did. As for the second question, it seems highly doubtful that Jackson would have remained with Philadelphia, but he wouldn't necessarily have ended up with the White Sox.

How good would Mack's "$100,000 Infield" team have been with Joe Jackson? They were damned good anyway, but take a look at this chart comparing Joe Jackson's 1911 numbers (his first full major league season) to those of the A's starting outfield:

Player	AB	R	RBI	OBP	Slug	RC/27
Jackson	547	126	83	.468	.590	10.92
Murphy	508	104	66	.398	.461	7.22
Lord	574	92	55	.355	.429	6.00
Oldring	495	84	59	.332	.394	5.06

Jackson's *on-base percentage* with the Indians was better than the *slugging percentage* of any of Philadelphia's starting outfielders. While acknowledging that Jackson's home park was an easier place to hit than the Athletics' home park, it seems obvious that his presence would have added more firepower to an already potent lineup. Although the A's did allow the fewest runs of any team in the American League in 1911, at least some of that was due to their park, and the real strength of the team was its lineup. In road games only, the A's ranked fourth in fewest runs allowed, but easily led the league in runs scored. The 1911 A's scored 477 runs in road games; the next-best team scored 378. Adding Jackson to that team may be a case of gilding the lily, but much of the fun in being a baseball fan is engaging in what-if scenarios. And Joe Jackson's career had more than its share of "what ifs."—Eddie

Does Winning Get Old?

One of the fundamental tenets of economics is the Law of Diminishing Marginal Returns. For example, if a person is thirsty, the third cola he drinks doesn't taste as good as the second which, in turn, didn't taste as good as the first. An inelegant example, perhaps, but I hope it serves to make the point.

Some people connected with baseball have wondered if the rule of diminishing marginal returns applies to the effect of winning on team attendance. Whether we realize it or not, situations are seldom judged against an objective "reality," but instead are judged against expectations. What I am trying to say is that the power of expectations could lead to diminishing marginal returns for winning.

Whether that is what happened to the Athletics in 1914 is hard to say from this distance. It is true, however, that despite winning the pennant, their attendance dropped dramatically even considering the overall drop in A.L. and N.L. attendance due to the "intrusion" of the Federal League and other factors. Take a look:

Year	Attendance	Rank	League Average	Percent Compared to League Average
1909	674,915	1 (of 8)	467,571	+44.3
1910	588,905	1 (of 8)	408,836	+44.0
1911	605,749	1 (of 8)	417,439	+45.1
1912	517,653	3 (of 8)	407,954	+26.9
1913	571,896	2 (of 8)	440,851	+29.7
1914	346,641	5 (of 8)	343,449	+0.9

As you can see, from 1909 through 1911 the A's led the league in attendance, and their turnout was incredibly consistent compared to the league average, right around 44+ percent. The Athletics' third-place finish in 1912 seems to have cost them some fans, though, because winning the pennant in 1913 didn't bring attendance back to the 1909–11 level.

None of that can really explain what happened in 1914. Of course, Mack broke up his great team partly because of the effect of Federal League competition on player salaries. As disappointing as the crowds were in 1914, things got a lot worse in '15, when the A's drew just 146,223 fans, last in the league and 52 percent worse than the league average. Supposedly, Mack once said, "Champions cost money." He also thought that fans did become apathetic when a team kept winning. His experience during this period no doubt colored his judgments.—Eddie

TEAM STATISTICS

Hitting

	Games by Position	Age	G	AB	R	H	2B	3B	HR	RBI	BB	SB	Avg	OBP	Slug
Stuffy McInnis	1B,97; SS,24	20	126	468	76	150	20	10	3	77	25	23	.321	.361	.425
Eddie Collins	2B,132	24	132	493	92	180	22	13	3	73	62	38	.365	.451	.481
Jack Barry	SS,127	24	127	442	73	117	18	7	1	63	38	30	.265	.333	.344
Home Run Baker	3B,148	25	148	592	96	198	42	14	11	115	40	38	.334	.379	.508
Danny Murphy	OF,136; 2B,4	34	141	508	104	167	27	11	6	66	50	22	.329	.398	.461
Rube Oldring	OF,119	27	121	495	84	147	11	14	3	59	21	21	.297	.332	.394
Bris Lord	OF,132	27	134	574	92	178	37	11	3	55	35	15	.310	.355	.429
Ira Thomas	C,103	30	103	297	33	81	14	3	0	39	23	4	.273	.341	.340
Amos Strunk	OF,62; 1B,2	22	74	215	42	55	7	2	1	21	35	13	.256	.363	.321
Jack Lapp	C,57; 1B,4	26	68	167	35	59	10	3	1	26	24	4	.353	.435	.467
Harry Davis	1B,53	37	57	183	27	36	9	1	1	22	24	2	.197	.297	.273
Claud Derrick	2B,21; SS,5; 1B,4	25	36	100	14	23	1	2	0	5	7	7	.230	.294	.280
Paddy Livingston	C,26	31	27	71	9	17	4	0	0	8	7	1	.239	.316	.296
Topsy Hartsel	OF,10	37	25	38	8	9	2	0	0	1	8	0	.237	.396	.289
Chester Emerson	OF,7	21	7	18	2	4	0	0	0	0	6	1	.222	.417	.222
Willie Hogan*	OF,6	26	7	19	1	2	1	0	0	2	0	0	.105	.105	.158
Earle Mack	3B,2	21	4	0	0	0	0	0	0	0	0	0	.000	.000	.000
Totals		27	152	5,199	**861**	1,540	237	93	**35**	**692**	424	226	**.296**	**.357**	**.398**

*Played for another team during season. Statistics are those compiled with 1911 Philadelphia Athletics only.

Pitching

	Threw	Age	Games	GS	CG	ShO	IP	H	HR	BB	SO	W	L	Pct	Sv	ERA
Jack Coombs	Right	28	47	**40**	26	1	337	**360**	8	119	185	**28**	12	.700	3	3.53
Eddie Plank	Left	35	40	30	24	6	257	237	2	77	149	23	8	.742	4	2.10
Cy Morgan	Right	32	38	30	15	2	250	217	0	113	136	15	7	.682	1	2.70
Chief Bender	Right	27	31	24	16	3	216	198	2	58	114	17	5	**.773**	2	2.16
Harry Krause	Left	23	27	19	12	1	169	155	2	47	85	11	8	.579	2	3.04
Doc Martin	Right	23	11	3	1	0	38	40	1	17	21	1	1	.500	0	4.50
Dave Danforth	Left	21	14	2	1	0	34	29	1	17	21	4	1	.800	1	3.74
Lefty Russell	Left	20	7	2	0	0	32	45	1	18	7	0	3	.000	0	7.67
Elmer Leonard	Right	22	5	1	1	0	19	26	0	10	10	2	2	.500	0	2.84
Boardwalk Brown	Right	24	2	1	1	0	12	12	0	2	6	0	1	.000	0	4.50
Lep Long	Right	22	4	0	0	0	8	15	0	5	4	0	0	—	0	4.50
Howard Armstrong	Right	21	1	0	0	0	3	3	0	1	0	0	1	.000	0	0.00
Allan Collamore	Right	24	2	0	0	0	2	6	0	3	1	0	1	.000	0	36.00
Totals		29	229	152	97	13	1,376	1,343	**17**	487	739	**101**	**50**	**.669**	**13**	3.01

CHAPTER 3

1912 New York Giants

By careful analysis it is not a difficult matter to ascertain why the New Yorks won. Their speed as a run-getting machine was much superior to that of any of their opponents. Every factor of Base Ball which can be studied demonstrates that fact. They led the National League in batting and they led it in base running. They were keenly alive to the opportunities which were offered to them to win games. . . . To earn the winning run, not by hook or crook, but to earn it by excelling opponents through superior play in a department where the opponents are weak, is the story of capturing a pennant.

—John Foster in *Spalding's Official Base Ball Guide* (1913 edition)

Record: 103-48, .682 (18th)
Two-Year (1912–13): 204-99, .673 (15th)
Three-Year (1911–13): 303-153, .664
  (12th)

SD Score: 3.32 (15th)
Two-Year: 5.81 (17th)
Three-Year: 7.84 (22d)

Results:
1911 National League Champions
1912 National League Champions
1913 National League Champions

Days in First Place: 151 of 179;
  clinched September 26

Winning Streak: 16 games
Longest Losing Streak: 4 games

Pennant Race: The Giants opened the 1912 season on the road and split six games. In the home opener on April 18, with the flag at half-mast to honor those poor souls recently lost on the *Titanic*, Christy Mathewson beat the Brooklyn Dodgers, 6–2. With that, the Giants embarked on a run that saw them win 27 of their next 30 games. And after the Giants beat the second-place Pirates on June 17, their lead ballooned to a dozen games, and the pennant race was essentially over.

Against the Contenders: The Giants went 12-8 against the Pirates, who wound up in second place, 10 games off the pace. But they went just 9-13 against the third-place Cubs.

Runs Scored: 823 (1st)

Runs Allowed: 571 (2d)

The Pirates allowed just 565 runs. The Giants and Bucs were the only N.L. clubs to allow fewer than 668. Thanks to Jeff Tesreau (1.96), Christy Mathewson (2.12), and Red Ames (2.46), who ranked first, second, and fifth in ERA, respectively, the club ERA was 2.58, easily the lowest in the loop. So how did Pittsburgh allow fewer runs? Simple, they committed an absurdly low number of errors (169), which would stand as the lowest full-season total of the century until 1921.

Pythagorean Record: 100-51

Manager: John McGraw

McGraw, of course, ranks among the game's greatest managers. "The Little General" managed for all or part of thirty-three seasons (all but two and a half of them with the Giants), and his teams won eleven National League pennants, including four straight from 1921 through 1924.

Regular Lineup

Player	Position	ROV	OW%
Beals Becker	CF	.281	.577
Larry Doyle	2B	.323	.707
Fred Snodgrass	LF	.276	.560

Ernie Shore's Bogus Save

On June 20, 1912, Ernie Shore made his major league debut as a member of the New York Giants. Shore entered in the ninth inning, with the Giants nursing a 21–2 lead over the Boston Braves. Perfect chance to get the kid some work, right? Shore got some work, all right. He finished the game, but not before Boston touched him for 8 hits and 10 runs (three of them earned). Shore was released soon after.

That single game with the Giants was not forgotten, however. To quote *Total Baseball*, "[B]eginning in 1967, a battalion of researchers commanded by David Neft foraged through the official records and newspaper box scores to provide freshly compiled figures for those who now had ERAs, RBI, slugging averages, saves, and all manner of wonderful things." Neft's researchers found Shore's 1912 appearance, of course. The save became an

Player	Position	ROV	OW%
Red Murray	RF	.271	.539
Fred Merkle	1B	.308	.665
Buck Herzog	3B	.269	.530
Chief Meyers	C	.351	.772
Art Fletcher	SS	.263	.506
Christy Mathewson	P		

at that time, a save was credited to any reliever who finished a victory, provided that pitcher was not eligible for the decision. Thus, when the first *Baseball Encyclopedia* appeared in 1969, Shore got a save.

The qualifications for a save got tougher in 1973, but nobody ever went back and took away saves from pitchers, which is why to this day Ernie Shore's line for 1912 still includes a 27.00 ERA and one save.—*Rob*

Stats 'n' Stuff

◆ John McGraw hated pitchers who couldn't throw strikes, and the 1912 staff was probably the best example of this. Giant pitchers issued only 338 free passes, 114 fewer than the second-best Reds. And Jeff Tesreau accounted for 106 of those 338 walks, which means the rest of the staff allowed just 1.85 walks per nine innings.

◆ The 1911 Giants own the major league stolen base record, with 347. In 1912

Clearly, this was an outstanding lineup, with every regular managing a better than .500 offensive winning percentage. The Giants might have scored a few more runs if the best hitters had been clustered together in the middle of the lineup, but when everybody can hit like this, you really can't go wrong.

Bench: Becker and Josh Devore were both left-handed-hitting outfielders, they both wound up hitting about the same, and Devore played almost as much as Becker. When the World Series rolled around, Devore played left field, Snodgrass shifted to center, and Becker sat (check this, as Snodgrass played some center field during the regular season).

Art Wilson backed up Meyers behind the plate, and Tillie Shafer served as New York's primary utility infielder. Aside from those three, the rest of the bench was mostly for decoration, though Moose McCormick did lead the National League with 11 pinch hits and 30 pinch-hit at-bats.

Scouting the Pitchers: Christy Mathewson (23-12, 2.12) is of course famous for his "fadeaway," an early version of the screwball that he'd learned from a minor league pitcher named Dave Williams back in 1898. However, the fadeaway hurt Matty's arm, so he didn't actually throw it much. The fadeaway was merely one of Mathewson's many pitches, as he also threw a fastball, a "slowball" (something like a knuckleball), a variety of curves (including a "drop curve" and an out curve), and even the occasional spitball.

Rube Marquard (26-11, 2.57) had learned the fadeaway from Mathewson, and before the 1911 season he also refined his changeup, thus adding two pitches to his primary offerings, a jumping fastball and a "drop ball" (slow curve), all thrown from a three-quarters delivery advised by Matty.

Rookie Jeff Tesreau (17-7, 1.96) relied on a spitball thrown with greater velocity than most.

Red Ames (11-5, 2.46) was famous for his inability to throw strikes and for his ability to pitch well in cold weather, though by 1912 he had, for the most part, conquered his control problems. Ames threw about as hard as anybody in the National League, and he complemented his heater with a sweeping curveball.

How Were They Built? In his autobiography, John McGraw wrote lovingly of his 1911 squad, but most of his comments are just as applicable to the 1912 team, which was essentially the same (save for the welcome addition of Jeff Tesreau, about whom more later). McGraw's book came out in 1923, and his Giants had just won two straight World Series. So of course everyone wanted him to compare his new pennant winners to his old ones.

> While I have a keen regard and admiration for my pennant-winning and world's championship club of 1921 and 1922, I can not truthfully say that it has ever given me the thrill and the glow that I used to get out of my speed marvels of 1911, the club that was beaten by the Athletics.
>
> I do not mean to say that the 1911 outfit, which practically stole their way into the pennant along the base lines, was a more powerful team than the one of 1922. I simply have a great love for it largely because of its speed on the bases and also because I developed nearly every man on that team. They were what you might call hand-raised. Other clubs I have built up by trades and shifts, by using what ability I may have at organization. Those 1911 boys, though, were my own.

What Brought Them Down? Unlike some teams, the Giants were not hurt by the rival Federal League, which opened play in 1913. McGraw supposedly received a pair of hugely lucrative offers from the Federals but turned them down, and none of his top players defected (thanks to some nice raises).

The Giants fell from the heights in 1914, but not without a fight. By the beginning of June, New York sat atop the N.L. standings, just as usual. And as late as early September, they were still in first place

they stole 319, third all-time behind the 1976 Athletics (341).

◆ Christy Mathewson won his 300th game on June 13, 3–2 over the Cubs. Though he tossed 27 complete games in 1912, somehow Matty didn't record a single shutout. It was the first and only full season of his career in which he wouldn't get one.

◆ A hardy bunch, Giant batters were struck by 69 pitched balls, 21 more than the runner-up Boston Braves.

Around the Majors

April 12 Tinker, Evers, and Chance play their last game together, as manager Chance replaces himself with Vic Saier at first base after today.

April 20 The Red Sox open Fenway Park with a 7–6 victory over the New York Highlanders, with 27,000 fans in attendance.

May 15 Ty Cobb is indefinitely suspended after assaulting a fan in the stands. Three days later, the rest of the Detroit Tigers protest Cobb's suspension by refusing to play. Manager Hughie Jennings signs local semi-pro players to fill out the roster, and the Tigers are drubbed by the Athletics, 24–2. Faced with the threat of permanent suspensions, the real Tigers return to work on May 19. Cobb's suspension is lifted on May 26.

September 6 Walter Johnson and Joe Wood hook up in one of the most anticipated pitching match-

before falling victim to Boston's "Miracle" Braves, who mounted one of the great stretch runs in the history of the game.

During the dynastic years, of course, the club's strength was its pitching staff. But by 1915, Mathewson was washed up, and Marquard had been waived the season before. That left Tesreau as the ace of the staff, with little help from his mates. In 1915, the Giants finished in last place for the first and only time in McGraw's twenty-nine full seasons as manager. They returned to the World Series in 1917 (and lost yet again), but with a mostly new group of players.

Most Valuable Giant: Christy Mathewson

Matty didn't win quite as many games as Marquard, and his ERA wasn't quite as low as Tesreau's, but his ERA was 0.45 lower than Marquard's, and he pitched 67 more innings than Tesreau. Plus, all things considered, he was the top N.L. pitcher of his era. Although Chief Meyers and Larry Doyle were very good players who had very good years, Mathewson was the on-field leader of the Giants.

Worst Regular: It's between Beals Becker and Fred Snodgrass. We'll go with Becker because over the course of his career he wasn't as good as Snodgrass.

Hall of Famers: Christy Mathewson, Rube Marquard, and of course John McGraw.

Our Hall of Famers: Matty and McGraw are both among the all-time greats at their spots. Marquard, on the other hand, was just one of many questionable candidates elected by the Veterans Committee in the late 1960s and early 1970s.

Marquard has been described by Bill James as "probably the worst starting pitcher in the Hall of Fame," and his career record is inferior to those of Wilbur Cooper, Charlie Root, and Bob Shawkey, none of whom have drawn much Hall of Fame support. The Hall's Veterans Committee elected seven new members in 1971, including Marquard, and the Committee's profligacy resulted in their power being severely cut back from that point.

The Pennant Race: Early on, the Giants were challenged by the Cincinnati Reds, who were 22-6 on May 19. However, the Reds managed only 53 victories the rest of the season, and the Giants just won and won and won, finishing with a comfy 10-game lead over the Pirates.

The 1912 World Series: See article, "Matty, Merkle, and Snow."

The Ballpark: The Giants played their home games in Brush Stadium, named for owner John T. Brush. The ballpark was renamed the Polo Grounds in 1920, after three earlier parks which had carried the same name. The dimensions were perhaps the most radical of the twentieth century, as fair territory was laid out something like a horseshoe. It was a mere 279 feet down the left-field line, and just 258 down the right-field line. But the distances increased sharply from there, to approximately 460 feet to left- and right-center, and 480-plus feet to straightaway center. Of course, in the dead-ball era it didn't matter much how close the fences were.

Brush Stadium was practically brand new because it was hurriedly built after the third Polo Grounds burned down on April 16, 1911. The Polo Grounds were demolished in 1964 (with the same wrecking ball that had taken down Brooklyn's Ebbets Field, four years earlier). Today, the site is occupied by the Polo Grounds Towers, four thirty-story apartment buildings.

Books about the 1912 Giants: The best book that deals specifically with the Giants of this period is Christy Mathewson's *Pitching in a Pinch* (New York: G. P. Putnam's Sons, 1912). Noel Hynd wrote a somewhat sloppily researched book called *The Giants of the Polo Grounds* (New York: Doubleday, 1988), which contains twenty-five pages on the 1911–13 Giants. And in 1996, Hynd published *Marquard & Seeley* (Hyannis, MA: Parnassus), a small book about the famous relationship between Giants pitcher Rube Marquard and vaudeville star Blossom Seeley. In 1998, Larry D. Mansch's painstakingly researched biography of Marquard, *Rube Marquard: The Life and Times of a Baseball Hall of Famer,* was published (Jefferson, NC: McFarland).

There are many, many books about John McGraw, including volumes by both him (*My Thirty Years in Baseball* [New York: Boni & Liveright, 1923]) and his wife, Blanche (*The Real McGraw* [New York: David M. McKay Co., 1953]). Charles Alexander's *John McGraw* (New York: Viking, 1988) is a comprehensive, scholarly account of

ups of all time. Johnson's 16-game winning streak had just been snapped 11 days earlier, and Wood was working on a 13-game streak. Wood's Red Sox beat Johnson's Senators, 1–0, and he too would run his winning streak to 16.

October 6 Pirates outfielder Owen "Chief" Wilson whacks his 36th triple, setting a single-season major league record that still stands.

They Took After Their Manager . . .

John McGraw was a commanding manager. He didn't manage by the seat of his pants; he knew what he wanted done, and he made sure it *got* done. As a player, McGraw is primarily remembered for being scrappy and feisty, but he had one truly *outstanding* skill: he got on base. McGraw's *career* on-base percentage was .465, which is the third highest in history behind only Ted Williams and Babe Ruth (minimum of

4,000 career plate appearances). In 1899, McGraw's OBP was .547 (in large part due to a league-leading 124 walks), which enabled him to lead the National League with 140 runs despite playing in only 117 games and rapping only 17 extra-base hits.

McGraw's first full year managing the New York Giants was 1903. From 1904 through 1914, the Giants led the league in on-base percentage *every year for a total of eleven consecutive seasons.* (McGraw managed the A.L. Orioles in 1901 and, you guessed it, they led the league in OBP.)

The 1908 Giants exceeded the league OBP by a greater margin than any other team in the twentieth century. Two other Giants teams (1905 and 1906) are among the handful of teams that posted OBPs more than 10 percent better than the league average in a season. From 1904 through 1924, a span of twenty-one seasons, the Giants led the National League in OBP *sixteen times.* The last five times that

John McGraw *(National Baseball Hall of Fame Library, Cooperstown, NY)*

McGraw's life and includes roughly twenty-five pages on the seasons covered in this chapter. Chief Meyers, Fred Snodgrass, and Rube Marquard are all featured in Lawrence S. Ritter's classic work of oral history, *The Glory of Their Times* (New York: Macmillan, 1966). Even better, all three can actually be *heard* in the wonderful audio version of that book, which was released in 1998.

Matty, Merkle, and Snow

The 1912 World Series opened in New York, and manager McGraw went with rookie Jeff Tesreau in game 1, apparently figuring he'd be more comfortable there than in Boston, site of games 2 and 3. Tesreau allowed three runs in the seventh, however, and wound up losing to Smokey Joe Wood, 4–3.

Mathewson started game 2 and pitched 11 innings but was lucky to escape with a 6–6 tie (the game was called on account of darkness) after five Giants errors, three of them by shortstop Art Fletcher. New York finally picked up a win in game 3, when Marquard tossed a complete game to defeat the Red Sox, 2–1.

The Series shifted to New York for game 4, which turned out to be a near-replica of the opener, Wood defeating Tesreau by a 3–1 score. Back in Boston for game 5, the Sox took a commanding three-games-to-one lead when Hugh Bedient tossed a three-hitter to beat Mathewson, 2–1. The Giants weren't finished yet, though. Marquard and Tesreau both went the distance in games 6 and 7, with the Giants driving Wood from the mound after only one inning in the latter contest, and suddenly the Series was even.

The eighth game of the 1912 Series remains one of the most famous of all for its dramatic and improbable conclusion. Game 8 was a rematch of game 5, Mathewson versus Bedient. The Giants grabbed a 1–0 lead in the third on Red Murray's RBI double, but the Red Sox tied the game on Olaf Henriksen's RBI double in the seventh. Because Henriksen had pinch-hit for Bedient, Joe Wood—so terrible just twenty-four hours earlier—came in to pitch the eighth for Boston. Wood allowed a baserunner that inning and another in the ninth, but held the Giants scoreless. Matty matched Wood, so the foes went to extra innings. With one out in the top of the tenth, Murray doubled again and came around to score when Tris Speaker fumbled Fred Merkle's base hit. Wood escaped the inning without further damage.

Thus, Christy Mathewson, the greatest N.L. pitcher of the era, took the mound in the bottom of the tenth with a chance to clinch the Giants' first World Championship since 1905. Pinch-hitter Clyde Engle led off with a high fly ball to center field. Fred Snodgrass camped under it, the ball dropped into his mitt . . . and then popped right back out, with Engle cruising into second base. Harry Hooper followed with a drive to deep center field, and this time Snodgrass made a brilliant running catch, with Engle tagging up and advancing to third.

That brought up second baseman Steve Yerkes, perhaps the weakest hitter in the Red Sox lineup. Chief Meyers once claimed of Mathewson, "I don't think he ever walked a man from being wild." But wild or not, Matty walked Yerkes, thus bringing up the far more dangerous Tris Speaker. However, Speaker lifted a routine pop fly in foul territory, midway between home plate and first base.

Speaker's foul pop is one of those plays that, if I had a time machine, I'd like to go back and see for myself because the differing accounts suggest a baseball version of *Rashomon*. According to Snodgrass, "Merkle didn't have to go thirty feet to get it, it was almost

McGraw's teams led the league in OBP (1917, 1921–24) they won pennants.

Of course, McGraw had been an important part of the successful Orioles teams of the 1890s and obviously understood the value of getting on base. I doubt if the actual phrase *on-base percentage* was used in McGraw's day, but he implicitly knew of its importance, and he made sure his players did, too.—*Eddie*

Tesreau's No-Hitter

Jeff Tesreau was a rookie in 1912, and a wild one at that. He issued 106 walks, easily the most among the Giant hurlers and tied for fourth-most in the National League. It was alright, though, because Tesreau also paced the National League with a 1.96 earned-run average (incidentally, 1912 was the first season that ERA was an official statistic).

Tesreau's given name was Charles, but the 6-foot-2-inch, 218-pounder was nicknamed "Jeff," or sometimes "Big Jeff," because of his resemblance to Jim Jeffries, the great heavyweight boxer. Tesreau was also called "the Ozark Bear," in honor of his southern Missouri heritage and his great size (some reports have him at 6-foot-4 and 240 pounds). Occasionally writers called him "the Human Bullfrog" because of his habit of jumping from team to team early in his professional career.

Tesreau relied on a hard spitball, and nearly ninety years later that still sounds like a hell of a pitch. Everything came together on September 6, when Tesreau no-hit the Phillies in Philadelphia. The only questionable scoring decision came when Dode Paskert led off the bottom of the first with a pop fly along the first-base line. First baseman Merkle and catcher Wilson converged on the ball, but nobody took charge until it was too late, and the ball bounced off Merkle's tardily outstretched glove.

Jeff Tesreau (*National Baseball Hall of Fame Library, Cooperstown, NY*)

in the first-base coaching box. Chief Meyers, our catcher, tried to catch it, but couldn't quite get there. It was too far from home plate. Matty could have put it in his hind pocket himself." According to Meyers,

I gave that pop-up the old college try, but it was too far away for me to get. Matty came over, too, but waited for Merkle to take it, and it fell right between all of us. I think the Red Sox dugout coached Merkle off it. The Boston bench called for Matty to take it, and called for me to take it, and I think that confused Fred. He was afraid of a collision. You see, the Red Sox bench was right there, near where the ball fell, and they just coached him off of it.

According to Harry Hooper, who was sitting on that Red Sox bench,

Steve Yerkes got a base on balls, and that brought up Tris Speaker. . . . Well, Spoke hit a little pop foul over near first base, and old Chief Meyers took off after it. He didn't have a chance, but Matty kept calling for him to take it. If he'd called for Merkle, it would have been an easy out. Or Matty could have taken it himself. But he kept calling for the Chief to take it, and poor Chief—he never was too fast to begin with—he lumbered down that line after it as fast as his big legs would carry him, stuck out his big catcher's mitt—and just missed it.

Spoke went back to the batter's box and yelled to Mathewson, "Well, you just called for the wrong man. It's gonna cost you this ball game."

And so it did. Whoever's fault it was, Speaker took advantage of the reprieve and lined a single into right field, scoring Engle and sending Yerkes to third base. Speaker moved up to second on the throw in, so Mathewson issued Duffy Lewis an intentional walk, thus loading the bases with only one out. Larry Gardner followed with a long fly to right field. Josh Devore caught the ball but had no chance to throw out Yerkes, who sprinted down the line to score the game-winning, Series-clinching win.

Of course, Snodgrass was anointed the goat of the Series. His error was immortalized as the "$30,000 muff," that amount being the approximate difference between what the Giants and Red Sox players split from the Series gate receipts. When Snodgrass died in 1974, his obituary in the *New York Times* was headlined, "Fred Snodgrass, 86, Dead; Ball Player Muffed 1912 Fly."—Rob

Hail to the Chief

Who is the *only* twentieth-century N.L. catcher to lead his league in on-base percentage? Well, given the title of this piece and where it appears, you can probably guess that the answer is John

An error was scored. Some observers thought it should have been scored a hit, but Merkle claimed to have stitch marks on his hand where the ball hit.

Tesreau was no one-year wonder. At the conclusion of his third major league season, he sported a 65-30 record and a 2.19 ERA, which I suspect would compare favorably with the first three seasons of just about any pitcher you might like to suggest, be it Mathewson (64-47, 2.27), Walter Johnson (32-48, 1.94), or Pete Alexander (69-38, 2.72).

His career petered out quickly, however, and by the end of the 1918 season Tesreau was pitching in semi-pro games in the New York area. In 1919 he took over as head baseball coach at Dartmouth College, where his charges included a number of future major leaguers, including Yankee third baseman Red Rolfe. Tesreau's life, like his pitching career, ended early. He died on September 24, 1946, at the age of fifty-seven.—*Rob*

The "Original" George Burns

Who is the only player of the twentieth century to lead his league in on-base percentage, runs scored, walks, and stolen bases in the same season? (I guess you could call that "The Leadoff Hitter Quadruple Crown.") The answer is George Burns of the New York Giants, who accomplished that feat in 1919.

Although he didn't become a regular until 1913, Burns did play briefly for the 1912 Giants. This George Burns, an outfielder, was no relation to "Tioga" George Burns (b. 1893), who played first base and was the American League MVP in 1926, nor to Nathan Birnbaum (b. 1896), who we would all come to know as George Burns the entertainer.

It is true that some other players have come close to matching Burns' feat (for example, Ty Cobb missed by one walk in 1915) and it's true that in the modern game a player who leads in runs

"Chief" Meyers, who posted a .441 on-base percentage in 1912. (Mickey Cochrane, also a leading character in this book, paced the American League in OBP in 1933 and is the only other major league catcher to accomplish such a feat. Of course, nobody had heard of OBP in those days, so neither Cochrane nor Meyers knew just how good they were.)

Meyers' 1912 season was the best of his nine-year career. It wasn't a fluke, though, as Meyers created runs at a rate better than the league average in every year except his last. Besides leading the league in OBP in 1912, Meyers finished fourth in the league in slugging and (barely) finished second, to future Giant Heinie Zimmerman, in RC/27. That's a hell of an offensive season for a catcher, and especially for a catcher who caught the best pitching staff in the league. No disrespect to John McGraw, but he probably wasted Meyers' hitting ability some by batting him seventh and eighth, presumably because that's where McGraw thought catchers were *supposed* to bat.

Meyers got a late start to his major league career and had a relatively short career, but lived a long life. A full-blooded Cahuilla Indian, Meyers was born in a small village in 1880, and when he was eleven or twelve his family moved to Riverside, California. After a few years of public school, Meyers made a meager living playing semi-pro baseball in the Southwest. Somehow, Meyers wangled a scholarship to Dartmouth College when he was twenty-five years old, though he couldn't play baseball for them because of his prior career as a professional. He left Dartmouth after one year, due to his mother's illness, and embarked on a true career as a professional ballplayer. In 1909, he debuted with the New York Giants at the ripe age of twenty-eight. Like nearly all catchers in his time, Meyers didn't last long, and by 1917 he was reduced to part-time duties with the Brooklyn Dodgers and Boston Braves in his last major league season.

In the late 1960s, half a century after his playing career, Meyers became famous once again, this time as one of the more erudite subjects in Larry Ritter's classic bestseller, *The Glory of Their Times*. As a result of the book, Meyers was invited to appear on *The Today Show*, where he delivered a rousing rendition of "Casey at the Bat." Meyers died on July 25, 1971, just four days short of his ninety-first birthday.—Eddie and Rob

Rube Marquard: "The Girl, the Big Streak, and Everything"

For the first few years of his major league career, Giants lefthander Richard William "Rube" Marquard was baseball's most famous failure. In 1907, his first professional season, Marquard went 23-13 with the Canton Chinamen (yes, that was their name) of the Central League. A year later, pitching for Indianapolis in the "fast" American Association, Marquard led the league with 28 wins and 250 strikeouts.

On June 30, 1908, Marquard tossed a three-hit shutout to beat the Louisville Colonels 3–0, and later that evening the owner of the Indianapolis club conducted a virtual auction of Marquard's contract, with representatives of ten major league teams in attendance. After a long evening, the New York Giants, represented by manager John McGraw and owner John T. Brush, took the prize with an $11,000 bid.

Eleven thousand dollars might not sound like much, but at the time it was the all-time record price for a baseball player. Marquard would be a Giant, though his contract required that he finish the season in Indianapolis. And he finished with a flourish, hurling a no-hitter in one of his last starts for the club.

With Indianapolis' season finally over, on September 16 Marquard—routinely described in newspapers as "the $11,000 Beauty" or something similar—joined the Giants, who were in the middle of one of the most famous pennant races in history. After using Marquard as a decoy in a few games, McGraw finally assigned a start to his young pitcher on September 25, against the Cincinnati Reds. Obviously suffering jitters, Marquard allowed five runs in five innings before he was yanked, and the Giants lost 7–1. Of course they would wind up losing the National League pennant to the Cubs by a single game.

Marquard didn't pitch poorly in 1909—he posted a 2.60 ERA that almost exactly equaled the league average—but poor luck resulted in a 5-13 record, and by the end of the season every newspaper in New York was referring to him as "the $11,000 Lemon." (Yes, even back then the sporting press in Gotham could be rough.)

Things got worse in 1910, as Marquard had so much trouble throwing strikes that McGraw wouldn't let him pitch in real games for

scored, walks, and OBP might be a big slugger who's not expected to steal bases. But the fact remains that Burns did something that neither Cobb nor Rickey Henderson nor Tim Raines nor anyone else has ever done. That season wasn't a fluke, either. Burns was a fine player and a major league regular for eleven seasons who led his league in runs scored and walks five times each.—*Eddie* weeks at a time, and he wound up working in only 13 games all season. McGraw would later write of Marquard's problems:

His main fault was of putting the ball over the plate with nothing on it, as we say. Rube had trouble with his control. After whipping a few curves—and he had a beauty—and some fast ones around the batter, he would find himself in the hole. So fearful was he of not being able to get the ball over when it came down to two-and-three that he would simply toss it over as straight as a string. In other words, he had so much stuff that he was afraid to use it.

Under the tutelage of the great Christy Mathewson and Giants coach Wilbert Robinson, Marquard did conquer his control problems. Though he walked 106 hitters in 1911, Marquard also topped the National League with 237 strikeouts, and his 24-7 record figured to a league-leading .774 winning percentage. He'd gone from Beauty to Lemon and now back to Beauty.

In 1912, Marquard led the National League with 26 wins. In the process, he became the most famous baseball pitcher in the country, although not the best baseball pitcher, as you can see from this comparison of Marquard to Mathewson over the two-year stretch of 1911 and 1912:

1911–12	W-L	Pct	Innings	Hits	BB	K	ERA
Mathewson	49-25	.662	617	614	72	275	2.06
Marquard	50-18	.735	572	507	186	412	2.53

Wins and losses aside (Marquard's 50 victories over the two seasons were tops in the National League) Matty still ranked as the ace of the Giants staff (and the best pitcher in the National League). He pitched more innings, and his ERA was significantly lower. Although Matty's arm wasn't what it once was, he compensated with incredible control.

But in the eyes of the public, Rube Marquard was tops, thanks to The Streak. Marquard's first start of the 1912 season came on April 16 in Boston, where he beat the Braves 8–2. Eight days later he won his second start, an 11–4 victory over the Phillies. And from there, he just kept winning. On May 20 in Cincinnati, he beat the Reds 5–0 for (surprisingly) his only shutout of the season. On June 19 in Boston, he beat the Braves for his fifteenth straight, the longest streak in the major leagues since 1890.

The streak finally ended on July 8, when the Cubs beat Marquard, 6–2. After starting the season 19-0, Marquard went just 7-11 the rest of the way, though that record was due as much to poor luck as poor pitching. No matter. His popularity was ensured. Marquard, baseball's most famous failure just a few years earlier, now ranked as baseball's most famous success. Shortly after the streak ended, he starred in *Rube Marquard Wins*, a silent movie that earned positive notices on its release in late August. And shortly after the 1912 World Series, Marquard began rehearsing a stage act with Blossom Seeley, a top vaudeville performer. Their show, "Breaking the Record, or The 19th Straight," toured the country and was a big hit. Wherever they went, the pair was met at train stations by newsmen and photographers.

But of more interest to some was the blossoming relationship between Marquard and Seeley (a.k.a. Mrs. Joe Kane). This resulted in some unpleasant scenes, the most unpleasant of which had Mr. Kane beating down the door of a hotel room in which Marquard and Seeley were staying, the latter two escaping down a fire escape. Seeley eventually got a divorce from Kane, and she and Marquard were wed on March 12, 1915. It was, in essence, an early, lesser version of the Joe DiMaggio–Marilyn Monroe story. And like that story, this one ended in divorce.

Marquard's vaudeville career, successful as it was, did not last long. He would eventually tire of the demands of Seeley's career, and the pair separated in 1919, then made it legal in 1920. By then, Marquard had been pitching for the Dodgers for five seasons, having negotiated his own trade from the Giants back in 1915, just a few months after tossing his first (and only) major league no-hitter. He pitched for Cincinnati in 1921, then spent four seasons with the Braves.

Even when nobody wanted him in the major leagues, Marquard's famous name still got him work. He managed, coached, and pitched sporadically in the minor leagues through 1932, and in 1931 he umpired in the Eastern League. As we noted earlier, Marquard was elected to the Hall of Fame in 1971, quite likely due, at least in part, to his chapter in *The Glory of Their Times*.

Finally, a revisionist note: Marquard generally claimed to have been born in 1889, and for many years that's what appeared in all the record books. That birth year would have meant that Marquard debuted with the Giants when he was not quite nineteen years old. However, Society for American Baseball Research member Fred Schuld recently discovered that Marquard was actually born in 1886 rather than 1889, meaning that he reached the majors when he was almost twenty-two. In addition, author Larry Mansch discovered that many of the stories Marquard told in *The Glory of Their Times*, particularly those involving his long-time estrangement from his father, were essentially fiction.—Rob

Charley Faust

If this chapter was concerned primarily with the 1911 Giants, then Charles Victor "Victory" Faust would certainly deserve a thousand-odd words in this book. But although this chapter is about the 1912 squad, Faust's story merits a mention.

On the morning of July 28, 1911, a thirty-year-old Kansas farmer named Charley Faust strolled into the Planter's Hotel in St. Louis, road quarters for the New York Giants. Someone pointed out John McGraw to Faust, who introduced himself to the Giants manager. Faust then told a strange tale. A few months back, he'd journeyed to Wichita, the nearest "big city," where he'd paid a fortune teller five dollars to divine his future. For his five bucks, Faust got a doozy. If he joined the New York Giants, he would become the greatest pitcher that ever lived. Once he helped the Giants win a pennant, he would meet a girl named Lulu, marry her, and sire a generation of baseball stars.

Now in July, with the Giants as far west as they ever got, Faust arrived in St. Louis and found himself talking to McGraw, manager of those same New York Giants.

McGraw, no doubt interested in a pleasant diversion from the oppressive St. Louis heat, invited Faust to the ballpark that afternoon. When Faust showed up at the park, he was wearing his Sunday best. McGraw gave him a glove and offered to catch his offerings.

Faust gave McGraw his signals, but of course all he had was a fastball that probably didn't break 65 miles an hour. After a few minutes of this, McGraw shrugged off his mitt and caught Faust bare-handed.

After McGraw tired of that particular foolishness, he reportedly told Faust, "Well, we're having batting practice now, so get a bat and go up there. I want to see you run, too, so run it out and see if you can score." Faust dribbled a grounder to shortstop, but the shortstop purposely bobbled the ball, then threw wildly to first base. As the ball went around the diamond haphazardly, Faust circled the bases, sliding into each of them and finally crossing the plate in a cloud of dust, still in his Sunday best. The players all had a grand time, and so did the early arrivals in the stands.

Such a grand time, in fact, that Faust eventually was given a uniform and became a big crowd pleaser performing pre-game workouts. He quickly gained fame as both a performer and a good-luck charm, and "The Kansas Jinx-Killer" even got into a couple of games late in the 1911 season.

The most popular legend about Faust holds that he was with the club from 1911 through 1913, during which time they won three National League pennants. But then he left the club and the Giants did *not* capture the flag in 1914.

Well, that's not exactly how it happened. Faust last appeared in a Giants uniform on April 21, 1912. Thereafter, he watched the team from the stands or, occasionally, from the end of the bench. According to researcher Gabe Schechter, Faust actually left the Giants for good in mid-July. The day Faust departed, Rube Marquard's record stood at 19-0. Within a week, Marquard lost three games, and the Giants took a nosedive in the standings before recovering to capture the pennant. By the time the 1912 World Series started, Faust was working as a carpenter in Pasadena, California. What's more, Faust spent all of 1913 on the West Coast, first in Pasadena and then in Seattle.

Faust did come back east in February of 1914, hoping to get his old job back or, barring that, more vaudeville work. Neither of those hopes were rewarded, and Faust returned to Seattle. As Giants center fielder Fred Snodgrass later told Larry Ritter,

That fall, I joined a group of big leaguers, and we made a barnstorming trip, starting in Chicago and going through the Northwest, and down the Coast and over to Honolulu. And in Seattle, who came down to the hotel to see me, but Charley Faust. And Charley Faust said to me, he said, "Snow, I'm not very well, but I think if you prevail upon Mr. McGraw to send me to Hot Springs a month before spring training, that I could get into shape and help you win another pennant." Unfortunately, that never came to pass, because Charlie Faust died that winter, and we did not win the pennant the next year.

Indeed, Faust was first hospitalized in the summer of 1914, after being arrested while wandering the streets of Portland and claiming that he had walked there from Seattle and was on his way to New York to save the Giants (who could have used him). After seven weeks he was sent back to Seattle, where he became so deranged that his brother had him committed to the Western Hospital for the Insane at Fort Steilacoom, Washington. He died of tuberculosis in June 1915 at the age of thirty-four.—Rob

Mac and Doc

John McGraw was, along with Clark Griffith in the American League, a pioneer of the bullpen. As player-manager of the New York Highlanders in 1905, Griffith frequently used himself as a reliever—actually, *rescue pitcher* was the preferred term then—while across town McGraw used Claud Elliott almost exclusively as a reliever.

Elliott pitched in only 10 games, but 8 of those were relief appearances. More important from a historical perspective is that Elliott recorded saves in six of those eight relief outings, thus leading the league in that category.

Of course, saves weren't actually recorded (and figured retroactively) until the 1960s, but McGraw clearly was using Elliott to protect late-inning leads, and this had never really been done before. For whatever reason, Elliott was gone the next year, replaced by George Cecil Ferguson.

Only nineteen years old in 1906, Ferguson pitched in 22 games, relieving in 21 of them, and he too led the National League in saves, with seven. What's more, his only start resulted in a complete-game shutout. Like Elliott, however, Ferguson didn't last long, as McGraw sent him to Boston before the 1908 season.

McGraw's next relief specialist was a righthander named James

Otis "Doc" Crandall, whose presence on the Giants was due solely to happenstance. McGraw had played for the Cedar Rapids club back in 1891, and he always had a soft spot for that franchise. Thus, sometime prior to the 1908 season, McGraw was looking over a list of players he could draft from the minor leagues when he noticed a Crandall with Cedar Rapids. "That's the fellow I'll take," McGraw supposedly told the Giants secretary, "and I'm taking him simply because he comes from Cedar Rapids. That's where I got my first start. This new fellow, I'll bet, is good." As McGraw relates in his autobiography, *My Thirty Years in Baseball,*

> I was right, too. Otie stepped right in and made good. Not only was he a good pitcher but he could sock the ball. New York fans know mighty well how we used him successfully as both a pinch hitter and a pinch pitcher.
>
> In a close, tight place—the bases full, for instance—Crandall was one of the coolest pitchers I ever saw. He had no fear, no nerves.

Crandall could indeed sock the ball. He posted a .285 lifetime batting average, and in 1912 he batted .313 with 19 RBI in only 80 at-bats. In 1908, his first campaign with the Giants, Crandall started 24 games, relieved in 8, and posted a 12-12 record with a 2.93 ERA. That last number looks pretty good, until you discover that the league ERA was 2.35. So in 1909 it was off to the bullpen for Crandall.

McGraw didn't use Crandall like he'd used Elliott and Ferguson. Crandall never led the National League in saves, but he did lead the league in relief victories three straight seasons, 1910 through 1912. Crandall was so effective as a reliever in 1910—7-1 with five saves— that Damon Runyon wrote, "Crandall is the Giants' ambulance corps. He is first aid to the injured . . . without an equal as an extinguisher of batting rallies and run riots. . . . He is the greatest relief pitcher in baseball." Crandall also started 18 games that season, and went 10-3 in that role. In fact, Crandall's record as a starter from 1910 through 1912 was 25-10, though it's likely that McGraw let his relief specialist start against only the N.L.'s weaker teams.

After a so-so 1913 season, Crandall jumped to the Federal League, and in 1915 he was one of that circuit's better pitchers (21-15, 2.59). However, he also pitched 313 innings that season, far more than he'd ever thrown before. After that, his arm was no stronger than a wet noodle. Crandall did pitch in the Pacific Coast League until he was forty-one, but he'll always be remembered as one of the game's first relief aces.—Rob

TEAM STATISTICS

Hitting

	Games by Position	Age	G	AB	R	H	2B	3B	HR	RBI	BB	SB	Avg	OBP	Slug
Chief Meyers	C,122	31	126	300	60	133	16	5	6	54	47	8	.358	.441	.477
Fred Merkle	1B,129	23	129	567	82	148	22	6	11	84	42	37	.309	.374	.449
Larry Doyle	2B,143	25	143	401	98	184	33	8	10	90	56	36	.330	.393	.471
Buck Herzog	3B,140	26	140	528	72	127	20	9	2	47	57	37	.263	.350	.355
Art Fletcher	SS,126; 2B,2; 3B,1	27	129	558	64	118	17	9	1	57	16	16	.282	.330	.372
Red Murray	OF,143	28	143	583	83	152	26	20	3	92	27	38	.277	.320	.413
Beals Becker	OF,117	25	125	587	66	106	18	8	6	58	54	30	.264	.354	.393
Fred Snodgrass	OF,116; 1B,27; 2B,1	24	146	244	91	144	24	9	3	69	70	43	.269	.362	.364
Josh Devore	OF,96	24	106	327	66	90	14	6	2	37	51	27	.275	.381	.373
Tillie Shafer	SS,31; 3B,16; 2B,15	23	78	163	48	47	4	1	0	23	30	22	.288	.408	.325
Art Wilson	C,61	26	65	121	17	35	6	0	3	19	13	2	.289	.358	.413
Doc Crandall	P,37; 1B,1; 2B,1	24	50	80	9	25	6	2	0	19	6	0	.313	.360	.438
George Burns	OF,23	22	29	51	11	15	4	0	0	3	8	7	.294	.400	.373
Heinie Groh	2B,12; SS,7; 3B,6	22	27	48	8	13	2	1	0	3	8	6	.271	.375	.354
Moose McCormick	OF,6; 1B,1	31	42	39	4	13	4	1	0	8	6	1	.333	.422	.487
Grover Hartley	C,25	23	25	34	3	8	2	1	0	7	0	2	.235	.257	.353
Dave Robertson	1B,1	22	3	2	0	1	0	0	0	1	0	1	.500	.500	.500
Totals		27		5,067	823	1,451	231	89	47	702	514	319	.286	.360	.395

Pitching

	Threw	Age	Games	GS	CG	ShO	IP	H	HR	BB	SO	W	L	Pct	Sv	ERA
Rube Marquard	Left	25	43	38	22	1	295	286	9	80	175	26	11	.703	1	2.57
Christy Mathewson	Right	33	43	34	27	0	310	311	5	34	134	23	12	.657	4	2.12
Jeff Tesreau	Right	23	36	28	19	3	243	177	2	106	119	17	7	.708	1	**1.96**
Red Ames	Right	29	33	22	9	2	179	194	3	35	83	11	5	.688	2	2.46
Hooks Wiltse	Left	31	28	17	5	0	134	140	7	28	58	9	6	.600	3	3.16
Doc Crandall	Right	24	37	10	7	0	162	181	7	35	60	13	7	.650	2	3.61
Al Demaree	Right	27	2	2	1	1	16	17	0	2	11	1	0	1.000	0	1.69
Lore Bader	Right	24	2	1	1	0	10	9	0	6	3	2	0	1.000	0	0.90
LaRue Kirby	Right	22	3	1	1	0	11	13	1	6	2	1	0	1.000	0	5.73
Ted Goulait	Right	22	1	1	1	0	7	11	0	4	6	0	0	—	0	6.43
Louis Drucke	Right	23	1	0	0	0	2	5	0	1	0	0	0	—	1	13.50
Ernie Shore	Right	21	1	0	0	0	1	8	1	1	1	0	0	—	1	27.00
Totals		27	230	154	93	8	1,370	1,352	36	**338**	652	**103**	**48**	**.682**	15	**2.58**

CHAPTER 4

Way Back When

THE BEST OF THE
NINETEENTH CENTURY

The great hitting aggregation of today, known as the Yanks, have to go a few more years at the pace they displayed in 1927, to class with the Baltimore club—the famous Orioles of the nineties.
— Maclean Kennedy in *The Great Teams of Baseball* (1929)

Talk about trying to hit a moving target. Major league baseball changed dramatically for much of the late nineteenth century. In 1890, there were three "major" leagues. In 1892, there was one. In 1881, a walk took seven balls. In 1884, the National League dropped it to six, but returned to seven in 1886 while the American Association dropped to six the same year. The four-ball walk (sounds like a dance, doesn't it?) didn't make its first appearance until 1889. Starting in 1885, the National League allowed one side of the bat to be flat, but not the American Association. As far as we can tell, flat bats were not made illegal until 1893. In 1876, the first year of the National League, the pitcher's box was 45 feet from home plate. That was changed to 50 feet in 1881, and to the modern distance of 60 feet, 6

inches in 1893. Until 1887, the batter could call for a high or low pitch.

The point of all this trivia is that trying to determine which were the best teams of the nineteenth century is made very difficult by all of the changes. Besides the rule and league changes (and changes in strategy) were the changes that occur in an industry, or any entity, in its early years, a maturation process if you will. I don't want to get too arcane, but the differences between the ability and performance of players and teams were almost certainly changing much more from year to year than at any time since. Changes of that nature can render almost any analytical tools useless.

Those warnings out of the way, we'll begin where most people think this should start, with the Orioles' teams of the mid-1890s. Baltimore joined the National League in 1892, after the demise of the American Association, which had included a Baltimore franchise in most seasons since 1882. The Orioles brought up the rear in 1892, their first season in the National League, with a splendid 46-101 record. They allowed 1,020 runs; the league average was 782. Their rise to the top was quick from there, however, just as their exit *out* of the National League would be quick.

Ned Hanlon was elected club president of the Orioles in 1893. To quote James H. Bready from his wonderful book on the history of baseball in Baltimore, *The Home Team*: "In judging men, and swapping ballplayers, Hanlon had moments akin to clairvoyance." Hanlon was field manager, general manager, director of scouting—you name it—only without all of the titles. He wasn't unusual in that regard at that time, of course, but the rise to power of the Orioles is directly attributable to him. Hanlon traded for many of the players who would turn the team into a powerhouse.

The Orioles won three straight National League pennants, 1894–96, and finished a strong second in 1897 (90-40, two games out of first) and 1898 (96-53, six games out). Their run differentials were far and away the best in the league in each of their pennant-winning seasons:

Year	Team	Run Differential
1894	Baltimore	+352
	Boston	+218
	Philadelphia	+177
1895	Baltimore	+363
	Cleveland	+197
	Philadelphia	+111
1896	Baltimore	+333
	Cleveland	+190
	Cincinnati	+163

Their SD scores were also outstanding (you didn't think we had forgotten those, did you?). As an aside, we were amazed at the stability of SD scores for the nineteenth century. We calculated them only for leagues in which every team played around 100 games or more. However, the best (and worst) SD scores of the nineteenth

The Big Apple and Charm City

John McGraw first became famous as a player with the Baltimore Orioles, but the bulk of his fame came later, as manager of the New York Giants.

A new version of the Orioles opened play in 1901, part of the brand-new American League. Two years later, however, the franchise moved to New York and became known as the Highlanders. Why did the American League Orioles move? Well, McGraw was involved in a bitter feud with A.L. president Ban Johnson and, during the 1902 season, McGraw—manager and part owner of the Orioles— secretly agreed to sell his Orioles stock to Giants ownership and manage the Giants. The new owners released several key Orioles players to sign with the Giants and other N.L. clubs, which left the Orioles without enough players to field a team. Ban Johnson ordered the franchise forfeited to the league, and it was moved to New York after the season.

New York's American League franchise eventually took the name *Yankees*, and it was made famous by Babe Ruth. Ruth was born and raised in Baltimore and began his professional career with the International League Orioles.

Finally, Wilbert Robinson, catcher on the 1890s Orioles, later managed the Brooklyn Dodgers for eighteen years, during which time the club was generally referred to as the *Robins*, in honor of Robinson.

So while fans of the Yankees and Orioles rarely see eye to eye these days, there is a strong connection between the baseball histories of their respective cities.—*Eddie*

century look like those of the twentieth century. Here are the Orioles' SD scores for 1894 through 1898, including three pennants and two second-place finishes:

Year	SD Score	Next-Best SD Score
1894	+2.93	+1.70
1895	+3.17	+1.64
1896	+3.08	+1.69
1897	+2.46*	—
1898	+2.97*	+2.48

*Orioles finished second in 1897 and 1898. They didn't have the top SD score in 1897, which is why no next-best score is listed.

Baltimore's five-year SD score, 14.60, is better than any twentieth-century team except the 1935–39 Yankees. In 1895, Baltimore's SD score was better than the next *two* best teams combined, and this was almost true for the 1894 and 1896 teams. All but one of the twentieth-century teams with a higher SD score than the 1898 Orioles finished in first place (the exception being the 1905 White Sox). The 1895 Orioles featured many players who would end up in the Hall of Fame: John McGraw, Willie Keeler, Hughie Jennings, Joe Kelley, Dan Brouthers (who was with the team in 1894 and part of 1895), and Wilbert Robinson. This may have been the most famous baseball team until the 1927 Yankees, known as much for their rough play as for their playing ability.

Baltimore lost its National League team in the consolidation that happened after the 1899 season, when the league contracted from twelve to eight teams. Unlike the Cleveland Spiders, who were totally non-competitive in 1899 because their owners had placed all of their good players on the other N.L. team they owned, Baltimore still had a decent team before the consolidation took place. In 1899, Baltimore's 86-62 record was good enough for fourth place in the twelve-team league. It is true that Baltimore's attendance dropped sharply after the 1897 season, even more sharply than the league as a whole. The Orioles' combined turnout for 1898 and 1899 was less than it had been in any one of the years from 1894 through 1897.

The St. Louis Browns of the American Association (then a major league) won four straight pennants from 1885 through 1888. Like the 1890s Orioles, the Browns were known for their rough play and for trying to intimidate opponents. Their first baseman and manager was none other than Charlie Comiskey, who would one day own the Chicago White Sox. The first three of these teams won the pennant by a double-digit margin, and two of them (1885 and 1887) posted winning percentages over .700. Take a look at the pitching staff for the 1885 St. Louis Browns:

Pitcher	G	GS	CG	IP	W	L	ERA
Bob Caruthers	53	53	53	482	40	13	2.07
Dave Foutz	47	46	46	408	33	14	2.63
Jumbo McGinnis	13	13	12	112	6	6	3.38

Don't ask where the rest of the pitchers are, because there aren't any more. Browns pitchers started 112 games and completed 111. Of course, that really wasn't unusual for that time in those days. Every American Association team had between 102 and 111 complete games in 1885. The Browns' 2.44 ERA was the best in the league (league ERA, 3.24).

If we had to pick one of these four teams as the best, we would pick the 1887 team for reasons that might best be explained by a chart:

Year	Runs Scored	Runs Allowed	Differential	Next-Best Differential	SD Score
1885	677	461	+216	+73	+2.79
1886	944	592	+352	+163	+3.74
1887	1131	761	+370	+147	+3.04
1888	789	501	+288	+233	+2.49

Or perhaps the 1886 team was the best; that team won the only undisputed World Championship for an American Association team. You see, although most people think that the World Series began in 1903, the champions of the National League and American Association did play each other in postseason series from 1884 through 1890. The 1886 St. Louis Browns defeated the Chicago N.L. team, then called the White Stockings, in that "World Series."

Tip O'Neill had a phenomenal year with the bat in 1887 for the

Browns' AA team. For that year only, walks were counted as base hits when computing averages. The modern encyclopedias don't use that rule. With the rule as we know it, O'Neill still hit .435 with a .490 OBP and a .691 slugging percentage, scoring 167 runs and driving in 123 in just 124 games. The league averages were .273 batting, .337 OBP, and .367 slugging. O'Neill led the league in runs, hits, doubles, homers, total bases, runs batted in, on-base percentage, and slugging percentage. It probably goes without saying that he led the league in runs created and runs created per 27 outs.

Jumping back to the 1890s National League, Baltimore's rival for supremacy for much of the decade was the Boston Beaneaters. The franchise wasn't really known as the Braves until around 1912 or 1913. Boston won the National League pennant in 1891, 1892, 1893, 1897, and 1898. (Actually, Boston won the first-half pennant in 1892—the league played a split season—and finished with the best overall record.) Of the first group of pennant winners, the 1891 club had the best run differential relative to its league as they led the league in both runs scored and fewest runs allowed. Neither the 1892 or 1893 club led the league in either category and, in fact, neither team even had the best run differential in the league.

Herman "Germany" Long and Harry Stovey were the two best position players on the 1891 team. Long was the shortstop and was a productive two-way player. His 784 OPS (.377 OBP, .407 slugging percentage) was much better than the league average 667 OPS (.325 OBP, .342 slugging). Long played sixteen years in the majors and was a remarkable player for the first half of his career. Stovey, an outfielder, was the team's best hitter, leading the league in slugging percentage (.498) and finishing third in OPS (870). Stovey also tied for the league lead in homers and was fifth in runs scored (Long was second), third in doubles, first in triples and total bases, and tied for second in RBI. He had been an outstanding player in the American Association in the 1880s while playing for Philadelphia.

In an era when the vast majority of a team's innings were still concentrated in just a few pitchers, the 1891 Boston club featured two of the nineteenth century's best—Hall of Famers John Clarkson and Kid Nichols. Clarkson had been a star with Cap Anson's Chicago teams before being sold to Boston in April 1888, when he was still among the elite pitchers in the game. His best year was probably 1889, when he led the league in wins (49), winning percentage (.721), innings

(620), strikeouts (284) and ERA (2.73). That's a pretty good year in any era. Clarkson was 33-19 with a 2.79 ERA in 1891; the National League ERA that season was 3.34.

Clarkson's post-baseball life was sad and short. He had always been known as temperamental while he played, a fact that helps explain his sale to Boston, but in retirement he went beyond temperamental. In May 1905, Clarkson was taken to a sanitarium in Michigan. The 1906 Reach guide reported that by December of 1905, he was a "hopeless physical and mental wreck." He died in February of 1909 at the McLean Hospital, a psychiatric facility in Massachusetts.

Kid Nichols may have been the very best pitcher of the nineteenth century. He certainly maintained a high level of performance for a long time:

Year	Innings	ERA	League ERA	W-L
1890	424	2.23	3.56	27-19
1891	425	2.39	3.34	30-17
1892	453	2.84	3.28	35-16
1893	425	3.52	4.66	34-14
1894	407	4.75	5.32	32-13
1895	380	3.41	4.78	26-16
1896	372	2.83	4.36	30-14
1897	368	2.64	4.30	31-11
1898	388	2.13	3.60	31-12
1890–98	3,642	2.97	4.15	276-132

He made the adjustment from the 50-foot pitching distance to the modern distance about as well as was humanly possible. Nichols' total of 297 wins in the 1890s was the most by any pitcher in the decade, 30 wins ahead of Cy Young.

As you can see, Nichols was still a force when Boston regained control of the N.L. standings from Baltimore in 1897. The epic 1897 race between Baltimore and Boston, settled in a three-game series in the last week of the season in Baltimore, has been chronicled in many books. Boston finished with a 93-39 record (.705 winning percentage) and a two-game edge over the Orioles. This Boston team was almost certainly better than the 1898 team:

Year	W-L Pct	Runs Scored	(Rank)	Runs Allowed	(Rank)	Differential
1897	.705	1,025	(1st)	665	(1st)	+360
1898	.685	872	(2d)	614	(1st)	+258

The 1898 team did not have the best run differential in the league, although they won the pennant by six games over the team that did (Baltimore, +310). Of the five Boston pennant winners in the 1890s, only two had the best run differential in the league, whereas all three of Baltimore's pennant winners in the decade had the best differentials, and by large margins, as mentioned earlier in the chapter.

It's a little more problematic to discuss teams that played before the mid-1880s. As I mentioned before, as with any new "system," the differences in relative ability among teams and players were changing far more rapidly from year to year than at any time since. Also, players were jumping teams, which led to the implementation of the reserve clause (the contract provision that bound a player to his team) around 1880.

The seasons were much shorter, too. In 1876, the first year of the National League, each team played between 57 and 70 games. Schedules of more than 100 games weren't adopted until 1884, another year in which three major leagues operated. All of these differences, relative to today, may help explain team performances like this:

Year	Team	W-L	Pct
1876	Chicago	52-14	.788
1877	Chicago	26-33	.441
1878	Chicago	30-30	.500
1879	Chicago	46-33	.582
1880	Chicago	67-17	.798

How good was this team? Who knows? Which team was the best of the nineteenth century? The Orioles were the most dominant team in the only major league of its day, at a time when baseball at this level had been evolving for twenty-plus years and when the rules most closely resembled those of today. Although Boston won more pennants and had the best one-year record and the best overall record of the 1890s, we think the evidence strongly suggests that the 1894–98

Orioles reached a level of performance higher than did any of the Boston teams of the 1890s.

Let's go back to our standby, the SD score. Here is a comparison of the Baltimore and Boston teams of the 1890s:

	SD Score	Next-Best SD Score
1894 Baltimore	+2.93	+1.70
1895 Baltimore	+3.17	+1.64
1896 Baltimore	+3.08	+1.69
1897 Baltimore	+2.46	Not the best score in the league
1898 Baltimore	+2.97	+2.48
1891 Boston	+2.81	+1.50
1892 Boston	+2.11	Not the best score in the league
1893 Boston	+2.33	Not the best score in the league
1897 Boston	+3.05	+2.46
1898 Boston	+2.48	Not the best score in the league

The St. Louis Browns team of 1885–88 was great in its league, but we think their run has to be discounted at least a little because it wasn't in the tougher National League. So, we would conclude that the 1895 (1894–98) Orioles were the best team of the nineteenth century.

1927 New York Yankees

There have been challenges to the title The Greatest Team Ever by fans, media and players, but I will be so bold as to defend the Yankees' designation on the basis of my experience as an active major league player for twenty years and, further, as the radio play-by-play broadcaster for the Cincinnati Reds for another twenty-five years. Although there have been many outstanding teams . . . I must say that I have never, never seen a team that I thought could beat the '27 bunch.

> —Waite Hoyt, who went 22-7 for the 1927 Yankees

Record: 110-44, .714 (5th)
Two-year (1927–28): 211-97, .685 (5th)
Three-year (1926–28): 302-160, .654 (20th)

SD Score: 3.69 (4th)
Two-year: 6.20 (7th)
Three-year: 7.77 (23d)

Results:
1926 American League Champions
1927 World Champions
1928 World Champions

Days in First Place: 174 of 174; clinched on September 13
The Yankees never fell below first place, leading wire to wire (including first-place ties). It wasn't until 1984 that another A.L. team, the Detroit Tigers, accomplished this feat.

Longest Winning Streak: 9 games
Longest Losing Streak: 4 games

The Pennant Race: The White Sox were only a few games behind the Yankees in early June, but they slumped and wound up in fifth place as New York went 45-13 in June and July to make the pennant race a non-issue. The Athletics finished in second place, 19 games off the pace.

Against the Contenders: As of the 1927 season, the Washington Senators were the last non-Yankee team to win the American League pennant (1925), and the Philadelphia Athletics would be the next non-Yankee team to win the flag (1929). Not coincidentally, those two teams finished third and second, respectively, behind the Bombers in '27. That season, New York was 14-8 against both "contenders," both of whom finished far off the pace.

Runs Scored: 975 (1st)

Runs Allowed: 599 (1st)

Pythagorean Record: 109-45

Manager: Miller Huggins

Regular Lineup:

Player	Position	ROV	OW%
Earle Combs	CF	.335	.714
Mark Koenig	SS	.254	.441
Babe Ruth	RF	.414	.854
Lou Gehrig	1B	.406	.844
Bob Meusel	LF	.315	.660
Tony Lazzeri	2B	.300	.613
Joe Dugan	3B	.244	.402
Pat Collins	C	.306	.633
Waite Hoyt	P		

The strength of the lineup is obvious, and these numbers reinforce the belief that Ruth and Gehrig still rank as the best one-two punch in baseball history. It must also be said that this lineup did contain two weak links in Koenig and Dugan.

Murderer's Row

"Murderer's Row" typically refers to the heart of the Yankee lineup—Ruth, Gehrig, Meusel, and Lazzeri—though sometimes leadoff man Combs is included, and sometimes the nickname is used to describe the entire lineup or even the whole team, as in "the Murderer's Row Yankees." However, this certainly wasn't the first use of the term. In fact, it's been traced as far back as 1858, when it was used to describe a lineup full of power hitters in a New York newspaper.

What's more, the 1926–28 Bronx Bombers weren't even the first Yankees to draw the nickname. Baseball researcher L. Robert Davids has traced "Murderer's Row" back to the 1919 club, whereas historian G. H. Fleming says the 1921 Yankees drew the moniker "not only because Babe Ruth hit fifty-nine home runs that year, but because for the first time in baseball history every member of the starting lineup hit at least four home runs during the season." Whatever the origin, when we think "Murderer's Row," we think Ruth-Gehrig-Meusel-Lazzeri . . . and for good reason.—*Rob*

The Lucky Hunchback, Part II

Eddie Bennett almost certainly ranks as the most sought-after and most "successful" mascot-batboy in major league history. When he was an infant, Bennett fell out of a baby carriage and sustained a spine injury. He developed a hunchback as a result, and his height topped out at 4½ feet. In 1919, the White Sox hired Bennett, then fifteen years old, as a batboy-mascot. The White Sox, of course, won the American League pennant. (As far as we know, Bennett had nothing to do with throwing the World Series.) The next season, Bennett was lured from Chicago by his hometown team, the Brooklyn Dodgers. They too won a pennant (and lost a

Bench: Johnny Grabowski served as the backup catcher, and saw action in 68 games. When Tony Lazzeri played shortstop, Ray Morehart took over at second base. All in all, this lineup was incredibly stable. Aside from the eight position players listed, plus Grabowski and Morehart, only five others saw any action at all!

Scouting the Pitchers: Paul Krichell, the Yankees' master scout, once said of ace Waite Hoyt (22-7, 2.64), "He had a good arm, meaning speed and stuff; a smart head, which meant control and pitching know-how; and he had guts. His physique was ideal—190 pounds, six feet tall—and he had width, bulk, and power in the region of the sacroiliac, which is the hinge of the entire pitching business." (Sacroiliac: "Of, relating to, or affecting the sacrum and ilium and their articulation or associated ligaments.")

In addition to the good fastball, thrown both overhand and three-quarters, Hoyt had a good palm ball and different curves.

Herb Pennock (19-8, 3.00) first came to the majors in 1912 with the Philadelphia Athletics, where he picked up a screwball from Chief Bender. He didn't actually throw that pitch too often, but he didn't throw many fastballs either. Pennock depended on his change-up and a great curve that he threw both overhand and sidearm.

Urban Shocker (18-6, 2.84) featured a spitball, thanks to a grandfather clause that allowed him and sixteen other major leaguers to continue throwing the spitter after such deliveries were outlawed in 1920.

Lefthander Dutch Reuther (13-6, 3.38) greatly enjoyed his libations, which led to him being released by a number of teams (including the Yankees after the '27 season, despite his fine stats). But he tossed a dazzling curveball, and used a particularly graceful delivery.

Nearly six-foot-two, big George Pipgras (10-3, 4.11) probably threw harder than anybody on the team, and in 1928 he paced the American League with 24 victories.

How were they built? The Yankees won American League pennants in 1921, 1922, and 1923, and they finished just two games behind the pennant-winning Senators in 1924. But in 1925, with Babe Ruth off his game and the Yankees plummeting to seventh place, general manager Ed Barrow got to work. Or at least that's the way he told it. In actuality, by 1925 the nucleus of the 1926–28 team was already in place.

Almost everyone knows about Lou Gehrig, who took over from Wally Pipp in June 1925. After legendary scout Paul Krichell saw Gehrig play at Columbia University, he simply told Barrow, "I've got another Babe Ruth." And, of course, Krichell wasn't far off. Gehrig signed with the Yankees in 1923 and played sporadically for the Yanks in '23 and '24 before replacing Pipp in '25. Also in 1925, Earle Combs replaced Whitey Witt in center field, but Combs too had been around in 1924.

The only real change in 1926 was at second base. In 1925, Tony Lazzeri was setting all kinds of Pacific Coast League records in Salt Lake City. Playing a 203-game schedule, *Lazzeri hit 60 home runs and drove in 222.* However, a number of teams passed on Lazzeri because he occasionally suffered epileptic fits. Barrow sent Krichell, his top scout, to Salt Lake City. Krichell was impressed, but warned Barrow that the stories about Lazzeri's epilepsy were true. Barrow's response? "As long as he doesn't take fits between three and six in the afternoon, that's good enough for me." The Yankees sent $50,000 and the promise of five ballplayers to Salt Lake City, and Lazzeri was a Yankee. (He did suffer a few fits while with New York, but never during a ballgame, and the public never learned about Lazzeri's epilepsy while he was in the majors.)

In his book, *My Fifty Years in Baseball,* Barrow was expansive in his praise of Lazzeri, commenting, "In our comeback from a calamitous seventh-place finish in 1925 to a championship in 1926 there is one player who stands out above all others—Tony Lazzeri. He was the making of that club, holding it together, guiding it, and inspiring it. He was one of the greatest ballplayers I have ever known." Lazzeri and Gehrig were the only two players linking the 1926–28 dynasty with the 1936–39 dynasty, though Lazzeri went to the Cubs in 1938 and Gehrig would play only a few games in '39.

What brought them down? For the Yankees, of course, "down" was a relative term. From 1926 through 1935, the Bombers won "only" four pennants but finished second five times and third once. Still, many people are surprised to learn that Ruth and Gehrig, teammates for ten seasons (1925 through 1934), played in just four World Series together (1926 through 1928, and 1932). Essentially, New York's pitching fell just a bit short, as they consistently led the American League in runs scored, even in the second-place years. Also, they

World Series). Riding that two-year streak, Bennett signed with the Yankees in 1921, and the Bombers immediately began a three-year pennant streak. Bennett remained with the Yankees until the middle of the 1933 season, when he was hit by a taxi and suffered a broken leg. No longer able to perform his batboy duties, Bennett fell into the bottle and died of acute alcoholism on January 16, 1935.—*Rob*

Walter Beall

Walter Beall, who pitched all of one inning (on May 30, against the Athletics) for the 1927 New York Yankees, owned one of the sharpest curveballs in history. But his control, or lack thereof, kept him from a long major league career.

In 1924, Beall paced the International League with a 2.75 ERA, and his 25 victories ranked behind only Lefty Grove. Late that August, the Yankees purchased Beall's contract for $50,000, a huge amount at the time (though not as huge as the

$100,600 the Athletics paid for Grove). In his first month with the Yankees, observers were awed by Beall's overhand curveball. Goose Goslin called it "the best curveball I ever saw." In his classic book, *The Hot Stove League*, Lee Allen wrote, "It was a curve that simply exploded and when he got it over the batters would grunt, swing, miss, and walk away, shaking their heads in wonder." Unfortunately for Beall, he didn't get it over nearly often enough, and his four seasons with the Yankees (and one with the Senators) were punctuated by frequent trips to the minor leagues. He did pitch 82 innings for the '26 Bombers, posting a 3.53 ERA. Beall finished his major-league career with 111 walks in 124 innings.—*Rob*

faced some stiff competition in the Philadelphia Athletics, about whom we'll read more later. In May 1929, Gordon Cobbledick asked Miller Huggins if his Yankees would soon shake off the cobwebs and catch the front-running Athletics. Huggins' reply was interesting on a number of levels.

No, Mr. Cobbledick. I don't think the Yanks are going to catch the Athletics. I don't think these Yanks are going to win any more pennants, or at least, not this one. They're getting older and they're becoming glutted with success. They've been in three World Series in a row, remember, and they've won the last two Series in four straight.

They've been getting fairly high salaries and they've taken a lot of money out of baseball, a whole lot of money. They have stock market investments and these investments are giving them excellent returns at the moment. When they pick up a newspaper now, they turn to the financial page first and the sports page later. Those things aren't good for a club, not a club which is trying to beat a club like the one Mr. Mack has.

First off, please note that some things never change. It isn't just ballplayers of our era who supposedly spend as much time talking about stocks and bonds as bunts and balks. And second, note the date of this exchange: May 1929. Five months later, the great majority of those stock market investments suddenly stopped giving the Yankees excellent returns. But even if Black Tuesday made the Yankees a little hungrier, it took them until 1932 to win another American League flag.

Most Valuable Yankee: As great as Gehrig was—.373 average, 47 home runs, an A.L.-best 175 RBI and a 1239 OPS—this was the Babe's year. Ruth played a tougher defensive position, he hit 60 home runs, and he topped the loop in both on-base percentage (.487) *and* slugging percentage (.772). According to *Total Baseball*, Ruth's '27 campaign ranks among the five greatest (non-pitching) performances of all time, along with two other Ruth seasons ('21 and '23), Barry Bonds in 1992, and Cal Ripken in 1984.

Worst Regular: The Yankee catchers—Collins and Grabowski, plus third-stringer Benny Bengough—collectively played in twenty-seven

Lou Gehrig and Babe Ruth *(National Baseball Hall of Fame Library, Cooperstown, NY)*

major league seasons, but in only one of those seasons did one of them play 100 or more games (Collins, 102 in 1926).

Hall of Famers: Ruth and Gehrig were both ushered into the Hallowed Halls as soon as possible. Number two starter Herb Pennock was elected by the Baseball Writers Association of America in 1948. Waite Hoyt, Earle Combs, and Tony Lazzeri were all elected by the Veterans Committee after long waits: Hoyt in 1969, Combs a year later, and Lazzeri in 1991. Manager Miller Huggins also was elected by the Veterans Committee, in 1964, as was Ed Barrow, in 1953.

Our Hall of Famers: Ruth and Gehrig are Ruth and Gehrig. Their Hall of Fame teammates, on the other hand, might all be considered marginal.

The 1927 World Series: See separate article, "The Myth of the 1927 Series."

The Ballpark: Every year from 1924 through 1931, more runs were scored by the Yankees and their opponents in Yankees' road games than in Yankee Stadium, despite the fact that every year in the same period more home runs were hit in Yankee Stadium than in Yankees' road games. The 1927 World Series was the third played in the Bronx. There would be many, many more (we're still counting).

Books about the 1927 Yankees: Relatively little has been written about the 1920s Yankees in general, but the '27 Yankees in particular have been the subject of many books, including John Mosedale's *The Greatest of All* (New York: The Dial Press, 1982) and G. H. Fleming's *Murderer's Row* (New York: Morrow, 1985). Fleming's book chronicles the team through contemporary newspaper accounts and includes a wonderful introduction by Waite Hoyt. There are, of course, numerous biographies of Ruth, the best of them being Robert Creamer's *Babe* (New York: Simon & Schuster, 1974) and Marshall Smelser's *The Life That Ruth Built* (New York: Quadrangle Books, 1975). There's one adult biography of Lou Gehrig: Ray Robinson's *Iron Horse: Lou Gehrig in His Time* (New York: W. W. Norton, 1990).

The Authors' Choice

When you're putting together a book proposal, one of the things you're supposed to do is make a list of the competition. That is, find out about similar books that have come before. Thus, after a bit of research, I found (and acquired) five books that treat the same subject as the one you're holding in your hands right now.

Two of those books, Tom Meany's *Baseball's Greatest Teams* (A. S. Barnes & Co., 1949) and Howard Siner's *Sweet Seasons: Baseball's Top Teams Since 1920* (Pharos Books, 1988), aren't particularly relevant to our discussion. Meany selected sixteen teams, one per franchise, and didn't attempt to rank them. And Siner's top twenty-five teams are simply the twenty-five post-1920 World Series winners with the best regular-season winning percentages.

It's the other three books that interest us, and here they are now!

- ◆ *Baseball's 10 Greatest Teams*, by Donald Honig (New York: Macmillan, 1982)
- ◆ *The Sporting News Selects Baseball's 25 Greatest Teams*, by Lowell Reidenbaugh (St. Louis: The Sporting News, 1988)
- ◆ *The Best & Worst Baseball Teams of All Time*, by Harry Hollingsworth (New York: S.P.I. Books, 1994)

The first two are similar in content. They both feature plenty of big black-and-white photos, along with anecdotal accounts of the teams. As it happens, all ten of Honig's teams are also featured in this book, though we differ on the exact years in a few cases. And of our fifteen teams, thirteen are in Reidenbaugh's book, the exceptions having come after The Sporting News published their book. Hollingsworth, on the other hand, used strict statistical measures in arriving at his list of greatest teams. His formula, in a nutshell, considers various measures of winning as 45 percent, offense as 30 percent, and pitching/defense as 25 percent. I'm not going to spend much space here on the results of all these methods. The point here is that all three authors arrived at the same conclusion: The 1927 New York Yankees were the greatest team of all time.

> Honig: "In selecting the greatest of all teams . . . one must bow again to legend and choose the 1927 New York Yankees in recognition of their awesome hitting, their depth of superb pitching, and their excellent defense. No other team quite matches this combination of outstanding talents."
>
> Reidenbaugh: "That the '27 Yanks have remained the standard by which all other teams are judged certainly attests to their overall might. They had hitting, pitching, defense, and that certain 'something.' The had so much of it that, pitcher Waite Hoyt explained, 'We felt we were superior people.' "
>
> Hollingsworth: "While they did not agree on anything else, recent

books and articles identifying the best baseball teams of all time *did* agree on the best single team: the 1927 New York Yankees. And our computer agreed."

The guys who didn't use a computer picked the '27 Yankees, and the guy who did use a computer picked the '27 Yankees. Eddie and I have attempted to come up with a happy medium between the two methods, but are we destined to arrive at the same answer as our predecessors? As I write this, I don't know yet. What I do know is that in 1927 the New York Yankees drew a line in the sand. Whether or not any team has been worthy of stepping across that line, we'll find out later in this book.—Rob

The Inefficient Bombers

The 1927 Yankees were in first place (or tied for first) every day of the season. The Yankees scored the most runs in the league and they allowed the fewest, one of only twenty-five teams that has done that. At +3.69, they posted the fourth-highest SD score of any team in this century. Their "predicted" record (109-45), based on their runs scored and allowed, was close to their actual record (110-44). They won their season series with every other team in the league. The '27 Yankees swept the World Series.

The 1927 Yankees had many individual leaders: Ruth led the league in runs scored, homers, walks, on-base percentage, and slugging percentage; Gehrig led in doubles, runs batted in, and extra-base hits; Combs led in hits and triples; Hoyt led in wins and winning percentage; and Wilcey Moore led in ERA and saves. I would argue that when one is comparing the greatest teams of all time, a real contender has to have some individual leaders, and the '27 Yankees obviously qualify.

The 1927 Yankees set the all-time major league record for slugging percentage, and they did it without benefit of the designated hitter. Their 872 team OPS is tied with that of the 1930 Yankees for the highest ever. That fact, however, leads to my minor criticism of the 1927 squad. Although their run total was very high (975 in 155 games), they probably didn't score as many runs as they should have. According to *Total Baseball*, they created 1,016 runs, meaning they were 41 runs, or about 4 percent, short of their "predicted" total.

Rather than run a long chart here, let me sum up what such a chart would show. Through 1998, twenty-one teams have scored 950-plus runs in one season. As measured by a ratio of actual runs scored to runs created, the Yankees were the second-least efficient of those teams. The average team was actually plus 2 percent in efficiency, whereas the Yankees were minus 4.2 percent. (The only team less efficient than the '27 Yankees was the '96 Cleveland Indians, at −5.4 percent.)

I think it's interesting to note that fifteen of the twenty-one teams outscored their RC. Just as teams that win a very high number of games usually exceed the number of wins that could be predicted from their run differential, it seems logical that teams that produce runs at this level would exceed, at least slightly, their "predicted" runs. Why did the Yankees score fewer runs than predicted? Of course, the real answer may just be random deviation. It might be that the 1927 Yankees' situational performance was not quite as good as its overall performance.

Even though most of the rigorous research on the effects of lineup sequence (including some done by yours truly) suggests that batting order has little effect on run production, I still can't shake the nagging feeling that the 1927 Yankees would have scored more runs if they had used someone other than Mark Koenig—Tony Lazzeri, maybe— in the number two slot. Koenig rapped only 34 extra-base hits in 526 at-bats and finished with a .320 on-base percentage. Lazzeri ended the season with 55 extra-base hits in 570 at-bats and a .383 on-base percentage. The extra-base hit total is relevant because Combs, the leadoff hitter, could run and had a .414 OBP. The number two hitter's OBP is important for obvious reasons, chief among them a pair of fellows named Ruth and Gehrig.

I'm not suggesting that a lineup change would have resulted in the Yankees scoring 100 more runs than they did, but perhaps they could have reached the 1,000 mark, thus becoming the first twentieth-century team to do so. That would have been fitting and yet another, stronger argument for this club's greatness.—Eddie

Ruth and His House

Yankee Stadium in 1927, just as it does now, featured a so-called short porch in right field. In '27, it was only 295 feet from home plate to the foul pole down the right-field line, which of course made it an inviting target for a pull hitter like Ruth. But what people forget is that it was 429 feet to right-center and 490 to straightaway center, and even the Babe didn't hit the ball 500 feet very often. And great as he was, he wasn't able to pull the ball severely *every* time.

So whenever you hear someone say Ruth was favored by Yankee Stadium—and people say it a lot—remind them of those dimensions. And conclude your refutation with the following fact: Ruth played a dozen seasons in the house that he built, and during those years he totaled 259 home runs at home and 252 elsewhere. Favored, indeed.—*Rob*

The Best of the Best

Obviously, Babe Ruth had many great seasons. Rob thought it would be a good idea if I picked his best.

Most students of the game know about Ruth's 1920 and 1921 seasons, his first two with the Yankees. He had those absurd slugging percentages (.847 in 1920, .846 in 1921) and was hitting more home runs than most other teams in the majors. The way I calculate offensive winning percentage, Ruth's was .906 in 1920 and "only" .881 in 1921 after adjusting for ballpark. Ruth's real offensive value (ROV) in both of those years was way over .400 (.461 in 1920 and .446 in 1921). In 1921, Ruth scored 177 runs and had 171 RBI in 152 games.

Some analysts talk about Ruth's 1923 season—the Yankees' first at Yankee Stadium—as his best. The league norm for scoring was lower in 1923 than in 1921, and Yankee Stadium was a tougher park to hit in than the Polo Grounds (the Yanks' home from 1913 through 1922). All Ruth did in 1923 was compile a .545 on-base percentage (with the help of an all-time record 170 walks) and a .764 slugging percentage. His real offensive value that year was .443, and his offensive winning percentage was .891.

Almost all fans know about Ruth's 1927 season. In fact, if you ask casual fans which was Ruth's greatest campaign, odds are they'll tell you it was '27 because that was the year the Babe hit 60 homers. That was also his last season with 400-plus total bases, and he posted the third highest single-season slugging percentage (.772) in history. For me, though, the essence of the Babe is captured by his 1919 season, his last with Boston. I'm not necessarily saying that's his best season, I just think it's the one that best captures his all-around greatness.

Ruth set his first single-season home run record in 1919, with 29. He did this in a hostile park for power hitters. Ruth hit just 9 of his 29 homers at home; he out-homered the Red Sox opposition in Fenway for the entire year, 9 to 3. There were 13 homers hit in Fenway in 1919, and 36 hit in Red Sox road games that year. The rest of the Red Sox team hit 4 homers (home and away) the entire season.

Besides home runs, Ruth led the league in the two most important offensive categories, on-base percentage (.456) and slugging percentage (.657), as well as leading the league in runs scored (103) and RBI (114). On top of that, Ruth pitched in 17 games, and went 9-5 with a better-than-league-average ERA for a team that finished under .500.

Stan Musial once argued that Ruth *had* to be the greatest player of all time because he could pitch *and* bat cleanup in the big leagues like the star of a high-school team. None of Ruth's seasons demonstrate that more clearly than 1919.—Eddie

The Greatest Player

In the summer of 1998, ESPN's Web site ran a poll asking users to select the "greatest baseball player ever." The choices were, in alphabetical order: Hank Aaron, Ty Cobb, Joe DiMaggio, Christy Mathewson, Willie Mays, Babe Ruth, and Ted Williams. You probably don't need us to tell you this, but that list is a little silly. I was actually working for ESPN.com at the time, but no one asked me for my list. Had I been asked, I'd have recommended replacing DiMaggio with Honus Wagner and Mathewson with Walter Johnson.

Anyway, Ruth "won" the poll, but both Eddie and I found *how* he won a little disturbing. You see, Ruth only pulled around 34 percent of the vote, which struck us as awfully low given that the Babe was clearly, *clearly* the greatest player in the history of the game. How can we be so confident? Well, Ruth is routinely acknowledged as one of the two greatest hitters of all time. The other candidate is Ted Williams. Give Teddy Ballgame those nearly five seasons he spent in the service, and he'd be right up there with Ruth in terms of career hitting value.

But—and this is a big but, yet one that people seem to forget—Ruth was also a fantastic pitcher for five years at the beginning of his career, five years in which he wasn't doing much hitting at all. If he had been playing the outfield all those years, Ruth quite likely would have finished with somewhere in the neighborhood of 800 home runs, in which case we wouldn't even be having this discussion.

You're right, though, we can't give Ruth credit for homers he didn't hit. But by the same token, we've got to give him credit for the victories he contributed as a pitcher, and he helped pitch the Red Sox to three American League pennants in four years. Add all that up and

A Different Game

On September 22 the Yankees beat the Tigers 8–7, thanks to Ruth's two-run homer in the bottom of the ninth. With jubilant fans pouring onto the grounds, Ruth carried his beloved bat around the bases. When he reached third, Babe was joined by a young boy, and the two of them proceeded home together. Both touched the plate, thus climaxing a wonderful afternoon for everybody.—*Rob*

Stats 'n' Stuff

◆ In 1909, the Chicago Cubs went 21-1 against the Boston Braves. In 1927, the Yankees just missed becoming the first team to go 22-0 against one team in the same season. The St. Louis Browns lost their first 21 to New York in '27, but in their last try the Brownies finally beat the Yanks, 6–2, on September 11.

◆ One of the dumbest, yet enduring clichés in sports is "The good teams win the close ones." Well, the 1927 Yankees were just 22-19 in one-run games. They made up for that by going 54-9 in games decided by four or more runs.

◆ The Yankees are the only team in major league history to feature the league's top three pitchers in ERA (Wilcy Moore, Waite Hoyt, and Urban Shocker) and the top four in winning percentage (same three, plus George Pipgras).

◆ They scored 10 or more runs in 26 games, going 25-1 in those contests. Their one loss was an eighteen-inning, 12–11 defeat to the Red Sox on September 5 at Fenway Park.

Around the Majors

May 30 Before 1927, there had been exactly six unassisted triple plays in major league history. Today, Cubs shortstop Jimmy Cooney makes it seven and, tomorrow, Tigers first baseman Johnny Neun makes it eight. Neun's trick snuffs a Cleveland rally in the ninth inning.

one is left with the conclusion that, indeed, the greatest, most valuable player in the history of the game was George Herman Ruth.—Rob

The Myth of the 1927 Series

Some years ago, I worked for a baseball writer named Bill James, and one of the things I did for Bill was to research and write a series of articles he called "Tracers." Essentially, the idea was to take old baseball stories—some of them well known, some of them not—and try to determine their accuracy. I've often thought an entire book of these would be fun, but I really wouldn't feel right about muscling in on Bill's action, so I haven't spent much time researching more of those old tales.

However, the following story qualifies for this book, and because it's so close to the topic at hand, I don't think Bill would mind:

Judge Landis selected October 5 [1927] as the day for opening the Series at Forbes Field, but many of the game's experts, including the New York delegation, always have insisted that the Yanks actually won the Series on the fourth, the day before it officially got under way. After the Pirates worked out, [manager Donie] Bush extended the courtesy of the field to his rivals. The Pirates dressed and most of them remained in the stands to observe the New Yorkers go through their exercises. And the Yankees put on a pyrotechnic display that had many of the Bucs whoozy. Ruth and Gehrig hit balls into and over the distant right-field stand as though it were a softball park, and Meusel and Lazzeri gave the left-field stands a similar treatment. Little 140-pound Lloyd Waner turned to his brother Paul and asked, "Gee, they're big guys; do they always hit that hard?"

—Fred Lieb in *The Story of the World Series*

Then, as the tale typically continues, the frightened Pirates barely put up a fight and are summarily swept by the powerful Bombers. Well, it's true, the Yankees certainly did sweep the Pirates. But it wasn't all that easy. The Yanks won games 1 and 4 by one run apiece, and game 2 was close (2–0, Yankees) until the bottom of the seventh.

The Pirates weren't exactly a bunch of Johnny-come-latelies themselves. They won 94 games in '27, thanks to a pair of legitimate stars (and future Hall of Famers) in Paul Waner and Kiki Cuyler. Also, Ray Kremer was a fine pitcher enjoying one of his finest seasons (19-8, 2.47). This same team had won the World Series just two years earlier.

Moreover, it seems a little strange to think that this was the first the Pirates had heard of Ruth and Gehrig et al. Ruth had been the most famous player in the game for nearly a decade, and the Yankees were defending American League champions. Could the Pirates really have been shocked to see them hitting the cover off the ball in batting practice? Donald Honig interviewed Lloyd Waner for his book, *The October Heroes*, and here's what Waner had to say:

> The famous story that has come out of the 1927 World Series concerns the first day, when we were supposed to have watched the Yankees taking batting practice. According to the story, which I have read and heard so many times, Paul and me and the rest of us were sitting there watching those big New Yorkers knock ball after ball out of sight and became so discouraged that we just about threw in the sponge right then and there. One story that I've read I don't know how many times has me turning to Paul and in a whispery voice saying, "Gee, they're big, aren't they?"
>
> That was the story. Well, I don't know how that got started. If you want to know the truth, I never even saw the Yankees work out that day. We had our workout first and I dressed and was leaving the ball park just as they were coming out on the field. I don't think Paul stayed out there either. We never spoke of it. I know some of our players stayed, but I never heard anybody talk about what they saw.
>
> I don't know where the story came from. Somebody made it up out of thin air, that's all I can say. Every time I hear that story I tell people it's not so, but it just keeps on going. I don't think Paul ever saw anything on a ball field that could scare him anyway. He was such a great hitter in his own right that he never had to take a back seat to anybody.

A quick aside about Paul Waner, since Lloyd brought him up: Paul was indeed a great hitter. Thanks to the inflated batting stats of the

June 19 Phillies pitcher Jack Scott tosses two complete games against the Reds, winning 3–1 and losing 3–0.

July 18 Ty Cobb, now with the Philadelphia Athletics, collects his 4,000th career hit, a double off Detroit's Sam Gibson.

July 27 New York Giants outfielder Mel Ott, all of eighteen years old, hits the fist home run of his career, an inside-the-park job. Ott will finish his career with 511 homers, and this is the only one that doesn't clear a fence.

1930s, a lot of players from that era are in the Hall of Fame who don't belong. In fact, Lloyd Waner is one of them. But Paul was an excellent player, one of the top three or four hitters in the National League for better than a decade.

Getting back to the point of this little essay, the Yankees did sweep the Pirates in fairly convincing fashion, outscoring them 23 to 10. But they did it because they were an awesome team, not because the Pirates were afraid of them.—Rob

Wilcy Moore, Relief Ace

One of general manager Ed Barrow's brighter moves (and there were a lot of them) was the acquisition of pitcher Wilcy Moore. The way Barrow told the story, he was flipping through *The Sporting News* one day in 1926 and noticed that somebody named Moore was 20-1 with the Greenville Spinners down in the Class B South Atlantic Association.

Barrow dispatched scout Bob Gilks to Greenville. "He can't pitch," Gilks reported back. "And anyway, he says he's thirty, but he must be forty." Barrow didn't care. "Anyone who can win that many games even in the Epworth League is worth what they're asking for him," Barrow said. Greenville was asking $3,500, and Barrow happily paid the price. (*Epworth League* was a popular term describing all players not part of Organized Baseball.)

Actually, Moore was only twenty-nine at the time, and he wound up 30-4 for the pennant-winning Spinners. There was a good reason nobody'd ever noticed Moore before. During the 1925 season, a batted ball fractured Moore's arm. When he came back, his wrist hurt when he pitched, so Moore dropped down to sidearm. Suddenly, he had a sinker that he'd never had before.

Moore earned a spot with the Yankees in the spring of '27. Class B to Yankee Stadium in six months . . . not a bad jump.

In his book, Ed Barrow vividly described Moore: "Wilcy was a character. He was a big, raw-boned, heavy-handed farmer from Hollis, Oklahoma, with a bald head, who threw a heavy ball that sank as it got to the plate. It was the perfect equipment for a relief pitcher, coming in with men on the bases."

Despite starting only a dozen games in 1927, Moore pitched 213 innings. That made him eligible for the American League ERA crown, which he won with a 2.28 mark, easily besting teammates Waite Hoyt (2.63) and Urban Shocker (2.84), who finished second and third in the league. Moore also went 19-7, 13 of those victories coming in relief, which was the record for a long time. He also saved 13 games. Come October, Moore saved game 1 of the World Series, and clinched the championship with a complete-game victory in game 4.

For whatever reason (overwork, as Moore later claimed?), he was never the same pitcher. Moore did save 10 games for the Red Sox in 1931, and pitched for the Yankees again in 1932 and 1933, but the magic was gone. When you're looking for differences between the awesome '27 Yankees and the merely-great '26 and '28 editions, an effective Wilcy Moore has to rank near the top of the list.—Rob

Men among Boys

Take a look at this chart of 1927 A.L. road games:

Team	Home Runs	Opponents' Home Runs	Differential	Ratio
New York	75	12	+63	6.25:1
Detroit	26	24	+2	1.08:1
Philadelphia	30	29	+1	1.03:1
Chicago	30	33	−3	0.91:1
Boston	23	27	−4	0.85:1
St. Louis	13	22	−9	0.59:1
Cleveland	16	26	−10	0.62:1
Washington	19	34	−15	0.56:1

Does that look right to you? Well, it is. The Yankees did indeed out-homer their opponents 75 to 12 in road games. (They out-homered the opposition "only" 83 to 30 in Yankee Stadium.) Much in the way that Babe Ruth was playing a different game than other players in the early 1920s, the 1927 Yankees were playing a different game than the other teams in the league. How much so? That +63 road home run differential is still the best of all time, as is that ridiculous 6.25 to 1 road home-run ratio. The following chart shows all teams (through 1998) that out-homered their opponents by 50 or more in road games:

Team	Home Runs	Opponents' Home Runs	Differential
1927 Yankees	75	12	+63
1936 Yankees	100	43	+57
1998 Braves	111	59	+52
1961 Yankees	128	78	+50
1963 Twins	113	63	+50
1965 Braves	98	48	+50

The 1965 Braves were the last team in a non-strike season to out-homer their opposition on the road by at least 2 to 1. (The 1981 Dodgers hit 45 homers on the road and their opponents hit 20 in 54 road games.)

Overall, the 1927 Yankees hit 158 home runs while their opponents hit just 42. That +116 differential remains the best in major league history and, as one might imagine, that percentage difference (276 percent more home runs than their opposition) is the best, by far, in major league history. Only one other team, the 1961 Yankees, out-homered their opponents by 100-plus in a season (240 to 137), although three other teams—the 1936 Yankees, 1947 Giants, and 1998 Braves—came very close. (By the way, those are the only five teams to have even a 90-homer advantage over their opposition in a season.)

To me, what makes the '27 Yankees' enormous advantage over their opponents more amazing is that it didn't happen at the very beginning of the "lively ball" era. By 1927, players and teams had seen the Ruth phenomenon for more than just a couple of seasons. It wasn't just Ruth, of course, who made this happen. With his 47 circuit clouts, Lou Gehrig out-homered four of the other seven clubs in the league. Obviously, the Yankee pitchers did their part as well, allowing the second-fewest number of homers in the league despite pitching in a home park that inflated home run rates (+27 percent from 1925 through 1927).

Some other notes: the 1927 Yankees hit almost as many homers as the next *three* highest teams in the league *combined*. Their slugging percentage was 90 points above the league average, and if one excludes the Yankees' numbers from the A.L. average, then they out-slugged the rest of the league by *103 points*. The Yankees hit nearly four times as many homers as the average of the rest of the teams in the league.

You could just go on and on with these types of comparisons. The 1927 New York Yankees were truly men among boys. They were, to borrow an expression from George Will as he described Babe Ruth, an Everest in Kansas.—Eddie

The Great Race

There was, of course, not much excitement in the American League pennant race. As often happens with great teams, this situation left the club to compete with history instead and, at least in this case, with each other. The year 1927 is remembered as Babe Ruth's year because he reached the magical figure of 60 home runs. But just as in 1961, for much of the 1927 season *two* Yankee sluggers were aiming for the record.

On July 3, Ruth hit his 26th home run, but that merely tied him with Gehrig, who'd hit his 26th two days earlier. Ruth soon passed Gehrig, but "Buster" wasn't done busting the ball quite yet. Gehrig hit his 34th and 35th homers in a doubleheader on July 30, thus moving back ahead of Ruth. (That second home run, by the way, bounced off the "running track" and into the stands. Until 1931, these hits were scored as homers rather than doubles. All of Ruth's 1927 home runs cleared the fence on the fly.) Gehrig hit two more on August 3, giving him 37 to Ruth's 34.

The Babe went ahead on August 27, blasting his 41st circuit clout off Browns hurler (and future *football* Hall of Famer) Ernie Nevers. Gehrig hung tough, though. On September 2, Ruth smote his 44th, but Gehrig hit his 42d and 43d as the Yankees destroyed the Athletics, 12–2. Three days later, Gehrig tied the Great Home Run Race with his 44th.

And then on September 6, Ruth took over. First, he hit three homers in a doubleheader split with the Red Sox. The next day he walloped two more, setting a record with five home runs in three games. Now the score was Ruth 49, Gehrig 45 (Lou had hit one on September 7). Somehow, Gehrig managed only two more home runs the rest of the way, while of course Ruth continued to maul opposing hurlers. He finished with 60, and 17 of them came in September. Ruth reached the magic number—breaking his own record of 59 set in 1921—on September 30, at 3:25 in the afternoon.—Rob

TEAM STATISTICS

Hitting

	Games by Position	Age	G	AB	R	H	2B	3B	HR	RBI	BB	SO	SB	Avg	OBP	Slug
Lou Gehrig	1B,155	24	**155**	584	149	218	**52**	18	47	**175**	109	84	10	.373	.474	.765
Tont Lazzeri	2B,113; SS,38; 3B,9	23	153	570	92	176	29	8	18	102	69	82	22	.309	.383	.482
Mark Koenig	SS,122	22	123	526	99	150	20	11	3	62	25	21	3	.285	.320	.382
Joe Dugan	3B,111	30	112	387	44	104	24	3	2	43	27	37	1	.269	.321	.362
Babe Ruth	OF,151	32	151	540	**158**	192	29	8	**60**	164	**138**	89	7	.356	**.487**	.772
Earle Combs	OF,152	28	152	**648**	137	**231**	36	**23**	6	64	62	31	15	.356	.414	.511
Bob Meusel	OF,131	30	135	516	75	174	47	9	8	103	45	58	24	.337	.393	.510
Pat Collins	C,89	30	92	251	38	69	9	3	7	36	54	24	0	.275	.407	.418
Ray Morehart	2B,53	27	73	195	45	50	7	2	1	20	29	18	4	.256	.353	.328
John Grabowski	C,68	27	70	195	29	54	2	4	0	25	20	15	0	.277	.350	.328
Cedric Durst	OF,36; 1B,2	30	65	129	18	32	4	3	0	25	6	7	0	.248	.281	.326
Mike Gazella	3B,44; SS,6	30	54	115	17	32	8	4	0	9	23	16	4	.278	.403	.417
Ben Paschal	OF,27	31	50	82	16	26	9	2	2	16	4	10	0	.317	.349	.549
Julie Wera	3B,19	25	38	42	7	10	3	0	1	8	1	5	0	.238	.273	.381
Benny Bengough	C,30	28	31	85	6	21	3	3	0	10	4	4	0	.247	.281	.353
Totals		28	155	5,347	**975**	**1,644**	291	**103**	158	908	635	605	90	**.307**	**.383**	**.489**

Pitching

	Threw	Age	Games	GS	CG	ShO	IP	H	HR	BB	SO	W	L	Pct	Sv	ERA
Waite Hoyt	Right	27	36	32	23	3	256	242	10	54	86	**22**	7	**.759**	1	2.63
Herb Pennock	Left	33	34	26	18	1	210	225	5	48	51	19	8	.704	2	3.00
Urban Shocker	Right	36	31	27	13	2	200	207	8	41	35	18	6	.750	0	2.84
Dutch Ruether	Left	33	27	26	12	3	184	202	8	52	45	13	6	.684	0	3.38
George Pipgras	Right	27	29	21	9	1	166	148	2	77	81	10	3	.769	0	4.11
Wilcy Moore	Right	30	50	12	6	1	213	185	3	59	75	19	7	.731	**13**	**2.28**
Myles Thomas	Right	29	21	9	1	0	89	111	4	43	25	7	4	.636	0	4.87
Bob Shawkey	Right	36	19	2	0	0	44	44	1	16	23	2	3	.400	4	2.89
Joe Giard	Left	28	16	0	0	0	27	38	1	19	10	0	0	—	0	8.00
Walter Beall	Right	27	1	0	0	0	1	1	0	0	0	0	0	—	0	9.00
Totals		31	264	155	82	**11**	1,390	**1,403**	42	**409**	431	**110**	44	.714	20	**3.20**

CHAPTER 6

1929 Philadelphia Athletics

The 1929 Philadelphia A's, not the '27 Yankees, may have been the greatest baseball club ever assembled.

—Cover of *Sports Illustrated*, August 19, 1996

Record: 104-46, .693 (12th)
Two-Year (1929–30): 206-98, .678 (11th)
Three-Year (1929–31): 313-143, .686 (3d)

SD Score: +2.97 (39th)
Two-Year: +4.96 (67th)
Three-Year: +7.22 (53d)

We could easily have used 1928–30 as our three-year period, and in some ways the Athletics would look even better had we done so. Although Philadelphia finished second to the Yankees in 1928 with a 98-55 record, their +2.89 SD score was outstanding (47th best of the century) and significantly better than their SD score in 1931 (+2.26). The A's two-year SD score for 1928 and 1929 (+5.86) is 13th best all-time, and their three-year SD score for 1928 through 1930 (+7.86) ranks 20th.

Results:
1929 World Champions
1930 World Champions
1931 American League Champions

Days in First Place: 159 of 174; clinched on September 14

Longest Winning Streak: 11 games
Longest Losing Streak: 4 games

The Pennant Race: No pennant race. The A's were nine up on the Yankees by July, and they went 56-29 from there.

Against the Contenders: Entering the season, the Athletics knew there was one, and only one, team they had to beat: the New York Yankees. And beat them they did, taking 14 of 22 games from the Bronx Bombers.

Runs Scored: 901 (2d)

The Detroit Tigers led the American League with 926 runs scored, but allowed 928 and finished in sixth place.

Runs Allowed: 615 (1st)

Permitting 615 runs in 1929 was a fairly amazing feat, especially when you consider that Philadelphia's Shibe Park was a pretty good place for hitters. The St. Louis Browns allowed the second-fewest runs in the league, which at 713 was nearly a hundred more than the A's.

Pythagorean Record: 100-50

Manager: Connie Mack

Regular Lineup:

Player	Position	ROV	OW%
Max Bishop	2B	.272	.508
Mule Haas	CF	.293	.584
Mickey Cochrane	C	.318	.661
Al Simmons	LF	.357	.759
Jimmie Foxx	1B	.376	.794
Bing Miller	RF	.314	.651
Sammy Hale	3B	.230	.335
Joe Boley	SS	.247	.407
Lefty Grove	P		

Bench: Jimmy Dykes.

An exaggeration, perhaps, but Dykes was the only non-pitcher with more than 100 at-bats. He spelled Boley at shortstop, Hale at

Why Not 1931?

Why did we—or for that matter, *Sports Illustrated*—select the 1929 Athletics as one of history's greatest teams, rather than one of Mack's later teams? After all, although the '29 A's won 104 games, the '31 squad won 107. And the '30 Athletics weren't exactly pikers, winning 102.

Well, one reason is that the '29 Athletics won the World Series, whereas the '31 A's fell to the Cardinals. But we don't disqualify a team just because it doesn't win the Series. The 1906 Cubs are here in this book, and anyway it's not as though the Athletics embarrassed themselves in 1931, taking St. Louis to seven games before losing the finale, 4–2. No, we picked the '29 A's because, aside from the records, nearly all the statistical indicators suggested that they were indeed the best team among the three.

As noted earlier, the Athletics went 313-143 from 1929 through 1931, for a three-year winning percentage that ranks third all-time. However, if we just look at their runs scored and allowed over the three seasons, the Athletics "should" have gone 290-166. That 23-game difference between their actual performance and their Pythagorean projection over a three-year span is— brace yourself—*the* largest difference this century, for any team. And most of those 23 games (18, to be precise) came in 1930 and 1931, strongly implying luck as a factor in these records. Here are the projected wins for the three seasons, beginning in 1929: 100, 93, and 97. On balance, then, we're convinced that, qualitatively, the '29 Athletics were the best of the three teams.—*Rob*

Stats 'n' Stuff

◆ Philadelphia pitchers led the majors with 573 strikeouts and were the only A.L. staff to record more strikeouts than walks (487).

third base, and occasionally Bishop at second, and actually finished the season with more at-bats (401) than Boley or Hale. In fact, by the end of the season, Dykes had replaced Hale at third, started all five games in the World Series, and earned the regular third-base job in 1930.

Cy Perkins, an Athletic since 1915, served as backup backstop, and Walt French was the number one pinch hitter.

Scouting the Pitchers: Lefty Grove (20-6, 2.82) succeeded Walter Johnson as baseball's greatest pitcher, and 1929 was the fifth of seven straight seasons in which he led the American League in strikeouts. Grove had a fastball and a curve, but his fastball was so overpowering that he didn't bother much with the curve until a few years later.

Connie Mack liked big pitchers. Grove and Rube Walberg (18-11, 3.59) both stood six feet two inches, and George Earnshaw (24-8, 3.29) was even bigger, at six-four. Like Grove, Walberg and Earnshaw both depended on outstanding fastballs.

Once you got past the Big Three, however, the A's were all junk. Eddie Rommell (12-2, 2.85) was a knuckleballer, forty-five-year-old Jack Quinn (11-9, 3.97) was a spitballer, and Howard Ehmke (7-2, 3.29) lobbed curves and change-ups.

How were they built? As we'll note in a separate article ("The Greatest Minor League Team of All Time"), a significant portion of the franchise—Lefty Grove, George Earnshaw, Joe Boley, and Max Bishop—was purchased from the Baltimore Orioles, perennial International League champs. According to Fred Lieb in his book *Connie Mack: Grand Old Man of Baseball*, the Athletics paid for Grove on the installment plan, $10,000 per year for ten years (plus $600 in interest).

Outfielder Al Simmons joined the club in 1923, after Mack paid the minor league Milwaukee Brewers $50,000. It's been reported that many teams were scared off by Simmons' unorthodox batting style (which soon earned him the nickname "Bucketfoot Al"), but if the Brewers were able to get $50,000 for him, there must have been at least *some* other teams in the bidding.

In 1924, the Athletics spent another fifty grand on Mickey Cochrane, an outfielder/catcher and a graduate of Boston University, who'd just hit .338 with Portland in the Pacific Coast League. Actually, that $50,000 purchased the entire Portland *franchise*, but it was worth it. Cochrane was quite raw behind the plate, and Mack considered leaving him in the outfield or even shifting him to third base. Instead, Mack assigned Cochrane to coach Kid Gleason and incumbent catcher Cy Perkins (once described by Yankees pitcher Waite Hoyt as "one of the greatest receiving catchers who ever lived"), and eventually Cochrane would become known as one of the league's top defensive catchers.

Jimmie Foxx was recommended to Mack by his old third baseman Home Run Baker, who in 1924 was managing a Class D club in the Eastern Shore League. Baker had signed the sixteen-year-old Foxx, who batted .296 in 76 games (mostly at catcher). Baker's last major league team had been the Yankees, and he offered to sell Foxx to New York for $2,500. Yankees manager Miller Huggins declined (leaving one to wonder what the Yankees would've done with both Foxx and Gehrig on their roster in the late 1920s).

Rebuffed by Huggins, Baker next contacted Mack, who was reportedly hesitant since he'd just signed Cochrane. Baker was a good salesman, though, and Mack coughed up the $2,500—one of the best investments he'd ever make. Foxx signed with the Athletics on December 1, 1924, and promptly dropped out of high school. He spent most of the next few years sitting on the bench next to Mack and played third base and even did some catching before settling in at first base.

What brought them down? Again according to Fred Lieb,

> There is an erroneous belief that Mack started to break up his second great team immediately after Pepper Martin derailed his Athletic Express in the 1931 World Series. Mack tried, to the very best of his ability, to make it four straight in 1932. No stars were sold, and he even paid a pretty price for Tony Freitas, crack Coast League southpaw, to bolster his pitching staff; and the pony left-hander paid a little dividend, winning a dozen games while losing five.

Indeed, the Athletics were more than respectable in 1932, winning 94 games. But in those days it took more than that to win a pennant. In the 1920s and 1930s combined, only four times were 94 victories enough to win the American League pennant. And in '32 it wasn't

◆ With 117 double plays, the Athletic defense turned by far the fewest in the American League. And no, it wasn't just because there weren't many baserunners out there to double up or that Athletic pitchers got all their outs on strikeouts. Over in the National League, the Cubs nearly matched the A's with 548 strikeouts, posted the second-lowest ERA in the loop, and yet still managed to lead the National League with 169 twin killings. It was probably a combination of fly-ball pitchers and inept infielders. In 1931, with new second basemen, Philadelphia ranked second in the league with 151 double plays.

◆ Mickey Cochrane ranks as one of the all-time great contact hitters, especially when you consider that he had pretty decent power and drew plenty of walks. His 1929 season best exemplified this, as he drew 69 walks and struck out only eight times.

Around the Majors

May 18 Dodgers rookie Johnny Frederick sets a N.L. record by scoring his eighth run in the last two games. Frederick also comes out of nowhere to lead the National League with 52 doubles. But Frederick will stake his real claim to fame in 1932, when he clouts six pinch-hit home runs in one season.

May 19 A sudden thunderstorm sends a standing-room-only crowd rushing for the Yankee Stadium exits. In the right-field bleachers, the stampede leaves two patrons dead and sixty-two injured.

July 5 The New York Giants introduce the first electric public-address system in major league history.

September 25 Yankees manager Miller Huggins dies of blood poisoning at the age of forty-nine. Successor and ex-Yankee pitcher Bob Shawkey will manage for one season, then be replaced by Joe McCarthy.

even close, as the New York Yankees shook their three-year pennant drought with 107 wins, matching exactly the '31 A's (though the Yankees lost two more games than had the Athletics, so their winning percentage wasn't quite as good).

The Athletics scored plenty of runs—981—more than they'd scored in any of the preceding three seasons, as Foxx belted 58 home runs, but their pitching suffered almost across the board. Grove was his typical self, leading the American League in ERA, but fellow starters George Earnshaw, Rube Walberg, and Roy Mahaffey posted a collective 49-36 record after combining for a 56-23 mark in 1931.

Mack claimed to have the highest payroll in the game, and with the Depression in full swing he and his co-owners felt the pinch like everyone else. Okay, probably *not* like everyone else. But they decided to cut costs nonetheless. On September 28, just as the 1932 World Series was getting under way, Mack sold Simmons, Haas, and Dykes to the White Sox for $150,000.

Earnshaw, Walberg, and Mahaffey all fell off again in 1933, and the Athletics wouldn't seriously contend again for almost forty years.

Most Valuable Athletic: The competition is between Lefty Grove and Al Simmons. Grove led the American League in winning percentage (.769), strikeouts (170), and ERA; Simmons topped the loop in RBI and was second in slugging percentage (.642) and batting average (.365).

Grove's 20 wins aren't all that impressive, at least not for Grove, who'd won 24 in 1928 and would average 27 wins per season from 1930 through 1933.

Total Baseball makes it no contest. They've got Simmons, born Aloysius Szymanski, as the second-most valuable player in the entire league (after Ruth), at 4.9 wins above average. However, a good portion of that 4.9 comes via 17 fielding runs, which is a lot for a left fielder and far more than he would get in a typical season. Take away half of those fielding runs and Simmons drops to around 4.1 wins above average. That's still better than Grove's 3.5, however, so we'll make Bucketfoot Al our MVA.

Worst Regular: This one's another two-man competition, between third baseman Sammy Hale and shortstop Joe Boley (born John Bolinski). Both were awful hitters and neither would have been a

Gold Glove candidate (if there were such a thing in 1929). We'll go with Boley, though. Hale, while never a great player, did have some good years and, in fact, played quite well just a season earlier. Boley was okay his rookie season (1927), but he was twenty-eight years old that year and got nothing but worse, eventually playing just 540 games in the majors.

Hall of Famers: The Athletics boasted three Hall of Famers (first baseman Jimmie Foxx, center fielder Al Simmons, and catcher Mickey Cochrane) in the starting lineup, and four on the days Lefty Grove pitched. And Grove pitched a lot—37 starts plus five relief appearances. Of course, Connie Mack is in the Hall, too.

That was nothing compared to 1928, though. In addition to all the Hall of Famers on the scene in 1929, in '28 Ty Cobb *and* Tris Speaker *and* Eddie Collins were Athletics. All three were at least forty years old, but Mack felt that their experience was beneficial for the many young prospects on the club. Philadelphia finished just 2½ games behind the Yankees in '28, and one can't help but wonder if, had Mack played Cobb and Speaker less (Collins only got into three games, then nine more in '29), the A's might not have somehow made up those 2½ games.

Well, it's possible. But although neither Cobb (95 games, 820 OPS) nor Speaker (64 games, 760 OPS) distinguished themselves, none of Mack's alternatives really did any better. So maybe Mack knew exactly what he was doing.

Our Hall of Famers: Foxx, Simmons, Cochrane, and Grove are all legitimate, and we wouldn't add any other Athletics. Knuckleballer Eddie Rommel was a fine pitcher (see separate article, "The Early Bloomer"), but not nearly fine enough. Spitballer Jack Quinn turned forty-six in 1929, yet he pitched another four seasons in the majors. Quinn was never a great pitcher, really, but he was a good pitcher for an awfully long time, and in twenty-three seasons one could argue that he was *bad* in only one of them. Still, he wasn't a Hall of Famer.

The 1929 World Series: If the Athletics had lost the 1929 World Series, Connie Mack would still be getting second-guessed today. For game 1 against the Chicago Cubs, Mack had a number of great options when deciding on a starting pitcher. With the A's having

October 5 On the last day of the season, Mel Ott of the Giants and Chuck Klein of the Phillies face off in a doubleheader, tied for the N.L. lead with 42 homers apiece. In the first game, Klein hits his 43d homer and Ott singles. From there, Philly pitchers issue five straight intentional (or at least, semi-intentional) walks to Ott, the last of them coming with the bases loaded. The same day, Phillies outfielder Lefty O'Doul collects 6 hits to finish the season with 254, the N.L. record.

clinched the pennant more than three weeks earlier, his staff was well rested, and it included a pair of 20-game winners in Lefty Grove and George Earnshaw. Instead, Mack called on Howard Ehmke. Ehmke had gone 7-2 with a 3.29 ERA during the season, but he was also thirty-five years old and hadn't pitched in weeks. Mack sent him on the road to scout the Cubs in September, and Ehmke responded with a 3–1 victory in the opener, striking out thirteen Chicago hitters, a new World Series record, with his variety of slow curves. Pitching Ehmke probably ranks as the single most unorthodox managerial move in Series history. And it worked.

The Athletics blasted the Cubs in game 2, 9–3, behind George Earnshaw and Lefty Grove, the latter held back for relief duties by Mack. Two days later in game 3, Earnshaw started again, and this time the Cubs went back to their hotel happy, with a 3–1 triumph.

Then game 4. If it had been two New York teams, or for that matter *any* two teams in the age of television, game 4 might be the most famous of them all. Ancient spitballer Jack Quinn started for the A's, and the Cubs jumped all over him, while Philadelphia could do nothing against Chicago's Charlie Root. So heading into the bottom of the seventh inning, the score was Cubs 8, Athletics 0. Then, disaster for the Cubs. Al Simmons led off with a home run to bust up Root's shutout, and five of the next six hitters singled. Cubs manager Joe McCarthy summoned Art Nehf from the bullpen, and he was greeted with a fly ball off the bat of Mule Haas. But center fielder Hack Wilson lost the ball in the sun, and Haas circled the bases for an inside-the-park home run. That made the score 8–7, and the A's weren't finished yet. They pasted two more relief pitchers and wound up scoring 10 runs in the inning. Mack called on Lefty Grove, who tossed two shutout innings to seal the most improbable victory in Series history.

And then they did it again in game 5. Ehmke started again for Philadelphia but was knocked out by a pair of Cub runs in the fourth. Pat Malone had been brilliant on the mound for Chicago, allowing just two hits through eight innings, and the A's came up in the bottom of the ninth still trailing, 2–0.

Pinch-hitter Walter French struck out, but Max Bishop singled over third base, and Mule Haas walloped Malone's second pitch over the right-field fence for a game-tying homer. Cochrane lined out to second baseman Rogers Hornsby to make the second out. Simmons kept the inning alive with a double, however, and Jimmie Foxx was intentionally walked. Bing Miller drove a double off the scoreboard, Simmons trotted home, and the A's were world champs once again.

Why didn't Mack start either Grove or Rube Walberg in the Series? Because both were lefties and, of the eight regulars in the Chicago lineup, seven batted right-handed, including sluggers Rogers Hornsby, Hack Wilson, Riggs Stephenson, and Kiki Cuyler. Grove pitched brilliantly in relief, by the way, striking out ten Cubs in six innings and saving both games in which he worked. As for Connie Mack . . . well, you don't second-guess the winners.

The Ballpark: The Athletics played their home games in Shibe Park (1909), the first concrete and steel stadium in the major leagues, located at North Twenty-first Street and West Lehigh Avenue. Shibe, relative to the rest of the American League, played almost exactly neutral in terms of run production. Over the three pennant seasons, only 1 percent more runs were scored (2,367) in Athletics road games than were scored (2,335) in Athletics home games. However, Shibe Park was an *excellent* place for power hitters. Over those same three seasons, Shibe saw 342 home runs, whereas only 253 circuit clouts were, umm, clouted in Philly's road games.

The Athletics shared Shibe with the Phillies from 1938 through 1954, and after the A's moved to Kansas City the Phils were the lone tenants through the 1970 season. The old ballpark was demolished in 1976, and the Deliverance Evangelical Church now stands on the site.

Books about the 1929 Athletics: Seventy years after the fact, Bill Kashatus' book, *Connie Mack's 1929 Triumph* (Jefferson, NC: McFarland & Co., 1999), was published. Kashatus writes extensively about not only the 1929 season, but also the construction of the team and its decline. Also in 1999, McFarland published David M. Jordan's *The Athletics of Philadelphia: Connie Mack's White Elephants, 1901–54.* Jordan devotes roughly twenty pages to the 1929–31 A's.

In his book *Connie Mack: Grand Old Man of Baseball* (New York: G. P. Putnam's Sons, 1945), Fred Lieb devotes thirty-odd pages to the 1928–32 Athletics. There are two well-done biographies of Jimmie Foxx: W. Harrison Daniel's *Jimmie Foxx: The Life and Times of a Baseball Hall of Famer* (Jefferson, NC: McFarland & Co, 1996) and Mark Millikin's *Jimmie Foxx, the Pride of Sudlersville* (Lanham, MD: Scarecrow Press, 1998). By the time you read this, new biographies of both Connie Mack and Lefty Grove will likely be available.

Mack's own book, *My 66 Years in the Big Leagues* (Philadelphia: John C. Winston Co., 1950), has surprisingly little information on this particular club.

The Early Bloomer

Eddie Rommel was that rarest of birds, a knuckleball pitcher. But Rommel was an even rarer sub-species of that group, because he did his best pitching early in his career.

Rommel specialized in what were once known as "freak" deliveries. In the minors he relied on a spitball, but the pitch was outlawed before he reached the majors, and thus he wasn't eligible to be grandfathered in, as seventeen major league pitchers were (in 1920).

So Rommel switched to the knuckleball. Most knuckleballers peak late, later by far than any other group of baseball players you might choose. Two knuckleballers are in the Hall of Fame (Hoyt Wilhelm and Phil Niekro), and the pair combined for the grand total of 52 victories before their thirtieth birthdays. Rommel, meanwhile, already could boast 108 career wins when he turned thirty.

How good was Rommel? He never really enjoyed any huge seasons, but he never really had any bad ones, either. In fact, according to *Total Baseball*, from 1920 through 1926 he was the fourth-best pitcher in the major leagues, as rated by total pitcher index:

Pitcher	TPI
Dolf Luque	22.3
Pete Alexander	19.7
Urban Shocker	19.7
Eddie Rommel	19.0
Walter Johnson	16.0

Only two Hall of Famers here (Alexander and Johnson), but they're all fine pitchers. Rommel declined somewhat after 1926, but when

1929 rolled around, he remained an effective pitcher. From 1927 through 1929, Rommel went 36-10, mostly in relief, for an eye-catching .783 winning percentage. In 1929 he went 12-2, with a 2.85 ERA that would have ranked second in the American League to Lefty Grove (2.81). Rommel pitched only four complete games and 114 innings, though, so he didn't qualify for the rankings. Nevertheless, Rommel hated his relatively new role, at least according to a 1938 edition of *The Sporting News*. Supposedly, Rommel, sick of seeing his younger teammates getting all the glory, threw a temper tantrum in the clubhouse before a game in Chicago: "I don't give a damn what happens out there this afternoon! I don't care two hoops in Hades if ten pitchers get their domes knocked off and we drop a twenty-run lead. I'm not doing any relief pitching today. Not for Mussolini, Rasputin, or Al Smith. It's a lousy job. I ain't a relief pitcher and that's final!"

That story sounds like it might have been embellished a bit by memory and/or a creative sportswriter, but the sentiment seems genuine enough. As the story goes, Rommel dutifully finished off a victory for Rube Walberg that very afternoon.

Rommel relieved once in the '29 World Series, allowing a run in the top of the seventh in game 4. As it happened, that made him the winner when the A's mounted their improbable comeback in the bottom of the inning.

On July 10, 1932, Rommel made perhaps the strangest relief appearance ever in one of the strangest games in major league history. In the second inning, he took the mound with the Athletics trailing Cleveland, 3–2. Four hours and 17 innings later, he staggered off the mound with an 18–17 victory, in which Rommel allowed 29 hits and 9 walks! Johnny Burnett cracked 8 of those 29 hits (plus another off the starter), but luckily for the A's, Jimmie Foxx weighed in with three home runs. Rommel finished the game with a one-two-three bottom half of the eighteenth inning.

All this came about as the result of some strange circumstances. This game was the third of a three-game series, the first two games of which were played in Philadelphia on Friday and Saturday. At that point, however, Sunday baseball was still illegal in Philadelphia, so after Saturday's contest the two clubs traveled to Cleveland to complete the series. Connie Mack saw little point in bringing his entire pitching staff to Ohio, so he left all his pitchers at home, except for Sunday's starter, Lew Krausse, and his top reliever, Rommel.

Anyway, that most improbable victory was the 171st of Rommel's major-league career and, coincidentally or not, the last. (It's generally thought that knuckleballers can throw an unlimited number of pitches without ill effects, but that's probably not the case. Arm strain aside, just being on the mound for all those innings takes its toll on a pitcher's legs.)

Rommel later coached with the A's for two seasons. Then, after a minor league apprenticeship, he served as an A.L. umpire from 1938 through 1959. In 1956 he became the first major league umpire to wear glasses on the field.—Rob

The Lefty

There are three candidates for the title "Best Left-Handed Pitcher Ever": Lefty Grove, Sandy Koufax, and Warren Spahn. Here are their lifetime statistics:

Pitcher	W-L	Pct	ERA
Grove	300-141	.680	3.06
Spahn	363-245	.597	3.09
Koufax	165-87	.655	2.76

Each of these three have something to offer. You want durability? Spahn won 363 games and pitched in the majors until he was forty-four. You want a sub-3.00 ERA? Koufax is your man.

But Grove . . . O, Lefty Grove. Durability? Grove pitched until he was forty-one, and he was still somewhat effective even then. In 1939, when he was thirty-nine, Grove led the American League with a .789 winning percentage (15-4) and a 2.54 ERA. Great stats? That career .680 winning mark ranks as the fourth highest of all time, behind Dave Foutz and Whitey Ford (both .690) and Bob Caruthers (.688). None of those three came close to Grove's 300 victories, with Ford leading the way at 236.

Essentially it comes down to this. Spahn was a great pitcher for a few seasons (though not consecutively), and a very good one for about two decades. Koufax was a great pitcher for a few seasons, and a decent one for a few more. But Grove was a great pitcher for many

Lefty Grove *(National Baseball Hall of Fame Library, Cooperstown, NY)*

seasons. He led his league in ERA nine times, more than Koufax (five) and Spahn (three) *combined*. If you adjust his career ERA for the era and ballparks in which he pitched, Grove's would be far lower than Spahn's and Koufax's.

In fact, *Total Baseball* does just that, with a stat they call *adjusted ERA* (abbreviated as ERA+), which is figured "by normalizing to the league average—which is done by dividing the league average ERA by the individual ERA—and then factoring in home park."

Warren Spahn was wonderful, with a 118 ERA+. Quite simply, this means that after adjusting for the league and ballpark contexts, his career ERA was 18 percent better than an average pitcher. Sandy Koufax was brilliant, with an ERA+ of 131. And Lefty Grove? His career ERA+ was 148. Think about that. For his *career*, Grove was 48 percent better than the American League. It's truly astounding, and Lefty's adjusted ERA ranks as not only the greatest among lefthanders, but the greatest of all time among all pitchers, just ahead of a fellow named Walter Johnson.

Was Grove the greatest pitcher ever? Maybe, maybe not. Johnson's got a great argument, and if you prefer modern pitchers, Roger

Clemens or Greg Maddux is your man. But no matter how you slice it, Lefty Grove deserves a crown as the King of the Southpaws.—Rob

Meanwhile, Over at the Baker Bowl . . .

If, in 1930, someone told you that in twenty-five years one of the Philadelphia baseball teams would be transplanted to Kansas City, and this someone asked you *which* team, what would you have said? You wouldn't have said the Athletics, that's for sure.

The Philadelphia Phillies, who played in the Baker Bowl (only six blocks from Shibe), were possibly baseball's lousiest franchise in the 1930s and early 1940s. The Phils won the National League pennant in 1915 and finished second in 1916 and 1917. But from 1918 through 1948, a period of thirty-one seasons, the Phils finished fourth once, fifth twice, sixth four times, seventh seven times, and eighth (last) seventeen times. Only once in those thirty-one seasons did the Phillies win more games than they lost (1932, 78-76), and in the thirteen seasons after that .500-plus campaign, the Phils finished in either seventh or eighth place *every* year. Remember, there were only eight teams in the league.

From 1929 through 1931 the Phillies went 189–272 (.410), which was actually pretty good compared to what would come later in the decade. Those same three seasons, the Athletics out-drew the Phillies, 2,188,303 to 865,056. But as you already know, things changed. When Connie Mack stopped caring about winning in the mid-1930s, the fans stopped caring about coming to the park, and neither club drew well. The Athletics stumbled, in a pedestrian manner, through the war years.

Meanwhile, all sorts of weird things were happening down the hall from Connie Mack's office (the Phils took up residence in Shibe Park in 1938). First, the National League essentially took over the franchise. Then a syndicate headed by New York businessman William Cox bought the Phillies. After less than a year, however, Cox was banned from baseball for, supposedly, betting on his club. Millionaire Bob Carpenter, a DuPont heir, next took ownership. He plowed plenty of money into building a farm system, and in 1950 the Phillies won their first National League pennant in thirty-five years.

Thus it was that, when a major league baseball team left the City of Brotherly Love in 1955, it was not the once-hapless Phillies, but rather the tradition-rich Athletics. Of course, those same Athletics wound up moving from Kansas City to Oakland and, within a few years, they might be somewhere else.—Rob

The Greatest Minor League Team

I am very proud of my Baltimore heritage. I mean, Baltimore gave America Babe Ruth and the national anthem. How many cities can match that? Baltimore was also home to the greatest minor league team of all time, the Baltimore Orioles franchise that from 1919 through 1925 won seven consecutive International League pennants. So what do they have to do with the 1929 Philadelphia Athletics, besides geographical and temporal proximity?

Well, for starters, Lefty Grove pitched for the Orioles from 1920 through 1924. Connie Mack purchased Grove from the Orioles for

Eddie Collins (*National Baseball Hall of Fame Library, Cooperstown, NY*)

Before Their Time

In May 1929, Athletics player-coach Eddie Collins turned forty-two years old. He could have passed for sixty-two. And Collins was the rule rather than the exception. In 1928, Ty Cobb also had played with the Athletics. He was forty-one and looked like he was sixty-one. Why did these fellows look so old? Well, before 1935, every major league game was played in the daytime. What's more, very few players wore sunglasses of any sort, and the bills of the caps were smaller than they would become. Thus, a ballplayer's three primary activities in the 1920s were hitting, fielding, and squinting, and not necessarily in that order. Of course, nobody'd ever heard of sunscreen back then; we can only imagine how many baseball players suffered from skin cancer in those days.—*Rob* more than $100,000, which was quite a lot of money in the 1920s. (Baltimore originally purchased Grove in 1920 from Martinsburg of the Blue Ridge League for the low, low price of $3,200.)

Remember, this was in the days before modern farm systems. Most minor league teams were independent entities. Grove's record with the Orioles was mind-numbing (109-36 or 108-36, depending on the source), and he led the International League in strikeouts the last four years he was there. Grove also led the American League in strikeouts his first seven years *there*, which means that he led his league in strike-outs an unbelievable *eleven straight times* from 1921 to 1931.

Lefty Grove alone would have been enough to link the Orioles championship teams and the A's championship teams, but there's much more. The leading winner on the 1929 A's was not Grove, but George Earnshaw (24-8). Where do you think he came from? Right, Baltimore. Earnshaw pitched for the Orioles from 1924 through early 1928. For the last of the Endless Chain Champs (as they were dubbed by the *Baseball Guide*) in 1925, Earnshaw went 29-11 and then beat Louisville three times in the Junior World Series as the Orioles won the series five games to three.

Mack bought Earnshaw for $70,000 in the middle of the 1928 sea-son, and the huge-for-his-time (6-foot-4) righthander debuted for the Athletics on June 3.

Okay, so we've got the two ace pitchers. How about the double-play combo? Max Bishop, the A's starting second baseman, and start-ing shortstop Joe Boley both played for the Orioles. In fact, Boley played for all seven pennant winners. Bishop, who played for the Orioles from 1918 to 1923, attended Baltimore City College, which despite the name is a high school. Of the four ex-Orioles who were part of the 1929–31 American League pennant winners, Bishop was the first to land in Philadelphia, when Connie Mack bought him for $25,000 after the 1923 season; Mack spent $65,000 on Boley after the 1926 season.

Before I get into some detail about the Orioles, I should say a bit about their mastermind, Jack Dunn. John Joseph Dunn was born in Meadville, Pennsylvania, (birthplace of Sharon Stone) in 1872 and enjoyed a decent major league career around the turn of the century, primarily as a pitcher. It was Jack Dunn who discovered Babe Ruth, assuming the role of Ruth's custodian when he was released from St. Mary's School for Boys in Baltimore. Dunn was also indirectly responsible for the most famous nickname in the history of sports. The most often repeated story of how George Herman Ruth became "Babe" holds that Ruth was very impressive in some exhibition games against major league clubs before the start of the 1914 season. When a sportswriter asked in amazement who Ruth was, the answer came from an Orioles coach, "That's Dunn's new babe." And in *Babe*, Robert Creamer's outstanding biography of Ruth, Creamer credits the Oriole players with giving Ruth his nickname during spring training, calling him "Dunnie's Babe."

Dunn felt compelled to sell Ruth to the Boston Red Sox in 1914, when Baltimore's Federal League team, the Terrapins, temporarily captured most of the Orioles' fan base, thus necessitating an infusion of cash. Dunn actually moved the Orioles to Richmond, Virginia, in 1915, but he sold that franchise in 1916, bought Jersey City's International League franchise, moved it to Baltimore, bought Terrapin Park (the Federal League had collapsed) and renamed it Oriole Park in honor of his "new" Orioles. (The current A.L. Orioles moved to Baltimore in 1954 from St. Louis, where they had been the Browns.)

Dunn was an aggressive, perceptive scout, though he certainly wasn't perfect. He gave tryouts to Home Run Baker (from Maryland's Eastern Shore) and Eddie Rommel (from Baltimore), but signed neither. He did like to sign local players, something that was particularly important in Baltimore, where parochial feelings have always been strong.

The streak of seven consecutive pennants began with the 1919 team that went 100-49 and won the pennant by 7½ games. In 1920 the Orioles added Lefty Grove, but the stars of the team were Jack Ogden, who had 27 wins; Harry Frank, who had 25; and Jack Bentley, who notched 16 wins and led the league in ERA *and* RBI. Yes, you read that right. Bentley was a first baseman first, and a pitcher second. Merwin Jacobson, who had 2,395 hits in his minor league career, paced the loop with 235 hits, 161 runs scored, and a .404 batting average. A strong Toronto team won 24 of its last 26 games, but the Orioles *won their last 25 games* to finish with a 110-43 record and take the pennant by 2½ lengths.

In 1921, the International League adopted a 168-game schedule, which just gave Baltimore a longer season to dominate. The Orioles started a 27-game winning streak in mid-May, a streak which remained the professional record for more than sixty years. Baltimore finished 119-47 and won the pennant by 20 games. Ogden's record was 31-8, Grove's was 25-10 with a 2.56 ERA and a league-leading 254 strikeouts. A newcomer, Tommy Thomas from Baltimore City College, won 24. Bentley led the league with 246 hits, 397 total bases, 47 doubles, 24 homers, and a .412 batting average. In his spare time, Bentley pitched his way to a 12-1 record and a 2.35 ERA.

Bentley was sold to the Giants for $72,500 (the most ever paid for a minor leaguer to that point) after another Orioles pennant in 1922 (115-52 record). In his last three years with the Orioles, Bentley batted .378, scored 340 runs and drove in 409, slugged .590, and went 41-6 with a 2.07 ERA.

Ogden led the league in wins for the third straight year in 1922. Unfortunately for Ogden, Dunn didn't sell him to a major league team—the St. Louis Browns—until after he was thirty. According to the Society for American Baseball Research's *Minor League Baseball Stars*, Ogden's .674 career winning percentage is the highest of any minor league pitcher with 200 or more wins (213-103), which is even more impressive when one considers that *all* of Ogden's minor league time was spent in the classy International League.

In 1923, Baltimore posted a 111-53 record and won the pennant by 11 games. Grove was 27-10 with 330 strikeouts (still, and almost certainly forever, the International League record). The real pitching star was oddball Rube Parnham, who won his last 20 decisions on the way to a 33-7 mark. The last two of those victories came in a closing-day doubleheader that Parnham pitched after he had jumped the team for about a week.

Baltimore won another easy pennant in 1924 (117-48 record, 19-game margin). It was Grove's last season with the Orioles; he was 27-6 with a 3.01 ERA and 231 strikeouts in 236 innings. Richard "Twitchy Dick" Porter led the league with a .364 batting average and chipped in with 116 runs, 125 RBI, and 23 homers. Porter later spent six years in the majors, most of that time with the Indians, who bought him for $40,000.

So for the five seasons ending in 1924, the Orioles' record was 572-243, which makes for a .702 winning percentage. They had won each of the last four International League pennants by at least 10 games, with an average margin of 15 games.

Without Grove, Bentley, Bishop, Jacobson, or Parnham (who skipped out again), Baltimore won its seventh straight pennant by four games over Toronto in 1925. George Earnshaw's season has already been mentioned, but Tommy Thomas went 32-12 in his last year with the Orioles, and Ogden was 28-11.

In essence, the Baltimore dynasty ended because the rest of the International League was tired of losing every year. The league finally surrendered to major league pressure and gave up its draft-exempt status. Before then, the International League had been the only top-level minor league that refused to allow major league teams to draft its players for a fixed price. Under the new arrangement, Dunn had to arrange sales every year before the annual draft, and that requirement ended the great Oriole teams.

In an independent high-level minor league, the Orioles won seven consecutive pennants. In six of those seasons they won more than two-thirds of their games, and in three of *those* seasons they won more than 70 percent of their games.

Lefty Grove, arguably the greatest pitcher ever, spent five seasons with the Orioles. Much of the core of a three-time American League pennant winner came from this team. This team sent many players to the major leagues, a number of whom were successful, including the greatest two-way player in the history of the high minors. These are all amazing accomplishments and yet, I'll say it again, the man responsible for building and maintaining this team, Jack Dunn, is almost completely forgotten today, except maybe in Baltimore. Dunn died of a heart attack in October 1928. One imagines that, had he lived, he would have greatly enjoyed seeing his former charges dominate the American League for three years.—Eddie

TEAM STATISTICS

Hitting

	Games by Position	Age	G	AB	R	H	2B	3B	HR	RBI	BB	SO	SB	Avg	OBP	Slug
Mickey Cochrane	C,135	26	135	514	113	170	37	8	7	95	69	8	7	.331	.412	.475
Jimmie Foxx	1B,142; 3B,8	21	149	517	123	183	23	9	33	117	103	**70**	9	.354	**.463**	.625
Max Bishop	2B,129	29	129	475	102	110	19	6	3	36	**128**	44	1	.232	.398	.316
Sammy Hale	3B,99; 2B,1	32	101	379	51	105	14	3	1	40	12	18	6	.277	.303	.338
Joe Boley	SS,88; 3B,1	32	91	303	36	76	17	6	2	47	24	16	1	.251	.310	.366
Bing Miller	OF,145	34	147	556	84	186	32	16	8	93	40	25	24	.335	.383	.493
Al Simmons	OF,142	27	143	581	114	212	41	9	34	**157**	31	38	4	365	.398	.642
Mule Haas	OF,139	25	139	578	115	181	41	9	16	82	34	38	0	.313	.356	.498
Jimmy Dykes	SS,60; 3B,45; 2B,12	32	119	401	76	131	34	6	13	79	51	25	8	.327	.412	.539
Homer Summa	OF,24	30	37	81	12	22	4	0	0	10	2	1	1	.272	.298	.321
Cy Perkins	C,38	33	38	76	4	16	4	0	0	9	5	4	0	.211	.259	.263
Jim Cronin	2B,10; SS,9; 3B,4	23	25	56	7	13	2	1	0	4	5	7	0	.232	.295	.304
Ossie Orwoll	P,12,OF,9	28	30	51	6	13	2	1	0	6	2	11	0	.255	.283	.333
George Burns*	1B,19	36	29	49	5	13	5	0	1	11	2	3	1	.265	.294	.429
Walt French		29	45	45	7	12	1	0	1	9	2	3	0	.267	.298	.356
Bud Morse	2B,8	24	8	27	1	2	0	0	0	0	0	2	0	.074	.074	.074
Bevo LeBourveau	OF,3	34	12	16	1	5	0	1	0	2	5	1	0	.313	.476	.438
Eric McNair	SS,4	20	4	8	2	4	1	0	0	3	0	0	1	.500	.500	.625
Eddie Collins		42	9	7	0	0	0	0	0	0	2	0	0	.000	.222	.000
Doc Cramer	OF,1	23	2	6	0	0	0	0	0	0	0	2	0	.000	.000	.000
Cloy Mattox	C,3	26	3	6	0	1	0	0	0	0	1	1	0	.167	.286	.167
Rudy Miller	3B,2	28	2	4	1	1	0	0	0	1	3	0	0	.250	.571	.250
Joe Hassler	SS,2	24	4	4	1	0	0	0	0	0	0	2	0	.000	.000	.000
Totals		29	151	5,204	901	1,539	288	76	122	845	543	440	63	.296	**.365**	.451

*Played for another team during season. Statistics are those compiled with 1929 Philadelphia Athletics only.

Pitching

	Threw	Age	Games	GS	CG	ShO	IP	H	HR	BB	SO	W	L	Pct	Sv	ERA
Lefty Grove	Left	29	42	**37**	21	2	275	278	8	81	**170**	20	6	**.769**	4	**2.81**
Rube Walberg	Left	32	40	33	20	3	268	256	22	99	94	18	11	.621	4	3.60
George Earnshaw	Right	29	44	33	13	2	255	233	8	**125**	149	**24**	8	.750	1	3.29
Jack Quinn	Right	45	35	18	7	0	161	182	8	39	41	11	9	.550	2	3.97
Bill Shores	Right	25	39	13	5	1	153	150	9	59	49	11	6	.647	7	3.60
Eddie Rommel	Right	31	32	6	4	0	114	135	10	34	25	12	2	.857	4	2.85
Howard Ehmke	Right	35	11	8	2	0	55	48	2	15	20	7	2	.778	0	3.29
Carroll Yerkes	Left	26	19	2	0	0	37	47	0	13	11	1	0	1.000	1	4.58
Ossie Orwoll	Left	28	12	0	0	0	30	32	6	6	12	0	2	.000	1	4.80
Bill Breckinridge	Right	21	3	1	0	0	10	10	0	16	2	0	0	—	0	7.20
Totals		31	277	151	72	8	1,357	**1,371**	73	487	**573**	**104**	**46**	**.693**	**24**	**3.44**

CHAPTER 7

1939 New York Yankees

This Yankee club is better than the much-talked-about 1927 outfit. This club
has great balance, brilliant youth, speed, pitching, everything.

—Yankees general manager Ed Barrow

Record: 106-45, .702 (9th)
Two-Year (1938–39): 205-98, .677 (13th)
Three-Year (1937–39): 307-150, .672
  (7th)

SD Score: 3.52 (9th)
Two-Year: 6.48 (5th)
Three-Year: 9.70 (2d)

Results:
1937 World Champions
1938 World Champions
1939 World Champions

Days in First Place: 159 of 168;
  clinched on September 16

Longest Winning Streak: 12 games
Longest Losing Streak: 6 games

The Pennant Race: At the close of play on May 31, the Yankees' record was 29-7, and for all intents and purposes the pennant race was over. The Red Sox got hot in July, reeling off a 12-game winning streak that included a 5-game sweep of the Yanks, but they never got closer than 10 games after that.

Against the Contenders: There weren't any contenders, but the Red Sox did capture the season series from New York, winning 11 of 19 games.

Runs Scored: 967 (1st)

Runs Allowed: 556 (1st)

No team was close to the Yankees in either category. More impressive, the 1939 Yankees are the only twentieth-century team to outscore its opponents by more than 400 runs.

Pythagorean Record: 111-40

Of the nine teams that played .700 or better baseball in the twentieth century, the 1939 Yankees are the only one to under-perform their Pythagorean projection.

Manager: Joe McCarthy

Regular Lineup:

Player	Position	ROV	OW%
Frankie Crosetti	SS	.246	.384
Red Rolfe	3B	.344	.716
Charlie Keller	RF	.364	.759
Joe DiMaggio	CF	.406	.830
Bill Dickey	C	.345	.717
George Selkirk	LF	.370	.771
Joe Gordon	2B	.315	.635
Babe Dahlgren	1B	.251	.406
Red Ruffing	P		

An imposing lineup, to say the least, with five regulars sporting .340+ real offensive values and .700+ offensive winning percentages.

Stats 'n' Stuff

◆ Yankees owner Colonel Jacob Ruppert dies on January 13.

◆ After three straight rain-outs, the Yankees finally open their season on April 20 against the Red Sox, in New York. The box score includes future Hall of Famers Lou Gehrig, Ted Williams, Joe DiMaggio, Bill Dickey, Bobby Doerr, Jimmie Foxx, Joe Cronin, and Lefty Grove.

◆ In the 1927 Yankees' first game, they beat Lefty Grove. In the 1939 Yankees' first game, they beat Lefty Grove.

◆ On May 27, George Selkirk cracks a pair of home runs off Athletics starter Robert Joyce. The next day, Joyce pitches in relief, and Selkirk hits two more home runs off him.

◆ On June 28, the Yankees hit eight home runs in the first game of a doubleheader with the A's, setting a single-game record. Then they hit five more in the nightcap for a total of thirteen, another major league record. The

Yanks win the opener 23–2, and the nightcap 10–0.

◆ Rookie pitcher Atley Donald runs his record to 12-0 with a victory over the St. Louis Browns on July 25.

The No-Trade Rule

By late 1939, the rest of the American League was mighty sick of the Yankees. In the previous four seasons, the Bombers had finished a composite 59 games ahead of the second-place teams, and there was no apparent end in sight.

So at the American League meetings on December 7, 1939, A.L. owners passed a rule which expressly prohibited a league champion from trading for, or purchasing, any players in its league, from the end of the championship season through the end of the next, or until it was eliminated from contention.

Yankees general manager Ed Barrow was less than concerned, to the point of nearly bursting with confidence. "I believe it wise

One has to wonder why the worst hitter in the lineup batted lead-off. Not many clubs bat their first baseman eighth, but the Yankees had a pretty good excuse for Babe Dahlgren, which we'll discuss below.

Bench: Bench? What bench? If the Yankees had a bench, you wouldn't know it from the record books. With Tommy Henrich playing in 99 games, the Bombers essentially had four regular outfielders, but he was about the only non-starter who had any fun at all.

Bill Dickey was the best catcher in the American League and played 128 games. Buddy Rosar caught 35 games. Arndt Jorgens, a native of Norway in his eleventh and final season with the Yankees, caught two games (and pinch-ran in another). Babe Dahlgren took over for Lou Gehrig on May 2 and played all but one game the rest of the season. The rest of the infield was amazingly stable, as Joe Gordon, Frank Crosetti, and Red Rolfe missed a *combined total* of one game all season (Gordon being the guilty party).

Why did everyone play so much? With the Yankees clinching the American League pennant in September and enjoying a huge lead for months before that, manager Joe McCarthy certainly could have afforded to rest his regulars from time to time. Why didn't he? We really can't say. We can say this, though: the Yanks didn't exactly look fatigued in the World Series. Given his reliance on a set lineup, McCarthy was frequently described as a "push-button manager." Perhaps, but it must also be said that he pushed a lot of buttons correctly.

Scouting the Pitchers: Joe McCarthy liked starters who could throw hard, so that's what most of them did. Future Hall of Famer Lefty Gomez (12-8, 3.41) depended on his lively fastball, though by 1939 his heater was starting to fade. Atley Donald (13-3, 3.71) threw hard, and Marius Russo's (8-3, 2.41) fastball was often compared to that of the usually incomparable Bob Feller. Monte Pearson (12-5, 4.50) and Bump Hadley (12-6, 2.98) were best known as curveball pitchers (though Hadley's most famous single pitch was a fastball that fractured the skull of Tigers player-manager Mickey Cochrane in 1937). Red Ruffing (21-7, 2.94) was the best hitter among the pitchers and, in fact, Red Ruffing is one of the best hitters among *all* pitchers, ever. When he was a boy, Ruffing lost a few toes (variously reported as two and four) in a mining accident, which makes his dual success seem all the more unlikely. Ruffing relied on his fastball and also used a curve-ball and a change-up that he learned in the middle of his career.

How were they built? The keys to the Yankees' success were their financial resources and brilliant management. Thanks to their success in the 1920s, their geographical location, and massive Yankee Stadium, the club always made plenty of dough when they were winning. But you need more than money to win pennants, as so many franchises in the 1990s have proved so well.

The Yankees were built by general manager Ed Barrow, the same man who constructed the 1927 team. Barrow thus ranks with Branch Rickey as one of the two greatest franchise builders in the history of the game. In his book, *The American Diamond*, Rickey devoted two pages to Barrow, concluding with, "A repeating winning club is not miraculous. It comes from job devotion and knowing players and above all putting them together properly. Ed Barrow was the number one man in my baseball acquaintance for making and maintaining a winning club."

Like all great executives, Barrow relied on talented lieutenants, including farm director George Weiss and scout Bill Essick. Nobody really "discovered" Joe DiMaggio, because after he hit in 61 straight games for the San Francisco Seals when he was only eighteen, every baseball executive in the country knew all about him. But Seals owner Charlie Graham wasn't ready to give up his drawing card quite yet, so DiMaggio remained in San Francisco for another season. Unfortunately, during the season DiMaggio tore up his knee (while jumping off a bus, not playing ball).

Legend has it that only the Yankees were willing to risk a bundle of cash on a young player with a gimpy knee, but that's not really true. Other clubs were still interested in DiMaggio after the injury. But this was during the Depression, and not many teams could *afford* to remain interested because, injury or not, Graham's asking price for DiMaggio was high. In 1933, George Weiss and scouts Essick and Joe Devine convinced Yankees owner Jacob Ruppert to go after DiMaggio. Ruppert agreed, and Essick told George Barrow, "Buy DiMaggio. I think you can get him cheap." Barrow ordered a battery of medical tests on DiMaggio's knee, and the knee passed. In return for DiMaggio's contract, Barrow sent Graham $25,000 and five minor leaguers—plus an extra year of Joe D, who played in San Francisco for one more season before reporting to the Yankees in 1936.

to let the New York club stand as it is and invite the others to knock it down," Barrow told *The Sporting News* just before the rule became official. "There is little that can be done to improve this Yankee club. It is the greatest team ever put together. That finally is sinking in all over baseball."

The funny thing about all this was, the Yankees of the late 1930s did not typically acquire players from other clubs during the season. They didn't need to, because they were incredibly deep and they typically had little competition anyway. The Yankees did pick up two useful pitchers (Monte Pearson and Steve Sundra) after the 1935 season, but they gave up a really good pitcher (Johnny Allen) to get those guys. From 1936 through 1939, the Yankees dealt for nine players, none of whom were very good.

When the Yankees failed to win in 1940, the no-trade rule was quickly repealed.

—*Rob*

May 2, 1939

If you've ever seen the movie *Pride of the Yankees,* you know that Gary Cooper gives an arresting performance as Lou Gehrig. But if all you know of May 2, 1939, is what you saw at the movies, then what you know is wrong.

In the film, the Yankees and Tigers are locked up in a tight game when the ballpark announcer shockingly intones, "Your attention, please. Dahlgren now playing first base for Gehrig." Of course, it didn't happen that way at all. If Dahlgren had replaced Gehrig during the game, then Lou's streak wouldn't have been snapped at all, at least not in that game. In reality, Dahlgren started the game at first base and, of course, Gehrig never played at all. By the way, Gary Cooper was not athletically inclined, so some of the batting sequences actually show Babe Herman, and the defensive scenes were filmed with Cooper throwing righty, and then the negative was reversed (Gehrig was a lefty, of course).

Joe Essick did discover Joe Gordon, who was playing shortstop for a company team in an industrial league. After signing with the Yankees, Gordon shifted to second base, and in 1938 he supplanted future Hall of Famer Tony Lazzeri with the big club.

In the 1930s, the Cleveland Indians engaged in a number of nefarious tactics in their hunt for young players. Tommy Henrich originally signed with the Tribe, but some questions arose as to whose property he actually was. Commissioner Kenesaw Mountain Landis was tiring of the Indians' shenanigans, and it apparently gave him some pleasure to declare the twenty-four-year-old Henrich a free agent in 1937. The Yankees outbid a number of other teams, Henrich signing for a $25,000 bonus.

What brought them down? Adolf Hitler, with a little help from Japanese militarists. True, the Yankees had something of an off season in 1940, finishing in third place. But they were only two games behind the first-place Tigers and obviously could have won yet another flag with a few breaks. Then they came back to capture three straight pennants and a pair of World Series, beginning in 1941.

Things got weird in 1944, when the St. Louis Browns won their first-ever (and last-ever) pennant. And after the always-solid Tigers won in 1945, in '46 the Red Sox captured their first flag since 1918. But in 1947, with enough butter and beef in the country for everyone, the Yankees became *The Yankees* once again. We'll have more on that edition of the Bombers later, but for now we'll tell you that from 1947 through 1964, the Yankees won fifteen pennants in eighteen tries, a run of success unmatched by any team in baseball or any other sport.

Most Valuable Yankee: DiMaggio was quite possibly the most valuable player in the major leagues despite missing six weeks with a torn calf muscle, and after the season he easily out-polled Jimmie Foxx for American League MVP honors.

Worst Regular: Babe Dahlgren

Hall of Famers: Lou Gehrig of course, though he played only eight games. DiMaggio and Dickey are both in, and so are Lefty Gomez, Red Ruffing, and manager Joe McCarthy.

Our Hall of Famers: Gehrig, DiMaggio, and Dickey are all more than deserving. Gomez and Ruffing are both questionable. Although his .649 career winning percentage ranks thirteenth on the all-time list, Gomez won "only" 189 games, and of course Lou Gehrig and Joe DiMaggio had something to do with Gomez' winning percentage. He did pitch brilliantly in 1934 (26-5, 2.33) and 1937 (21-11, 2.33), but two great seasons do not a Hall of Famer make.

Ruffing won 273 games, but he also lost 225. Ruffing was one of the best-hitting pitchers in the history of the game, and he probably does deserve a little extra credit for that. Ruffing was just 39-96 with the Red Sox before he got traded to the Yankees in 1930, and apologists claim that pitching for a crummy team hurt his record. That's true. But it's also true that Ruffing really did become a better pitcher once he left Boston, above and beyond the wins and the losses. Call it better coaching or natural maturation or whatever you want, but Ruffing went 231-124 as a Yankee. He capped his career in pinstripes with a 5-1 record and a 1.77 ERA in 1946, when he was forty-two years old. The next year he signed with the White Sox and went 3-5 with a 6.11 ERA.

One can make an interesting Hall of Fame argument for Joe Gordon. He's a classic case of a guy who played brilliantly for a decade but didn't play at all after that. Gordon was a better hitter than Boston's Bobby Doerr and just as good a fielder (more on that below). But Doerr's in the Hall of Fame and Gordon's not because Doerr played fourteen seasons and Gordon played only eleven (and also, perhaps, because Doerr had more friends on the Veterans Committee). Their key career percentages—on-base and slugging—are practically identical: .362 and .461 for Doerr, .357 and .466 for Gordon. I'll save you the trouble and figure their OPSs . . . yep, 823 for both of them. And Gordon played in Yankee Stadium, a significantly tougher park for hitters than Boston's Fenway.

Gordon was an outstanding defensive second baseman. Senators manager Bucky Harris observed, "If the outfield behind Gordon weren't so great, Joe would make the darndest catches an infielder ever made. He'd play second base, short center field, and part of right field."

Joe McCarthy absolutely loved Joe Gordon. In the documentary *When It Was a Game*, Tommy Henrich related the following scene:

Finally, the May 2 contest in Detroit wasn't close at all. Suggesting just how much they would miss Gehrig as the season continued, the Yankees destroyed the Tigers, 22–2, with Dahlgren connecting for a double and a homer.

Gehrig remained with the club all season, suiting up daily. He even played three innings of an exhibition game against Kansas City on June 12. In his only at-bat, Gehrig grounded out weakly, and he messed up a couple of plays at first base. After the game, he boarded a plane for Rochester, Minnesota, home of the Mayo Clinic. It was there that doctors diagnosed the amyotrophic lateral sclerosis—soon to be known as Lou Gehrig's Disease—that would kill him in two years.

On July 4, Gehrig delivered his famous farewell speech to a packed Yankee Stadium. Six months later, he became the first player in major league history to have his number (4) retired.—*Rob*

Around the Majors

April 20 Ted Williams makes his American League debut in Boston's season opener at Yankee Stadium. It's the only official game to include both Williams, who doubles, and Lou Gehrig, who goes hitless. "The Splendid Splinter" will go on to lead the American League with 145 RBI.

June 12 The National Baseball Hall of Fame is dedicated in Cooperstown, New York. Babe Ruth, Ty Cobb, Honus Wagner, Walter Johnson, Grover Cleveland Alexander, Nap Lajoie, George Sisler, Eddie Collins, Tris Speaker, Cy Young, and Connie Mack are all on hand to accept their plaques.

July 23 The Dodgers and Cardinals test a yellow baseball, and the Brooklyns don't much enjoy the canary-colored sphere, dropping a 12–0 decision. The yellow ball, which had been used at least once in 1938, will be tested in a few other games

Somebody was saying, "McCarthy, you like Joe Gordon, don't you?"

He says, "I sure do."

"Why do you like him?"

He says, "I'll show you why. . . . Hey Joe, come over here." He says, "What's your battin' average?"

Gordon says, "I don't know."

"What's your fieldin' average?"

"I don't know."

Gordon walked away and McCarthy says, "That's what I like. All he does is come to beat you."

Does Joe Gordon deserve a plaque in Cooperstown? That's really a philosophical question. The current Hall of Fame voting rules stipulate that a player must spend ten seasons in the major leagues, and Gordon has eleven to his credit (granted, he spent 1944 and 1945 in the service). In eight of those eleven seasons, he was one of the two best second baseman in the American League. Is that a Hall of Famer? Like we said, that's a philosophical question. But given the number of marginal Hall of Famers already in, we can't quite support his candidacy.

The 1939 World Series: The Yankees faced off against the Cincinnati Reds, winners of their first pennant in twenty years and heavy underdogs. Game 1 was a nail-biter, as the score was tied at one apiece heading into the bottom of the ninth. Red Rolfe led off with a ground-out, but Charlie Keller followed with a triple to right center. After DiMaggio was intentionally walked, Bill Dickey singled over second base to plate Keller with the winning run.

In game 2, Yankee starter Monte Pearson carried a no-hitter into the eighth and finished with a two-hitter and a 4–0 victory. Two days later, the Series resumed in Cincinnati, but it did the Reds no good. Lefty Gomez lasted only an inning before retiring because of injury, and the Yankees totaled only five hits the entire game. However, four of those five hits were home runs—two for Keller, one each for Dickey and DiMaggio—and the Bombers rolled to a 7–3 triumph, Bump Hadley collecting the victory with eight innings of relief.

Game 4 was another heartbreaker for the National Leaguers, who owned a 4–2 lead going into the ninth. Keller and DiMaggio opened the inning with singles, but Dickey followed with a double-play grounder that the Reds botched. New York eventually scored twice, forcing extra frames. In the top of the tenth, the Yankees scored three runs, two of them unearned, with the help of three Cincinnati errors. In the bottom of the tenth, the Reds collected a pair of singles, but Wally Berger's liner to shortstop ended the Series.

The Ballpark: Yankee Stadium was little changed from its 1927 configuration (see page 98), though in general the fences were moved back slightly down the left-field line and in straightaway left and moved closer in left-center and straightaway center fields. The Stadium was, of course, very tough on right-handed power hitters because of "Death Valley" in left-center. In his first four seasons as a Yankee (1936–39), Joe DiMaggio hit 83 home runs on the road, but only 54 at home.

Books about the 1939 Yankees: Talmage Boston's *1939: Baseball's Pivotal Year* (Fort Worth, TX: The Summit Group, 1994) includes chapters on both Gehrig and DiMaggio. Tommy Henrich did a book in 1992 with Bill Gilbert, *Five O'Clock Lightning: Ruth, Gehrig, DiMaggio, Mantle and the Glory Years of the NY Yankees* (New York: Birch Lane Press, 1992). That subtitle is a bit curious, seeing as how Henrich joined the Yankees two years after Ruth departed and left the Yankees a year before Mantle arrived. However, there are roughly 100 pages on the Gehrig/DiMaggio teams. Of course, numerous biographies have been written about both Gehrig and DiMaggio, although a definitive, well-researched biography of either has yet to be written.

later this season before the idea is dropped.

September 9 Appendicitis ends the season of Red Sox first baseman Jimmie Foxx, but he'll end up leading the American League with 35 homers anyway.

Four Straight

It wasn't just that the Yankees won four straight World Series (as we'll see later in the book, the 1949–53 Bombers would win *five* straight), but rather *how* they won those four straight Series.

In 1936, the Yankees needed six games to stop the Giants in the first one-city World Series since 1923 (another Yankees-over-Giants affair). In 1937, the Yankees beat the Giants once again, this time in five games. In 1938 and 1939, the Yankees swept the Cubs and Reds, respectively. So that's sixteen wins and three losses in four years. Sixteen and three works out to an .842 winning percentage.

How does that compare to other Series streakers? The list of teams that won three (or more) straight World Series is a short one: the 1936–39 Yankees, the 1949–53 Yankees, and the 1972–74 A's. Let's break those teams down into three-year groups and rank them by World Series winning percentage. To the right of those are the composite numbers for the three teams (three years for the A's, four for the 1936–39 Yanks, five for the 1949–53 Yanks).

1937–39 Yankees	12-1, .923	1936–39 Yankees	16-3, .842
1936–38 Yankees	12-3, .800		
1949–51 Yankees	12-3, .800	1949–53 Yankees	20-8, .714
1950–52 Yankees	12-5, .706		
1951–53 Yankees	12-7, .632		
1972–74 A's	12-7, .632	1972–74 A's	12-7, .632

Now, you might say I stacked the deck here, rating the 1936–38 Yanks ahead of the 1949–51 Yanks, and the 1951–53 Yankees ahead of the 1972–74 Oakland A's. Ah, but there is a method to my madness. In the case of winning-percentage ties, I ranked the teams according to run differential. The 1936–38 Yankees were +49 in the World Series, the 1949–51 Yankees +14. The 1951–53 Yankees were +23, whereas the 1972–74 A's were—hold on to your caps—*minus 3*.

It doesn't take a genius, then, to see that the 1936–39 Yankees dominated in World Series play like no team before or since, at least when you're looking at three- or four-year stretches.—Rob

Why '39

Although none of the teams in this book were one-year wonders, we did decide to focus on one season when writing the team chapters. Obviously, the Yankees absolutely dominated the American League from 1936 through 1939, so how did we arrive at '39? First, let's look at the Yanks' records those four seasons:

Year	W-L	Pct
1936	102-51	.667
1937	102-52	.662
1938	99-53	.651
1939	106-45	.702

The 1939 team had the best record and was the only one of these four to post a .700+ winning percentage. Only nine teams in the twentieth century have posted such a winning percentage. (By the way, three of those nine are Yankees teams, the other two being the 1927 and 1998 Bombers.) Let's look at SD scores:

Year	SD Score
1936	+3.12
1937	+3.22
1938	+2.97
1939	+3.52

The SD scores match almost exactly the winning percentages. The 1939 Yankees' SD score is also among the top ten of this century (and yes, the '27 and '98 Yankees are in the top ten as well). Even though the '38 Yankees had the worst SD score of the four, the 1938–39 Yankees have the highest two-year SD score for this team. Likewise, the 1937–39 SD score is higher than the 1936–38 SD score.

The 1939 Yankees had the best run differential (+411) of *any* team in the twentieth century. Here are the run differentials for the four teams:

Year	Runs Scored	Runs Allowed	Differential
1936	1065	731	+334
1937	979	671	+308
1938	966	710	+256
1939	967	556	+411

Let's see, how about the number of days spent in first place? The '39 club spent 159 days atop the A.L. standings, more than the 1936 (141 days in first), 1937 (143), or 1938 (87) squads.

Looking at all this data, it seems obvious that the 1939 team was the best of the four. So, what objections could be made to that year? Probably the biggest objection for some people is that 1939 is the year Lou Gehrig's streak and career ended, early in May. However, I think that fact argues in favor of the 1939 team. Can you imagine having to replace a player who may have been the greatest ever at his position . . . and having an even better season as a team?

The performance of the outfield of the 1939 team was certainly the best of the four and was one of the most productive outfields of all time:

Player	Plate Appearances	Runs	RBI	OBP	Slug	RC/27
DiMaggio	524	108	123	.448	.671	11.71
Selkirk	537	103	101	.452	.517	9.57
Keller	490	87	83	.447	.500	9.21
A.L. Avg				.352	.407	5.21

Though he missed nearly six weeks, it was one of DiMaggio's best seasons, winning him the first of three American League MVP awards.

Any way you slice it, the 1939 Yankees were the best of the four great teams from 1936 to 1939. And any way you slice it, the 1936–39 Yankees were the best four-year team in baseball history.—Eddie

What Might Have Been

You know what's really scary about the '39 Yankees? They quite easily could have been significantly better than they were.

First, there was Joe DiMaggio. Great as he was (DiMaggio batted .381, knocked in 126 runs, and won the American League MVP award), he could have been better. In late April, DiMaggio tore a calf muscle and wound up missing the better part of six weeks. It's not unreasonable to assume that the Yankees would have won at least one more game had DiMaggio been available all season. (On the other hand, they did go 28-7 in his absence, so perhaps he wasn't missed at all.)

And of course, there was Lou Gehrig. Most of you are no doubt familiar with his story, so suffice it to say that Gehrig left the lineup on

Lou Gehrig and Babe Dahlgren *(National Baseball Hall of Fame Library, Cooperstown, NY)*

McCarthy's Bullpen

Yankees manager Joe McCarthy didn't really have a bullpen in the traditional sense of the word. Nine different Yankee pitchers pitched in at least 20 games, and eight of those nine started at least 10 games. There were plenty of starts to go around because, although McCarthy didn't believe in resting his everyday players, he also didn't believe in working his starters too hard. Red Ruffing led the staff with 28 starts.

So McCarthy's bullpen was whichever starter wasn't tired—and John Joseph Murphy. They called him "Grandma" and "Fireman" and "Fordham Johnny," and he threw a wicked curveball. If Otis "Doc" Crandall was the best relief pitcher of the 'teens and Fred "Firpo" Marberry was the best relief pitcher of the 1920s, then Johnny "Grandma" Murphy was the best relief pitcher of the 1930s. Between 1935 and 1943, Murphy led the

May 2 and did not return. In his place, the Yankees installed Babe Dahlgren at first base. Dahlgren, putting it bluntly, was awful. He had some power—15 home runs—but batted just .235 and was godawful slow. Dahlgren was probably the worst regular first baseman in the American League—either him or Washington's Mickey Vernon. And although Vernon was only twenty-one years old and would eventually become a pretty fair country ballplayer, Dahlgren was *never* any good. According to *Total Baseball*, Dahlgren was roughly four wins worse than an A.L.-average first baseman (granted, the American

American League in relief victories six times and saves four times.

Joe McCarthy wasn't really ahead of the curve (Marberry had saved 22 games for the Senators back in 1926) but he certainly wasn't behind it, either. Murphy's 19 saves in 1939 were the second-highest total to that time and would remain the second-most in A.L. history until Joe Page recorded 27 saves in 1949.

Murphy aside, McCarthy wasn't really a big fan of relief pitchers. From 1937 through 1939, the Yankees led the American League in complete games every year. If the game was on the line and his starter was having problems, McCarthy would happily summon Murphy from the bullpen. Otherwise, it was the starter's game to win or lose.—*Rob*

A Deep Staff

How deep was the Yankee pitching staff in 1939? Well, consider the following story. On May 31, en route from Boston to Cleveland, the

League at that time featured a number of fine first basemen in Hank Greenberg, Jimmie Foxx, Hal Trosky, and George McQuinn).

How good would a healthy Gehrig have been in 1939? We can't say for sure, but it's not hard to make a pretty good guess. Gehrig didn't turn thirty-six years old until June 19 that season, and if you make a list of the all-time greatest hitters, you'll find that practically all of them were still quite effective into their mid- and late thirties. Just two seasons earlier, in 1937, Gehrig had driven in 159 runs and led the league with a .473 on-base percentage.

He was just fair in 1938, but that was almost certainly due to the early stages of the disease that would eventually kill him. Anyway, Gehrig's TPRs from 1934 through 1937 look like this: 7.8, 4.8, 6.4, and 4.3, followed by the 1.2 in '38.

Given that progression, and Gehrig's incredible talent, it seems quite reasonable to assume that a healthy Iron Horse would have been at least three games better than an average A.L. first baseman in 1939. So if you combine Dahlgren's –4 with Gehrig's +3, you come up with a net difference of seven games. Remember, we're being conservative here. Throw in the one game that DiMaggio's injury might have cost the Yankees, and all of a sudden you're looking at 114-odd wins. And with 114 wins, you've got to start talking about the '39 team in the same breath as the '27 club, just as Ed Barrow did.—Rob

The Best Job in the World, Part I

Have you ever heard of Arndt Jorgens? If you haven't, don't feel bad. True, Jorgens played eleven seasons in the major leagues (1929 through 1939), but he compiled just 738 at-bats. Fortunately for Jorgens, all eleven of those seasons came with the New York Yankees, which means that he was the recipient of five World Series winner's shares (1932 and 1936 through 1939).

Tommy Henrich joined the Yankees in 1937, by which time Jorgens had gone from backing up Bill Dickey to backing up Buddy Rosar, who backed up Bill Dickey. Over his last three seasons, Jorgens saw action in only 25 games: 13 in '37, 9 in '38, and 3 in '39. Still, Jorgens made an impression on Henrich, who told Bill Gilbert in *Five O'Clock Lightning*:

Even our third-string catcher, Arndt Jorgens, stayed on top of the guys when they made a mistake or he thought they weren't giving 100 percent. Arndt was born in Norway, and he never played more than fifty-eight games in any season, but he was in the big leagues for eleven years and was a Yankee that entire time. Why? Because McCarthy loved his attitude.

He was a little guy for a catcher, only five-feet-nine and 165 pounds, but that didn't stop him from his self-appointed role of staying on top of the rest of us. His position as a third-stringer didn't make any difference, either. He'd yell at us first-stringers anyhow. He saw me clowning in the dugout before a game in my rookie year and he let me have it. "C'mon, Tom! Bear down!" And I did.

Jorgens' attitude and his 3 games played (out of 152) presumably earned him a full Series share, which in 1939 equaled $5,541.89. That was almost certainly more than Jorgens' salary for the entire regular season. As I said, it was the best job in the world.—Rob

Whither Batting Average?

Okay, what does this chart show?

Team	Avg	AB	Runs	Hits	HR	RBI
Boston Red Sox	.299	5230	902	1566	98	860
Washington Nationals	.293	5474	814	1602	85	767
Cleveland Indians	.281	5356	847	1506	113	797
St. Louis Browns	.281	5333	755	1498	92	713
Chicago White Sox	.277	5199	709	1439	67	657
New York Yankees	.274	5410	966	1480	174	917
Detroit Tigers	.272	5270	862	1434	137	804
Philadelphia Athletics	.270	5229	726	1410	98	686

This is how final A.L. team batting statistics would have been printed in a 1938 newspaper. (Yes, I know this chapter's mostly about the '39 Yankees; please bear with me while I make a point.) Pretty silly, huh? The Yankees led the American League in runs scored,

Bombers stopped off for an exhibition game against the Toronto Maple Leafs. Now, the Maple Leafs weren't a great team (they would finish the season with a 63-90 record, last in the International League), but the International League was one of the top three minor leagues in the country.

Like most managers, Joe McCarthy didn't want to waste one of his starters in a meaningless game. But whereas in our time the manager will simply call up a pitcher from the minors to start an in-season exhibition, before the advent of air travel teams didn't yank their minor leaguers up and down like yo-yos.

So instead, McCarthy called on a righthander named Paul Schreiber. Though he'd pitched a few games for the Brooklyn Dodgers back in 1922 and 1923, by 1939 Schreiber was thirty-five years old, and he'd been gainfully employed as the Yankees' batting-practice pitcher since 1937. Maybe some of the Yankee magic had rubbed off on him, because Schreiber limited the Maple Leafs to six hits and a single unearned run, as New York took a 4–1 decision behind Tommy Henrich's two-run homer.

In the 1940 *Spalding-Reach Official Baseball Guide* (covering the '39 season), Schreiber's photo appears along with all the other Yankees, and he was accorded a full World Series share after the Bombers won their fourth straight. In fact, Schreiber collected a total of $26,822.45 in Series money from 1937 through 1943. This was a huge amount of money, considering that his salary from the club was somewhere in the neighborhood of $3,500 per season.

When Schreiber wasn't giving the Yankee hitters those fat pitches, he fooled around with a knuckleball. And in September of 1945, Schreiber—still the Yanks' batting-practice pitcher and now forty-two years old—pitched in his first major league game in nearly 22 years. Manager Joe McCarthy explained, "I put him on the

which is sort of the point of the game, yet they show up *sixth* in this table. Unfortunately, that's also how they would be printed in 2000. WAKE UP, AMERICA! IT'S THE TWENTY-FIRST CENTURY! BATTING AVERAGE REALLY DOESN'T MATTER! None, I repeat, *none* of those awesome Yankee teams from 1936 through 1939 led the American League in batting average, including the 1938 club, which finished sixth among eight teams. However, all four of those teams led the league in runs scored, and by an average margin of *90 more runs than the second-best team*. Look at the chart. The two teams just ahead of the Yankees in batting average in 1938 scored 211 fewer runs and 257 fewer runs than the Yankees. If batting average is so important, how could that happen? Let's look again at the 1936–39 Yankees:

Year	Avg	Runs	OBP	Slug	OPS
			Ranking		
1936	3	1	1	1	1
1937	3	1	2	1	1
1938	6	1	2	1	1
1939	2	1	1	1	1

Okay, which columns resemble each other the most? Actually, you could turn this into an S.A.T.-type question: Which series does not belong?

Why do people have such a hard time letting go of batting average? On-base percentage and slugging percentage are *more* important, *more* significant, *more* meaningful, *more everything* than batting average. Batting average is a red herring. Let go of it, friends. It's not that important.

If you were a student taking a test, would you rather get a grade of 60 or a grade of 90? No, it's not a trick question. A score on a test is supposed to mirror how much of the subject the student understands or can explain. Well, if run production is the subject and batting average is the student taking the test, batting average only gets a grade of 60. OPS gets a grade of close to 90.

Offensively, the name of the game is to score runs, period. Team batting statistics should be listed in the order of team runs scored. Individual batting statistics should be listed in order of OPS because that correlates better with run production than batting average, or either on-base percentage or slugging percentage separately. Tradition, you say? When tradition is wrong, the hell with tradition.—Eddie

Pitchers Love Pinstripes

Obviously, the quality of the team had much to do with this, but the Yankees have had a lot of pitchers—many of whom aren't really household names—compile great records for a season or group of seasons. Maybe this started with a pitcher who has some notoriety, but whose "fame" rests on something a very notable Yankee did *against* him. If he is remembered today, Tom Zachary is remembered as the pitcher who allowed Babe Ruth's 60th homer in 1927. Two years later, however, as a member *of* the Yankees, Zachary set a major league record that still stands for the most wins in a season without a loss, 12. Besides the perfect record, Zachary's 2.48 ERA was nearly two runs per game better than the league average, he completed 7 of his 11 starts (the highest complete game percentage of any Yankee with 10-plus GS in 1929), he pitched two shutouts and had two saves. Not a bad year, but unfortunately for Zachary it was his only full year in pinstripes and it was not a pennant year for the Yankees.

Although Red Ruffing is in the Hall of Fame, his career shows a dramatic contrast looking at his Yankee and non-Yankee days. During his nearly fifteen seasons with the Yankees, Ruffing was 231-124 with a 3.47 ERA. In his time with the Red Sox and White Sox, he was 42-101 with a 4.68 ERA. As Bill James has pointed out, Ruffing had a better record than the rest of the pitchers on the Yankees while he was there, but a worse record than the rest of the pitchers on the bad teams he played for.

Monte Pearson was a good pitcher with Cleveland before he joined the Yankees in a trade in December 1935 (Johnny Allen to Cleveland for Pearson and pitcher Steve Sundra). In his last year in Cleveland, however, he was 8-13 with a 4.90 ERA. In Pearson's first four years with the Yankees (1936–39), he was 56-22 with a 3.83 ERA. Sundra chipped in with an 11-1 record for the 1939 Yankees.

Atley Donald never played for anyone except the Yankees in the majors. What fame he may have is as the Yankee scout who signed Ron Guidry. (Donald really did more than sign Guidry: he quietly

pitching staff because he throws a knuckleball in batting practice and nobody hits it. I figure I can use him in relief and maybe he can fool somebody else."

Schreiber did indeed fool somebody else, tossing 3⅓ innings of hitless relief against the Detroit Tigers (who would clinch the pennant in a few weeks) in his first outing.

Later in the same series, Schreiber relieved once more. This time he permitted four hits and two runs in one inning, and never again pitched in a game that counted.

Citing budget constraints, the Yankees let Schreiber go after the 1945 season. He quickly signed with the Red Sox as a batting-practice pitcher, and in 1947 he earned a promotion to pitching coach, in which capacity he served through the 1958 season.—*Rob* "arranged" for Guidry to drop out of college and make himself eligible for the 1971 draft.) Donald's first full major league season was 1939; his record was 13-3. For his brief eight-season career, Donald's record was 65-33; for his first five full seasons, it was 47-18. Combined, Atley Donald and Steve Sundra were 24-4 for the Yankees in 1939, and no one can say with a straight face that those two guys are famous.

Later Yankees teams had similar success (or luck, depending on your perspective) with pitchers, many of whom had not done well with other clubs but who flourished while playing in New York. The potent Yankee lineups no doubt played a big part in their transformation, but these players must also have benefited from better coaching, a much greater commitment to winning, and being used in a more resourceful way.—Eddie

TEAM STATISTICS

Hitting

	Games by Position	Age	G	AB	R	H	2B	3B	HR	RBI	BB	SO	SB	Avg	OBP	Slug
Babe Dahlgren	1B,144	27	144	531	71	125	18	6	15	89	57	54	2	.235	.312	.377
Joe Gordon	2B,151	24	151	567	92	161	32	5	28	111	75	57	11	.284	.370	.506
Frankie Crosetti	SS,152	28	152	**656**	109	153	25	5	10	56	65	81	11	.233	.315	.332
Red Rolfe	3B,152	30	152	648	**139**	**213**	**46**	10	14	80	81	41	7	.329	.404	.495
Charlie Keller	OF,105	22	111	398	87	133	21	6	11	83	81	49	6	.334	.447	.500
Joe DiMaggio	OF,117	24	120	462	108	176	32	6	30	126	52	20	3	**.381**	.448	.671
George Selkirk	OF,124	31	128	418	103	128	17	4	21	101	103	49	12	.306	.452	.517
Bill Dickey	C,126	32	128	480	98	145	23	3	24	105	77	37	5	.302	.403	.513
Tommy Henrich	OF,88; 1B,1	26	99	347	64	96	18	4	9	57	51	23	7	.277	.371	.429
Buddy Rosar	C,35	24	43	105	18	29	5	1	0	12	13	10	4	.276	.356	.343
Jake Powell	OF,23	30	31	86	12	21	4	1	1	9	3	8	1	.244	.270	.349
Joe Gallagher*	OF,12	25	14	41	8	10	0	1	2	9	3	8	1	.244	.311	.439
Lou Gehrig	1B,8	36	8	28	2	4	0	0	0	1	5	1	0	.143	.273	.143
Bill Knickerbocker	2B,2; SS,2	27	6	13	2	2	1	0	0	1	0	0	0	.154	.154	.231
Art Jorgens	C,2	34	3	0	1	0	0	0	0	0	0	0	0	—	—	—
Totals		27	152	5,300	**967**	1,521	259	55	**166**	**904**	**701**	543	72	.287	**.374**	**.451**

*Played for another team during season. Statistics are those compiled with 1939 New York Yankees only.

Pitching

	Threw	Age	Games	GS	CG	ShO	IP	H	HR	BB	SO	W	L	Pct	Sv	ERA
Red Ruffing	Right	35	28	28	22	5	233	211	15	75	95	21	7	.750	0	2.93
Lefty Gomez	Left	30	26	26	14	2	198	173	11	84	102	12	8	.600	0	3.41
Bump Hadley	Right	34	26	18	7	1	154	132	10	85	65	12	6	.667	2	2.98
Atley Donald	Right	28	24	20	11	1	153	144	12	60	55	13	3	**.813**	1	3.71
Monte Pearson	Right	29	22	20	8	0	146	151	9	70	76	12	5	.706	0	4.49
Oral Hildebrand	Right	32	21	15	7	1	127	102	11	41	50	10	4	.714	2	3.06
Marius Russo	Left	24	21	11	9	2	116	86	6	41	55	8	3	.727	2	2.41
Steve Sundra	Right	29	24	11	8	1	121	110	7	56	27	11	1	.917	0	2.76
Johnny Murphy	Right	30	38	0	0	0	61	57	2	28	30	3	6	.333	19	4.40
Wes Ferrell	Right	31	3	3	1	0	19	14	2	17	6	1	2	.333	0	4.66
Spud Chandler	Right	31	11	0	0	0	19	26	0	9	4	3	0	1.000	0	2.84
Marv Breuer	Right	25	1	0	0	0	1	2	0	1	0	0	0	—	0	9.00
Totals		30	245	152	**87**	**15**	1,349	**1,208**	85	567	565	**106**	**45**	**.702**	**26**	**3.31**

CHAPTER 8

The Worst Teams of All Time

J ust as the conversation about the greatest teams of all time usually starts with the 1927 New York Yankees, the conversation about the *worst* teams of all time usually begins with the 1962 **New York Mets.** In their first season, the Mets won 40 games, lost 120, and finished 60½ games out of first place.

What some people don't know is that the 1962 Mets' .250 winning percentage is not the worst of all time, nor even the worst of the twentieth century. The **1916 Philadelphia Athletics** won 36 games and lost 117, which works out to a neat .235 winning percentage. They finished 54½ games out of first place *and 40 games behind the team that finished next to last.* Take a look at the 1916 A.L. standings:

Team	W	L	Pct	GB
Boston Red Sox	91	63	.591	—
Chicago White Sox	89	65	.578	2.0
Detroit Tigers	87	67	.565	4.0
New York Yankees	80	74	.519	11.0

The Money Game

I suppose this might be the appropriate place to launch into a short dissertation on the economics of baseball and about what Mack did to his 1910–14 powerhouse and, later on, his 1929–31 pennant winners. I am writing this late in 1998, just a few days after Kevin Brown signed the first $100 million contract in baseball history. Baseball people are bemoaning the increasing disparity between the haves and the have-nots and the increasing influence of money on the game. Before I offer my opinion, I want to remind people that *for most of its history, baseball has been about the haves and have-nots.* It's been about the Yankees winning 29 pennants in 44 seasons and the St. Louis Browns winning one pennant in 52 seasons. In a way, of course, this book is about the ultimate haves.

At present, the ratio of revenue from the very top to the very bottom teams is about 4 to 1. In 1935, when almost all revenue was

Team	W	L	Pct	GB
St. Louis Browns	79	75	.513	12.0
Cleveland Indians	77	77	.500	14.0
Washington Senators	76	77	.497	14.5
Philadelphia Athletics	36	117	.235	54.5

Every team in the league except the Athletics spent at least three days in first place. The seventh-place Senators, who missed a chance at .500 because one of their games with the Athletics was rained out, were in first place for 16 days, and the sixth-place Indians spent 47 days in first, more than any other team except the pennant-winning Red Sox. Another quirky thing about this league and the Athletics were the consistent records of the A's against every other team in the league:

Opponent	Athletics' 1916 Record
Boston	6-16
Chicago	4-18
Detroit	4-18
New York	7-15
St. Louis	5-17
Cleveland	4-18
Washington	6-15

That's just bizarre. The 1962 Mets, for example, were 9-9 against the Cubs (who went 59-103), 2-16 against the Dodgers, and 6-12 against the Braves. Anyway, the 1916 Athletics were truly terrible. They are the only team in the twentieth century whose offensive and defensive SD score components were both −2.00 or worse. Their overall SD score, −4.39, is horrendous. Remember, when a team's SD score is +3.00 or higher, that's outstanding.

However, the 1916 A's did make an impact on the pennant race. With Boston, Chicago, and Detroit all bunched together, the Athletics beat the Tigers in the only game of a one-game series on September 18. That, coupled with Boston's win over Chicago that day, knocked Detroit out of first place for good.

Philadelphia's best month was May, when they were 11-14. Their worst month? Would you believe a 2-28 July? For a long time, that .067 July winning percentage was the worst by any team, for any month, in the twentieth century. That record stood until April 1988, when my then-employers, the Baltimore Orioles, went 1-22 (.043).

Nap Lajoie played second base for the '16 Athletics. Lajoie's place in history is the subject of debate among baseball analysts. In the fifth edition of *Total Baseball*, Lajoie's total baseball rating is the second highest of all time, behind only Babe Ruth. Many analysts, including Bill James, argue that the "linear weights" method used in *Total Baseball* gives Lajoie too much credit for his defense, and that that "flaw" makes Lajoie look like a better player than he was. Indeed, in that same edition of *Total Baseball*, Lajoie is credited with more career fielding runs than any other player in baseball history. Anyway, Lajoie was forty-one years old in 1916, his last season in the majors. He created 2.46 runs per 27 outs; the league average that year was 3.68, and Lajoie's career average was 7.04. In other words, he was a big part of the problem.

Other Athletics of note were Stuffy McInnis, Wally Schang, and Bullet Joe Bush. Bush, who would go 26-7 in 1922 for the pennant-winning Yankees and finish with 196 career wins, went 15-24 for Philadelphia despite a 2.57 ERA (just two years earlier, when he was twenty-one years old, Bush went 17-12 with a 3.06 ERA for the "same" team). Two other Athletics starters, Jack Nabors and Tom Sheehan, combined for a 2-36 record (or 2-34, depending on the source).

As noted elsewhere in this book, just two years earlier (in 1914) the Athletics won the American League pennant, and in 1913 they won the World Series. People moaned about the quick fall of the Florida Marlins, who won the World Series in 1997 and had the worst record in baseball in 1998. Everything old is new again. Philadelphia went from a World Series title and a pennant in consecutive seasons to the worst record in baseball the next two seasons, and a total of *seven straight* last-place finishes, a streak that didn't end until 1922 and is highly unlikely to be matched by the Marlins.

I doubt any team has ever declined as much and as fast as the Athletics did after Mack sold off most of his good players. In 1914, they posted a 3.05 SD score. In 1915, their SD score was −3.00, and in 1916 it was even worse, −4.39. I don't think I have to check to see if any other team went from +3.00 or better to −3.00 or worse in a single year. The 1962 Mets were worse than the 1916 Athletics but,

derived from ticket sales, the Browns drew about 81,000 fans *for their entire home schedule*, while the Tigers drew more than a million. That ratio is a heck of a lot bigger than 4 to 1. In 1928 the Cubs drew over 1.1 million fans, whereas the Phillies drew about 182,000. Putting aside for a moment the issue of whether such a disparity in revenue and team quality is good for the game, baseball has been like that the majority of the time. This issue is nothing new.

As to how I feel, it seems apparent that it's bad for the game if just five or six teams can compete for all the marbles. In the long run, what will be the value of any team's broadcast rights if a great percentage of the games are against overmatched opponents? Many baseball historians think the Yankees' dominance from the late 1940s through the mid-1960s contributed to the malaise that infected the sport. A return to a similar condition, with very few teams being able to compete, will have negative consequences for owners and players alike.—*Eddie*

Be Careful What You Wish For . . .

For most of my life, I've wanted to work in baseball. Early on, I especially wanted to work for the Baltimore Orioles, my hometown team, and I did work for them in a full-time position for six years. I was born and raised in Baltimore, and I lived there until I was thirty-five. I grew up as an Orioles (and Colts) fanatic, and I was blessed in being able to watch one of the greatest baseball teams of all time, the 1969–71 Orioles. I only wish I had known it then. I won't bore anyone with the story of how I got a job with the Orioles. Suffice it to say, they hired me on full-time in January of 1988. Yes, 1988.

Some people think that the 1988 Orioles were one of the worst teams of all time. Obviously, we were not a good club. The 0-21 start was the first tip-off. Our baseball people moaned

as one of the first expansion teams, at least the Mets had a good excuse.

So we've established the fact that the 1962 Mets didn't have the worst record of the twentieth century. They wouldn't have had the worst record of the nineteenth century, either. Even though they played outside the period we're discussing in this book, no treatment of the worst teams of all time would be complete without some mention of the 1899 **Cleveland Spiders**.

The 1890s were bad times for the National Pastime. Beginning in 1892, the National League had a monopoly on major league baseball. During this decade, ownership of multiple teams came into vogue; that is, various owners would have parts of more than one team. As bad as some things are today in baseball, at least that doesn't happen any more. With multiple ownership, really bad things began to happen. If the same ownership group owned two teams, for example, the weaker team would inevitably find itself losing most or all of its best players to the stronger team, so the latter could compete with the other similarly situated teams. The effect of this was to create a hybrid major/minor league, where teams would play against their *de facto* farm team(s), but the games counted in the standings. From 1892 through 1899, the last-place teams finished an average of 59 games behind the first-place teams, and finished fewer than 50 games out of first place just once in those eight seasons.

For the most part, the Spiders benefited during those seasons, and finished in second place in both 1895 and 1896. Cleveland fell to fifth place in 1897, however. And in 1898, with the Spiders in the middle of another so-so season and suffering poor attendance, club owner Frank De Haas Robison arranged to have nearly every home game for the last two months rescheduled for the road.

The following spring, with the few remaining fans threatening a boycott, Robison purchased controlling interest in the N.L.'s St. Louis Cardinals. And shortly thereafter, Robison arranged a "trade" whereby St. Louis received Cleveland's best players, including future Hall of Famers Cy Young, Jesse Burkett, and Bobby Wallace, and Cleveland received a motley collection of has-beens and never-wases. This questionable transaction didn't make pennant winners out of St. Louis, but it did make history for the Cleveland club. Here are the 1899 N.L. standings:

Team	W	L	Pct	GB
Brooklyn Superbas	101	47	.682	—
Boston Beaneaters	95	57	.625	8.0
Philadelphia Phillies	94	58	.618	9.0
Baltimore Orioles	86	62	.581	15.0
St. Louis Perfectos	84	67	.556	18.5
Cincinnati Reds	83	67	.553	19.0
Pittsburgh Pirates	76	73	.510	25.5
Chicago Cubs	75	73	.507	26.0
Louisville Colonels	75	77	.493	28.0
New York Giants	60	90	.400	42.0
Washington Senators	54	98	.355	49.0
Cleveland Spiders	20	134	.130	84.0

Yes, the Spiders finished 84 games out of first place. They also finished 35 games out of *eleventh* place.

The Spiders were swept by Brooklyn (0-14) and Cincinnati (0-14), and won only one game against Chicago, New York, and St. Louis. Just for the heck of it, I figured SD scores for the 1899 National League. Pennant-winning Brooklyn was tops, at a modest +1.82. How bad were the Spiders? Negative 5.63.

With such distorted standings and runs scored/allowed totals, I'm not sure how to interpret those numbers. (Also, I'm not going to tell you, just yet, if that's the worst SD score I've ever seen.) The Spiders scored 529 runs; the next-worst team scored 734, and the league average was 804. Cleveland allowed 1,252 runs; the next worst was 983. The Spiders' best month was May, when they went 7-19. They were 1-34 from September 1 through the end of the season. They were 1-40 in their last 41 games.

My favorite player on the Spiders was Harry Colliflower. A left-handed "pitcher," he was 1-11 with an 8.17 ERA (the league ERA was 3.85). He allowed 152 hits in 98 innings, striking out eight and walking 41. Yet he was not a bad hitter. Colliflower played six games in the outfield and four at first base and batted .303. His .676 OPS was better than the team's regular first baseman, not to mention the regular catcher, the regular second baseman, the regular third baseman, the regular shortstop, and two of the regular outfielders. It was Colliflower's only year in the majors.

about bad luck during the losing streak but, given the run differential for those 21 games, our record was pretty much what it should have been. I don't have the exact figures, but I remember calculating our Pythagorean record for those 21 games at something like 2-19.

The 1988 Orioles' final record was 54-107, the worst in baseball by half a game. (Atlanta finished 54-106 after losing their first ten games of the season.) In addition to the horrible start, Baltimore lost 17 of its final 20 games. The only three games we won in that span were the three games started by Bob Milacki (his first three major league appearances).

It's difficult to explain just how bad one feels when working for a team that starts 0-21. I had a hard time sleeping, for one thing, and eventually I stopped watching the road games on television. Thus, I didn't know we had broken the streak until a friend called with congratulations. Even though I had been with the club for only a few months, I was beginning to hear that famous remark: "Be careful what you wish for, you may get it." I did have some concerns that most or all of the baseball people might be fired because of the team's horrible start, which would have meant a very short baseball career for me.

The 1988 Orioles' SD score was –3.75, the fourteenth worst of the twentieth century. The 1987–88 Orioles' SD score was –6.16, the twenty-fifth worst two-year score of the century. Almost everyone associated with the team complained about our pitching and defense but, in fact, the offense was the bigger culprit. We allowed 789 runs in 1988, about 12 percent worse than the league average. But we scored only 550 runs, *22 percent fewer than the league average.* Those 550 runs were, and are, the fewest scored by any Orioles club over a 162-game schedule. Everyday second baseman Billy Ripken was horrible (.260 on-base

The Spiders also had pitcher Jim Hughey, who tied for the team lead in wins (4), but also lost 30 games and posted a 5.41 ERA. He allowed 403 hits in 283 innings. Hughey finished his major league career with a 29-80 record. Another interesting pitcher was Frank Bates, who played part of the year in St. Louis and may have been part of the "trade" that sent Lave Cross from Cleveland to St. Louis. Bates' Cleveland numbers were: 1-18, with a 7.24 ERA, 13 strikeouts, and 105 walks in 153 innings.

The starting second baseman was Joe Quinn, who led the team with 72 RBI and a .286 average. His 657 OPS ranked eighth among N.L. starting second basemen. At least Quinn enjoyed a bit of glory in his career, as he was a member of the dynastic Baltimore Orioles from 1896 through 1898. One can only imagine his thoughts during the 1899 season.

The 1899 Spiders and the 1916 Athletics are similar in that they had both been winning immediately preceding their decline. Of course, the Spiders were not as good as the Athletics. In 1895, Cleveland's record was 84-46 and they finished in second place. They finished second again in 1896 (80-48) and had winning records in 1897 (69-62) and 1898 (81-68). The two teams are also similar in that their declines were essentially planned by management and were not a function of poor personnel decisions.

Cleveland was one of four N.L. franchises that were eliminated after the 1899 season. A new Cleveland franchise joined the American League in 1901, and the club eventually became known as the Indians, reportedly in honor of an old-time Spider of American Indian descent, Lou Sockalexis.

Heading back into the twentieth century, another candidate for the worst team of all time is either the **1938** or **1939 Philadelphia Phillies**. Take a look at the amazing similarity between those two seasons:

Year	W-L	Pct	Scored	Allowed	SD Score
1938	45-105	.300	550	840	–4.02
1939	45-106	.298	553	856	–4.01

That degree of resemblance between consecutive seasons for the same team is, as you might suspect, extremely uncommon. Only six teams in the twentieth century have had an SD score of –4.00 or worse for even a single season, and no other team "achieved" that in consecutive seasons (although one other team, which we'll get to later, was very close).

It may have been just a coincidence, but 1938 was the year the Phillies moved out of the tiny Baker Bowl and became co-tenants of Shibe Park with the Athletics. That season, the Phillies and Athletics both finished in last place in their respective leagues. (In 1939, the Athletics climbed all the way to seventh, ahead of another power-house, the 43-111 St. Louis Browns.)

Eight times during the 1930s, the Phillies finished last or next-to-last. They posted only one winning season (78-76 in 1932) and only one season (also 1932) when they finished fewer than 31 games out of first place. For the decade, their average record was 58-94, their average finish was seventh place, and the average number of games they finished out of first place was about 36.

The bad times continued for the Phillies, as they were last every year from 1938 through 1942, for a total of five straight last-place finishes. In February of 1943, the National League took control of the Phillies and sold them to William Cox, who owned the club just long enough to be banned from baseball for betting on his team. The club was then sold to the Carpenter family, which owned the team until the early 1980s.

This team (1938–39) was the one for which Hugh "Losing Pitcher" Mulcahy toiled. In 1938, Mulcahy went 10-20 with a 4.61 ERA. In 1939, he was 9-16 with a 4.99 ERA. He led the Phils both years in starts and innings. In fairness, Mulcahy probably wasn't that bad a pitcher—he just happened to be the workhorse for a terrible team.

Two Phillies hurlers were rescued and ended up contributing to the N.L. pennant winners in 1939 to 1941. Bucky Walters pitched for the Phillies from 1934 until June 13, 1938 (he went 4-8 with a 5.23 ERA as a Phillie that year), when he was traded to Cincinnati for Spud Davis, Al Hollingsworth, and cash. The Reds won the National League pennant in 1939 and 1940, and Walters was one of Cincinnati's, and the league's, best players, topping the loop in wins and ERA both seasons. I wonder if Walters celebrated on June 13 every year after the trade.

Kirby Higbe's first full big league season was spent primarily with the 1939 Phillies (10-14, 4.85 with Philadelphia), who acquired him

percentage, .258 slugging), but a bigger problem was the lack of production from many of the corner players: Ken Gerhart, 600 OPS; Rene Gonzales, 529 OPS; Rick Schu, 679 OPS; Larry Sheets, 645 OPS; Jim Traber, 585 OPS.

Actually, Gerhart played a lot of games in center field and Gonzales played a few games at second and short, but you get the point. This team got next to nothing from most of the players at positions that are expected to make offensive contributions.

The 1988 season also included a genuinely sad event. Edward Bennett Williams, who had owned the team since 1979, died in August after a long battle with cancer.

Despite the terrible season, our fans supported us. We weren't anywhere near the bottom of the league in attendance and drew 82 percent of the league average, which is pretty good for a team that starts 0-21 and finishes 54-107.

The next year, amazingly enough, our record improved by 32½ games and we almost won the A.L. East. We spent 117 days in first place and weren't eliminated until the next-to-last game of the season.

As mentioned, in 1988 the O's had scored 22 percent fewer runs than the league average, and allowed 12 percent more than the league. In 1989, the club was slightly better than the league in both runs scored and allowed, which means that we made a much greater improvement in the former. Nevertheless, people in the organization attributed our greatly improved record to "better pitching and defense." Some things never change.

The dramatic turnaround, and the fact that the team only spent two years at a particularly low level (the O's were 67-95 in 1987), are why I don't consider the '88 Orioles one of the worst teams of all time.

It certainly was an interesting first two years in baseball. I am fortunate to

from the Cubs in May. In November of 1940, Higbe was traded to the Dodgers for Vito Tamulis, Bill Crouch, Mickey Livingston, and cash. In 1941, Higbe went 22-9 with a 3.14 ERA for pennant-winning Brooklyn. Supposedly, the Dodgers were also interested in Hugh Mulcahy, but when the first military draft lottery was held on November 18, 1940, he had drawn a low number, which meant he was more likely to be inducted earlier rather than later. Mulcahy was inducted into the Army on March 8, 1941, and didn't pitch again until 1945. Timing is everything, I guess.

Speaking of timing, before the birth of the Mets, many people considered the 1952 Pittsburgh Pirates one of the worst teams of all time. Joe Garagiola played for that club, and he spent many years as a broadcaster making fun of it. Speaking of Garagiola, he was actually one of the few Pirates to have a decent year in 1952. He posted a .369 on-base percentage, a .410 slugging percentage (better than the league averages in both cases), and he was a catcher.

The 1952 Pirates' record was 42-112, and they ended the season 54½ games out of first place. Their −3.39 SD score is one of the ten worst of the twentieth century. That performance was not an anomaly. Pittsburgh suffered through nine consecutive losing seasons (1949–57) and finished last or next-to-last every season from 1950 through 1957. Looking at SD scores for periods of up to five consecutive seasons, a Pirates team from this era is among the worst in each time frame. (The 1952–53 Pirates have the eleventh-worst two-year SD score in the twentieth century, the 1952–54 Pirates have the fifth-worst three-year SD score, the 1952–55 Pirates have the fifth-worst four-year SD score, and Pittsburgh has two entries in the five-year rankings: the 1951–55 team has the sixth-worst SD score and the 1950–54 Pirates have the ninth-worst SD score.)

As opposed to the Spiders and Athletics, the Pirates were not particularly successful immediately preceding their nadir, but became very successful immediately after. In 1958, the Pirates finished in second place (84-70), eight games behind the Braves. They had a regrouping year in 1959, but still finished in the first division (remember that phrase?) at 78-76. Of course, in 1960 the Pirates won the National League pennant and a very memorable World Series. The Pirates had some up-and-down seasons in the 1960s, but they were never anywhere near as bad as they had been for most of the 1950s, and they contended for the National League pennant in 1962, 1965, and 1966.

Let me go back to the 1952 club, if I may. This is the team that brought us a now-famous admonition. After the 1952 season, in which he led the league in homers for the seventh straight time, Ralph Kiner felt he deserved a raise. Pirates president Branch Rickey, earlier the architect of dynasties in St. Louis and Brooklyn, supposedly responded to Kiner's request with, "We could have finished last without you."

It bears repeating: Kiner led the National League in homers his first seven seasons, the last one being 1952, which turned out to be his last full year with the Pirates. On June 4, 1953, he was traded to the Cubs in a ten-player deal that also sent Joe Garagiola to Chicago and netted a substantial amount of cash ($150,000) for Pittsburgh. Kiner had turned thirty years old after the 1952 season, and Rickey always preferred to trade a player a year too early rather than a year too late.

The image of Kiner has changed dramatically compared to when he was playing. The truth is that Kiner was a very productive player and was viewed as such during his career. Kiner played only ten years due to back problems, but he scored 100-plus runs six times and drove in 100-plus runs six times. He led his league three times in slugging percentage and once in on-base percentage. His career marks in those two categories are very good: .548 career slugging, .398 career on-base. Rogers Hornsby is said to have once sneered that if you shake a tree, ten gloves will fall out—but no bats. Given Hornsby's skills, that was obviously something of a self-serving statement, but the fact is that if a player can really hit, he will play. Kiner could really hit.

It might also be said that Kiner was a gate draw and worth the money he was asking. Although I can't prove that Kiner was the sole or even the main reason, the Pirates did draw pretty well for a bad team. For example, despite a last-place finish in 1950—and remember that the Pirates did not have a good 1949 season—they drew 1,166,267 fans, which was more than the N.L. average of 1,040,077. The pennant-winning Phillies drew 1,217,035, essentially the same as the last-place Pirates.

Although Pittsburgh's attendance kept deteriorating as the team struggled, even their 1952 attendance wasn't awful under the circumstances. The Pirates drew 686,673 fans in 1952, not too far from the league average of 792,394, and they had better attendance than Cincinnati or Boston. Of course, that was the Braves' last year in Boston. Pittsburgh's attendance really dropped in the first two full

have been with a team that made two postseason appearances, including a trip to the World Series, but unless I am with a team that wins the World Series, I doubt I will have any more fun than I did in 1989. I also hope I never have to endure another season like 1988, although the "suffering" was tempered by the fact that it was my first season with a big league team, and with my hometown team, to boot. Maybe it's okay to get what you wish for.—*Eddie* years without Kiner, dipping under 500,000 in both 1954 and 1955, while league attendance was going up.

One could obviously argue that it was the monotony of losing and not the departure of Kiner that caused Pittsburgh's attendance to drop so sharply. I would argue that it was both. The team endured a horrible season of historic proportions in 1952 and *then* traded Kiner in the middle of the next season, which probably represented a total breach of faith for Pirates fans. Looking at it like this, the Pirates' attendance for 1949–51 was quite remarkable. Today, most people think that Pittsburgh is not a good baseball town. Clearly, though, this was not always the case.

Pittsburgh's attendance increased dramatically in 1956, perhaps due to the Pirates' 21-16 start. Turnout dropped a little in 1957 with another last-place finish, but increased sharply as the Pirates returned to contention in 1958.

Two regular players on the 1952 Pirates were still around to enjoy the good times, including the 1960 World Championship. Dick Groat, the National League's MVP in '60, debuted in June 1952 and played regularly from then through the 1966 season. Bob Friend was in his second major league season in 1952 and had the third-most starts on the team behind two former Cardinals, Murry Dickson and Howie Pollet. Although Pittsburgh's Vern Law won the Cy Young award in 1960, Friend led the Pirates that year in starts and innings pitched and went 18-12. In 1952, Friend went 7-17.

Dickson "lost" 21 games for the '52 Pirates, but he's a great example of how a pitcher's record, particularly for one season, can be so misleading. First of all, Dickson's 3.57 ERA in 1952 was better than the league average. More important, however, a pitcher's record is quite often a function of things over which he has no control. His record also has to be placed in context. In Dickson's case, his 14-21 record for a 42-112 team is damn good. That means, of course, that the Pirates were 28-91 in games in which Dickson didn't get the decision.

As for the team, their best record for one month came in August, when they went 10-20, whereas their worst was 4-18 in September. Just like the 1916 A's, the Pirates had an impact on the pennant race, although it was somewhat indirect. The pennant-winning Dodgers beat the Pirates 19 of 22 games. The Dodgers, in fact, were 38-6 against the league's two bottom feeders, Pittsburgh and Boston. The second-place Giants were 28-16 against those same two teams, so despite the Giants' head-to-head domination of Brooklyn (winning 14 of the 22 games), New York finished 4½ games behind the Dodgers.

It must be said that in choosing these teams, the same temporal criterion was applied as was applied for the best teams. In plain English, although the focus is on one particular year (except for the practically identical 1938–39 Phillies), the team had to be in the middle of a bad period to be considered. For example, one will not find the 1935 Boston Braves here, despite their 38-115 record and their −3.05 SD score because, when looking at the relevant period, that season was an aberration. They were .500 or better in 1932, 1933, and 1934 and were near .500 from 1936 through 1938. In addition, the 1935 Braves' SD score is not one of the 50 worst of the twentieth century.

First in war, first in peace, and last in the American League. That famous saying originated long before the American League, honoring George Washington as "First in war, first in peace, first in the hearts of his countrymen." But the newer version was long used to describe Washington, D.C.'s baseball franchise, which spent most of its history languishing at or near the bottom of the A.L. standings. The **1904 Washington Senators** were almost certainly the worst Senators team ever, and this is no small feat.

Washington didn't have a winning record until its twelfth season as a member of the American League (1912). Two of the early teams, in 1904 and 1909, posted sub-.300 winning percentages. The Senators finished last or next-to-last every year from 1903 through 1911.

The 1904 Senators set a record, since broken, by losing their first 13 games on the way to a 38-113 season. (Yes, this is another record broken by those powerhouse 1988 Orioles.) Okay, the Senators actually had one tie in there, but they were 0-13 for all practical purposes. They finished 55½ games behind pennant-winning Boston, 23½ games behind seventh-place Detroit. Their SD score was −3.82, the eleventh worst of the century. Their two-year SD score (1903–04) of −7.61 is the third worst of the century.

Malachi Kittridge began the 1904 season as catcher and manager, but after Washington's 1-16 start, outfielder Patsy Donovan assumed the managerial duties. In an era of low-scoring games, the Senators had a really anemic offense. Of the eleven Washington players with 250-plus plate appearances, only three had an OBP above .300 and,

The Washington Whats?

Wherever you read about Washington's A.L. franchise, including in this book, the club is almost invariably called "the Senators." Technically, however, that's not really right.

In 1901, Washington opened play with the rest of the new American League. That team was officially dubbed "Senators" and remained so through 1905. In 1906, after five seasons of futility, management, led by money man Thomas Noyes, proposed changing the club's name. According to historian Marc Okkonen, "[T]he public was invited to suggest new names, but in the end the club elected to restore one of their old nineteenth-century names, NATIONALS [sic], and even displayed the nickname prominently on the players' shirt fronts." The silly thing about all this was that a number of N.L. clubs were commonly called "Nationals," and of course Washington wasn't *in* the National League.

So for the most part, newspapers continued to refer to the club as the Senators, though "Nats" was convenient in headlines, and the two names essentially were used interchangeably as long as the franchise remained in Washington. However, not long after the passing of long-time owner Clark Griffith in 1955, the club was officially renamed "Senators," and that is how we remember them.—*Rob*

The '35 Braves

As Eddie notes, the 1935 Boston Braves don't really deserve to be mentioned among the worst teams of all

even then, the highest was just .313, posted by outfielder Frank Huelsman. Of the same group of eleven Senators position players, seven had slugging percentages below .300.

The Senators' pitching was no prize, either. The American League ERA was 2.60 (again, this was an era characterized by low run production) and seven of the eight clubs finished at 2.83 or lower. Then you've got the Senators, at 3.62. Washington's ERA was worse than the next-worst ERA (St. Louis, 2.83) by more than the margin which separated the next-worst ERA from the *best* ERA (Boston, 2.12).

The Senators lost 20 of 22 games to the first-place Boston Americans, and 18 of 22 to the second-place New York Highlanders, the third-place Chicago White Sox, and the fourth-place Cleveland Blues. Given that New York finished just 1½ games out of first, can we say that Washington had an indirect impact on the pennant race? Does it really matter? Washington did almost manage a season split with sixth-place St. Louis, winning 10 of 21.

Okay, now the Mets. After studying this issue for quite some time, I feel pretty comfortable in asserting that the **1962 New York Mets** were the worst baseball team of the twentieth century. In case you have forgotten the beginning of this chapter, I will repeat that their record was 40-120, and they finished 60½ games out of first place. What I have not told you before is that their −5.91 SD score is *by far the worst of the century, and it is even worse than that of the 1899 Cleveland Spiders.* In fact, the pitching/defense component of the '62 Mets SD score (−4.27) would, by itself, rank as the fifth-worst SD score of the century. Part of that result was due to the Polo Grounds, which was a hitter's park relative to the other N.L. parks in 1962–63. However, most of it was the Mets. In 1962, they allowed more runs on the road (438) than any other team in the league, in addition to allowing more than 500 runs in their home games.

Their team ERA was 5.04, which was last, of course, and was far worse than the league ERA of 3.94. Their defense was worse than their pitching. The 1962 and 1963 Mets are the only major league teams since 1950 to commit more than 200 errors in a season (exactly 210 each season). The 1962 club allowed the staggering total of 147 *unearned* runs, nearly one per game. For comparison's sake, the most errors committed by any team in 1997 was 135, and the most unearned runs allowed was 87. Looking at multiple seasons, the early Mets have a clean sweep of last place of SD scores for the twentieth century:

Period	SD Score	Rank
1962	−5.91	Last
1962–63	−9.90	Last
1962–64	−12.75	Last
1962–65	−16.04	Last
1962–66	−18.30	Last

For all of these except the five-season period of 1962–66, the Mets' SD score is *by far* the worst of the century. Here are the bottom five for the one-season through four-season periods:

One Season		Two Seasons		Three Seasons		Four Seasons	
Team	SD Score	Team	SD Score	Team	SD Score	Team	SD Score
1962		1962–63		1962–64		1962–65	
Mets	−5.91	Mets	−9.90	Mets	−12.75	Mets	−16.04
1916		1938–39		1938–40		1938–41	
Athletics	−4.39	Phillies	−8.04	Phillies	−11.08	Phillies	−14.74
1919		1903–04		1939–41		1916–19	
Athletics	−4.35	Senators	−7.61	Phillies	−10.71	Athletics	−14.08
1943		1918–19		1918–20		1939–42	
Athletics	−4.31	Athletics	−7.43	Athletics	−10.47	Phillies	−13.96
1938		1919–20		1952–54		1952–55	
Phillies	−4.02	Athletics	−7.38	Pirates	−10.23	Pirates	−13.54

The 1962–63 Mets missed by the smallest of margins matching the 1938–39 Phillies for consecutive SD scores of −4.00 or worse. The 1963 Mets had an SD score of −3.99. So one could certainly not claim that the 1962 Mets were an aberration. The '62 Mets were 22-58 at home and 18-62 on the road. They opened the season with 9 consecutive losses and also lost 17 straight. Their longest winning streak was three games. This is actually one area where the Mets aren't the worst among these terrible teams. The 1916 Athletics lost 20 straight, and their longest winning streak was *two* games.

For such a bad team, the '62 Mets had some players who either were famous or would become famous. Richie Ashburn played center field and had a good year, with a .424 OBP in 135 games. Gil Hodges played in 54 games and still showed some power with nine

time, because they were really just a mediocre team going through a terrible season. However, the Braves were incredibly interesting for a number of reasons, and I can't let this chance pass without at least throwing a few facts your way.

First off, there was their entirely out-of-character record. From 1932 through 1938, the Braves won between 71 and 83 games (average, 77.5) every season except for 1935, when they went 38-115! In 1934 the Braves were 78-73 and, in 1936, they were 71-83. Given those numbers, Boston's '35 performance might be considered the flukiest of all time.

Second, there was Wally Berger's season, perhaps the greatest ever by a player on a terrible team. Berger hit 34 home runs to lead the National League. No other Brave hit more than six. He knocked in 130 runs to lead the National League. No other Brave knocked in more than 60. Do you know how hard it is to drive in 130 runs when your team scores only 575?

And third, there was Babe Ruth. I noted that Berger was the only Brave to hit more than six home runs. Well, the guy who hit six was Ruth. The Bambino batted just .181 in 28 games, with only seven hits aside from the six circuit clouts. The highlight of the season, for Ruth and the Braves, came on May 25. With three mighty swings, Babe blasted three titanic home runs over the right-field wall at Pittsburgh's Forbes Field. But Ruth, bloated and playing on sore legs, was useless in the outfield (no designated hitter back then!), and on June 2 he announced his retirement.—*Rob*

homers in 127 at-bats. "Marvelous" Marv Throneberry was the regular first baseman after being acquired from the Orioles in early May. The "first" Frank Thomas hit 34 homers for the 1962 Mets. He gained more notoriety later for fighting with Dick Allen when they were teammates in Philadelphia. Roger Craig, later the guru of the split-finger fastball, led the team in wins and innings pitched although, of course, his record was 10-24.

Maybe I'm stating the obvious, but if this team hadn't played in New York and been managed much of the time by Casey Stengel, they would not be remembered so fondly. I'm sure Philadelphia fans weren't so tolerant of all of the poor Athletics and Phillies teams they had. In fact, the early Mets weren't really supported all that well by New York fans. Granting that they played in an obsolete facility, the 1962 Mets were actually outdrawn slightly by their expansion counterpart, the Houston Colt .45's, who also were playing in a run-down park and were not playing in the nation's largest city. The 1969 Royals, playing in an old ballpark and a relatively small city, drew virtually the same number of fans as did the 1962 Mets.

To me, there is nothing cute or funny about a team as bad as the early Mets. Maybe my experience with the 1988 Orioles has soured me on teams like that, but I see nothing positive about losing three games out of every four. Plain and simple, the Mets sucked. One might accuse me of overstating the significance of a winning baseball team, but professional sports franchises are in business primarily to do one thing—*win*.

Besides their poor record, one of the strange things about the 1962 Mets was their catchers. Seven different players caught for the team, six of those in 10+ games, and yet none caught in more than 56 games. The other nine N.L. teams used a total of 34 catchers, 11 of whom caught in 70 or more games. Of course, bad teams tend to use more players than do good teams. The record for most players used in a season is held by the 1915 Philadelphia Athletics, who used 58. The '62 Mets used "only" 45 players.

So there they are, the worst teams of all time. Despite revenue sharing and the amateur draft, if the current and ever-widening gap between the haves and have-nots continues to grow, we could very well see a team that is the "equal" of the teams in this chapter in the not too distant future.

CHAPTER 9

1942 St. Louis Cardinals

They were, and to this day still are, the most underrated great team in major league baseball history. They were a youthful, hustling team, convinced that they could not be beat. They never gave up, no matter how many runs behind they might be. When baseball fans talk about great teams of baseball's past, the 1942 St. Louis Cardinals are hardly mentioned. They should be. They deserve a better place in the history of the game.

—Rick Van Blair, writing in *Dugout to Foxhole: Interviews with Baseball Players Whose Careers Were Affected by World War II*

Record: 106-48, .688 (15th)
Two-Year (1942–43): 211-97 (5th)
Three-Year (1943–44): 316-146 (4th)

SD Score: +2.94 (42d)
Two-Year: +5.73 (22d)
Three-Year: +8.78 (6th)

Results:
1942 World Champions
1943 National League Champions
1944 World Champions

Days in First Place: 16 of 166; clinched on September 27

The Cardinals spent far less time in first place than any other team in this book, as the Dodgers sat atop the standings for 148 days.

Longest Winning Streak: 8 games
Longest Losing Streak: 4 games

Kings of Konsistency

If you enjoy symmetry, you have to like the 1942–44 St. Louis Cardinals because of three numbers: 106, 105, and 105.

I think it's safe to say that no team has ever come so close to posting exactly the same record three years straight. Now, this would perhaps be less interesting if the numbers were 81, 81, and 82, or even 93, 93, and 94. But they're not. They're 106, 105, and 105, and those 322 victories, spread almost exactly equally among three seasons, represent a thrilling sort of consistency, a consistency the likes of which most of us can only dream about.—*Rob*

The Pennant Race: See separate article, "Down the Stretch They Come."

Against the Contenders: St. Louis went 13-9 against Brooklyn.

Runs Scored: 755 (1st)

Runs Allowed: 482 (1st)

Pythagorean Record: 107-47

Manager: Billy Southworth. See article, "The Forgotten Man(ager)."

Regular Lineup:

Player	Position	ROV	OW%
Jimmy Brown	2B	.234	.462
Terry Moore	CF	.275	.627
Enos Slaughter	RF	.332	.787
Stan Musial	LF	.324	.771
Walker Cooper	C	.259	.568
Johnny Hopp	1B	.267	.600
Whitey Kurowski	3B	.255	.553
Marty Marion	SS	.258	.566
Mort Cooper	P		

Enos Slaughter is famous for his hustle, but in his prime he could hit a little, too. Slaughter created 128 runs in 1942, tops in the National League, and he and Musial gave the Cardinals an awesome force in the middle of the lineup.

Their nickname has been mostly forgotten, but in their time the Cardinals of the early '40s were known as the "St. Louis Swifties." According to Fred Lieb, "[T]hey were always running. Unlike McGraw's 1911 Giants, who stole a pennant with 347 larcenies, Southworth's 1942 champions didn't go in much for stolen bases, but they ran on any pretext. . . . No club ever took more reckless chances on the bases, and none had a higher percentage of successful risks." Almost to a man, when members of the club reminisce about the '42

Cardinals, they echo Lieb's comments. First to third, first to third, first to third . . . it's almost like a mantra for those guys. And in the 1947 Sporting News Guide, Connie Mack is quoted as saying, "In 1942 the St. Louis Cardinals defeated the Yankees in the World's [*sic*] Series because the Cardinals knew that the Yankee outfielders were careless in returning the ball to the infield. The Redbirds literally stole the title on the bases."

Terry Moore was universally regarded as the outstanding defensive center fielder of his era, and Marty Marion also was brilliant with the glove.

Bench: Aside from the regulars, five Cardinals batted at least 150 times. This statistic was due, for the most part, to manager Billy Southworth's infield machinations. When the season opened, the regulars were Ray Sanders at first base, Creepy Crespi at second, Marty Marion at short, and Jimmy Brown at third. By season's end, only Marion was still in his original spot. Johnny Hopp was at first base, rookie Whitey Kurowski was at third, and Jimmy Brown had been shifted from third to second. Interestingly, Sanders and Hopp finished with practically identical stats: .258 batting average, 3 homers, and 37 RBI in 95 games for Hopp, and .252 average, 5 homers, and 39 RBI in 95 games for Sanders (their on-base percentages and slugging percentages were similar, too).

Ken O'Dea backed up Walker Cooper. Harry "The Hat" Walker served as the Cardinals' fourth outfielder and hit .314, but with little power. Coaker Tripplett was the club's fifth outfielder, seeing action in 64 games.

Scouting the Pitchers: Lefthander Howie Pollet was famous for his change-up; ace Mort Cooper threw hard and featured a great forkball.

How Were They Built? Branch Rickey. Rickey took over as business manager of the moribund St. Louis Cardinals before the 1917 season. By 1921 they were competitive, and the Cardinals won National League pennants in 1926, 1928, 1930, 1931, 1934, and 1935. Those last two clubs, paced by personalities like Dizzy Dean, Pepper Martin, and Leo Durocher, are remembered fondly as "The Gas House Gang." But when the Gas House Gang got old, there weren't enough suitable replacements, and the Cardinals dropped from contention in 1937 and 1938.

Over the course of the decade, however, Rickey had been building a huge network of minor league clubs, some owned by the Cardinals and others loosely connected to the club. Thus, by the late '30s, the Cardinals either owned or were affiliated with teams scattered across the continent, from hell to breakfast. At its peak in 1940, the Cardinal empire numbered 33 clubs at all levels: major (1), AA (3), A-1 (1), B (4), C (4), and D (20!). Of the 32 minor league teams, the Cardinals owned 15 outright and had working agreements with the other 17. Stan Musial, Terry Moore, Enos Slaughter, Marty Marion, Johnny Beazley, the Cooper brothers . . . all were products of Rickey's far-flung farm system. All those players meant two things for Rickey: pennants, and extra cash in his pocket. Every time the Cardinals had a youngster ready for the big leagues, Rickey would sell one of his veterans to another club and, as stipulated in his contract by then, he pocketed 10 percent of the sale price.

What Brought Them Down? Branch Rickey. There had long been antipathy between Rickey and Cardinals owner Sam Breadon, and things finally came to a head in 1942. On October 19, exactly two weeks after his Cardinals had disposed of the Yankees in the World Series, Rickey resigned. Shortly thereafter, he accepted a position as general manager of the Brooklyn Dodgers.

The day that Rickey left the Cardinals, they got worse, and the day he joined the Dodgers, they got better—at least on paper. It took some time for Rickey's departure to show up on the field, as the Cardinals won pennants in 1943, 1944, and 1946 before the Dodgers established their hegemony over the National League in 1947. But with Rickey gone, the Cardinal organization simply didn't produce like it once had. By the late '40s, Stan Musial was the only star left, and by the early '50s the Cardinals weren't contending for anything but third place.

Most Valuable Cardinal: Mort Cooper, who topped the National League with 22 wins and a 1.78 ERA, was not only the most valuable Cardinal, but officially the National League's MVP. Enos Slaughter, a future Hall of Famer enjoying his best season, finished second in the MVP vote. For more on the Cardinals and the MVP, see separate article, "The Red Monopoly."

Worst Regular: Jimmy Brown was versatile, if nothing else. He played 82 games at second base, 66 at third, and 12 at shortstop. Brown was always a halfway-decent hitter . . . until 1942, when he set career lows with a .256 batting average and .320 slugging percentage. In 1943 Brown batted just .182 before getting drafted, and his comeback with the Pirates in '46 didn't last long.

Hall of Famers: Stan Musial and Enos Slaughter.

Our Hall of Famers: Musial's one of the all-time greats. Slaughter was admitted to the Hallowed Hall in 1985 by the Veterans Committee, and we all know how picky they're not. In all fairness, though, Slaughter did draw substantial support from the BBWAA (Baseball Writers of America Association). In 1979, the last year those voters could consider him, Slaughter drew 297 votes, with 324 needed for enshrinement. Slaughter finished just behind future Hall of Famer Duke Snider (308) and ahead of seven men who would make it later on.

Too, Slaughter spent three of his prime seasons, 1943 through 1945, in the service of his country. He finished his career with 2,383 hits, but give him another three seasons and 180 hits per, and all of a sudden you're looking at damn near 3,000.

Ultimately, Slaughter's career stats don't merit inclusion in the Hall. But give him credit for the war years—and I think all those guys deserve the benefit of the doubt—and Country Slaughter's no disgrace to Cooperstown. (By the way, Slaughter just missed playing for another team in this book, the 1953 Yankees, as he was traded to the Yanks after the '53 season. He did play for three American League pennant winners, the 1956–58 Yankees.)

You can make an argument for manager Billy Southworth getting into the Hall of Fame, but more on him later.

The 1942 World Series: Things were back to normal in the American League, as the Yankees won 103 games and cruised home to a nine-game edge over the second-place Boston Red Sox. The Yankees, because they were *The Yankees*, entered the World Series as big favorites over the Cardinals. And the prophets looked prophetic after game 1, in which the Cardinals made four errors and didn't pick up their first base hit until the eighth inning, eventually dropping a 7–4 decision.

But St. Louis took game 2, 4–3, and Ernie White spun a six-hit shutout to beat the Bombers in game 3. Game 1 loser Mort Cooper was roughed up again in game 4, but his mates rescued him with a six-run fourth, then scored two runs in the seventh on their way to a 9–6 triumph. Game 2 winner Johnny Beazley picked up another victory in game 5, though it wasn't easy. The score was 2–2 until the top of the ninth, when Whitey Kurowski smacked a two-run homer down the left-field line. In the bottom of the inning, the first two Yankees reached base, but catcher Walker Cooper picked Joe Gordon off second base, and Beazley retired the next two batters to clinch the World Championship.

The Ballpark: Sportsman's Park. Marty Marion once said, "Being an infielder, I used to call it 'The Brickyard.' It was the worst infield in baseball. You really had to guard yourself. I didn't want a bad hop to knock my teeth out. We had two teams playing in the ballpark and the field never got any rest. And, with the hot summers, even the infield grass had trouble surviving." The site of Sportsman's Park is now occupied by the Herbert Hoover Boys' Club, and a baseball diamond is in place where the major league one used to be.

Books about the 1942 Cardinals: There are a number of books about World War II–era baseball, all of which were sources for this chapter. Bill Borst's *The Best of Seasons* (Jefferson, NC: McFarland, 1995) is a day-by-day account of both the 1944 Cardinals and the 1944 St. Louis Browns, both of whom won their respective pennants. Stan Musial has done a pair of books with St. Louis sportswriter Bob Broeg: *Stan Musial: The Man's Own Story* (Garden City, NY: Doubleday, 1964) and *The Man, Stan: Musial, Then and Now* (St. Louis: Bethany, 1977). The two best books on Branch Rickey are Murray Polner's *Branch Rickey* (New York: Atheneum, 1982), and *Branch Rickey's Little Blue Book* (New York: Macmillan, 1995), a collection of his notes and short essays.

Mort, Stan, and Slats: The Red Monopoly

For three years running, 1942 through 1944, St. Louis Cardinals players were named National League MVP. That's not so surprising, given that the Cards won the pennant in each of those seasons.

Walker and Mort Cooper *(National Baseball Hall of Fame Library, Cooperstown, NY)*

What might be surprising, however, is that three *different* Cardinals won the MVP. And continuing with that theme, you might be surprised to see how *many* Cardinals figured in the voting.

As we've seen, Mort Cooper and Enos Slaughter finished one-two in the 1942 voting. Marty Marion finished 7th. Walker Cooper and Stan Musial finished 11th and 12th, respectively. Johnny Beazley and Jimmy Brown finished tied for 13th. Terry Moore finished 18th, Whitey Kurowski tied for 25th. (Jimmy Brown, as we noted above, was not a good player in 1942. So how did he finish right behind Beazley, who won 21 games? Well, "intangibles" probably had something to with it. In the book *Players' Choice: Major League Baseball Players Vote on the All-Time Greats,* Max Lanier names Brown as the "Ball Player Who Did Most to Inspire His Team.")

In 1943 Musial and Walker Cooper moved from 12th and 11th to first and second. Walker's brother Mort led the National League in victories for the second straight season, but he failed to pace the league in ERA again and finished fifth in the MVP voting. Marion finished 13th, and new second baseman Lou Klein finished 23d.

It was Marion's turn in 1944, as he became one of the more questionable MVPs ever, not to mention the first shortstop to win the award in either league. Musial finished fourth, Walker Cooper eighth, and brother Mort ninth. Ray Sanders and Johnny Hopp (by '44, Hopp was almost exclusively an outfielder) figured in the voting, too, and three other Cardinals were also mentioned.—Rob

Captain Terry

When you read interviews with various 1942 Cardinals, two things keep popping up: their ability, willingness, or intention to take the extra base whenever possible, and the leadership of center fielder Terry Moore. They also talk about Moore's defensive skills. Max Lanier pitched in front of both Moore and Willie Mays, and Lanier called Moore "the greatest outfielder I ever played with." Moore actually practiced bare-handed catches and reportedly performed the trick a number of times in real games. If there'd been Gold Gloves in the 1940s, Moore would almost certainly have won a mantel's worth.

But as great a center fielder as Moore was, that wasn't what his teammates remembered most about him. Rather, they remembered him as the good-natured enforcer, the veteran who kept the kids in line, reminding everybody of why they were all out there sweating their asses off in wool uniforms day after day. Here's what a few of Moore's teammates have said on the subject over the years:

> Terry Moore was a great team leader as well as a great competitor and center fielder. He really could chew out anyone he didn't think was giving 100 percent.
>
> —*Stan Musial*

We were a close team and Terry Moore was a lot of that. . . . We traveled by train and had more time together, but Terry was our captain and was respected by everyone on the club. He would do more talking to players than the manager did; everyone respected him for that.

—Harry Walker

We were an intent ballclub that played together. We had a good captain in Terry Moore. You could say that he was the father of the ballclub. If we had any troubles or anything, we would go to Terry. He's the one that kept us in good spirits. . . .

It's true that if we made a mistake, Terry Moore would pinch the back of our neck and tell us what we did wrong. And he had bear claws for hands, so you felt it.

—Whitey Kurowski

Surprisingly, Moore didn't spend many years around the game after retiring in 1948. He coached with the Cardinals for five seasons, managed the Phillies for half a season, coached with the Cards for a couple more years, and then left baseball for good, managing a bowling alley in his retirement.—Rob

The Forgotten Man(ager)

Billy Southworth managed the St. Louis Cardinals from mid-1940 through 1945. For those five-plus seasons, the Cards won 577 games and lost 301, for an incredible .657 winning percentage. Yet, Billy Southworth is not a member of the National Baseball Hall of Fame, and even most diehard baseball aficionados would be hard-pressed to identify the manager of baseball's most successful World War II–era team.

So who *was* Billy Southworth, anyway? And why has he been forgotten? In his younger days, Southworth was an outfielder by trade. He broke in with the Cleveland Naps in 1913, but didn't really play until 1918 with the Pirates. In 1919, Southworth served as the club's regular left fielder and paced the National League with 14 triples. After stints with the Boston Braves and New York Giants,

Roomies

The St. Louis Cardinals and the St. Louis Browns shared Sportsman's Park, and in 1944 Cardinals manager Billy Southworth and Browns manager Luke Sewell and their wives shared an apartment. This worked out nicely because neither of them was ever in St. Louis at the same time.

The arrangement fell apart in October, however. To no one's surprise, the Cardinals had cruised to another pennant. Meanwhile, the Browns had won their first (and only) American League pennant in franchise history. It certainly wouldn't have been comfortable for both the Southworths and Sewells to occupy the same residence, so the Southworths moved into a vacant apartment for the duration of the World Series.

Southworth's Cards won the Series, but tragedy struck just a few months later. Billy Southworth, Jr., survived twenty-five missions over Europe as a bomber pilot. On February

15, 1945, however, Billy's B-29 overshot LaGuardia Field while attempting an emergency landing and crashed into Flushing Bay. On impact, the huge bomber broke into two flaming sections and sank. Five airmen were rescued, but Southworth and four other crewmen were killed. Before the war, Billy Jr. had played in the minor leagues for five years, and he played briefly in the International League in 1940.—*Rob*

Around the Majors

January 15 The Chicago Cubs have every intention of installing lights at Wrigley Field for the 1942 season, but today they cancel those plans because of the military's need for the materials.

April 21 All four major league games played today result in shutouts, including Reds pitcher Johnny Vander Meer's 1–0 triumph over the Cardinals in eleven innings.

May 13 Boston Braves knuckleball pitcher Jim Tobin

Billy Southworth *(National Baseball Hall of Fame Library, Cooperstown, NY)*

Southworth was traded to the Cardinals in 1926, and he led St. Louis with six runs in their World Series upset of the Yankees that fall.

In 1927, Southworth batted .301 (but with little power) in 92 games, and .301 without power in 1927 wasn't worth a whole lot. The Cardinals offered him a job as player-manager of their Rochester farm club, and he took it. In 1928, without Southworth, St. Louis won the National League pennant but lost the World Series to New York. *With* player-manager Southworth, who batted .361, Rochester won the International League pennant.

Southworth got his first chance to manage the Cardinals in 1929, under strange circumstances. Bill McKechnie had managed St. Louis to the National League pennant in 1928, but after the Cards were swept by the Yankees in the World Series, club owner Sam Breadon demoted McKechnie to Rochester and replaced him with Southworth.

Southworth had played under tough guys like George Stallings, John McGraw, and Rogers Hornsby, and so that's what he thought managers were supposed to be like. His new players, most of them well-paid veterans who had been Southworth's teammates just two seasons earlier, didn't take kindly to "Billy the Kid" and his ministrations. The Cards sat atop the standings on June 4, but then they started slipping, and by July 5 they were in fourth place with a 43-45 record. Shortly thereafter, Breadon brought McKechnie back to St. Louis and sent Southworth back to Rochester. Breadon loved to change managers.

The Cardinals finished 1929 in fourth place, while Southworth's Red Wings won another International League pennant (he batted .349 in 37 games). The Cards beat the Philadelphia Athletics in the 1931 World Series. Southworth was still in Rochester, however, where he guided the Wings to their (and his) fourth straight pennant. In 1932, Southworth managed the Columbus Redbirds to a second-place finish in the American Association. In 1933, he was back in the major leagues as a coach with the New York Giants. And in 1934, Billy Southworth was out of baseball.

Given another chance by Branch Rickey, Southworth managed Cardinal farm teams in Asheville and Memphis from 1935 through 1938. In 1939, he skippered Rochester once again, this time to a second-place finish. Also in 1939, the St. Louis Cardinals finished in second place, with a 92-61 record. Yet on the morning of June 7, 1940, the National League standings showed the Cardinals in sixth place, with a 14-24 mark. Sam Breadon still owned the club and, overriding the objections of Branch Rickey, he fired manager Ray Blades and summoned Southworth from Rochester. Like I said, Breadon loved to change managers.

By the time Southworth arrived, the team had gone 1-5 under interim manager Mike Gonzalez, dropping to seventh place. But the Redbirds responded to Southworth. Or perhaps they just started getting some breaks. Either way, the club started winning, with a 69-40 record the rest of the way, which landed them in third place. In *The St. Louis Cardinals*, Fred Lieb wrote of Southworth,

He is the friend of every man on the team, and they know it. They come to him with personal problems, as well as those concerning baseball. Even if a man has made a stupid blunder, Billy doesn't bawl out the player until next day. Then both he and the athlete have had a night's sleep on it. He is a strict disciplinarian, but not in the sense that McGraw and George Stallings were

blasts three straight home runs to beat the Cubs at Braves Field, 6–5.

June 21 White Sox knuckleballer Ted Lyons wins his 250th game. Lyons will complete all 20 of his games this season, and lead the American League with a 2.10 ERA before joining the U.S. Marines at age forty-two.

July 6 The American League tops the National League in the All-Star Game, 3–1. The only N.L. run comes on Dodger catcher Mickey Owen's solo home run. In 421 regular-season at-bats this season, Owen hits exactly zero homers.

July 19 Dodgers center fielder Pete Reiser crashes into the wall at Sportsman's Park while chasing Enos Slaughter's long fly. Reiser is hitting .379 at the time but, after suffering a concussion, his average drops to .310 by season's end, and the 1941 batting champion is never the same player again.

September 13 Cubs shortstop Lennie Merullo commits four errors in one game. His newborn son is named "Boots."

September 23 In the last start of his major league career, Dodgers pitcher Larry French throws a one-hit shutout against the Phillies, recording his 197th career victory before joining the U.S. Navy.

Ten Greatest Stretch Runs

What makes a great stretch run? Ideally, it involves a team that overcame a large deficit in the latter stages of the season, thus allowing it to beat out another good team.

10. *1974 Baltimore Orioles* The Orioles overcame an eight-game deficit in late August with a 28-6 run to end the season.

9. *1977 Kansas City Royals* As of early August, the top clubs in the A.L. West were all bunched up, but the Royals won 38 of their last 47 games to pull away. Included in that run were

clubhouse despots. The Cardinals just don't step out of the traces, because that wouldn't be playing fair with Billy. He is known as baseball's "little gentleman," but he can carry an iron fist in his velvet glove. No one puts anything over on him, and one of his first rules on the club was that no Cardinal should go to the front office except to get his pay check. That rule wasn't always in effect.

Billy Southworth probably wasn't a certifiable genius, but Lieb's description is a pretty good prescription for success. Essentially, it boils down to this: *make sure everybody knows who's running the team without getting obnoxious about it.* Oh, and having a bunch of great players helps a little, too.

After the 1945 season, in which the Cardinals finished three games behind the pennant-winning Cubs, Southworth received a hefty contract offer from Lou Perini, president of the Boston Braves. Though he still had a year to run on his contract with St. Louis, Southworth persuaded Breadon to release him. Eddie Dyer was hired to manage the Cardinals, who did win the pennant (and World Series) in 1946. It would be their last title until 1964.

With all the players coming back from the war, the Cardinals had a fair amount of surplus talent, and a number of Southworth's old St. Louis charges ended up with the Braves. In fact, so many ex-Redbirds eventually made their way to Boston that the club was known in some quarters as the "Cape Cod Cardinals."

Southworth needed the help because he was taking over a club that hadn't finished in the first division—that is, higher than fifth—since 1934. In 1946, Southworth's first season, the Braves finished fourth. They finished third in 1947. In 1948, the Braves won the National League pennant, their first in thirty-four years. The Cardinals finished second, 6½ games back.

What kind of manager was Southworth? Well, he sure did like to bunt. We are not big fans of the sacrifice bunt, but you've got to admit that it worked for Southworth. He managed the Cardinals for five full seasons, 1941–45, and the Cards led the National League in sacrifice hits in 1941, 1942, 1943, and 1944. In 1945, they were second.

Southworth's St. Louis clubs featured fine pitching and wonderful defense up the middle, so his idea was to get ahead as soon as possible, and then hang on. And, as we've noted elsewhere in this chapter, although Southworth's teams didn't steal a lot of bases, he was obsessed with taking the extra base. The result of all this? Southworth's teams won. They won a lot. The chart below lists the all-time leaders in managerial winning percentage, with a minimum of 1,500 games and considering only those men who managed the majority of their games after 1900.

Manager	Wins	Losses	Winning Percentage
Joe McCarthy	2,125	1,333	.615
Billy Southworth	1,044	704	.597
Frank Chance	946	648	.593
John McGraw	2,763	1,948	.586
Al Lopez	1,410	1,004	.584
Earl Weaver	1,480	1,060	.583
Fred Clarke	1,602	1,181	.576
Davey Johnson*	1,062	812	.567
Walt Alston	2,040	1,613	.558
Bobby Cox*	1,521	1,204	.558

*Through the 1999 season.

Of these ten managers, seven are in the Hall of Fame. (Two of those, Chance and Clarke, are in as players, though it's hard to imagine Chance making the Hall had he not managed the Chicago Cubs when he did.) The three who aren't in the Hall of Fame are Billy Southworth, Bobby Cox, and Davey Johnson, and of course Cox and Johnson aren't eligible yet. So why isn't Southworth in the Hall? Two reasons, probably. One, his managerial career was relatively brief. And two, it's possible that his pennants are discounted by voters because they came during the war.

To the first of these, there can be little argument. Although there aren't really any *de facto* standards for Hall of Fame managers, most of them did manage longer than Southworth. As for the second reason, it doesn't hold much water. Say what you will about wartime talent, but Southworth was working under the same system as everyone else. Does Billy Southworth deserve a plaque in Cooperstown? Yes or no, we do know that he deserves to be remembered as one of the more effective managers in the history of the game.—Rob

10- and 16-game winning streaks.

8. *1930 St. Louis Cardinals*
On the morning of August 11, the Cards trailed the first-place Dodgers by 11 games. But they went 38-10 from there (including 21-4 in September) to wind up taking the pennant by two games over the Cubs.

7. *1969 New York Mets*
On August 14, the famously hapless Mets were 9½ games behind the Cubs in the N.L. East standings. As late as September 3, the Cubs still led by 5 games. But Chicago collapsed, losing 17 of their last 24. Meanwhile, the Mets won 24 of their last 32 and finished with a comfortable 8-game lead.

6. *1993 Atlanta Braves*
On July 18, when the Braves acquired first baseman Fred McGriff, they were eight games behind the front-running San Francisco Giants in the N.L. West. But from

that point, they went 51-18. That left them with 104 victories, just one more than the Giants.

5. *1978 New York Yankees*
On July 19, the Yankees were mired in fourth place, 14 games behind the A.L. East–leading Boston Red Sox. They went 52-21 the rest of the way, including a victory over Boston in a one-game playoff for the division title.

4. *1935 Chicago Cubs*
At the end of August, the defending champion St. Louis Cardinals boasted a 2½-game lead over the Cubs. But Chicago promptly won 21 straight games, the second-longest streak of the century, and finished with a four-game edge over the Redbirds.

3. *1914 Boston Braves*
When August began, the Braves were 44-45 and nine games behind the first-place Giants. Boston went 50-14 the rest of the

1941, A Prequel

The 1941 National League pennant race was the first ever in which two teams, in this case the Brooklyn Dodgers and St. Louis Cardinals, spent virtually the entire season trading first place. The Dodgers finally clinched the pennant with two days left in the season, and the Cards wound up 2½ lengths off the pace despite winning 97 games.

This was an amazing accomplishment, considering the devastating series of injuries suffered by St. Louis. Johnny Mize suffered a broken finger and a sore shoulder, and his homers fell from 43 in 1940 to 16 in 1941. Walker Cooper broke his collarbone and missed a few weeks. Staff ace Mort Cooper was out of action from June 17 to August 3 and had to have bone spurs removed from his right elbow. On August 10, Enos Slaughter collided with Terry Moore in the outfield, and Slaughter was lost for nearly five weeks with a broken collarbone. And finally, late in August the Cardinals lost Moore, who ended up in the hospital after being struck in the head by an Art Johnson fastball.

What is now remembered as the key game of the pennant race took place on Saturday, September 13, in St. Louis. The Cardinals entered this finale of a three-game series against Brooklyn trailing the Dodgers by one game. If they won, they'd be tied for first place, with each team having 14 more games to play. Whitlow Wyatt and Mort Cooper matched zeroes on the scoreboard for seven innings, with Cooper carrying a no-hitter into the eighth. In the top of that inning, however, Brooklyn outfielder Dixie Walker lined a double into the gap in right-center, bringing up Billy Herman. On second base, Walker stole the sign—curveball—from St. Louis catcher Gus Mancuso and relayed the message to Herman. Herman sat on the curve, Cooper threw the curve, and Herman drilled the curve off the right-field fence for an RBI double. The Dodgers would score no more, but the damage had been done. It was still 1–0 in the bottom of the ninth when Wyatt struck out pinch-hitter Slaughter on three straight fastballs, ending the game and giving the Dodgers a two-game lead that they would never relinquish.

In light of the Cardinals' second-place finish despite all the injuries, two things happened. One, Billy Southworth was named National League Manager of the Year by *The Sporting News* and, two, St. Louis was favored to win the flag heading into the 1942 season.—Rob

Down the Stretch They Come

The '42 Cardinals are best known for their amazing stretch run. St. Louis won 43 of their last 51 games and came back from a double-digit deficit in games in early August to edge out the Dodgers for the N.L. flag. The story of the 1942 National League pennant race revolves so much around the Cards and Dodgers that *The Sports Encyclopedia: Baseball* credits the Redbirds' doubleheader sweep of Brooklyn on August 4 as the beginning of their pennant push.

However, when I went through the National League box scores for August and September, I found something quite different. The Cardinals' 43-of-51 run did begin with a doubleheader sweep, but it was against the Pirates on August 9. On August 4, St. Louis lost at Cincinnati, and Brooklyn tied the Giants 1–1 at the Polo Grounds because the game was called early on account of wartime dim-out regulations.

After winning 5 of 7 games from August 9 to August 13, the Cardinals won 8 straight games, their longest streak of the stretch (they also enjoyed three 6-game winning streaks). The Cards chopped off a big chunk of the Dodgers' lead during the second half of August, winning 17 of 19 games from August 14 through the end of the month, including 3 of 4 from Brooklyn, beginning August 24.

The two middle games of that series were classics, as St. Louis won each 2–1 in extra innings. On August 25, in front of what was, up to that time, the biggest-ever crowd (33,527) for a night game in St. Louis, the Cardinals won a 14-inning nail-biter. The game was scoreless until the Dodgers scored a run in the top of the 13th. The Cards tied it with a run in the home half of the 13th, and won it in the 14th. Dodger manager Leo Durocher and coach Charley Dressen were both thrown out of the game in the 12th inning for arguing balls and strikes. Mort Cooper pitched a complete game; yes, all 14 innings for the Cardinals.

That was Cooper's 16th victory. Mort, brother of Cards' catcher Walker Cooper, changed jerseys with almost every start so the number he was wearing would match the number of the win he was trying for. He wore No. 14 (former St. Louis catcher Gus Mancuso's number) when he got his 14th win, his brother's No. 15 when he won his 15th, Cards catcher Ken O'Dea's No. 16 when he won number 16, Erv Dusak's No. 17 when he got that win (Dusak was in the minors), Lon Warneke's old No. 18, and teammate Harry Gumbert's

way, earning themselves the nickname "Miracle Braves" and, even better, the National League pennant.

2. 1942 St. Louis Cardinals
See the article, "Down the Stretch They Come."

1. *1951 New York Giants*
Perhaps the most famous stretch run in history was when the Giants came back from 13½ down on August 11 to beat out the Dodgers. Their 39-8 record from August 12 to season's end includes their 2-1 record against Brooklyn in the pennant playoff, the culmination of the famous Miracle at Coogan's Bluff.

Beazley's Bizarre Career

On September 28, 1941, Johnny Beazley pitched his first major league game. He permitted ten hits and three walks, but gave up just one run over nine innings to beat the Cubs at Wrigley Field, 3–1. That would be his only appearance with the Cardinals in '41, but in 1942 Beazley was a mainstay of the staff, finishing second in the National League in winning percentage (.778), ERA (2.13), and victories (21). (Dodgers hurler Larry French went 15-4 to take the percentage crown, while Beazley's teammate Mort Cooper topped the National League in ERA and wins.)

Described by Fred Lieb as "a cocky Tennesseean," Beazley capped his wonderful year with two triumphs over the Yankees in the World Series. And then, like so many other young men, he put on the uniform of his country. Stationed with the Army Air Force in Texas, Beazley pitched some, but not often enough to really keep his arm in shape. The Cardinals came in for an exhibition game against the base team and, after getting hit hard early, Beazley reached back for something extra. His right shoulder would never be the same.

Still only twenty-eight years old, Beazley rejoined the Cardinals in 1946 and

No. 19. Unfortunately, the game accounts don't say whether he continued this ritual through the end of the season, but he finished with 22 wins and was rewarded with the National League's MVP award. Anyway, on August 26 the Cardinals needed only 10 innings for their second straight 2–1 squeaker.

St. Louis and Brooklyn met again, this time in Brooklyn, for a two-game series September 11 and 12. In the first game, Mort Cooper picked up his 20th win and 8th shutout of the season (a three-hitter), in St. Louis' 3–0 win. That victory moved the Cardinals to within one game of the Dodgers, and on September 12 they evened the pennant race with yet another 2–1 victory, this one credited to Max Lanier.

St. Louis went ahead for good the next day, as the Cards split a doubleheader with the Phillies and the Dodgers got swept by the Reds. The Cardinals simply would not lose. They went 21-4 in September, including a 12-2 mark after they tied the Dodgers on the 12th. The Dodgers didn't play poorly, 16-10 in September and 10-4 after the 12th. They even won their last eight games. But Brooklyn simply could not recover from a stretch of five losses in six games from the 11th through the 17th because the Cardinals almost never lost. St. Louis clinched the pennant with a win in the first game of a doubleheader on September 27, the last day of the season.

If there seem to be a lot of one-run Cardinals' wins during this stretch, you weren't imagining it. St. Louis played 14 one-run games of these final 51 and had tremendous success, winning 13. However, if you're thinking that St. Louis was exceptionally lucky, they were also 17-3 in games decided by four or more runs. Not counting extra innings, St. Louis outscored its opponents in every inning during their stretch run:

	Inning								
	1	2	3	4	5	6	7	8	9
Cardinals	29	19	31	21	44	33	25	25	22
Opponents	12	16	17	19	14	29	16	14	5

Overall, they outscored their opposition 254 to 143, which translates into a Pythagorean record of 38-13. The Cardinals' opponents scored two runs or less in 29 of these 51 games. St. Louis scored five or more runs in 29 of these 51 games. The Cardinals had an amazing

25-3 record at home and a not-so-shabby 18-5 record on the road. They had a winning record against every other N.L. team during their 51-game stretch run:

Cardinals vs.	W	L
Brooklyn Dodgers	5	1
Boston Braves	5	0
Chicago Cubs	8	2
Cincinnati Reds	9	0
New York Giants	2	1
Philadelphia Phillies	6	1
Pittsburgh Pirates	8	3

If Brooklyn had just been able to split its last six games with St. Louis, the Dodgers would have won the pennant.

Mort Cooper probably sewed up the MVP award during these games, as he went 9-2 with four shutouts and a superb 1.52 ERA. Johnny Beazley had an even better record, 9-1 and a fine 2.17 ERA, on his way to a 21-6 mark for the season and a 2.13 ERA. Howie Krist was 5-0 over this stretch.

Stan Musial led the Cards in slugging percentage (.491) and RBI (32) during the Cards' finishing kick. His slugging and average (.319) were very similar to his overall numbers for the year (.490 and .315).

Enos Slaughter led the club with 36 runs scored, a .429 on-base percentage, and a .326 batting average. Slaughter played in the first 50 games of the Cards' pennant push before finally resting on Day 51, after his club had clinched the flag. That batting average notwithstanding, Slaughter may have been somewhat fatigued. Only one of his 17 triples on the season came in his last 50 games, and his slugging percentage was .519 before the stretch run, but only .442 after (those wool uniforms got awfully hot in the long St. Louis summer).

The 1942 Cardinals' run to the pennant was most remarkable and, given the circumstances and the outcome, it's probably the most significant stretch drive in major league history.—Eddie

lost the opener to Pittsburgh, 6–4. Pitching on and off, Beazley posted a 7-5 record during the regular season. His World Series action was limited to one scoreless inning in St. Louis' game 5 loss to the Red Sox. Joe Garagiola, who joined the Cards in 1946, later said of Beazley, "He'd had that *good* overhand curveball, but now it was a shame to watch him try to pitch. You could catch him with a Kleenex."

In 1947, Beazley followed Billy Southworth to Boston, where he would total 13 games—four of them starts—and 46 innings over the next three seasons. He retired with a 31-12 record in the major leagues and a .721 winning percentage that ranks as the second-highest ever among pitchers with at least 350 innings. (The number one man on the list is Howie Krist [.771], who was Beazley's teammate in St. Louis for parts of two seasons.)—*Rob*

TEAM STATS

Hitting

	Games by Position	Age	G	AB	R	H	2B	3B	HR	RBI	BB	SB	Avg	OBP	Slug
Walker Cooper	C,115	27	125	438	58	123	32	7	7	65	29	4	.281	.327	.434
Johnny Hopp	1B,88	25	95	314	41	81	16	7	3	37	36	14	.258	.334	.382
Creepy Crespi	2B,83; SS,5	24	93	292	33	71	4	2	0	35	27	4	.243	.309	.271
Whitey Kurowski	3B,104; SS,1; OF,1	24	115	366	51	93	17	3	9	42	33	7	.254	.326	.391
Marty Marion	SS,147	24	147	485	66	134	**38**	5	0	54	48	8	.276	.343	.375
Enos Slaughter	OF,151	26	152	591	100	**188**	31	**17**	13	98	88	9	.318	.412	.494
Stan Musial	OF,135	21	140	467	87	147	32	10	10	72	62	6	.315	.397	.490
Terry Moore	OF,126; 3B,1	30	130	489	80	141	26	3	6	49	56	10	.288	.364	.391
Jimmy Brown	2B,82; 3B,66; SS,12	32	145	**606**	75	155	28	4	1	71	52	4	.256	.315	.320
Ray Sanders	1B,77	25	95	282	37	71	17	2	5	39	42	2	.252	.351	.379
Ken O'Dea	C,49	29	58	192	22	45	7	1	5	32	17	0	.234	.297	.350
Harry Walker	OF,56; 2B,2	25	74	191	38	60	12	2	0	16	11	2	.314	.355	.398
Coaker Triplett	OF,46	30	64	154	18	42	7	4	1	23	17	1	.273	.345	.390
Erv Dusak	OF,8; 3B,1	21	12	27	4	5	3	0	0	3	3	0	.185	.267	.296
Buddy Blattner	SS,13; 2B,3	22	19	23	3	1	0	0	0	1	3	0	.043	.185	.043
Gus Mancuso*	C,3	36	5	13	0	1	0	0	0	1	0	0	.077	.077	.077
Sam Narron	C,2	28	10	10	0	4	0	0	0	1	0	0	.400	.400	.400
Estel Crabtree		38	10	9	1	3	2	0	0	2	1	0	.333	.400	.556
Jeff Cross	SS,1	23	1	4	0	1	0	0	0	1	0	0	.250	.250	.250
Totals		26		**5,421**	755	1,454	282	69	60	**680**	551	71	**.268**	**.338**	**.379**

*Played for another team during season. Statistics are those compiled with 1942 St. Louis Cardinals only.

Pitching

	Threw	Age	Games	GS	CG	ShO	IP	H	HR	BB	SO	W	L	Pct	Sv	ERA
Mort Cooper	Right	29	37	35	22	**10**	279	207	9	68	152	**22**	7	.759	0	**1.78**
Johnny Beazley	Right	24	43	23	13	3	215	181	4	73	91	21	6	.778	3	2.13
Harry Gumbert	Right	32	38	19	5	0	163	156	3	59	52	9	5	.643	5	3.26
Max Lanier	Left	26	34	20	8	2	161	137	4	60	93	13	8	.619	2	2.96
Ernie White	Left	25	26	19	7	1	128	113	11	41	67	7	5	.583	2	2.52
Murry Dickson	Right	25	36	7	2	0	121	91	1	61	66	6	3	.667	2	2.91
Howie Krist	Right	26	34	8	3	0	118	103	2	43	47	13	3	**.813**	1	2.51
Howie Pollet	Left	21	27	13	5	2	108	102	7	39	42	7	5	.583	0	2.88
Lon Warneke*	Right	33	12	12	5	0	82	76	8	15	31	6	4	.600	0	3.29
Bill Lohrman*	Right	29	5	0	0	0	13	11	0	2	6	1	1	.500	0	1.42
Whitey Moore*	Right	30	9	0	0	0	12	10	0	11	1	0	1	.000	0	4.38
Bill Beckmann*	Right	34	2	0	0	0	7	4	0	1	3	1	0	1.000	0	0.00
Clyde Shoun*	Left	30	2	0	0	0	2	1	0	0	0	0	0	.000	0	0.00
Totals		26	305	156	70	**18**	1,410	**1,192**	49	473	**651**	**106**	**48**	.688	15	**2.55**

*Played for another team during season. Statistics are those compiled with 1942 St. Louis Cardinals only.

1953 New York Yankees

The reason this club hasn't made a deal is why should we? When you got players good enough to win a pennant on the road and a World Series on the road, which is where they win the majority of their games and against a tremendous club like the Dodgers, which you know is a great ball club because, why, they have played us more games in the World Series than anybody ever since we've been in the World Series for four years, then why would you want to change? If the players are good enough to win four years they should be good enough to win five.

—Yankees manager Casey Stengel, at a press luncheon in May 1953

Record: 99-52, .656 (45th)
Two-Year (1952–53): 194-111, .636 (55th)
Three-Year (1951–53): 292-167, 636 (45th)

SD Score: 2.72 (70th)
Two-Year: 5.22 (45th)
Three-Year: 7.68 (30th)

Results:
1951 World Champions
1952 World Champions
1953 World Champions

Days in First Place: 158 of 167; clinched on September 14

Longest Winning Streak: 18 games
Longest Losing Streak: 9 games
The winning streak was one game short of the A.L. record, set by the 1906 White Sox and tied by the '47 Yankees. The losing streak is the longest ever by any A.L. team that finished first in its league or division.

The Pennant Race: One interesting thing about these Yankees was their relatively small margins of victory in the consecutive pennant seasons. In 1949, they finished one game ahead of the Red Sox, thanks to a pair of victories over Boston on the season's final two days. In 1950, they finished three games ahead of Detroit. In 1951, they finished five games ahead of Cleveland, and in 1952 they finished a mere two games ahead of the Indians.

In the preseason polls of the baseball writers before each of those four campaigns, the Yankees finished second. The Red Sox were favored from 1949 through 1951, and then the Indians won the straw poll in 1952. But, of course, the Yankees finished atop the A.L. standings all four of those seasons, and in 1953 the Bronx Bombers finally were favored in the preseason poll. Mind you, they still didn't blow away the competition, finishing with an 8½-game lead over the second-place Indians. But the Yanks grabbed first place for good in the middle of May, and their 18-game winning streak that started on May 27 put away the competition.

Against the Contenders: The Yankees split their season series, 11-11, with the Cleveland Indians. New York fared slightly better against the third-place White Sox, taking 13 of 22.

Runs Scored: 801 (1st)

Runs Allowed: 547 (1st)

The 1953 Yankees were the only one of the five-time World Series champs to lead the league in both runs scored and fewest runs allowed. In fact, the 1952 Yankees are the only other one of those teams to lead the league in either category; they allowed the fewest runs in the league.

Pythagorean Record: 101-50

Manager: Casey Stengel

Regular Lineup:

Player	Position	ROV	OW%
Gil McDougald	3B	.294	.635
Joe Collins	1B	.299	.652

The Best Job in the World, Part II

A few notes on Charlie Silvera, Yogi Berra's backup, who played on seven World Series teams and picked up the winner's share six times:

◆ They called Silvera "the Arndt Jorgens of the 1950s."

◆ In nine years with the Yankees, Silvera batted 429 times, hit one homer, and scored 33 runs.

◆ Silvera played regularly only once. Late in 1949, Berra missed six weeks with a broken thumb, and Silvera batted .315 until Berra returned with a week to play. The Yankees wound up beating out the Red Sox by one game for the A.L. flag.

◆ According to Silvera, "Without me the Yankees wouldn't have won five straight. There wouldn't have been any dynasty."

◆ Silvera's six Series winner's and one loser's share added up to

Player	Position	ROV	OW%
Hank Bauer	RF	.320	.713
Yogi Berra	C	.326	.728
Mickey Mantle	CF	.340	.762
Gene Woodling	LF	.329	.736
Billy Martin	2B	.255	.490
Phil Rizzuto	SS	.285	.606
Whitey Ford	P		

This lineup was amazingly productive, with Billy Martin the weakest link but still a pretty good player when you consider his solid defense at second base.

Bench: As everyone knows, Casey Stengel loved to use everybody on the roster and, unless you were a big star, you probably weren't going to play every day. However, his hand was forced in 1953, as injuries limited Mantle to 121 games in the outfield. Speedy Irv Noren filled in for Mantle most of the time. Don Bollweg played first base when Joe Collins didn't, and Bill Renna batted .314 with pretty good power as the club's fifth outfielder.

Scouting the Pitchers: See separate articles, "Superchief" and "The Big Three."

How Were They Built? In general, the Yankees got their pitchers from other organizations, and they liked to trade for veteran hitters to fill holes. But the backbone of the club, the lineup, was generally populated by products of the farm system, which was stocked thanks to ample financial resources and a talented staff, led by general manager George Weiss and scout Tom Greenwade.

Greenwade will forever be remembered as the man who discovered Mickey Mantle in a small town called Commerce, Oklahoma. As Greenwade later remembered, "I saw him hit one over the fence left-handed and then I saw him turn around and whack one off the other fence from the right side. And then I saw him run. That was enough for me." Mantle was only sixteen years old then, so the Yankees waited. And when Mantle graduated in 1949, Greenwade returned. With a straight face, he told Mickey's father, "I'm afraid Mickey may never reach the Yankees. Right now I'd have to rate him a lousy short-stop. Sloppy. Erratic arm. And he's small. Get him in front of some really strong pitching. . . . However, I'm willing to take a risk." Mantle signed for $400 a month, plus a $1,100 bonus. Baseball was different back then.

What Brought Them Down? Down? The Yankees won nine American League pennants in ten years, and in the only one of those years they didn't win, 1954, they won 103 games. One of baseball's all-time oddities is that Casey Stengel's winningest team, his '54 Yankees, did *not* win a pennant. Of course, the Yankees didn't win forever, but the story of their eventual downfall will be told in another chapter.

Most Valuable Yankee: Yogi Berra

Mantle was great, but he didn't really play enough. In the early 1950s, Berra might have been the most respected player in the game. He won American League MVP awards in 1951, 1954, and 1955. He finished fourth in the MVP balloting in 1952, and in '53 he finished second behind Indians third baseman Al Rosen, who simply blew everybody else away. Berra also finished third in 1950 and second in 1956.

Worst Regular: Billy Martin (at least until the World Series)

Hall of Famers: Mickey Mantle, Yogi Berra, Whitey Ford, Phil Rizzuto, and Casey Stengel.

Our Hall of Famers: Mantle, Berra, and Ford are all legitimate, with Mantle and Berra both among the three or four all-time best at their positions.

Rizzuto, who was elected by the Veterans Committee in 1994, is a marginal Hall of Famer, based on his record. If you're interested in the cases for and against Rizzuto, you should find a copy of Bill James' book on the Hall of Fame, *The Politics of Glory*, which was titled *Whatever Happened to the Hall of Fame?* in paperback. I've always felt negatively about Rizzuto being in the Hall, but I have to admit he's got a pretty good case if you give him credit for the three years he missed during World War II. Of course, there are others about whom you could say the same, and most of them have not been elected.

$46,426.25, which was pretty good change in those days. Not bad for a guy who actually played in just one of those seven World Series.

In the 1950s, Charlie Silvera was one of the luckiest men in the world.—*Rob*

Around the Majors

April 13 The brand-new Milwaukee Braves, relocated from Boston (in the first franchise shift in fifty years), beat Cincinnati 2–0 in their first game. The next day, the Braves win their first home game when Billy Bruton homers in the bottom of the tenth inning.

May 6 St. Louis Browns rookie Bobo Holloman throws a no-hitter to beat the Athletics in his first major league start. Holloman will win only two more games in his career.

May 10 Pittsburgh's Johnny and Eddie O'Brien become the first twins to play for the same major league team. For much of the season, they'll make up the Pirates' double-play combination.

June 18 Red Sox rookie Gene Stephens collects three hits in the seventh inning, thus becoming the first major league player to get three hits in one frame. Boston scores 17 runs in the

The 1953 World Series: Billy Martin, the least productive regular during the regular season, came through big in the World Series against the Brooklyn Dodgers, who the Yankees had previously beaten in 1941, 1947, 1949, and 1952.

Cy Young, who had pitched in the first World Series fifty years earlier, threw out the ceremonial first pitch before game 1. And in the first inning of the opener, Martin's bases-loaded triple gave the Yankees a 4–0 lead. The Dodgers battled back, but New York sealed the game with three runs in the bottom of the eighth on their way to a 9–5 victory.

It was Mickey Mantle's turn in game 2. In the bottom of the eighth, he broke up a 2–2 tie with a two-run homer into the left-field stands, and the game ended as a 4–2 Yankee triumph. After two games in the Bronx, the Series shifted to Brooklyn, where the Dodgers evened things up with 3–2 and 7–3 victories. In game 3, Dodgers righthander Carl Erskine struck out fourteen Yankees to break Howard Ehmke's World Series record. Yankees left fielder Gene Woodling led off game 5 with a home run over the wall in left field, and Mantle made the score 6–1 with a grand slam in the third inning. Billy Martin also homered in the seventh, and the Yankees rolled to an 11–7 win.

Back at Yankee Stadium for game 6, the Bombers owned a 3–0 lead after two innings, but the Dodger bullpen clamped down after that. Whitey Ford permitted just one Brooklyn run in seven innings, and after eight frames the Dodgers still trailed 3–1. Allie Reynolds had relieved Ford after the seventh, and he escaped the eighth with no damage. In the ninth, however, Dodgers center fielder Duke Snider drew a walk, and right fielder Carl Furillo followed with a dramatic home run into the right-field stands, thus tying the game. Reynolds rebounded to strike out the next two hitters, and the contest was tied at three going to the bottom of the ninth. Hank Bauer led off and coaxed a walk from Dodgers reliever Clem Labine. Yogi Berra followed with a line drive, but right at Furillo. Mantle then chopped a grounder between third base and the mound and beat the throw to first for an infield hit, with Bauer stopping at second base. So with Bauer only 180 feet away from the plate, Billy Martin singled up the middle (his twelfth hit, tying a World Series record), and Bauer came across with the Series-clinching run. The Yankees were world champs for the fifth year in a row, and Dodgers manager Charlie Dressen snarled, "We were beaten by a .257 hitter."

The Ballpark: Unchanged since 1939. With its spacious dimensions and ample foul ground, Yankee Stadium generally played as one of the top two or three pitcher's parks in the American League.

Books about the 1953 Yankees: Dom Forker's *The Men of Autumn* (Dallas, TX: Taylor, 1989) contains interviews with twenty-three Yankees from the 1949–53 period, including greats like Allie Reynolds, Phil Rizzuto, and Yogi Berra, and some not-so-greats like Frank Shea, Cliff Mapes, and Tom Ferrick. There's a whole library of books about Mantle, and the same is true of Billy Martin. The single best source for information on the Yankees of this era is Peter Golenbock's *Dynasty: The New York Yankees 1949–1964* (New York: Prentice-Hall, 1975); however, beware the factual errors.

Superchief

How many thirty-seven-year-old pitchers have led their league in ERA, strikeouts, and shutouts? Allie Reynolds did it in 1952, and for good measure he went 20-8 and saved six games. Reynolds was the oldest pitcher since 1920 to win 20 games for the first time. (Why start at 1920? A 20-win season didn't mean as much before then. From 1901 through 1919, the average win total for the league leader was 29; since then, the average is 23.) Reynolds is also one of just nine pitchers to lead a major league in ERA after the age of thirty-five.

Reynolds' career was most remarkable. His rookie season was 1943, when he was twenty-eight years old and led the American League in strikeouts. Then he retired after the 1954 season, even though he was still quite effective (13-4, 3.32 ERA, seven saves). Reynolds' record in his eight years as a Yankee was 131-60 (.686) with eight straight winning seasons and only one of those below .600. He finished in the top five in the league in winning percentage four times; the top five in ERA twice; and in the top five in strikeouts, strikeouts per nine innings, and opponents' batting average five times each. A lot of people think his best year was 1951, when he threw two no-hitters, one of which clinched the American League pennant on September 28. That year, he was third in the league in winning percentage, first in shutouts, fourth in saves, fourth in strikeouts per in-

inning on their way to a 23–3 trouncing of Detroit.

September 27 With teammate Mickey Vernon in danger of losing the batting title in the last game of the season, his Washington Senators teammates make an out on purpose so he won't have to bat again.

Stats 'n' Stuff

◆ With Mickey Mantle injured for part of the season, no Yankee came close to leading the American League in a hitting category, though Mantle did finish third with 105 runs scored and Berra finished (a distant) fourth with 27 home runs.

◆ The Yankee pitchers fared better. Eddie Lopat led the American League in ERA (2.42) and winning percentage (.800), Vic Raschi led in opponents' batting average (.283), and Johnny Sain boasted the best strikeout to walk ratio (1.87).

◆ On May 12, with Cleveland only a game behind the Yankees, Whitey

Ford tossed a one-hitter to beat the Indians, 7–0. The Tribe's only hit was pitcher Early Wynn's infield single in the sixth.

◆ The Yankees and St. Louis Browns combined to use forty-one players in a game on May 17, setting a new major league record.

◆ June 14 saw the end of the Yankees' franchise-record winning streak (18 games) and the end of the Browns' franchise-record losing streak (14 games), as Duane Pillette beat the Yanks 3–1 at Yankee Stadium.

◆ On August 17, Bob Kuzava shut out the Athletics 9–0, despite allowing 11 hits.

nings pitched, fifth in ERA, first in VERA, and first in opponents' batting average.

Reynolds finished in the top five in the league in shutouts and saves three times in his career, more than any other pitcher. In honor of Reynolds, I calculated a statistic, which I am calling the Allie Reynolds number (ARN), that is an amalgamation of shutouts and saves figured in the same way as Bill James' power/speed number.

$$ARN = \frac{(2 \times \text{shutouts} \times \text{saves})}{(\text{shutouts} + \text{saves})}$$

A pitcher with 50 saves and no shutouts has an ARN of 0, and a pitcher with 10 shutouts and no saves has an ARN of 0. Here are the only pitchers since 1920 with an ARN of 6.00 or higher in a season:

Player	Year	Shutouts	Saves	ARN
Carl Hubbell	1933	10	5	6.67
Carl Hubbell	1934	5	8	6.15
Dizzy Dean	1934	7	7	7.00
Allie Reynolds	1951	7	7	7.00
Allie Reynolds	1952	6	6	6.00
Luis Tiant	1966	5	8	6.15

Reynolds' double duty certainly did not pass without notice by the sporting press, the broadcasters, or Reynolds' own manager. In the days before the Cy Young award, Reynolds received MVP votes in five different seasons, finishing third in 1951 and second in 1952. Yankees broadcaster Mel Allen recalled, "Allie was one of the best pitchers I ever saw. He was a big-game pitcher. I can't think of any other pitcher, offhand, who got off the bench and ran down to the bullpen in big-moment situations like he did."

In 15 World Series games, Reynolds went 7-2 with a 2.79 ERA. Two of his nine starts resulted in complete-game shutouts, and he converted four saves in five chances. In game 1 of the 1949 Series, Reynolds beat Don Newcombe, 1–0, with a nine-strikeout two-hitter, in one of the best pitchers' duels in Series history. He earned the save in game 4 with 3⅓ perfect innings, including five strikeouts. In the 1950 Series, he pitched a 10-inning complete game to beat the

Phillies 2–1 in game 2, and he got the last out in the game 4 clincher. In 1952, with the Dodgers up two games to one, Reynolds helped the Yankees even the series with a 10-strikeout, four-hit shutout in game 4. And working in relief, he saved game 6 and earned the victory in game 7.

It's not altogether clear that Reynolds liked his dual pitching role, but he was such an effective reliever that Stengel considered using him exclusively out of the bullpen. According to Reynolds, he agreed to the move but it never happened because the Yankees decided they didn't have an adequate replacement for him in the rotation.

So who was this guy, and why is he almost forgotten today? Teammate Jerry Coleman calls Reynolds a "Hall of Fame pitcher without the numbers" and says that Reynolds was one of the few pitchers he's seen who could pitch a game just with his fastball, such was its quality. Reynolds also threw a great curve and slider. According to Coleman, Joe DiMaggio was responsible for Reynolds ending up with the Yankees. After the 1946 season, the Yankees were eager to trade Joe Gordon, their star second baseman. The Indians coveted Gordon, and they offered either Red Embree or Reynolds in return. DiMaggio recommended Reynolds, and MacPhail made the deal. As for why he retired while still pitching well, here is Reynolds himself from Dom Forker's book, *The Men of Autumn*:

> I retired after the 1954 season. That year I was 13-3. Not too bad for a guy who was 37. But I had recently been in a bus crash. I had hurt my back. It was a difficult injury in a difficult place. Afterwards I had running problems. I could no longer condition myself. I would pitch with back spasms. Then I would have to go to the dugout for cold spray. I couldn't put up with that for too long. In 1954 I didn't want to play anyway. The game didn't appeal to me any more. It took me away from my family too much.

Actually, Reynolds was thirty-nine and went 13-4 in 1954, and when interviewed by Peter Golenbock years before the Forker book, Reynolds suggested that his '54 record contributed to his decision to retire. "I had a nice record," Reynolds recalled, "but with that record I couldn't expect not to get a cut in salary, and this would have hurt me."

Times have sure changed, haven't they? Can you imagine going

13-4 these days and getting a salary cut? (By the way, the bus mishap occurred in July 1953, in Philadelphia. According to Mickey Mantle, Reynolds later got a cash settlement from the bus company for lost wages.) Not to harp on the same theme too much, but Reynolds is another player whose reputation today is just a small fraction of the true level of his accomplishments. He was probably the best pitcher on a team that won five consecutive World Series titles, and he was a better pitcher than a lot of guys in the Hall of Fame.—Eddie

The Big Three

Although Allie Reynolds clearly was the leader of the staff from 1949 through 1953 due to his ability to start and relieve, he had plenty of help from Vic Raschi and Ed Lopat. Here are the combined stats for all three pitchers, "The Big Three," for those five seasons:

1949–53	W-L	Pct	Innings	Hits	BB	K	ERA
Reynolds	83-41	.669	1,065	920	519	637	3.22
Raschi	92-40	.697	1,194	1,036	503	646	3.36
Lopat	80-36	.690	1,013	971	290	341	2.98

As great as Reynolds was, his winning percentage was actually the lowest of the trio, and his ERA was right in the middle.

Eddie Lopat threw five or six different pitches, none of which would have impressed the radar gun. As White Sox manager Paul Richards once said of Lopat, "It is bad enough to be beaten, but it is worse when you are beaten by a pitcher who has nothing."

Vic Raschi did throw hard (though not as hard as Reynolds), and he mixed in a great sinker as well. In his autobiography, Casey Stengel wrote, "Raschi was the greatest pitcher I ever had to be sure to win. It looked like we would never make any mistakes when he was pitching. And he never would give in any time that he pitched, even when his stuff was ordinary. . . . He wasn't a graceful pitcher—he just put so much on it."

One of the things that made the 1953 season the Yankees' best in this stretch was that, in addition to The Big Three, young Whitey

Ford returned from a two-year stint in the U.S. Army. Back in 1950 Ford had joined the Yankees for the second half of the season and won his first nine straight decisions. Ford didn't miss a beat in 1953, going 18-6 with a 3.00 ERA.

It's often been pointed out that The Big Three wasn't nearly as successful when they weren't pitching for the Yankees, and this is true to an extent. With the Yankees, the trio combined for an incredible 364-169 record. That works out to a .683 winning percentage. (Perhaps not coincidentally, that's nearly the same as the .690 career mark posted by Whitey Ford, who spent his entire career with the Yankees.) Away from the Yankees, The Big Three went 116-116, which of course is a .500 winning percentage. But it should be noted that a significant portion of the difference between .683 and .500 must be chalked up to the teams for which they pitched. The Big Three combined for a 3.52 non-Yankees ERA, not much higher than their 3.32 composite ERA as Yankees.

Dom Forker has suggested that The Big Three be inducted into the Hall of Fame *en masse*, a la Tinker, Evers, and Chance. That's a patently ridiculous suggestion, of course. Better that we remember them for what they were: a group of fine pitchers who found themselves in the right place at the right time.—Rob

Don Bollweg?

During the Yankees' long run of dominance from 1947 through 1964, one thing often said by baseball people was that some players could be transformed into good players if they were traded to the Yankees. Somehow, some way, just putting on the pinstripes could make a player better than he had ever been, or ever would be if he left the Yankees. One of the "examples" that sticks with me is Pedro Ramos in 1964. Ramos spent most of the year as a swingman with Cleveland, for whom he was 7-10 with a 5.14 ERA. Traded to the Yankees in September (late-season acquisitions of key players was another New York trademark of this era), Ramos took over short-relief duties. Pitching in 13 games, he went 1-0 with eight saves and a 1.25 ERA, with 21 strikeouts and zero walks in 22 innings.

Don Bollweg was a backup first baseman and pinch hitter with

Don Bollweg *(National Baseball Hall of Fame Library, Cooperstown, NY)*

the 1953 Yankees. He'd had cups of coffee with the Cardinals in 1950 and 1951, a total of 21 plate appearances, and didn't do anything in that brief trial. In May of '51, St. Louis traded Bollweg to the Yankees, and in 1952 he was MVP of the minor league American Association, batting .325 and scoring 108 runs for the champion Kansas City Blues. Bollweg's true rookie season came with New York in 1953, when he was thirty-two years old. Although he didn't play much, just 70 games and 178 plate appearances, Bollweg was productive when he did play: .384 on-base percentage, .503 slugging percentage, and 7.58 runs created per 27 outs (the league average was 4.46).

He would finally get a chance to play a little in 1954; unfortunately for Bollweg, it was with the Athletics, then playing their last season in Philadelphia. He was part of an eleven-player trade between the Yankees and Athletics in December of 1953. The Yankees traded Bollweg and Vic Power, among others, for Eddie Robinson and others. For the only time in his career, Bollweg played in more than 100 games and had more than 300 plate appearances. How'd he do? Not so well; he was below the league averages in all the aforementioned categories.

Bollweg played a little for the Athletics in their first season in Kansas City in 1955, but that was his last major league action. His decline after his one year with Yankees could be attributed to age, but that still doesn't explain why he did *so* well while with the Yankees. Bollweg's career non-Yankees OBP was .315, his non-Yankees *slugging* percentage was .340. His RC/27 was 70 percent better than the league average with the Yankees, and 12 percent worse than average the rest of his career. Am I stretching to try to make the point? Perhaps, but the point has been made. Besides, "Bollweg" is a neat name.—Eddie

The Greatest Catcher

Coincidentally or not, four claimants to the title of greatest catcher of all time played on teams that are in this book. Alphabetically, they are: Johnny Bench, Yogi Berra, Roy Campanella, and Mickey Cochrane. Obviously, if you were a general manager and were told that your catcher had to be one of these guys in his prime, I don't think you'd be too upset.

Much of the evaluation of a catcher revolves around things that are difficult to measure, such as calling a game or blocking pitches. Ideally, one would like to compare, for example, the ERA of their pitching staff with and without them behind the plate. But we don't have that data for these guys and, besides, during the time they were regulars, they played in a lot of games, which probably wouldn't leave us with enough "other" games to make a meaningful comparison. Bench caught 125-plus games in ten different seasons. Berra did it seven times and led the league in games caught in eight consecutive seasons (1950–57). Campanella didn't catch quite as many games per year, but did lead the league four times in games caught. Like Campanella, Cochrane had a relatively short career, but he did lead the league in games caught in five of his eleven seasons as a regular.

Gold Gloves have been awarded only since 1957, so that leaves Cochrane completely out, essentially leaves Campanella out (his last season was 1957), and leaves out the majority of Berra's career. So the fact that Bench won ten Gold Gloves is impressive, but not that useful in this comparison. Campanella would probably have won his share, and Cochrane might have as well.

This group of four catchers won ten MVP awards, crediting Cochrane with his pre-BBWAA award in 1928. That's not too shabby.

It is true that in Berra's first two full big league seasons he played a fair number of games in the outfield so Aaron Robinson and Gus Niarhos could catch. It is also true that many people say that Berra's defense improved markedly after he began to catch every day, thanks in part to the teachings of coach Bill Dickey. Whitey Ford once remarked of Berra, "I very seldom shook him off. I think he knew the hitters probably better than I did. He could almost outguess them. . . . A batter couldn't believe the combination of pitches he would call for. I'll tell you, he outguessed a lot of good hitters. He had a natural instinct."

Hitting? Well, this is something that we can measure with some degree of accuracy. All of these catchers were productive hitters. Bench, Berra, and Cochrane were better than the overall league average in runs created per 27 outs (RC/27) every year that they were regular catchers. Nagging injuries kept Campanella from doing this, but he finished in the top five in his league in RC/27 four times, more than any of the other players in this group. In terms of where they ranked among catchers in their league while they played, Berra and Cochrane dominate. They each led their league's catchers in RC/27 ten times. Campanella led six times and, somewhat surprisingly, Bench led "only" four times.

I have concocted a method to rate these four players as hitters, trying to combine quantity and quality of performance. Basically, all I did was to calculate their RC/27 rate relative to their league and multiply that times the number of plate appearances they had. Yes, that ignores the fact that Bench and Berra played a few hundred games at other positions, but we can't control for everything. It is also true that the offensive statistics of these players were affected in different degrees by the home ballpark they played in, but we have to start somewhere and this is a pretty good place to start. All right, once again I calculated each player's relative career RC/27 rate and multiplied that times his career plate appearances. Here goes:

Player	Plate Appearances	Player RC/27	League RC/27	Relative RC/27	Net RC/27
Bench	8,669	5.47	4.07	1.34	11,651
Berra	8,361	6.14	4.45	1.38	11,536

Player	Plate Appearances	Player RC/27	League RC/27	Relative RC/27	Net RC/27
Campanella	4,816	6.17	4.48	1.38	6,633
Cochrane	6,206	7.60	5.08	1.50	9,825

Let's use Bench as an example. He had 8,669 career plate appearances, his career RC/27 rate was 5.47, and the league average during the time he played was 4.07. Dividing 5.47 by 4.07 gives us 1.34, meaning that, for his career, Bench was 34 percent more productive offensively (as measured by runs created) than the league average player. Multiplying 1.34 times 8,669 gives us 11,651. I don't know what to call this except "net" RC/27.

As you can see, this method says that, over the course of their careers, Bench and Berra were basically the same offensive player, but given their similar number of plate appearances and similar relative RC/27 rates, this is no surprise. I'm not sure how this would come out if we just focused on the seasons as a regular catcher, except that Campanella and Cochrane wouldn't change much. Campanella never played a game in the field at any position other than catcher, and Cochrane played the grand total of one game in the outfield, his only defensive game not as a catcher. Well, let's see what happens if we use only those seasons in which these players caught in at least 100 games (the number in parentheses next to the player's name is the number of seasons he caught 100-plus games):

Player	Plate Appearances	Player RC/27	League RC/27	Relative RC/27	Net RC/27
Bench (13)	7,607	5.69	4.07	1.40	10,620
Berra (10)	5,782	6.46	4.48	1.44	8,334
Campanella (9)	4,531	6.23	4.48	1.39	6,298
Cochrane (11)	5,902	7.59	5.06	1.50	8,854

This slice of the data leaves Bench out in front of the pack and lifts Cochrane to number two. Bench gets "extra" credit because he had more seasons and plate appearances as a regular catcher, which seems fair given the demands of the position. Confused? I hope not. Even in this day of meticulous record keeping, it is difficult to evaluate much of what a catcher does. All four of these catchers were out-

The Mantle Brothers

You want a good story? How about an outfield consisting of three Mantles? Well, it was always a long shot, but Mickey Mantle had twin brothers a few years younger than him named Ray and Roy. And they played ball. For whatever reason (lack of talent?), the pair wasn't scouted much out of high school, but in 1953 they did well in semi-professional ball, and Mickey asked the Yankees to take a look.

The twins drove to New York in the spring of 1954, and as Mickey later told the story, "I . . . brought them to Yankee Stadium. A half hour later Roy and Ray were in pinstripes, hitting batting practice pitchers with ease—long drives and sharp hits through the infield. Casey scratched his chin and said to me, 'What do they feed you boys in Oklahoma?' "

Roy and Ray both signed professional contracts with the Yankees, and that summer they played together

back near home, with McAllister in the Class D Sooner State League. They did their big brother proud, too. Oddly enough, Roy hit .325 and Ray hit .324 (though Ray only played in 12 games, as compared to 45 for Roy).

In 1955, both were invited to the Yankees' instructional camp and, according to Mickey, they were faster than everybody except him. Roy and Ray were assigned to Class C, but Roy injured his leg and Ray got drafted into the Army, and neither played professionally again.—*Rob*

standing players, but given Johnny Bench's defensive reputation and his offensive contributions as a catcher, it seems as though he may have a slightly better claim to the title of greatest catcher of all time than his three esteemed colleagues. And if you want a different answer, ask me again in five years.—Eddie

(Fairy) Tale of the Tape

The following note appears on the 1953 American League page in *Total Baseball*:

April 17 Mickey Mantle hits the longest home run in Griffith Stadium history, a 565-foot shot off Chuck Stobbs of the Washington Senators. The Yanks win, 7–3.

I don't mean to pick on *Total Baseball*. It's the best one-volume baseball encyclopedia available, and if someday I'm exiled to a desert island and am allowed to take along one book, this is the one. No, I could have found similar citations in any number of books, but I used *Total Baseball* because it's "The Official Encyclopedia of Major League Baseball." Thus, one might argue that Mickey Mantle's 565-foot home run is an "official" fact. Except it's not. Yes, it's a fact that on April 17, 1953, Mickey Mantle hit a long, long home run off Washington's Chuck Stobbs. And it's also a fact that the Yankees beat the Senators at Griffith Stadium, 7–3. It's that "565" that bothers me, because that number is a fiction, yet it's trotted out every time people start talking about so-called tape-measure home runs.

New York's publicity director, Red Patterson, was sitting in the press box when Mantle homered. After scurrying outside, he supposedly found the ball, took precise measurements, and then— presto!—Patterson announced to the world that Mickey Mantle had hit a baseball 565 feet! What actually happened was that the baseball cleared the bleachers, then glanced off the stadium's football scoreboard before coming to earth and bouncing some distance. A boy retrieved the ball and later showed Patterson where he'd found it. So Patterson's "565" actually included an undetermined amount of rolling, and this doesn't even take into account the margin for error in the little boy's memory or the almost-certain error in measurement. Did Patterson hire a team of surveyors to determine the exact distance from home plate to the ball's final resting place? Probably not.

That's not to say Mantle's blast wasn't titanic, because it was. In all the years that American League and Negro League teams played at Griffith Stadium, nobody else ever carried the bleachers in left-center field. But 565? No way. Home run expert William J. Jenkinson has estimated the actual bat-to-ground distance of Mantle's clout at 510 feet, and I'm inclined to accept that as a realistic number.—Rob

TEAM STATISTICS

Hitting

	Games by Position	Age	G	AB	R	H	2B	3B	HR	RBI	BB	SO	SB	Avg	OBP	Slug
Yogi Berra	C,133	28	137	503	80	149	23	5	27	108	50	32	0	.296	.363	.523
Joe Collins	1B,113; OF,4	30	127	387	72	104	11	2	17	44	59	36	2	.269	.365	.439
Billy Martin	2B,146; SS,18	25	149	587	72	151	24	6	15	75	43	56	6	.257	.314	.395
Gil McDougald	3B,136; 2B,26	25	141	541	82	154	27	7	10	83	60	65	3	.285	.361	.416
Phil Rizzuto	SS,133	35	134	413	54	112	21	3	2	54	71	39	4	.271	.383	.351
Hank Bauer	OF,126	30	133	437	77	133	20	6	10	57	59	45	2	.304	.394	.446
Mickey Mantle	OF,121; SS,1	21	127	461	105	136	24	3	21	92	79	90	8	.295	.398	.497
Gene Woodling	OF,119	30	125	395	64	121	26	4	10	58	82	29	2	.306	.429	.468
Irv Noren	OF,96	28	109	345	55	92	12	6	6	46	42	39	3	.267	.350	.388
Don Bollweg	1B,43	32	70	155	24	46	6	4	6	24	21	31	1	.297	.384	.503
Bill Renna	OF,40	28	61	121	19	38	6	3	2	13	13	31	0	.314	.385	.463
Johnny Mize	1B,15	40	81	104	6	26	3	0	4	27	12	17	0	.250	.339	.394
Charlie Silvera	C,39; 3B,1	28	42	82	11	23	3	1	0	12	9	5	0	.280	.352	.341
Andy Carey	3B,40; SS,2; 2B,1	21	51	81	14	26	5	0	4	8	9	12	2	.321	.389	.531
Willie Miranda*	SS,45	27	48	58	12	13	0	0	1	5	5	10	1	.224	.286	.276
Gus Triandos	1B,12; C5	22	18	51	5	8	2	0	1	6	3	9	0	.157	.204	.255
Loren Babe*	3B,5	25	5	18	2	6	1	0	2	6	0	2	0	.333	.333	.722
Jerry Coleman	2B,7; SS,1	28	8	10	1	2	0	0	0	0	0	2	0	.200	.200	.200
Ralph Houk	C,8	33	8	9	2	2	0	0	0	1	0	1	0	.222	.222	.222
Bob Cerv		27	8	6	0	0	0	0	0	0	1	1	0	.000	.143	.000
Jim Brideweser	SS,3	26	7	3	3	3	0	1	0	3	1	0	0	1.000	1.000	1.667
Art Schult		25	7	0	3	0	0	0	0	0	0	0	0	—	—	—
Frank Verdi	SS,1	27	1	0	0	0	0	0	0	0	0	0	0	—	—	—
Totals		28		5,194	801	1,420	226	52	139	762	656	644	34	.273	.359	.417

*Played for another team during season. Statistics are those compiled with 1953 New York Yankees only.

Pitching

	Threw	Age	Games	GS	CG	ShO	IP	H	HR	BB	SO	W	L	Pct	Sv	ERA
Whitey Ford	Left	24	32	30	11	3	207	187	13	110	110	18	6	.750	0	3.00
Johnny Sain	Right	35	40	19	10	1	189	189	16	45	84	14	7	.667	9	3.00
Vic Raschi	Right	34	28	26	7	4	181	150	11	55	76	13	6	.684	1	3.33
Ed Lopat	Left	35	25	24	9	3	178	169	13	32	50	16	4	**.800**	0	**2.42**
Allie Reynolds	Right	38	41	15	5	1	145	140	9	61	86	13	7	.650	13	3.41
Jim McDonald	Right	26	27	18	6	2	130	128	4	39	43	9	7	.563	0	3.82
Ewell Blackwell	Right	30	8	4	0	0	20	17	2	13	11	2	0	1.000	1	3.66
Steve Kraly	Left	24	5	3	0	0	25	19	2	16	8	0	2	.000	1	3.24
Tom Gorman	Left	28	40	1	0	0	77	65	5	32	38	4	5	.444	6	3.39
Bob Kuzava	Right	30	33	6	2	2	92	92	9	34	48	6	5	.545	4	3.31
Ray Scarborough*	Right	35	25	1	0	0	55	52	4	26	20	2	2	.500	2	3.29
Bill Miller	Left	25	13	3	0	0	34	46	3	19	17	2	1	.667	1	4.76
Art Schallock	Left	29	7	1	0	0	21	30	2	15	13	0	0	—	1	2.95
Johnny Schmitz*	Left	32	3	0	0	0	4	2	1	3	0	0	0	—	0	2.08
Totals		32	327	151	50	**18**	1,358	**1,286**	94	500	604	**99**	52	.656	39	3.20

*Played for another team during season. Statistics are those compiled with 1953 New York Yankees only.

CHAPTER 11

1955 Brooklyn Dodgers

This was a team that simply never made a mistake. . . . It was an extraordinary team in every way. The infield was Hodges, Gilliam, Reese, and Robinson. The outfield was Snider, Furillo, and Amoros. The catcher, of course, was Campanella.

Not only could they all hit the ball out of the park, they could all field their positions with anyone. With it all, it was a particularly confident team. Not cocky, not complacent, just absolutely sure of itself.

—Sandy Koufax, in his 1966 autobiography, *Koufax*

Record: 98-55, .641 (68th)

Two-Year Record (1954–55): .619 (92d)

Three-Year Record (1953–55): .640 (39th)

SD Score: 3.03 (33d)

Two-Year: 3.73 (182d)

Three-Year: 6.52 (91st)

Results:

1953 National League Champions

1954, second place, National League

1955 World Champions

Days in First Place: 166 of 167; the Dodgers clinched on September 8, thus breaking their own N.L. record, set back on September 12, 1953.

Longest Winning Streak: 11 games

Longest Losing Streak: 5 games

The Pennant Race: The Dodgers won their first 10 games and 22 of their first 24. By July they boasted a huge lead over the second-place Milwaukee Braves and wound up 13½ games on top.

Against the Contenders: Aside from the Dodgers, only the up-and-coming Braves (85-69) and the defending champion New York Giants (80-74) finished above .500. Brooklyn didn't mess around with either club, taking 15 of 22 from the Braves and 13 of 22 from the Giants.

Runs Scored: 857 (1st)

Runs Allowed: 650 (1st)

Brooklyn's pitching/defense doesn't look all *that* impressive, as four other clubs were within 34 runs of the Dodgers. But the Dodgers destroyed the competition with their bats, as those 857 runs were 96 more than the runner-up Reds.

Pythagorean Record: 95-58

Manager: Walter Alston

Regular Lineup:

Player	Position	ROV	OW%
Jim Gilliam	2B	.248	.456
Pee Wee Reese	SS	.268	.536
Duke Snider	CF	.351	.780
Roy Campanella	C	.328	.728
Carl Furillo	RF	.306	.668
Gil Hodges	1B	.305	.665
Jackie Robinson	3B	.276	.566
Sandy Amoros	LF	.268	.535
Don Newcombe	P		

Bench: Aside from the regulars, only three position players batted more than 100 times. Don Hoak (279 at-bats) played third base nearly as often as Jackie Robinson, who was fat and suffered aching

Stats 'n' Stuff

◆ On April 21, the Dodgers won their tenth straight game to set a major league record (later broken) for most victories to open a season.

◆ Tommy Lasorda started his first major league game on May 5 and tied a major league record with three wild pitches in the same inning.

◆ On May 10, Don Newcombe tossed a one-hitter at the Cubs, running Brooklyn's second-longest winning streak to 11 games and leaving their overall record at 22-2.

◆ Frank Kellert's home run on September 20 was Brooklyn's 200th of 1955, thus making the Dodgers the first franchise to reach the 200 mark in two different seasons (they blasted 208 in 1953).

Before the Gerbil

For a generation (two generations?) of baseball fans, Don Zimmer is a little round man who sits on the bench, chews tobacco, and talks like Boomhauer in *King of the Hill.* You know, the guy Bill Lee dubbed "The Gerbil" back in the 1970s.

In 1955, though, Don Zimmer was a baseball player, and a good one. What's more—you'd never have thunk it—Zimmer's forte was defense. At shortstop.

According to Don Drysdale, "I've seen a lot of infielders in my day, but I never saw a man with a better throwing arm than 'Popeye.' None. The man had an absolute gun." Al Campanis once called Zimmer "a Stanky with ability . . . the outstanding man in our organization."

Zimmer had a big problem, though. He kept getting hit in the head by baseballs. On July 7, 1953, Zimmer was leading the American Association with 23 home runs and 63 RBI when he had his skull fractured by a Jim Kirk fastball. Near death, Zimmer was unconscious for three weeks and in the hospital for seven. He didn't play again that season. On June 23, 1956, Zimmer had

legs. Don Zimmer split time at second with Gilliam, who typically played left field when Amoros didn't. Rube Walker backed up Campanella. Oh, and pitching ace Don Newcombe racked up 117 at-bats, thanks to a team-leading 21 pinch-hit at-bats (see article, "Newk's Big Year").

Scouting the Pitchers: Don Newcombe was all power—a fearsome fastball and a hard curve that broke so sharply umpires suspected him of throwing spitballs. Carl Erskine, who threw no-hitters in 1952 and 1956, was famous for his overhand curveball, and his fastball was good enough to keep the hitters guessing. Johnny Podres, only twenty-two years old, went just 9-10 in the regular season but showed enough to earn the starting assignment in game 7 of the World Series, in which he dazzled the Yankees with his fastball, hard curve, and occasional change-up. Top reliever Clem Labine threw sinking fastballs and curves.

How Were They Built? Like the '42 Cardinals, the '55 Dodgers were constructed by Branch Rickey, who hired on with Brooklyn shortly after resigning from St. Louis in October of 1942. Rickey was forced out by owner Walter O'Malley after the 1950 season, but of the eight non-pitching regulars on the '55 team, four—Duke Snider, Roy Campanella, Jackie Robinson, and Gil Hodges—had been signed and developed when Rickey was still running the show.

Of course, the story of the Brooklyn club's role in the integration of the game has been told, and told well, many times. Here, we'll just mention in passing that the Dodgers' willingness to sign black players gave them a huge edge over their opponents. In 1951, for example, Roy Campanella was the National League's MVP, Don Newcombe won 20 games, and Jackie Robinson was the N.L.'s best second baseman. Meanwhile, there were still some teams that didn't have *any* black players.

Shortstop Pee Wee Reese, a future Hall of Famer whose last good season was 1955, originally was property of the Boston Red Sox. But in 1939, Boston manager Joe Cronin was also the club's shortstop, and he thought he had a few years left as a player. So that July the Dodgers purchased Reese for $75,000. He took over the shortstop job in Flatbush the next summer and remained the Dodgers' regular shortstop until 1957.

Roy Campanella *(National Baseball Hall of Fame Library, Cooperstown, NY)*

What Brought Them Down? The Dodgers were old. In 1955, Campanella and Furillo were both thirty-three, and Robinson and Reese were both thirty-six. Duke Snider was only twenty-eight, but he didn't age well and had problems staying in the lineup after the Dodgers moved to Los Angeles in 1958.

Alston was able to eke out one more pennant from this geriatric crew in 1956 (they lost another World Series to the Yankees), but they finished 11 games behind Milwaukee in 1957, and *21 games* behind the Braves in '58.

When the Boys of Summer got old, there just weren't any replacements. These were the Dodgers, though, and so they made do. Although the lineup in '55 was old, the pitching staff wasn't. And in 1959, when the Dodgers returned to the top of the N.L. standings, all

his cheekbone fractured by a Hal Jeffcoat fastball, and he didn't play again that season.

Zimmer just couldn't get out of the way. Two of the National League's most intimidating pitchers, Drysdale and Sal Maglie, were themselves afraid of hurting the little infielder. Maglie once said he "hated to pitch against him. I didn't dare throw at him because I knew he'd freeze." And Drysdale wrote, "When we [the Dodgers] traded him to the Cubs for Perranoski in 1960, Popeye scared me half to death. He stood in there, right over the plate, daring you to come inside on him. He had a motto about that, too: 'If you're going to hit me, don't wound me. Get me good. I don't want to lie there quivering. I want to get it over with. Just end it.' "

Zimmer hit 15 home runs and slugged .443 for the Dodgers in 1955, but though he would hang around in the majors for another decade, Zimmer was never worth much with the stick after the Jeffcoat beaning.—*Rob*

Around the Majors

April 12 Major League Baseball comes to Kansas City, as the Athletics open their first season after moving from Philadelphia. The A's will draw 1,393,054 fans in 1955 (behind only the Giants and Yankees), but never approach that figure again before moving to Oakland in 1968.

April 14 Eight years after Jackie Robinson joined the Dodgers, Elston Howard becomes the first black New York Yankee. Casey Stengel comments famously, "Well, when they finally get me a nigger, I get the only one who can't run." (Stengel and Howard generally admired each other, in case you're wondering.)

May 28 Ted Williams opened the season on the retired list, but today he "unretires," and he will join the Red Sox two days later. He'll go on to hit .356 with a .501 on-base percentage and a .703 slugging percentage, all of which would easily

seven pitchers who started more than three games were twenty-nine or younger.

Most Valuable Dodger: One thing's for sure, the MVP voters liked the Dodgers. Roy Campanella finished first, with 226 points in the balloting. Duke Snider was right behind, with 221. (Interestingly, it appears that a clerical error may have kept Snider from tying Campanella for first place. Campanella was listed on the MVP ballots submitted by all 24 voters, but Snider was listed on only 23. However, on the ballot that did not include Snider, Campanella was listed *twice*, in both first place and sixth. Thus, it seems likely that this voter meant to list Snider sixth, or perhaps even first. Had this ballot simply been invalidated, Snider would have been the MVP. Had the BBWAA given that sixth-place slot on the ballot to Snider, he and Campanella would have been tied with 226 points each. Instead, the BBWAA altered the ballot by simply eliminating the sixth slot and moving everybody up one.)

Which was truly more valuable? Well, Snider's batting stats were superior to Campanella's, though not by a lot. Snider played 148 games, Campanella 123. Campanella was considered a great defensive catcher, whereas Snider was perhaps the third-best defensive center fielder in the league, after Willie Mays and Richie Ashburn. Snider gets the edge in our book, primarily because he played 25 more games, and also because catchers in the 1950s didn't really have to worry about baserunners.

Worst Regular: Amoros was just okay and played only against right-handed pitchers.

Hall of Famers: Roy Campanella, Jackie Robinson, Pee Wee Reese, Duke Snider, and Sandy Koufax. Snider was a great player, though perhaps not as great as people remember, and he was clearly not as valuable as his New York counterparts, Mays and Mantle. Robinson was also a great player, *greater* than people remember, or at least for different reasons than people remember. For more on Robinson, see separate article, "Jackie's Greatness." Reese is in the middle of the pack when you're talking about Hall of Fame shortstops. He was better than Joe Tinker and Phil Rizzuto and Luis Aparicio, not as good as Arky Vaughan and Honus Wagner and Luke Appling. Manager Walter Alston is in the Hall, too.

Our Hall of Famers: We don't have any arguments with the afore-mentioned five. A lot of people want to put Gil Hodges in the Hall, but he really doesn't belong unless you give him a fair amount of extra credit for managing the '69 Mets. For more on Hodges, see article, "Saint Gilbert."

The 1955 World Series: After losing five previous World Series to the Yankees, the Dodgers finally beat them in a thrilling seven-game affair. For more, see article, "Amoros and Gilliam."

The Ballpark: Cozy Ebbets Field was a wonderful place for power hitters, especially lefty power hitters, because it was only 297 feet down the right-field line. But it wasn't a bad place for righty hitters, either, as the distance to both power alleys was only about 350 feet.

Books about the 1955 Dodgers: Gee, where do you want to start? It's possible that no single team has been written about more than the early 1950s Brooklyn Dodgers. The two best books specifically about the Dodgers are Roger Kahn's classic, *The Boys of Summer* (New York: Harper & Row, 1972), and Peter Golenbock's *Bums* (New York: G. P. Putnam's Sons, 1984). Jackie Robinson has been an enormously popular subject in recent years, and the best of these books are probably David Falkner's *Great Time Coming* (New York: Simon and Schuster, 1995), and Arnold Rampersad's comprehensive *Jackie Robinson: A Biography* (New York: Alfred A. Knopf, 1997).

Amoros and Gilliam

The 1955 World Series was the Dodgers' eighth, and they'd lost their first seven. From 1947 through 1953, the Dodgers and the New York Yankees met in four World Series and, of course, the Yankees won all of them. They took '54 off, and then went at each other again in 1955 (and '56, too).

By 1955, then, Dodger fans were feeling cursed. As fan Bill Reddy told Peter Golenbock, "The frustration was overwhelming. It gave you a feeling that God and everybody was against you. What the hell. What could you do? Wait for the next year? But next year never

have led the American League had Williams played enough to qualify.

July 19 Tigers reliever Babe Birrer tosses four innings and hits a pair of three-run homers. The same day, Pirates starter Vern Law pitches eighteen innings to beat Milwaukee, 4–3.

Why Not '53?

Almost everyone thinks that the best of the "Boys of Summer" teams was the 1953 club. They had a great record (105-49), gaudy offensive numbers (955 runs scored, 187 more than the next-best teams), and the fact that they still lost the World Series to the Yankees is just part of the folklore. In some quarters, the Dodgers are more lovable *because* they were losers.

So why did we pick 1955? The two biggest reasons were the SD scores and the World Series. Believe it or not, the 1955 Dodgers had a better SD score, 3.03 versus 2.80 for the 1953 team. This is not a book about the greatest hitting teams of all time but about the greatest *teams* of all time. The 1955 Dodgers scored the most runs in the league, just like the '53 team, but the '55 team also *allowed* the fewest runs in the league, despite playing half their games in Ebbets Field. The 1953 Dodgers were third in the league in runs allowed.

The 1955 Dodgers were also a potent offensive team, leading the majors in runs scored, home runs, on-base percentage, slugging percentage, and batting average. When you add the SD score advantage—the 1955 club ranks 33d in this century; the 1953 team is not in the top 50—to the fact that the '55 Dodgers won the World Series, the choice seems fairly clear.

A few other points in favor of 1955. If one excludes games against the hapless Pirates, last-place finishers in 1953 and 1955, the records of the two teams are virtually identical (1955, 84-47; 1953, 85-47). How much credit should be given for beating up more on a bad

seemed to come." "Next year" came in '55, though. And the 1955 World Series is one of those that will forever be remembered for one particular moment. Before we get to that particular moment, however, let's set the scene.

The Yankees took game 1, 6–5, but it was Jackie Robinson who stole the show. With two outs in the eighth inning and Whitey Ford on the mound, Robinson attempted to steal home. You've seen it on TV. Robinson slides into home, where Yogi's waiting with the ball. The umpire (Bill Summers) gives Jackie the, umm, benefit of the doubt, and Yogi jumps up and down, bellowing all the while but to no avail.

The Yankees won game 2, 4–2, and it looked like the same, sad story for the Dodgers and their fans. The Series shifted to Ebbets Field for game 3, though, and the Dodgers started doing what they'd done all year—score runs, and lots of them. Brooklyn won the next three games in the Series, outscoring the Yankees 21–11 in the process.

Back in the Bronx for game 6, the Yanks avoided elimination with a 5–1 victory. New York scored all five of their runs in the first inning, and Whitey Ford cruised with a complete-game four-hitter.

Leading 1–0 after five innings of game 7, the Dodgers added another run in the sixth on Gil Hodges' sac fly. With two outs and the bases loaded, Walt Alston sent George Shuba up to pinch-hit for second baseman Don Zimmer. Shuba grounded out, ending the threat, and Alston needed a new second baseman. He summoned Jim Gilliam in from left field and sent Sandy Amoros out to left field. It was the same move he'd been making all season.

Billy Martin led off the bottom of the sixth with a walk, and Gil McDougald followed with a bunt single. That brought up Yogi Berra, who sliced a drive down the left-field line. Amoros sprinted over, snagged the ball to retire Berra, and fired the ball to shortstop Pee Wee Reese, who easily doubled up McDougald by tossing to Gil Hodges at first. Hank Bauer then grounded out to Reese, and the Yankee threat was over. New York collected a pair of singles in the eighth, but Dodger starter Johnny Podres wriggled out of that mess, too. And in the bottom of the ninth, with the Dodgers still leading 2–0, Elston Howard grounded out to Reese, ending the game and the Series.

The Dodgers were finally World Champs. And if you read about the 1955 World Series, you'd think they never could have done it without Walter Alston and Sandy Amoros. Here's how various writers have described that fateful play:

> From the Yankee point of view the play was full of irony, as Gilliam, a right-handed thrower, would probably not have been able to make the catch.
> —Lee Allen, *The World Series*

> Amoros . . . set his eye on the ball and set his heart on having it. Moving like a hungry hound, he sped toward the foul line and reached there just in time to seize the ball before it hit the grass.
> —Robert Smith, *World Series: The Games and the Players*

> Amoros was playing well in left-center for Yogi, and had to come a long way even to get near the ball. Running full tilt right at the stands, he made a last moment lunge and clutched the ball with extended gloved hand just a few inches in fair territory. It generally was conceded that Gilliam, righthander, could not have made this catch with his gloved left hand.
> —Fred Lieb, *Official Baseball Guide and Record Book* (1956)

> Had Junior Gilliam still been in left, the Dodgers would have lost the game and the Series, for even with Gilliam's good speed, he would not have caught Berra's ball. Gilliam, moreover, was right-handed, which would have made the catch very difficult. Of all the moves Alston ever made, this one must have been blessed, because he needed a man with special attributes to make the catch. And Sandy Amoros was there.
> —Peter Golenbock, *Bums*

Well, I'm not so sure about all this. First of all, if there's any evidence that Amoros was faster than Gilliam, I haven't seen it yet. In Amoros' first three seasons, he totaled 200 singles and walks, and stole 12 bases. In Gilliam's first season, he totaled 214 singles and walks, and stole 21 bases.

Also in his first season, Gilliam led the National League with 17 triples.

Make no mistake, Amoros could run. In 1956, he tripled eight

team? In addition, the Pirates were almost certainly worse in 1953 than in 1955.

The Dodgers got out of the gate very quickly in '55, winning 22 of their first 24 games and holding a 13-game lead at the end of June. If they wound up coasting a little bit with that huge lead, they certainly wouldn't have been the first (or last) team to do so. The '55 team clinched the pennant earlier than the '53 team and spent more days in first place. Given all of the relevant considerations, our choice of 1955 instead of 1953 seems perfectly logical and consistent with the bulk of the evidence.—*Eddie* times in 292 at-bats, which is an impressive ratio. But I'm fairly certain that if Amoros and Gilliam faced off in a 40-yard dash, there wouldn't be more than a snake's eyelash of difference between the two of them, and Gilliam would break the tape first. Of course, speed's not everything in the outfield. There's positioning, and getting a good jump on the ball, and so on. The important thing is how many plays you make.

Which brings me to my second point: based on how many plays Amoros and Gilliam actually *did make* in 1955, there's no reason to think Amoros had better range. Thanks to the late Allan Roth and our friends at Retrosheet, we've got complete play-by-play data for the Dodgers in the '50s. Here are Amoros' and Gilliam's stats in left field for 1955 only:

1955	Games	Innings	Putouts	PO/9
Amoros	102	856	188	1.98
Gilliam	40	304	80	2.37

Does it look to you as though Amoros was a better outfielder than Gilliam? Amoros made 1.98 plays per nine innings. Gilliam made 2.37 plays per nine innings, or roughly 20 percent more. Ah, but the sample size is a tad small, isn't it? Well, in 1956 Amoros and Gilliam were used in essentially the same way, with Gilliam in the lineup every day, and Amoros in left field when Gilliam played second base. Below are their stats in left field for 1955 and 1956 combined:

1955–56	Games	Innings	Putouts	PO/9
Amoros	182	1,523	301	1.78
Gilliam	93	716	177	2.22

Wow. Apparently the 1955 stats were no fluke, as Gilliam was even better over the two-year period. All this leads me to believe that Gilliam possessed significantly better range than Amoros, which would likely have compensated for the difference in their "handedness."

And finally, if you actually watch the play in question (and I've seen it many, many times) you'll see that Amoros' catch doesn't approach "miraculous." It was a fine running catch, but he didn't have to dive or pluck the ball off his shoetops. He caught it in full stride, just a tad below waist level.

Conclusions? Shifting Gilliam to second base and replacing him with Amoros wasn't a particularly brilliant move. It was the natural thing to do, and Alston had been doing it all season. And even if Gilliam had still been in left field when Yogi hit that slicing liner, the ball probably would have been caught, and the Dodgers probably still would have won the World Series.—Rob

Saint Gilbert

Few things elicit more sentiment than a good or great baseball player who left the earth a little early. Ross Youngs is in the Hall of Fame because he died when he was thirty. Some people will swear up and down that Roberto Clemente was a better player than Henry Aaron and Frank Robinson. And then there's Gil Hodges, who suffered a fatal heart attack in 1972, two days before his forty-eighth birthday.

There's no better way to make a fifty-year-old baseball fan teary-eyed than to start talking about the erstwhile Dodger first baseman. And there's no better way to make a fifty-year-old baseball fan angry than to argue that Hodges does not belong in the Hall of Fame. Nevertheless, let me give you some stats for two sluggers, roughly contemporary:

	Hits	HR	RBI	OBP	Slug	MVP
Player A	1,921	370	1,274	.361	.487	0
Player B	1,730	374	1,159	.362	.489	0

Player A is Gil Hodges. Player B is Rocky Colavito. Colavito is almost never discussed as a Hall of Fame candidate. When he first became eligible for the Hall, in 1974, he drew two votes. In 1975, that dropped to one vote and Colavito dropped off the ballot. Statistically, though, there's not much difference between Colavito and Hodges, with Hodges holding about a season's edge in both hits and RBI. Their career OPSs, as you can see, are virtually identical, as are their home runs.

Hodges was an excellent defensive first baseman and won the first three Gold Gloves awarded for the position. Colavito never won a

Gold Glove in right field, but his throwing arm was feared around the American League, and he set a league record for consecutive errorless games.

Hodges was named to eight All-Star teams. Colavito was named to six All-Star teams.

Hodges knocked in 100-plus runs seven times and scored 100-plus runs three times. Colavito knocked in 100-plus runs six times and scored 100-plus runs once.

Of course, Colavito spent most of his career in Cleveland and Detroit, mostly with mediocre teams, and he never played in the postseason. Hodges, as you know, was a key performer for the 1950s Brooklyn Dodgers teams that have been immortalized as "The Boys of Summer." All right, so let's say Hodges gets extra credit for playing with good teams, and let's say he was a slightly more productive hitter. Then what about Boog Powell?

Player	Hits	HR	RBI	OBP	Slug	Postseasons
Powell	1776	339	1187	.364	.462	6
Hodges	1921	370	1274	.361	.487	6

Both Powell and Hodges were regulars or semi-regulars with six postseason teams. Both were first basemen. Hodges was a better first baseman, certainly, but Powell had soft hands and was fairly mobile until late in his career. Although Hodges' batting stats look slightly more impressive, you have to remember (1) that Powell was active in the late 1960s, a great era for pitchers, and (2) the ballparks.

Hodges spent a decade playing his home games in Ebbets Field, a great place for right-handed power hitters. In 1951, Hodges led the National League with 24 road home runs (along with 16 at home). In each of his other seasons in Brooklyn, he hit more homers at home than on the road. In fact, of his 370 career home runs, only 160 came on the road. Let's look at home-run breakdowns for the three players we've been discussing:

	Total HR	Home HR	Road HR
Hodges	370	210	160
Colavito	374	193	181
Powell	339	150	189

In case you're wondering, Colavito finished third, fourth, and fifth in various MVP balloting. Powell won the MVP in 1970 and also finished second and third in other years.

Hodges, on the other hand, never particularly impressed contemporary observers. In 1949, he finished 11th in the MVP vote, behind Dodger teammates Jackie Robinson, Pee Wee Reese, Carl Furillo, and Don Newcombe. In 1950, Hodges finished eighth in the MVP vote, tops among Dodgers. In 1951, he finished 16th, behind Roy Campanella, Preacher Roe, Robinson, and Reese. In 1952, he finished 19th, behind Joe Black, Robinson, Reese, Snider, and Campanella. In 1953, he finished 14th, behind Campanella, Snider, Carl Erskine, Furillo, Reese, and Robinson. In 1954, Hodges finished 10th, behind Snider and Reese.

In 1955, as we've already seen, Campanella won the MVP. Snider, Newcombe, Reese, Clem Labine, and Furillo all garnered votes. Hodges didn't appear on the ballot of even one voter. In 1956, the Dodgers won again. This time Brooklyn ace Don Newcombe was named MVP. Seven other Dodgers were listed on MVP ballots. For the second straight season, Hodges wasn't among them. The Dodgers won another pennant in 1959, though by then they were in Los Angeles. That was Hodges' last good season, and he finished 18th in the MVP voting, behind teammates Wally Moon, Charlie Neal, and Roger Craig.

That's a pretty amazing thing, for a supposed Hall of Famer never to have finished higher than eighth in the MVP voting. By my count, 44 Hall of Fame non-pitchers were regulars for at least one season after World War II. Of those 44, 24 won at least one MVP award, leaving 20 who did *not* win an MVP. Of those 20, 12 finished as high as second in the voting, leaving eight who didn't finish first or second. Of those eight, three finished as high as third in the voting, leaving five who didn't finish first, second, or third. Of those five, three finished as high as fourth in the voting, leaving two who didn't finish first, second, third, or fourth. Those two players were the aforementioned Pee Wee Reese and Phillies center fielder Richie Ashburn. Reese finished fifth once, sixth twice, and eighth three times. In other words, he matched or exceeded Hodges' best finish in the MVP voting six times. Ashburn's best finish in the voting was seventh, and he did it twice. So you've got 44 Hall of Famers, and *every one of them* was considered more valuable in his best season than Hodges was in *his* best season.

The "Boys of Summer" Brooklyn Dodgers were a wonderful team, and Gil Hodges was a fine player. But he was generally only the sixth-best player on the club, behind Robinson, Campanella, Snider, Reese, and Newcombe. Yes, those players all provided stiff MVP competition, but remember too that players for pennant-winning teams typically get a boost. Hodges never led his league in an official statistical category, and there's absolutely no reason to think he'd have done better in the MVP voting had he been with the Pirates or the Phillies.

The evidence is quite clear. When he was actually playing the game, observers did *not* consider Hodges a great player, a Hall of Fame–caliber player. So if you put Hodges in, what do you say to Rocky Colavito and Boog Powell, not to mention Lee May and Dwight Evans and Jim Rice and Roy Sievers and Frank Howard?

Wait, I think I'm forgetting something. . . . Ah yes, the 1969 Mets. Look, managing the Mets to a World Championship was a remarkable accomplishment, and I suspect that many of those who support Hodges as a Hall of Fame candidate are combining his playing career and his managing career, since you can't really justify his enshrinement based purely on one or the other.

Joe Torre's in almost exactly the same boat. Both men were great players for a few years, but not really great enough for long enough to get in the Hall. Both initially struggled as managers, but eventually led New York teams to championships. I'm not going to run any more stats, but I'll tell you that Torre's career numbers compare well to those of Hodges.

Granted, there is a rule that might justify the election of Hodges. According to Veterans Committee Rule 6(C), "Those whose careers involved stints as both players and managers/executives/umpires may be considered for their overall contributions to the game; however, the specific category in which such individuals fall for purposes of election shall be determined by the role in which they were most prominent." This rule certainly might explain the elections of players like Hughie Jennings and Red Schoendienst. However, that last clause is scary, because when you start putting in guys for their dual contributions but count them as players, you lower the standards for the players who are still out. What's more, there are many players in the same boat, including current figures of the game like Dusty Baker and, of course, Torre. They can't all go in, and they shouldn't.—Rob

Newk's Big Year

In 1955, Don Newcombe was the best pitcher in the National League, with his only competition being Philadelphia's Robin Roberts:

Player	ERA	W-L	Win%	Innings	CG	K	BB
Newcombe	3.20	20-5	.800	234	17	143	38
Roberts	3.28	23-14	.622	305	26	160	53

Well, maybe not. It all depends on how much stock you put in winning percentage. Either of them would have been worthy Cy Young winners had the award existed. (Newcombe did win the first Cy Young, one year later.)

The season wasn't without its rough spots, though. On May 5, Newcombe refused to pitch batting practice, and eventually Alston ordered him to remove his uniform and consider himself indefinitely suspended. The next day, he apologized and offered to bear any burden. Accordingly, that night in Philadelphia, he earned a victory with two innings of hitless relief. And four days later, Newcombe tossed a one-hit shutout in Chicago, running the Dodgers' winning streak to 11 games.

Anyway, this article isn't about Newcombe's pitching, wondrous though it was. It's about his hitting. In 1955, Newcombe posted some of the greatest hitting stats ever by a pitcher. In 117 at-bats, he batted .359 with nine doubles, seven home runs, and 23 RBI. Those nine doubles and seven homers, plus a triple, gave Newk a .632 slugging percentage. That triple, by the way, came on May 26 against Pittsburgh, and Newcombe followed up by stealing home. It was the only time in the 1950s that a National League pitcher swiped home plate. All of which got us to wondering, where does Newcombe's 1955 season rank on the all-time list of best-hitting pitchers? After a fairly exhaustive search, including all the pitchers who batted at least 75 times in a season, we came up with the following:

Player	Year	AB	Avg	HR	RBI	OBP	SLG
Wes Ferrell	1935	150	.347	7	32	.427	.533
Don Newcombe	1955	117	.359	7	23	.395	.632
Wes Ferrell	1931	116	.319	9	30	.373	.621

More Than a Pioneer

I had seen Robinson in a couple of the Montreal exhibition games, and that was all it took to convince me that I wanted him. He was still playing second base with Montreal . . . and you could see how he could move in the field and could run the bases. But most of all, you could see he was a really good hitter.

—Leo Durocher in *Nice Guys Finish Last*

Jackie Robinson certainly doesn't suffer from any lack of fame. Robinson is the only player to have his number retired by every major league team, and one could argue that Robinson trails only Ruth when it comes to name recognition among the general populace. Of course, Robinson owes the great majority of his fame to his status as the first black major leaguer of the twentieth century. He was a pioneer. That story has been told in many books. Your library probably has a shelf full of those books, and I can heartily recommend at least three of them.

What sometimes gets forgotten, unfortunately, is that Robinson was a great *player*. He finished his career with a .311 batting average, he had a great batting eye, and he reached double figures in home runs in nine of his ten seasons. That's a powerful combination, and one can reasonably argue that Robinson was the best player on a great team— Robinson or Roy Campanella. But while Campanella mixed in some mediocre seasons with his great ones, Jackie never really had an off year.

In 1998, The Sporting News selected "Baseball's 100 Greatest Players." They got a lot of stuff wrong, but they got some stuff right, too. They ranked Jackie Robinson No. 44 on the all-time list, and he just might have been that good. Pioneer or no pioneer.—*Rob*

Player	Year	AB	Avg	HR	RBI	OBP	SLG
Walter Johnson	1925	97	.433	2	20	.455	.577
Line Drive Nelson	1937	113	.354	4	29	.387	.549
Red Ruffing	1930	110	.364	4	22	.402	.582
Babe Ruth	1915	92	.315	4	21	.376	.576
Bob Lemon	1949	108	.269	7	19	.331	.556
Jack Bentley	1923	89	.427	1	14	.446	.573
Schoolboy Rowe	1935	109	.312	3	28	.380	.459

Those of you with even one eagle eye probably noticed something about this list—it's almost all guys who pitched (and hit!) in the 1920s and 1930s, the chief exceptions being Newcombe and Bob Lemon. We didn't make any sort of meaningful adjustments for historical context because, well, it's not worth the trouble.

Ferrell was the best hitting pitcher in the history of the game, and Red Ruffing was fantastic. Johnson's .433 season, at the age of thirty-seven, was completely out of context with the rest of his career. Lynn Nelson was called "Line Drive" not because he hit a lot of line drives, but because he allowed a lot of them, which is why he didn't last long in the majors. Ruth you know about. Lemon was an excellent hitter and a Hall of Fame pitcher to boot. Rowe was a good hitting pitcher for a long time.

Jack Bentley was a brilliant double threat in the minor leagues; in 1921 with Baltimore, he played first base and pitched, batting .412 with a 12-1 record on the mound. Though Bentley was clearly talented enough to hit major league pitching, he was limited to pitching and pinch-hitting on joining the New York Giants in 1923 because the Giants had future Hall of Famer George Kelly at first base.

Newcombe's season is the most recent on the list, which makes it all the more impressive.—Rob

Karl and Sandy

Karl Spooner's 1955 pitching line isn't too shabby: 29 games, 14 of them starts, with an 8-6 record and a 3.65 ERA. Yet for Dodger fans, those numbers were a huge disappointment.

In 1954, twenty-three-year-old Karl Benjamin Spooner won 21 games for Fort Worth and topped the Texas League with 262 strikeouts in 238 innings. He was a modest six feet tall and 185 pounds, but he had great stuff. As Dodgers relief pitcher Clem Labine later told Peter Golenbock, "That man had a fastball that was unbelievable, not for sheer speed, but for how much the ball moved."

Brooklyn called up Spooner in September, and he proceeded to make one of the most auspicious debuts in the history of the game. In his first start, he beat New York 3–0, striking out fifteen Giants in the process. In his second start, he beat Pittsburgh 1–0, striking out twelve Pirates. Two games, two complete-game shutouts, 27 strikeouts. Oh, and five hits allowed. It's unlikely that any rookie pitcher ever did better in his first two starts, and those 27 Ks in consecutive games were an N.L. record (since broken) for *any* pitcher in two straight games, rookie or not. Needless to say, Dodger fans were more than a little excited to see what Spooner would do in 1955. That March, in spring training, Spooner went in to pitch against the White Sox. As he told Peter Golenbock,

> I threw a real good curveball to Jim Rivera, struck him out, and I felt a kind of a pull in my shoulder, but it didn't hurt that much, and so I finished the inning and the next inning. After I took a shower and was dressing, jiminy crickets, it started hurting real bad, and I could hardly even put my damn shirt on. And that's when I told the trainer. He rubbed me down real good, put some diathermy on me. Of course, back then they didn't know near what they know today about arms.

They didn't, indeed. Though Spooner pitched decently in 1955, his arm was never the same. He went back to the minors in 1956, had an operation in 1957, pitched a little more minor league ball in 1958, and that was it.

As if Spooner weren't enough, the '55 Dodgers roster also included Sandy Koufax, which means that the Dodgers just might have possessed the most impressive collection of left-handed pitching specimens in the history of the game. Koufax was a bonus baby, so even though he was only nineteen years old, the Dodgers weren't allowed to send him to one of their farm clubs. Koufax rarely pitched, but with Brooklyn boasting a 10-game lead on August 27, Sandy made his second start, against Cincinnati. He threw a two-hit shutout and struck out fourteen Reds. A week later he started again, and shut out the Pirates on five hits.

Amazingly enough, Koufax would not record another shutout until 1959. From 1956 through 1960, he won 34 games, lost 38, and posted a 4.17 ERA. But in 1962 the Dodgers moved into Dodger Stadium, a year later Major League Baseball expanded the strike zone, and (not coincidentally) Sandy Koufax became *Sandy Koufax*.—Rob

The Boys of OBP

The "Boys of Summer" Dodgers team has been romanticized almost to no end. The great camaraderie, the teamwork, the playing smarts have all been cited as main reasons for the team's success. The power of Campanella, Hodges, and Snider; the baserunning of Robinson; the defensive play of Reese, Furillo, and Gilliam are given some credit, but the Dodgers are often depicted as a group that won as much with will as with skill.

I never played pro ball, so maybe I'm missing some respect for chemistry, for the ability of some teams to get more out of less through hard work and determination. I'll tell you what, though, most teams that win consistently have consistently good numbers in more than one area of the game. Performance in baseball is largely, though not completely, *measurable.*

The one thing that this Dodgers team did better than almost any other in baseball history was *get on base.* In the eleven seasons starting in 1946 (the Dodgers' loss to the Cardinals in a best-of-three pennant playoff) and ending with the Dodgers last pennant in Brooklyn in 1956, they led the league in on-base percentage *nine times.* True, some of that was attributable to Ebbets Field, a good hitter's park, but most of it was the good Dodger hitters. Besides, much of Ebbets Field's impact on scoring came via the long ball and not via higher batting/on-base averages. From 1946 through 1956, overall run production at Ebbets Field was inflated less than home runs in eight of those eleven seasons.

The Dodger club that showed this skill to the fullest was the 1955 entry. Their .365 on-base percentage was 11.3 percent better than the

.328 league average. Only six teams in the century exceeded their league average by a greater margin. Six of the eight Dodger regulars posted OBPs over .370, and the worst OBP among the group was Jim Gilliam's respectable .341 mark. Seven of the eight regulars, Gil Hodges being the exception, walked at least as often as they struck out. Among the other 56 National League regulars in 1955, only 21 had at least as many walks as strikeouts.

As we've noted elsewhere in this chapter, though Branch Rickey hadn't worked for the Brooklyn organization in some years, his players and his philosophies still served the Dodgers well. Rickey once wrote, "The greatest single difference between a major-league and a minor-league batsman is the difference in his judgment of the strike zone. The major leaguer knows better the difference between a ball and a strike. He knows better whether to swing or take a pitch." You can talk about guts, determination, teamwork, and so on, but when a team's OBP is so much better than the league average, that team is almost certainly going to win some games. Since 1901, teams that have led their league in on-base percentage have a collective .581 winning percentage. Eighty-eight percent of them had winning records, 43 percent finished first in their league or division, and 19 percent won 100 or more games. On-base percentage correlates better with winning than any other percentage or rate statistic, *including ERA.* Whether they knew that or not, the Boys of Summer *played* like they knew. Call them "The Boys of OBP."—Eddie

TEAM STATISTICS

Hitting

	Games by Position	Age	G	AB	R	H	2B	3B	HR	RBI	BB	SO	SB	Avg	OBP	Slug
Roy Campanella	C,121	33	123	446	81	142	20	1	32	107	56	41	2	.318	.395	.583
Gil Hodges	1B,139; OF,16	31	150	546	75	158	24	5	27	102	80	91	2	.289	.377	.500
Jim Gilliam	2B,99; OF,46	26	147	538	110	134	20	8	7	40	70	37	15	.249	.341	.355
Jackie Robinson	3B,84; OF,10; 1B,1; 2B,1	36	105	317	51	81	6	2	8	36	61	18	12	.256	.378	.363
Pee Wee Reese	SS,142	36	145	553	99	156	29	4	10	61	78	60	8	.282	.371	.403
Duke Snider	OF,146	28	148	538	126	166	34	6	42	136	104	87	9	.309	.418	.628
Carl Furillo	OF,140	33	140	523	83	164	24	3	26	95	43	43	4	.314	.371	.520
Sandy Amoros	OF,109	25	119	388	59	96	16	7	10	51	55	45	10	.247	.347	.402
Don Zimmer	2B,62; SS, 21; 3B,8	24	88	280	38	67	10	1	15	50	19	66	5	.239	.289	.443
Don Hoak	3B,78	27	94	279	50	67	13	3	5	19	46	50	9	.240	.350	.362
Rube Walker	C,35	29	48	103	6	26	5	0	2	13	15	11	1	.252	.342	.359
Frank Kellert	1B,22	30	39	80	12	26	4	2	4	19	9	10	0	.325	.385	.575
George Shuba	OF,9	30	44	51	8	14	2	0	1	8	11	10	0	.275	.422	.373
Dixie Howell	C,13	35	16	42	2	11	4	0	0	5	1	7	0	.262	.273	.357
Walt Moryn	OF,7	29	11	19	3	5	1	0	1	3	5	4	0	.263	.417	.474
Bob Borkowski*	OF,9	29	9	19	2	2	0	0	0	0	1	6	0	.105	.150	.105
Bert Hamric		27	2	1	0	0	0	0	0	0	0	1	0	.000	.000	.000
Totals		30	154	5,193	857	1,406	230	44	201	800	674	718	79	.271	.365	.448

*Played for another team during season. Statistics are those compiled with 1955 Brooklyn Dodgers only.

Pitching

	Threw	Age	Games	GS	CG	ShO	IP	H	HR	BB	SO	W	L	Pct	Sv	ERA
Don Newcombe	Right	29	34	31	17	1	234	222	35	38	143	20	5	**.800**	0	3.20
Carl Erskine	Right	28	31	29	7	2	195	185	29	64	84	11	8	.579	1	3.79
Johnny Podres	Left	22	27	24	5	2	159	160	15	57	114	9	10	.474	0	3.95
Billy Loes	Right	25	22	19	6	0	128	116	16	46	85	10	4	.714	0	3.59
Karl Spooner	Left	24	29	14	2	1	99	79	8	41	78	8	6	.571	2	3.65
Clem Labine	Right	28	**60**	8	1	0	144	121	12	55	67	13	5	.722	11	3.24
Russ Meyer	Right	31	18	11	2	1	73	86	8	31	26	6	2	.750	0	5.42
Roger Craig	Right	25	21	10	3	0	91	81	8	43	48	5	3	.625	2	2.78
Ed Roebuck	Right	23	27	0	0	0	84	96	14	24	33	5	6	.455	12	4.71
Don Bessent	Right	24	24	2	1	0	63	51	7	21	29	8	1	.888	3	2.70
Jim Hughes	Right	32	24	0	0	0	43	41	10	19	20	0	2	.000	6	4.22
Sandy Koufax	Left	19	12	5	2	2	42	33	2	28	30	2	2	.500	0	3.02
Joe Black*	Right	31	6	0	0	0	15	15	1	5	9	1	0	1.000	0	2.93
Chuck Templeton	Left	23	4	0	0	0	5	5	2	5	3	0	1	.000	0	11.57
Tom Lasorda	Left	27	4	1	0	0	4	5	1	6	4	0	0	—	0	13.50
Totals		26	154	154	46	11	1,378	1,296	168	483	**773**	**98**	**55**	**.641**	**37**	**3.68**

*Played for another team during season. Statistics are those compiled with 1955 Brooklyn Dodgers only.

CHAPTER 12

There Were Others

THE GREATEST BLACK TEAMS

In all the books about the greatest teams, you'll find not a single mention of Josh Gibson. Or Cool Papa Bell or Satchel Paige or any of the other players elected to the Hall of Fame based on their service in baseball's Negro Leagues. In a way, that's quite understandable because Negro League teams played irregular schedules and kept reliable records only sporadically.

Still, it somehow doesn't seem right to ignore those teams completely. In his book *Baseball Between the Lies*, Bob Carroll has a chapter titled "The Most Overrated Teams Ever." Tops on Carroll's list? None other than the 1927 New York Yankees. His reasons for ranking the '27 Yanks "first" include (1) a lineup with some holes that didn't score as many runs as people think, and (2) a pitching staff that was some-

thing less than immortal. But Carroll saves the heavy ammunition for last:

[T]here's another reason I'm leery of hanging "The Greatest" tag on the '27 team. Or even the '36 club. How can a team be the greatest ever when it never had to face a significant number of the best players in America? . . . In my book there can't be a pre-Jackie Robinson "best ever." Anything monochrome is overrated.

Well, maybe. But for the purposes of this book, we're ignoring the chromality of the teams in question. Why? Because what we want to know is which teams, given the conditions that existed *at that time*, were the best. Still, Carroll's admonition got us to thinking, which *was* the best Negro League team? Before we go any further, though, a bit of background is probably in order (but if you already know this stuff, feel free to skip the next few paragraphs).

Most people think that Jackie Robinson was the first African American to play in the major leagues, but that's not precisely true. In 1884, catcher Moses Fleetwood Walker and his brother Welday played with Toledo in the American Association, which then was a major league. They were the last known blacks in the major leagues until Robinson, sixty-three years later, but for a few years after that, blacks did play in the minors.

However, integrated professional teams quickly became impractical, so next came all-black minor league teams. From 1889 through 1891, the famed New York Cuban Giants competed in three different minor leagues and twice finished second to Harrisburg, Pennsylvania, another all-black team. The last all-black team in the minors was the 1898 New York Celeron club of the Iron & Oil League. They went 8-42 and finished in the basement. The following season, an African American named Bill Galloway played in the minors. After Galloway, no known black would play in so-called Organized Baseball until 1946, when Jackie Robinson debuted with the Montreal Royals.

Most of the all-black teams in the nineteenth century performed as independents, taking on all comers and making what money they could and, by the twentieth century, that's what all of them were doing. Most of the best clubs were along the Atlantic coast, but there were some good teams in the Midwest, too. Some of those pre-1920 teams were undoubtedly talented, but we have almost no way to compare them to each other because there weren't any leagues and there weren't any records kept.

In 1920, however, ex-player and impresario Rube Foster, owner of the (Chicago) American Giants, organized the Negro National League, comprising his Giants and seven other top clubs. And in 1923, the six-team Eastern Colored League came together. The E.C.L. survived into the spring of 1928, whereas the N.N.L. lasted through 1931. A new Negro National League opened play in 1932, mostly with eastern teams. And in 1937, the Negro American League was organized. Both of them essentially fell apart as competitive entities by the early 1950s, though the Negro American League did struggle along until 1960.

So when people talk about the Negro Leagues, it's these leagues that they're referring to, but it's worth understanding that a single entity called the Negro Leagues never existed (and thus, it's actually a little silly to capitalize the N and the L). Therefore, when selecting the greatest all–African American teams, we're essentially restricted to the thirty-odd years between the formation of the Negro National League and the beginnings of integration in Major League Baseball. It's only for those three decades that we've got league standings and (often incomplete) statistics that allow us to compare teams to each other.

Given that (1) we're drawing our fifteen top Major League Baseball teams from about ninety-five seasons (1902–99), and (2) there were only about thirty Negro League seasons (1920–50), in terms of proportionality it makes sense to pick the top five Negro League teams. So that's what we'll do.

Now for the comparisons. It's easy to have opinions about the Negro Leagues, but not so easy to back them up with facts. However, elsewhere in this book we're trying to use the facts at hand, and consistency being the hobgoblin of our little minds, let's be consistent here. Aside from opinions, then, what do we have to go on? I've come up with four indicators that might be at least a little helpful:

1. Regular-season winning percentage
2. All-Stars
3. Hall of Famers on roster
4. Negro World Series results

Each of these has its own problems. To wit:

1. Regular-season winning percentage isn't derived from large samples of games. When it comes down to it, the 154 or 162 games we usually look at for American and National League teams isn't even a great sample. So what do you do with the 1923 Hilldale Giants, who played 49 Eastern Colored League games? Or the 1939 Kansas City Monarchs, who played just 24 contests against Negro American League opponents? This, perhaps, almost necessitates looking at more than one season for the teams in question.
2. All-Stars were selected only from 1933 through 1950. What's more, they were chosen through ballots printed in the *Chicago De-*

fender and the *Pittsburgh Courier*. Not exactly the most scientific of methods.

3. It's instructive to look at Hall of Famers, but again we're talking about a small sample size. Only sixteen players have been elected as representatives of the Negro Leagues. We can expand the pool of players by including Negro Leaguers who were elected for their service in Major League Baseball. Henry Aaron, Ernie Banks, and Larry Doby, for example, all played for pennant-winning teams in the Negro Leagues. But this pool is heavily biased in favor of players in the '30s and '40s. By the time the Hall got around to honoring Negro Leaguers, there simply weren't many people around who could still remember the players of the 1920s. And given the dearth of meaningful statistics from those days, remembrances are about all you've got to go on.

   Another problem with Hall of Famers is that just because they were on the roster doesn't mean they were always around. Satchel Paige, for one, would quite often jump his teams in the middle of the season, or at least take off for a few days in favor of a big barnstorming paycheck.

4. The Negro League World Series, aside from the obvious problem with the sample size—best-of-seven or best-of-nine series—was played only seven times, 1924 through 1927 (Negro National League versus Eastern Colored League) and then 1944 through 1946 (Negro National League versus Negro American League).

I'm not suggesting that all this data will result in some Grand Unified Formula telling us which team was the greatest, but at least it's a start. I entered all the data into a spreadsheet, and then I . . . well, I eyeballed it. Yes, I know it's not very scientific. Okay, it's not scientific at all. But given the elusive nature of Negro Leagues data, it might be the best we can do. So without further introduction, here are my picks for the five greatest teams in Negro Leagues history.

5. Newark Eagles, 1946–47
The Newark Eagles of 1946–47 were a pretty awesome team, featuring three future Hall of Famers. The pitching staff was anchored by thirty-year-old Leon Day, who some say threw as hard as Satchel Paige. The middle of the infield was manned by shortstop Monte

Irvin and second baseman Larry Doby, both of whom would eventually enjoy great success as outfielders in the major leagues.

In '46, the Eagles placed five players on the All-Star team: the aforementioned trio, plus catcher Leon Ruffin and third baseman Murray Watkins. They dominated the competition in both halves of the season, finishing with 47 wins and 16 losses (the next-best record was posted by the New York Cubans, at 28-21). Newark capped their season with a seven-game triumph over the Kansas City Monarchs in the Negro World Series.

Leon Day was off to Mexico City in 1947, but Doby and Irvin led the Eagles to a first-half title. Unfortunately, second-half standings weren't published and there was no World Series, so it's hard to say just how good the '47 Eagles were.

4. Kansas City Monarchs, 1923–26

The Monarchs were a good team, we're just not sure how *great* they were. Over the course of their history, however, the Monarchs were the best-run, most consistent black team, and it just seems like they belong here somewhere.

Mind you, the Monarchs were excellent in the mid-1920s. They may have featured just one future Hall of Famer—Joe "Bullet" Rogan, inducted in 1998—but they were the dominant team in the Negro National League of the time. Beginning in 1923, the Monarchs won four straight pennants, and over those same four seasons they went 231-99 (.700) in league games.

In 1924, the Monarchs faced off against the Hilldale club, champs of the Eastern Colored League, in the first "World Series" involving black teams. Led by third baseman Judy Johnson, Hilldale was itself a fantastic club, and the best-of-nine series went the distance before Kansas City prevailed in the game 10 finale, 5–0 (game 3 ended in a tie). The two clubs met again in the 1925 World Series, and this time Hilldale romped over the Monarchs, five games to one. In 1926, the Monarchs were topped by the Chicago American Giants, five games to four, in a playoff for the National Negro League pennant.

3. St. Louis Stars, 1928–30

Up the middle, the Stars employed a pair of future Hall of Famers in shortstop Willie Wells and center fielder Cool Papa Bell. Mule Suttles, who rivals Josh Gibson as the most powerful man in Negro

Leagues history, manned first base. In 1928, St. Louis won both the first and second halves of the season, finishing 66-26 overall. The next season they dropped to 59-33, second behind the 62-17 Monarchs. But in 1930, the Stars finished with their best record ever, 65-22. Their combined record for those three seasons was 190-81, which works out to a .701 winning percentage.

Regrettably, the Stars never got a chance to face off against the Eastern Colored League champs because the E.C.L. came apart during the 1928 season. The St. Louis club would die a quick death. After going 11-11 in the first half of the '31 season, the Stars disbanded. Not long after, so did the rest of the Negro National League.

2. Homestead Grays, 1943–45

At another point in this book, we suggest that perhaps wartime teams really can't be taken too seriously because the talent base was so depleted. However, this wasn't so true in the Negro Leagues, as most of the top black players played right on through the early '40s. And the Homestead Grays of Pennsylvania were clearly the best black team during the war. From 1943 through 1945 they won three straight Negro National League pennants and combined for a 90-34 (.726) record. Homestead featured a trio of all-time greats, aging though they were, in Cool Papa Bell (forty years old in 1943), Josh Gibson (an old thirty-one), and Buck Leonard (thirty-five). In both '43 and '44, the Grays aced the Birmingham Black Barons in the World Series, but in the last hurrah for Bell, Gibson, and Leonard, the Grays were swept four straight by the Cleveland Buckeyes in the '45 Series.

1. Pittsburgh Crawfords, 1934–36

Most authorities on the Negro Leagues wind up picking this squad as the greatest ever. In the Society for American Baseball Research's *The Negro Leagues Book*, Merl Kleinknecht describes the 1935 Crawfords as "arguably the greatest black team in history." In *The Biographical Encyclopedia of the Negro Baseball Leagues*, James A. Riley writes, "Although their existence as a team was brief, the Pittsburgh Crawfords are considered the greatest team in the history of black baseball." We concur. Given their talent, there's no reason to think that the Crawfords at their best couldn't have played with just about *any* team, anywhere, at any time. After all, how many major league teams have ever boasted five Hall of Famers? The Crawfords could put on the field, all at once, Cool Papa Bell in center field, Oscar Charleston at first base, Judy Johnson at third, Josh Gibson behind the plate, and Satchel Paige on the mound. True, Paige didn't actually pitch much for the Crawfords in 1935 (he was off barnstorming, making piles of money for himself) but Leroy Matlock went 19-0 in Satchel's absence.

The Crawfords finished third in 1934, sort of, as their 29-17 combined record (the season was split into halves) was just a few percentage points behind the Chicago American Giants (28-15) and the Philadelphia Stars (23-13). But Pittsburgh won Negro National League pennants in both 1935 (39-15) and 1936 (36-24).

Like the great St. Louis Stars team, the Craws dynasty didn't last long. In 1937, most of the stars left to play in Dominica for dictator Rafael Trujillo's team. In 1939 the Pittsburgh Crawfords became the Toledo Crawfords, and a year later they were the Indianapolis Crawfords. But in their time, the Pittsburgh Crawfords probably were as talented as any baseball team on the planet, whatever the chromality of their players.—Rob

1961 New York Yankees

It is doubtful that any team in baseball history, with perhaps the 1927 Yankees the exception, could have beaten [the 1961 Yankees] in this World Series, the quality of Yankee play from both regulars and substitutes was so incredibly good. The 1961 team was a most awesome machine.

—Peter Golenbock in *Dynasty*

Record: 109-53,.673 (27th)
Two-Year (1961–62): 205-119, .633 (63d)
Three-Year (1961–63): 309-176, .637
  (44th)

SD Score: 2.97 (40th)
Two-Year: 5.34 (39th)
Three-Year: 7.77 (25th)

Results:
1961 World Champions
1962 World Champions
1963 American League Champions

Days in First Place: 83 of 175; clinched
  on September 20

Longest Winning Streak: 13 games
Longest Losing Streak: 4 games

The Pennant Race: On June 6, the Cleveland Indians ran their winning streak to eight games and grabbed first place at the same time. On June 6 it was Detroit's turn, as the Tigers' 4–2 victory over the Yankees elevated *them* to the top of the standings. First place went back and forth for the next six weeks, but the Yankees finally went ahead for good on July 25 with a doubleheader sweep of the White Sox (Maris homering twice in each game). They surged from that point and were never passed.

Against the Contenders: The third-place Orioles finished 14 games off the pace, leaving Detroit as the only real contenders. The Tigers won 101 games, an incredible number for a second-place team, and they held their own against the Yankees by winning 8 of their 18 match-ups.

Runs Scored: 827 (2d)

Runs Allowed: 612 (2d)

The Yankees are the only team featured in this book that didn't lead its league in either runs scored or runs allowed, but they were not far off from leading in both. The second-place Tigers scored 841 runs, 14 more than the Yankees. The third-place Orioles allowed 588, 24 fewer than the Yankees.

Pythagorean Record: 103-59

Manager: Ralph Houk

A native of Lawrence, Kansas, Houk served as a U.S. Army officer in World War II and saw rough action in Europe, winning a Silver Star for bravery. By 1947 he was serving as backup catcher with the Yankees, and he slapped a pinch-hit single in game 6 of the World Series that year. Houk soon lost his job to Charlie Silvera, however, and from 1950 through 1953 Houk was New York's third-string catcher. And when we say third-string, we mean *third-string*. Though he was on the roster all season long for all four of those seasons, Houk batted only 29 times. All that time on the bench went to good use, however, and in 1955 Houk began a three-year stint managing the Yankees' Triple-A farm club in Denver. After guiding the Bears to one third- and two second-place finishes, Houk returned to New York as a coach. In 1961, he took over as manager from the deposed Casey Stengel.

Regular Lineup:

Player	Position	ROV	OW%
Bobby Richardson	2B	.225	.355
Tony Kubek	SS	.261	.510
Roger Maris	RF	.343	.763
Mickey Mantle	CF	.410	.868
Yogi Berra	LF	.293	.626
Elston Howard	C	.344	.764
Bill Skowron	1B	.276	.569
Clete Boyer	3B	.241	.425
Whitey Ford	P		

Mantle's .868 offensive winning percentage is the highest posted by any player in this book for the given season. Bobby Richardson wasn't your ideal leadoff man, and there's no doubt that dropping him to eighth would have resulted in a few more runs scored.

Bench: With one or two notable exceptions, the Yankee bench was extraordinarily weak. Johnny Blanchard we'll read about later. And veteran slugger Bob Cerv (who played briefly for the '53 Yanks) hit six homers in 118 at-bats. But the rest of the reserves were almost uniformly ineffective. Hector Lopez, who started against lefthanders and served as a defensive sub for Berra, posted a 597 OPS, almost ridiculously awful.

Aside from those three, six other Yankee reserves collected more than a dozen at-bats. Billy Gardner led the way with a .212 batting average. The other five combined for a .135 average, zero doubles, zero triples, and one home run in 104 at-bats. Jack Reed, who batted only thirteen times all season, gained a small degree of fame as "Mickey Mantle's caddy," much as Sammy Byrd became "Babe Ruth's Legs" thirty years earlier.

Scouting the Pitchers: In his first nine seasons as a Yankee, Whitey Ford had started more than 30 games only once. But with Ralph Houk replacing Casey Stengel as manager in 1961, Ford finally got a chance to start every fourth day, and he responded with a brilliant 25-4 record. Ford's curveball was famous around the league, but the curve only worked because Ford's fastball was better than average, too. He was smart, and he threw enough illegal pitches—spitballs, mudballs, scuffballs—to keep the hitters guessing.

Ford was essentially impossible to run against, the Terry Mulholland of his era. In 1961, three brave souls attempted to steal a base with Ford on the mound, and all three were gunned down. Oh, and he also picked off six guys. It's quite possible that no other pitcher in major league history has thrown 250-plus innings without permitting a stolen base.

In 1988 Ralph Houk did a book with Bob Creamer, *Season of Glory: The Amazing Saga of the 1961 New York Yankees*, and Houk was good about giving in-depth scouting reports on just about everybody on the team, including the pitchers. Of Ralph Terry (16-3, 3.16), Houk observed, "Ralph had all the pitches. He had a good fastball, maybe not a Bob Feller fastball or even a Whitey Ford fastball, but a good one, and he had a real good breaking ball that helped make his fastball better. He had that slider, and he had the change."

Only twenty-one years old, Bill Stafford (14-9, 2.68) posted the second-best ERA in the American League, but a relatively pedestrian record thanks to poor luck. Houk later described Stafford: "He was big and he was fairly strong and he had a good curveball, a good fastball, a fair change. Those are the three basic pitches and he had them."

Relief ace Luis Arroyo (15-5, 2.19, 29 saves) gained fame for his screwball, which many have said made the lefthander more effective against righty hitters than lefties. However, Arroyo actually performed somewhat better against the lefties, at least in 1961.

How Were They Built? For the most part, the Yankees were a home-grown club, with the organization drawing on ample financial resources to stock their farm clubs. In 1958 the Yankees boasted ten minor-league affiliates, tops in the American League, and it wasn't until 1965 that any other American League team had *more* affiliates than the Yankees. When they did make deals, as often as not they were with the Kansas City Athletics, then owned by Arnold Johnson, who previously had owned the Kansas City Blues, a Yankee farm team. That's where they got Roger Maris, but let's backtrack a little.

In 1955, Maris was still in the minor leagues and property of the Cleveland Indians. Word got back to Yankees general manager George Weiss that this kid was worth watching, but Weiss soon discovered that the Indians weren't interested in trading Maris. As the story goes, Weiss decided to check further on Maris anyway and sent a representative to Fargo, North Dakota, Maris' hometown, to conduct a background check. All reports were positive, and Weiss bided his time. Maris reached the majors two years later and, in June 1958, the Indians traded him to the Kansas City Athletics. After the 1959 season, Weiss finally got his man, as Maris came to the Yankees in a seven-player deal. Maris was just one of eight ex–Kansas City Athletics on the roster in 1961, the others including starting third baseman Clete Boyer and number two starter Ralph Terry.

From March 1955 through June 1961, the clubs made seventeen deals involving 64 players, and legend holds that the Yankees were continually robbing the Athletics blind. However, Kansas City got some pretty good players from the Yankees, too. Norm Siebern, part of the Maris deal, became perhaps the best player in Kansas City A's history, at least until 1967 when guys like Catfish Hunter and Reggie Jackson came up.

What Brought Them Down? It took them forty-five years, but it finally happened. From 1921 through 1964, the New York Yankees won 29 pennants. They finished second or third in thirteen other seasons. That leaves two seasons, 1925 and 1945, in which the Yankees finished lower than third. In '25, they finished seventh because Babe Ruth was suffering through his worst season. And in '45, they finished fourth because all their good players were wearing olive drab and saluting.

But when the crash finally came, it came fast and hard. After winning their fifth straight American League pennant in 1964, the Yankees were topped by the St. Louis Cardinals in a seven-game World Series. Yogi Berra, who piloted New York to the pennant in his first year as skipper, was fired. To replace him, the Yankees lured Cardinals manager Johnny Keane away from St. Louis. In 1965, the Yankees finished sixth. And in 1966, the Yankees finished last (tenth) for the first time since 1912.

In his book *October 1964*, David Halberstam echoes a common argument, that the Yankees' decline was in large part due to the organization's unwillingness to scout and sign talented black ballplayers. But just as important, early in the 1962 season Yankees owners Dan Topping and Del Webb decided to sell the club at the earliest opportunity and to spend as little money as possible in the interim. Predictably, the farm system suffered, and the organization simply didn't produce many good young players in the '60s.

Most Valuable Yankee: If you're reading this book, you probably already know that Roger Maris hit 61 home runs in 1961, thus breaking the record set by Babe Ruth in 1927. Maris also led the American League with 142 RBI (more on this later). These are impressive numbers, the kind of numbers that normally get a guy the MVP award. Yet somehow, the MVP voters almost got it right. They almost voted for Mickey Mantle instead. Maris hit 61 home runs, but Mantle hit 54. Maris finished with 142 RBI, Mantle with 128. Maris scored 132 runs, and so did Mantle. Mantle would have done better in these prime categories, but a freak illness cost him the last week of the season. By that time, however, the Yankees had already clinched the pennant. Mantle's .868 offensive winning percentage was more than a hundred points better than Maris' .763.

Mantle's 1138 OPS (on-base percentage plus slugging percentage) in 1961 ranks 45th on the all-time list. Maris' 996 OPS in 1961 doesn't rank anywhere near the top 100. Mantle played center field, a tougher position than right field where Maris played. Mantle slugged .731 with runners on base; Maris slugged .661 in the same situation. Mickey Mantle was clearly the American League's most valuable player in 1961. But Maris finished first in the voting with 202 points. Mantle was right behind, at 198. Like I said, the voters almost got it right.

Worst Regular: Clete Boyer

Almost as bad a hitter as Bobby Richardson, Boyer didn't play as important a defensive role, though he was certainly a fine defensive third baseman. Yogi Berra wasn't so hot, either. Given that he was essentially immobile in left field and was platooned, Berra simply didn't add a whole lot.

Hall of Famers: Mickey Mantle, Yogi Berra, and Whitey Ford.

Our Hall of Famers: Mickey Mantle, Yogi Berra, and Whitey Ford. Mantle ranks among the top three center fielders of all time (with Cobb and Mays), Berra ranks among the top three catchers of all time (with Cochrane and Bench), and Whitey Ford's .690 career winning percentage was the best of the twentieth century.

The only other Hall of Fame candidate on the roster is Roger Maris. With Mark McGwire and Sammy Sosa both chasing, and eventually breaking, Maris' record in 1998, there was renewed sentiment for the latter's enshrinement. And sentiment is about the only argument for Maris being in the Hall of Fame. Without going into all the gory details, let us remember that while the Hall's voting rules don't prohibit the election of Maris, they do discourage such an election. According to Rule 6, "No automatic elections based on performances such as a batting average of .400 or more for one (1) year, pitching a perfect game or similar outstanding achievement shall be permitted." Ask yourself, if Maris hadn't enjoyed the one huge season, would his name *ever* come up in Hall of Fame discussions?

The 1961 World Series: Yankees 4, Reds 1

The Yankees, not surprisingly, entered the Series as huge favorites, getting 12–5 odds where people took bets. In fact, the joke going around in New York was that the Yankees would win in three games.

The Series opened in the Bronx, and Cincinnati was never really in the game as Whitey Ford tossed a two-hitter to beat the Reds, 2–0. But Cincy came back in game 2, Joey Jay stopping the Yankees on four hits, with Yogi Berra's two-run homer accounting for all the New York scoring in the 6–2 affair.

Game 3, in Cincinnati, saw the critical point of the Series. With the Reds leading 1–0 in the seventh, Berra faced Reds starter Bob Purkey with two out and Kubek on second. Berra lofted a pop fly into short right field but, just as Frank Robinson was catching the ball, second baseman Elio Chacon ran into Robinson, jarring the ball loose. Kubek scored, and the Yankees eventually stole a 3–2 victory thanks to solo home runs from John Blanchard and Roger Maris. It was no contest after that, as the Bombers destroyed the Reds in games 4 and 5, 7–0 and 13–5.

Stats 'n' Stuff

◆ What is the record for fewest doubles in a season by a 50-homer hitter? Sixteen, by both Mantle and Maris in 1961.

◆ The Yankees hit 240 home runs to set a major league record, which didn't leave much power to spare. Tony Kubek led the club with 38 doubles, nobody else hit more than 23, and the Yankees finished last in the league in that category.

◆ Bobby Richardson and Tony Kubek, the number one and two hitters in the lineup, combined for a .300 on-base percentage and just 164 runs in 315 games.

◆ Utility infielder Joe DeMaestri, in his final major league season, finished his career in a 0-for-20 slump.

Around the Majors

April 10 The expansion Washington Senators play their first-ever game, but lose 4–3 to the White Sox in front of a crowd that includes President Kennedy.

The next day, the "old" Washington Senators, now the Minnesota Twins, play *their* first game, beating the New York Yankees 3–0. Also on April 11, the brand-new Los Angeles Angels play their first-ever game and beat the Orioles 7–2.

April 28 Five days after his fortieth birthday, Braves lefthander Warren Spahn throws a no-hitter at the San Francisco Giants. The 1–0 shutout leaves Spahn 10 victories short of 300. He'll throw a two-hitter in his next start, and he wins his 300th game on August 11.

June 16 Lew Krausse, Jr., fresh out of high school, debuts for the Kansas City Athletics with a three-hit shutout of the Angels. Krausse's father pitched for the Philadelphia Athletics in 1931.

July 5 Roger Maris is mistakenly credited with two RBI rather than one. This has ramifications because Maris winds up leading the American League with 142 RBI, one more than Orioles first baseman Jim Gentile.

The Ballpark: Unchanged since 1953.

Books about the 1961 Yankees: As you'd expect, there's no shortage of information on the team. In the late 1980s, two books were published that specifically concerned the '61 Yankees. In 1987, Tony Kubek and Terry Pluto published *Sixty-One: The Team, The Record, The Men* (New York: Macmillan, 1987). A year later, Ralph Houk and Bob Creamer followed with *Season of Glory: The Amazing Saga of the 1961 New York Yankees* (New York: G. P. Putnam's Sons, 1988). Both books are better than most of their kind, probably because Pluto and Creamer are both exceptionally talented collaborators. Houk also did a book back in 1962, *Ballplayers Are Human, Too*. The title is more interesting than the contents, but it's not bad. Dom Forker's *Sweet Seasons: Recollections of the 1955–64 New York Yankees* (Taylor, 1990) is exactly what it sounds like. The lives of the Yankee stars have been well chronicled, to say the least. There are books about Whitey, there are books about Mickey, and there are books about Whitey and Mickey together.

Breaking Them Down

In the *1991 Elias Baseball Analyst*, the editors revisited the 1961 Yankees, and they came up with some awfully interesting stuff:

◆ The Yankees went 44-37 on the road. Ho hum. But at home, they were 65-16! And that difference was due almost entirely to the pitching staff. Although the Yankees scored 411 runs at home and 416 on the road—virtually the same—they *allowed* 361 on the road and only 251 at home. Here's the home/away data in a chart:

Average Runs Scored		Average Runs Allowed	
Home	Road	Home	Road
5.07	5.14	3.10	4.46

Those are bizarre numbers, and I don't really know how to explain them. Yankee Stadium was supposed to be a good place for left-handed pitchers.

◆ Everyone knows that Roger Maris didn't draw even one intentional walk all season, mostly because Mantle was batting behind him. Maris did bat sixth the first six weeks of the season, and Mantle missed the last week with an injury.

When Mantle was on deck (475 at-bats), Maris batted .293 and slugged .682.

When Mantle was not on deck (115 at-bats), Maris batted .174 and slugged .365.

◆ While we're talking about Roger Maris, it's worth noting that, like Babe Ruth and Lou Gehrig before him, this left-handed slugger did *not* take particular advantage of the cozy distance down the right-field line. He hit 30 home runs in Yankee Stadium and 31 on the road.

The Ol' Perfessor and the Major

Much has been made of the differences between the way Casey Stengel and his successor, Ralph Houk, handled the Yankees' starting pitching. The usual example given is Whitey Ford. In each of Stengel's last three seasons as Yankee manager (1958–60), Ford made 29 starts. His career high in wins under Stengel was 19. In Houk's first year as Yankee manager (1961), Ford started 39 games, won 25 of them, and earned the Cy Young award (and back then they were only giving out one for both leagues).

I thought I would enter the data and see just how Stengel and Houk differed. Here are the results:

	Pitcher 1 Avg GS	Pitcher 2 Avg GS	Pitcher 3 Avg GS	Pitchers 1–3 Avg GS
Stengel (1949–60)	31.2	28.3	23.5	83.0
Stengel (1957–60)	29.3	26.3	22.0	77.5
Houk (1961–64)	38.0	34.3	30.8	103.0

Although some sources now list Maris and Gentile as co-leaders, others still credit Maris with that extra RBI and the title.

August 20 After 23 straight losses, a new National League record, the Phillies finally win a game, as they beat the Braves 7–4, thus ending Milwaukee's 10-game winning streak.

Blanchard's Big Year

When the 1961 season opened, Johnny Blanchard was a twenty-eight-year-old catcher stuck behind Yogi Berra and Elston Howard. His career batting average was .211, and he'd hit six home runs in 161 at-bats. No matter. In 1961, Blanchard hit 21 home runs. And he hit those 21 homers in only 243 at-bats, thus becoming the first major leaguer to hit 20 or more homers in fewer than 250 at-bats. Blanchard is one of two major leaguers to hit home runs in four consecutive at-bats, yet finish his career with fewer than 100 home runs. (The other is Art Shamsky.)

There's always been this opinion floating around that Blanchard was truly a productive hitter, that his inability to break into the starting lineup is yet another testament to the incredible strength of the Yankee organization. The truth, I suspect, is somewhat different. In 1961 Blanchard was twenty-eight years old, and that's a fairly common age for a player to enjoy a career year. In 1962, he got almost exactly the same amount of playing time as in 1961. The result? (See table below.)

Will the real Johnny Blanchard please stand up? Actually, neither one of these stats lines represents the real Johnny Blanchard. The real Johnny Blanchard is somewhere in the middle. He's the dead-pull hitter, slower than Manhattan traffic, who finished his major league career with a .320 on-base percentage and a .441 slugging percentage. Pretty good numbers for a catcher, but the fact is that

Well, obviously the *facts* are consistent with the *notion* that Houk and Stengel used their starting pitchers differently. Also notice that Stengel's use became "less" traditional the longer he managed. Houk's number three starter averaged more starts than Stengel's number one starter over Stengel's last four seasons as manager.

The way Houk used his rotation is similar to the way Earl Weaver would use his, a decade later, in Baltimore. Weaver believed in concentrating as many starts at the top of his rotation as he could. As he usually did, Weaver expressed his philosophy succinctly: "It's easier to find four good starters than five." Here is the same chart for Weaver, 1969–71:

	Pitcher 1 Avg GS	Pitcher 2 Avg GS	Pitcher 3 Avg GS	Pitchers 1–3 Avg GS
Weaver (1969–71)	39.3	38.7	36.3	114.3

Which way is better? Well, all three of these managers were extremely successful in the time periods under consideration. Whitey Ford pitched very well for Stengel, compiling a 133-59 record with a 2.70 ERA and twice leading the league in ERA. He pitched very well under Houk, too: 66-19 with a 2.96 ERA before Houk moved up to the front office. Ford finally succumbed to injuries in 1966–67, but he was in his late thirties by then, and one would be hard pressed to blame his decline on his increased usage.

If a pitcher can maintain his effectiveness at higher innings totals, it seems like common sense that he should be used more, but pitcher performance is unpredictable and one also has to consider the long-term impact of higher yearly workloads. During the period discussed here, the team had total control over the player for his entire career, and it may have made sense to worry about the long run. Today, a team can be assured of having a player for only six years, so the long-term future may not be as much of a concern. Taken to its extreme,

Table: John Blanchard

Year	Games	At-Bats	Runs	HR	RBI	Avg	OBP	Slug
1961	93	243	38	21	54	.305	.383	.613
1962	93	246	33	13	39	.232	.313	.419

that viewpoint could lead to teams pushing pitchers to the limit (and beyond) and burning them out faster, which isn't good for the game as a whole.—Eddie

Batting First . . . Bobby Richardson?

Bobby Richardson was a wonderful second baseman, famous for his quick pivot on the double play. He wasn't Bill Mazeroski or anything, but he was the closest to Maz in the American League.

Richardson couldn't hit a lick, though. When he played for Casey Stengel, he sometimes batted ninth. That's right, ninth at a time when pitchers still batted in the American League. Don Larsen and Tommy Byrne were pretty good hitters, for pitchers, and Stengel would occasionally bat them eighth. Stengel frequently replaced Richardson with a pinch-hitter—sometimes in the first inning.

According to Richardson in *The Bobby Richardson Story*:

He jumped on me once about my habit of swinging at the first good pitch. Casey thought I ought to take more strikes. "You can't get many walks if you're a first-ball hitter," he'd say. After I tried his way unsuccessfully for a while, he looked over at me during a subsequent meeting and growled, "Just forget that taking business; you were better the other way!"

Stengel was no fool. Though he let Richardson hit the way he wanted to, he also kept him at the bottom of the order, where he could do the least damage. As a hitter, Richardson combined two lousy qualities: he had little power, and he *never* walked. Richardson would typically draw around 30 freebies in a season. (For what it's worth, he struck out even less often than he walked.)

In 1961, the Yankees fired Stengel and hired Ralph Houk, who, in the mid-1950s, had managed Richardson for two seasons in Denver. Houk, in his infinite wisdom, moved Richardson from eighth to first in the batting order! Batting just ahead of Roger Maris and Mickey Mantle, Richardson played 162 games and scored the grand total of 80 runs.

I rest Casey Stengel's case.—Rob

Bronx Hurlers?

Although the 1932 Yankees had a slightly better home winning percentage, the '61 Bombers own the record for home victories in one season, with 65. Makes sense, right? All those lefty sluggers taking advantage of the short porch in right, right? [buzzer sound] WRONG! The 1961 Yankees actually scored more runs on the road than at home (416 to 411) and hit more homers on the road than at home (128 to 112). The runs scored totals are a little misleading, because when you're 65-16 at home, you're not batting too often in your half of the ninth. However, their OPS at home (787) wasn't that much better than their road OPS (756), and their home slugging percentage (.447) wasn't that much better than their road slugging percentage (.436). As we've noted, Roger Maris hit more home runs on the road (31-30), and so did Mickey Mantle (30-24).

The Yankee players who really benefited from The House That Ruth Built were those guys who played Ruth's original position—pitcher. Let me show you some numbers, courtesy of *The 1991 Elias Baseball Analyst*:

Pitcher	Home ERA	Road ERA
Arroyo (left)	1.44	3.04
Coates (right)	2.68	4.45
Daley (left)	2.88	5.06
Ford (left)	2.65	3.84
Sheldon (right)	2.33	5.45
Stafford (right)	2.26	3.15
Terry (right)	2.79	3.45
Turley (right)	4.91	6.33
Team	2.77	4.18

As you can see, it wasn't just the left-handed pitchers who were helped by Yankee Stadium. The pitcher with the biggest home/road differential was righthander Rollie Sheldon.

The 1961 Yankees allowed just 251 runs in their 81 home games. Although that's not the lowest total ever in a 162-game schedule (the 1964 White Sox allowed just 213 runs at home all year), it's certainly an outstanding figure.

Mickey Mantle and Roger Maris *(National Baseball Hall of Fame Library, Cooperstown, NY)*

Something else was afoot at Yankee Stadium in 1961. Although it's true that the Pythagorean method is less "reliable" the fewer games you've got, something will tell you that the following is still unusual: the Pythagorean record for home games was 58-23; the actual record for home games was 65-16. You can call it *Yankee mystique* or *stochastic variation*, or even *luck*, but the Yankees were certainly very "efficient" at home in 1961, and it was hardly just a function of being the Bronx *Bombers.*—Eddie

Was Mantle a Good Clutch Hitter?

A criticism of "macro" offensive statistics, like linear weights or pre-1998 versions of runs created, is that they didn't consider a player's situational performance—that is, his performance with runners in scoring position, his performance late in close games, or whatever. One argument for excluding situational hitting is that, in a given year, the number of plate appearances in such a subset of the player's season becomes statistically less than meaningful. In addition, it is only since the mid-1980s that we've had wide access to such data, and when one looks at this data over time, the majority of players' numbers with runners in scoring position are very consistent with their overall numbers. However, that is not true for all players.

Mickey Mantle was a great player, that cannot be disputed. However, his career resumé has one disturbing flaw: seemingly low RBI totals in some of his seasons. For example, he had five seasons with 300+ total bases, all before 1962, playing for the best team in baseball. In only two of those seasons did he have 100-plus RBI, granting that he had 99 in one of those seasons. For a player batting third or fourth on a good team, that is not impressive. His ratio of RBI to total bases (RBI/TB) should be comfortably over one-third.

Unfortunately for us, play-by-play data for Mantle's Yankees is incomplete except for 1961, so we can't just look at his numbers with runners in scoring position. We can, however, look more closely at his RBI/TB ratios and compare him to his peers in the league and, closer to home, on his own team. The following is a very detailed chart that looks at Mantle's RBI/TB ratios year by year, except for 1963 when he missed most of the season with an injury. The league ranks shown are among all players with 350 or more plate appearances in that season.

Year	RBI	Mantle Total Bases	Ratio	League Rank	Yankees ahead of Mantle	League Leader
1951	65	151	.430	5 (of 61)	None	Clyde Vollmer (.483)
1952	87	291	.299	33 (of 52)	Berra (6th, .384) McDougald (7th, .380) Woodling (25th, .326)	Billy Hitchcock (.471)
1953	92	229	.402	6 (of 60)	None	Clyde Vollmer (.463)
1954	102	285	.358	16 (of 62)	Berra (4th, .439)	Larry Doby (.452)

Year	RBI	Mantle Total Bases	Ratio	League Rank	Yankees ahead of Mantle	League Leader
1955	99	316	.313	30 (of 54)	Woodling (11th, .374) Carey (12th, .374) Berra (4th, .439) Noren (7th, .424)	Ray Boone (.487)
1956	130	376	.346	17 (of 57)	Berra (11th, .378) Skowron (13th, .367) Bauer (15th, .350) Carey (16th, .350)	Dick Gernert (.459)
1957	94	315	.298	29 (of 55)	Skowron (5th, .409) Berra (9th, .389) Howard (23d, .326)	Sherm Lollar (.507)
1958	97	307	.316	23 (of 56)	Berra (1st, .441) Skowron (10th, .371) Howard (12th, .367) McDougald (17th, .344)	Yogi Berra (.441)
1959	75	278	.270	42 (of 57)	Lopez (6th, .377) Siebern (19th, .346)	Gus Triandos (.432)

Year	RBI	Mantle Total Bases	Ratio	League Rank	Yankees ahead of Mantle	League Leader
1960	94	294	.320	27 (of 59)	Howard (20th, .346) Berra (26th, .317) Bauer (31st, .305) Berra (4th, .388) Maris (5th, .386) Howard (20th, .342) Skowron (26th, .320)	Jim Gentile (.510)
1961	128	353	.363	18 (of 76)	Maris (8th, .388)	Jim Gentile (.449)
1962	89	228	.390	6 (of 77)	None	Willie Kirkland (.456)
1964	111	275	.404	2 (of 75)	None	Bob Chance (.444)
1965	46	163	.282	50 (of 83)	Kubek (16th, .350) Howard (21st, .333) Pepitone (44th, .297)	Felix Mantilla (.414)
1966	56	179	.313	29 (of 80)	Maris (22d, .323)	Ed Kirkpatrick (.431)
1967	55	191	.288	43 (of 76)	Pepitone (14th, .339) Whitaker (29th, .316) Tresh (33d, .314)	Harmon Killebrew (.370)

Year	RBI	Mantle Total Bases	Ratio	League Rank	Yankees ahead of Mantle	League Leader
1968	54	173	.312	23 (of 71)	Robinson (38th, .302) Pepitone (5th, .366) Tresh (11th, .333) Kosco (12th, .331)	Ken Harrelson (.394)

What might we conclude from this data? "The other teams wouldn't let Mantle beat them, so they pitched around him with runners on, especially if the runs were important." Well, maybe that's part of the answer, because Mantle was a feared hitter who took a lot of walks. You can't get an RBI if you walk with runners on second and third. That's not to say that the walk has no value, it's just that the value doesn't show up in the RBI column. Although Yogi Berra was no doubt a feared hitter, he wasn't as patient at the plate and probably "expanded" his hitting zone with runners on. However, it is a stark contrast between Mantle's and Berra's RBI/TB ratios while playing on the same team. In Mantle's first ten seasons with the Yankees, he led the team twice and finished in the top ten in the league twice. During the same period, Berra led the team six times and finished in the league's top ten six times. From 1954 to 1960, Mantle never finished higher than third on his own team or higher than sixteenth in the league. That data does raise a red flag.

Let me quickly add that I do not advocate RBI/TB ratio as the "be all and end all" measure of hitting with runners in scoring position when that data is not available. For example, even though Roger Maris' RBI/TB ratio was better than Mantle's in 1961, Mantle's numbers with runners in scoring position were better (Mantle: 1420 OPS; Maris: 1127 OPS). I am just saying that this is an area that requires more investigation.—Eddie

Ode to a Moose

This isn't a poem for Bullwinkle, even though *Rocky & Bullwinkle* was one of my favorite cartoons when I was a kid. No, this story is about a Yankee first baseman named Bill "Moose" Skowron.

Before it was remodeled in 1974–75 and again in 1985, Yankee Stadium had extreme dimensions that were flat-out unfavorable for right-handed power hitters. It goes without saying that the layout was part of the charm of The House That Ruth Built (e.g., the monuments being in play), but the park did affect the numbers of Yankees hitters. Bill Dickey, a left-handed hitter, blasted 135 of his 202 (67 percent) career homers in Yankee Stadium. That is the highest percentage of homers at home among the 205 players with 200 or more career homers through 1998. (What's more, from 1935 through 1939, Dickey hit 88 of his 116 homers at home.) What the park giveth, the park could taketh away. Joe DiMaggio hit just 148 of his 361 (41 percent) career homers in Yankee Stadium, the sixth *lowest* percentage of homers at home for players with 200-plus career homers.

All of which brings us to the Moose. Skowron's career home/road home run totals were 86 at home and 125 on the road. His home-run percentage in home games, 41 percent, is the *fourth-lowest* percentage among players with 200-plus career homers. Even this underestimates the impact of Yankee Stadium on his career totals because Skowron, unlike Dickey and DiMaggio, didn't spend his entire career in pinstripes. While with the Yankees, Skowron hit only 60 of his 165 home runs at home, just 36.4 percent.

Here are the ten lowest career percentages in history:

Player	AB	HR	Home HR	Home HR%
Goose Goslin	8,656	248	92	37.1
Tim Wallach	8,099	260	103	39.6
Sid Gordon	4,992	202	82	40.6
Bill Skowron	5,547	211	86	40.8
Joe Adcock	6,606	336	137	40.8
Joe DiMaggio	6,821	361	148	41.0
Pedro Guerrero	5,392	215	90	41.9
Bill Nicholson	5,546	235	99	42.1

Player	AB	HR	Home HR	Home HR%
Roberto Clemente	9,454	240	102	42.5
George Brett	10,349	317	136	42.9

Skowron was traded to the Dodgers in November 1962 and thus got a measure of "revenge" when the Dodgers swept the Yankees in the 1963 World Series. Moose played in all four games, going 5-for-13 with a homer, three RBI, and two runs scored in a Series that saw a total of just 16 runs.

Just as a person's behavior is a function of genetics and environment, a player's statistics are a function of his ability and his environment. It is unlikely that Bill Skowron would have been a Hall of Famer under any circumstances, but his career track record is more impressive than it appears at first glance because for most of his career he played in a ballpark very hostile to his kind of player.—Eddie

Diamond Jim and the Phantom Ribbie

In all the commotion over Mantle, Maris, and Norm Cash (who hit .361 for the Tigers), Baltimore first baseman Jim Gentile's 1961 season has gotten lost in the sauce, along with half of an RBI title.

Gentile made major contributions to the first modern "season of smash." He hit 46 home runs in 1961 and no doubt lost a few to Memorial Stadium, which at that time was a big park. He hit 30 homers on the road. The major league record for road homers in a season is 32, set by Babe Ruth in 1927 and equaled by Mark McGwire in 1998. Gentile hit five grand slams in '61, and two of those came in consecutive innings on May 9.

He finished second to Roger Maris in RBI, with 141, or did he? SABR member Ron Rakowski has unearthed a phantom RBI for Maris in 1961. Specifically, he found that on July 5 (Cleveland at New York), the official records credited Maris with two RBI when he really had only one. The play in question occurred in the third inning of that game. Tony Kubek led off the inning by striking out, but he got to first base on a passed ball by Cleveland catcher Johnny Romano on the third strike. Maris then singled to right field, sending Kubek to third. Cleveland right fielder Willie Kirkland attempted to throw Kubek out at third, but his throw was late and Indians third baseman Bubba Phillips threw back toward first base to try to get Maris rounding the bag. Phillips' throw went into the stands, however, and Kubek was waved home by the umpire while Maris jogged to third.

It seems impossible to award Maris an RBI on this play, but Maris is credited with two RBI on the official sheet (he hit a solo home run in the seventh inning). Anyway, Rakowski checked several newspapers and came up with nine independent sources that indicate Maris had only one RBI that day. Even the box scores from the Associated Press and *The Sporting News* had Maris with only one RBI on July 5. According to Major League Baseball, Maris' official 1961 RBI total is still 142, one more than Gentile's, but it's quite likely that Maris will officially lose one RBI soon, which will drop him into a tie with Gentile.

The revisionist research is not all bad for Roger Maris, however. Maris and Mantle are officially credited with co-leading the American League with 132 runs apiece. However, a run credited to Mickey Mantle on September 10 was really scored by Bill Skowron. Thus, Maris really led the league in runs scored, all by his lonesome. It makes you think that if these totals for such a visible player in a relatively modern season are wrong, then what other errors lurk in the record books?

As for Jim Gentile, his moment in the sun was fairly short. He spent many seasons trapped in the Dodgers farm system behind Gil Hodges. Finally liberated by the Orioles in 1960, Gentile was already twenty-six years old. He was traded to Kansas City after the 1963 season in exchange for Norm Siebern. Talk is that Diamond Jim couldn't always control his temper, and that may have hastened his early exit from the majors. The numbers say that Gentile was a good player in 1960, a legitimately great player in 1961, and a good player for a few more years. Gentile's last season in the majors (he did play in Japan later) was 1966; he was just thirty-two years old. The irony in that, of course, is that 1966 marked the Orioles' first World Series title.—Eddie

TEAM STATISTICS

Hitting

	Games by Position	Age	G	AB	R	H	2B	3B	HR	RBI	BB	SO	SB	Avg	OBP	Slug
Elston Howard	C,111; 1B,9	32	129	446	64	155	17	5	21	77	28	65	0	.348	.387	.549
Bill Skowron	1B,149	30	150	561	76	150	23	4	28	89	35	108	0	.267	.318	.472
Bobby Richardson	2B,161	25	162	662	80	173	17	5	3	49	30	23	9	.261	.295	.316
Tony Kubek	SS,145	24	153	617	84	170	38	6	8	46	27	60	1	.276	.306	.395
Clete Boyer	3B,141; SS,12; OF,1	24	148	504	61	113	19	5	11	55	63	83	1	.224	.308	.347
Yogi Berra	OF,87; C,15	36	119	395	62	107	11	0	22	61	35	28	2	.271	.330	.466
Mickey Mantle	OF,150	29	153	514	**132**	163	16	6	54	128	**126**	112	12	.317	.448	**.687**
Roger Maris	OF,160	26	161	590	**132**	159	16	4	**61**	**141**	94	67	0	.269	.372	.620
Johnny Blanchard	C,48; OF,15	28	93	243	38	74	10	1	21	54	27	28	1	.305	.382	.613
Hector Lopez	OF,72	31	93	243	27	54	7	2	3	22	24	38	1	.222	.292	.305
Bob Cerv*	OF,30; 1B,3	35	57	118	17	32	5	1	6	20	12	17	1	.271	.344	.483
Billy Gardner*	3B,33; 2B,6	33	41	99	11	21	5	0	1	2	6	18	0	.212	.278	.293
Joe DeMaestri	SS,18; 2B,5; 3B,4	32	30	41	1	6	0	0	0	2	0	13	0	.146	.146	.146
Deron Johnson*	3B,8	22	13	19	1	2	0	0	0	2	2	5	0	.105	.182	.105
Earl Torgeson*	1B,8	37	22	18	3	2	0	0	0	0	8	3	0	.111	.385	.111
Jack Reed	OF,27	28	28	13	4	2	0	0	0	1	1	1	0	.154	.214	.154
Bob Hale*	1B,5	27	11	13	2	2	0	0	1	1	0	0	0	.154	.154	.385
Jesse Gonder		25	15	12	2	4	1	0	0	3	3	1	0	.333	.467	.417
Tom Tresh	SS,3	23	9	8	1	2	0	0	0	0	0	1	0	.250	.250	.250
Lee Thomas*		25	2	2	0	1	0	0	0	0	0	0	0	.500	.500	.500
Totals		28	163	5,559	827	1,461	194	40	**240**	**782**	543	785	28	.263	.337	**.442**

*Played for another team during season. Statistics are those compiled with 1961 New York Yankees only.

Pitching

	Threw	Age	Games	GS	CG	ShO	IP	H	HR	BB	SO	W	L	Pct	Sv	ERA
Whitey Ford	Left	32	**39**	39	11	3	**283**	242	23	92	209	**25**	4	**.862**	0	3.21
Bill Stafford	Right	21	36	25	8	3	195	168	13	59	101	14	9	.609	2	2.68
Ralph Terry	Right	25	31	27	9	2	188	162	19	42	86	16	3	.842	0	3.15
Rollie Sheldon	Right	24	35	21	6	2	163	149	17	55	84	11	5	.688	0	3.60
Bud Daley*	Left	28	23	17	7	0	130	127	17	51	83	8	9	.471	0	3.96
Jim Coates	Right	28	43	11	4	1	141	128	15	53	80	11	5	.688	5	3.44
Luis Arroyo	Left	34	**65**	0	0	0	119	83	5	49	87	15	5	.750	**29**	2.19
Bob Turley	Right	30	15	12	1	0	72	74	11	51	48	3	5	.375	0	5.75
Art Ditmar*	Right	32	12	8	1	0	54	59	9	14	24	2	3	.400	0	4.64
Hal Reniff	Right	22	25	0	0	0	45	31	1	31	21	2	0	1.000	2	2.58
Tex Clevenger*	Right	28	21	0	0	0	32	35	3	21	14	1	1	.500	0	4.83
Danny McDevitt*	Left	28	8	2	0	0	13	18	2	8	8	1	2	.333	1	7.62
Al Downing	Left	20	5	1	0	0	9	7	0	12	12	0	1	.000	0	8.00
Ryne Duren*	Right	32	4	0	0	0	5	2	2	4	7	0	1	.000	0	5.40
Johnny James*	Right	27	1	0	0	0	1	1	0	0	2	0	0	—	0	0.00
Duke Maas	Right	32	1	0	0	0	⅓	2	0	0	0	0	0	—	0	54.00
Totals		27	364	163	47	14	1,451	1,288	137	542	866	**109**	**53**	**.673**	**39**	3.46

*Played for another team during season. Statistics are those compiled with 1961 New York Yankees only.

CHAPTER 14

1970 Baltimore Orioles

"They were so good fundamentally that it was boring to watch, but baseball people, players, managers, writers, appreciated how great the team was. It had everything: pitching, defense, and hitting. Everybody knew we were going to win in those years [1969–71]."

—*Merv Rettenmund*

Record: 108-54, .667 (tie, 33d)
Two-Year (1969–70): 217-107, .670
  (17th)
Three-Year (1969–71): 318-164, .660
  (16th)

SD Score: +3.31 (16th)
Two-Year: +6.64 (2d)
Three-Year: +9.86 (1st)

Results:
1969 American League Champions
1970 World Champions
1971 American League Champions

Days in First Place: 169 of 171;
  clinched on September 17

Longest Winning Streak: 11 games
Longest Losing Streak: 3 games

Attendance in Charm City

In these days of Oriole Park at Camden Yards, when every game is a sellout—rain or shine, great team or mediocre—it's easy to assume that fans in Baltimore have always supported their team with such gusto. However, 'twas not always this way. As we've seen, from 1969 through 1971 the Orioles were easily the best team in the American League, winning nearly two-thirds of their games and advancing to the World Series each year. You wouldn't know it from the attendance figures, though. Over the course of those three seasons, the O's drew a total of 3,142,175 paying customers, which ranked fifth in the American League over that span, well behind Boston (5,107,256) and Detroit (4,669,847) and somewhat behind Minnesota (3,552,073) and New York (3,275,646). What's more, the Orioles weren't even able to sell out their postseason games. Why this relative

The Pennant Race: When July dawned, the resurgent New York Yankees trailed the Orioles by "only" six games. But the Yankees slumped in July, and then the Orioles went 44-15 over the season's last two months to win going away.

Against the Contenders: Contenders? There really wasn't any such thing, and we're not just talking about 1970, when the second-place Yankees finished 15 games off the pace. In '69 the O's finished 19 games ahead of the runner-up Tigers, and in '71 they beat the (again) second-place Detroit team by an even dozen. For the record, though, in 1970 the Orioles took 11 of 18 from the Bronx Bombers.

Runs Scored: 792 (1st)

Runs Allowed: 574 (1st)

Pythagorean Record: 104-58

Manager: Earl Weaver

Regular Lineup:

Player	Position	ROV	OW%
Don Buford	LF	.311	.715
Paul Blair	CF	.277	.606
Boog Powell	1B	.335	.773
Frank Robinson	RF	.324	.748
Brooks Robinson	3B	.269	.579
Elrod Hendricks	C	.254	.519
Davey Johnson	2B	.275	.600
Mark Belanger	SS	.215	.345
Mike Cuellar	P		

Bench: Andy Etchebarren, who batted righty, was usually behind the plate against lefty starters. Merv Rettenmund had a marvelous season as the O's fourth outfielder, batting .322 with 18 homers and a .544 slugging percentage. Terry Crowley, a lefty, was Weaver's top pinch-hitter (and you know how Weaver loved his pinch-hitters) going 9-

for-31 in that role. Chico Salmon picked up 172 at-bats as the club's chief utility infielder.

Scouting the Pitchers: The Orioles boasted a pair of 24-game winners in Mike Cuellar (24-8, 3.48) and Dave McNally (24-9, 3.22). Like a lot of Latin pitchers, Cuellar brought a passel of pitches to the mound. He was best known for his screwball and fastball, but he also mixed in a slider and a slow curve. McNally depended on his fastball and his curve, plus a slider that he rediscovered before the 1968 season after a five-year absence.

Jim Palmer (20-10, 2.71) won "only" 20 games in 1970, but of course he turned out to be the best of the bunch. A 20-year-old sensation back in 1966 (he pitched a shutout in the World Series), Palmer missed most of 1967 and all of '68 with something called "biceptal tendonitis." He came back better than ever in 1969, his stock in trade a high fastball that resulted in more pop-ups and fly balls than strikeouts. Palmer mixed in a curve and change-up, too.

How Were They Built? See separate article, "We Grow 'em on the Farm."

What Brought Them Down? An interesting question, this. Although Earl Weaver should probably be regarded as the top manager of his time, the fact remains that Weaver's teams went seven straight seasons, 1972 through 1978, without reaching the World Series, and the Orioles won just two American League East titles during that span.

So what happened? Well, for one thing, the Hall of Famers got old. Frank Robinson went to Los Angeles in 1972, and by 1971 Brooks Robinson was practically helpless at the plate. Also, big Boog Powell, as you might have expected, didn't age well and was practically washed up at age thirty-four when he went to Cleveland.

Mind you, the Orioles never collapsed or came close to collapsing. With Weaver in charge and Jim Palmer in the rotation, that simply wasn't going to happen. From '72 through '78, Baltimore averaged 90 wins per season, and they always won more than they lost. In fact, some analysts consider Weaver's performance in the mid-1970s more impressive than his performance in the early 1970s because he kept a team with no superstar position players in the pennant hunt just about every season.

apathy? Five letters: C-O-L-T-S. From the mid-1950s through the early 1970s, Baltimore was a football town, and no town loved their football team more than Baltimore loved the Colts.—*Rob*

Boog Powell *(National Baseball Hall of Fame Library, Cooperstown, NY)*

Most Valuable Oriole: You were probably thinking one of the Robinsons, right? Think again. Frank Robinson posted a 922 OPS, but he played only 132 games and finished with just 78 RBI. Brooks Robinson played almost every game (he supposedly had an incentive clause in his contract that rewarded him for doing so), but his 767 OPS was nothing special. No, the most valuable Oriole was first baseman John Wesley "Boog" Powell. What's more, Powell was officially the American League's MVP in 1970, after finishing second in the voting to Harmon Killebrew in 1969. Interestingly, Powell's stats were virtually identical those two seasons:

	Games	Runs	Hits	2B	3B	HR	RBI	Avg	OBP	Slug	OPS
1969	152	83	162	25	0	37	121	.304	.383	.559	942
1970	154	82	156	28	0	35	114	.297	.412	.549	961

The only real difference was Powell's walks (not shown here), which went from 72 in 1969 to 104 in 1970. That's why his on-base percentage went up 19 points in '70 (in case you were wondering).

We remember Powell as a big, fat guy, but in his prime he was fairly nimble around the bag. Mark Belanger, who knew a little something about defense, said of his first baseman, "I'm not saying this because I play with the guy, but the guy is nothing but great. He has a fantastic pair of hands."

After finishing second and then first in those two MVP votes, Powell was never quite the same player. His MVP support after 1970 consisted of one eighth-, one ninth- and one-and-a-half tenth-place votes, all in 1975 when, reunited with manager Frank Robinson, he slugged 27 homers as Cleveland's first baseman. A year later he hit .215, and in 1977 the thirty-six-year-old Powell ended his career as a pinch-hitter for the Dodgers.

Worst Regular: Yes, Mark Belanger was a brilliant defensive shortstop. But in 1970 he was such a terrible hitter (more on that later) that he wins this one.

Hall of Famers: Brooks Robinson, Frank Robinson, Jim Palmer, and Earl Weaver.

Our Hall of Famers: Same four. Those guys are all locks, and there's nobody else on the team who has a case. Well, that's not precisely true. Rookie infielder Bobby Grich got into 30 games in 1970, and the more sabermetrically inclined will try to convince you that Grich was one of the great second basemen of all time. We're inclined to agree, but the Hall of Fame voters were not. In 1992, his first year of eligibility, Grich drew only 11 votes and, thus, fell off the ballot. Given that Grich's skills—good glove, medium power, lots of walks—tend to be overlooked by just about everybody, he'll likely spend eternity as one of the game's great underrated players.

The 1970 American League Championship Series: For the second straight year, the Orioles swept the Minnesota Twins to reach the World Series. But whereas the '69 ALCS had at least been competitive, with two of Baltimore's three victories coming by a single run, in 1970 the Orioles destroyed the Twins, outscoring them 27–10 in the series.

The 1970 World Series: The 1970 World Series will forever be remembered for the scintillating defensive play of Brooks Robinson.

Good Field, No Hit

In 1969, shortstop Mark Belanger batted .287, posted a solid 696 OPS, and created 4.34 runs per 27 outs, all those numbers better than league average. But in 1970, Belanger turned into the weak-hitting glove man we all remember. His numbers—.303 on-base, .259 slugging (!), .218 batting average—speak for themselves. Belanger's OPS ranked last among the fifty-six American League players who qualified for the batting title, and 111th among the 115 A.L. players with 250-plus plate appearances.

What the overall numbers fail to show is that, for the first half of the year, Belanger was *much* worse than his season totals. In 255 at-bats through the end of June, Belanger's numbers looked like this: .246 on-base, .212 slugging, .173 batting. Despite all this, Earl Weaver kept playing Belanger because of his defense. Belanger did not win the Gold Glove in 1970.

He had won his first in 1969 and would win seven more, and his not winning it in 1970 could be yet another example of how Gold Gloves can be won and lost based on a player's hitting instead of his fielding. Why else would Weaver have continued to play him?

Belanger's offensive "contributions" notwithstanding, the 1970 Orioles led the American League in runs scored despite playing their home games in a pitcher's park. Belanger wasn't bad in 1971 (685 OPS and a better-than-league-average 4.39 RC/27) and he was okay in 1976, but for the rest of his career he was a Gold Glove shortstop who simply couldn't hit.
—*Eddie*

The Control Artist

By the time the 1970 World Series rolled around, Orioles reliever Dick Hall was forty years old; he'd turned forty on September 27. Roger Angell wrote that Hall pitched "with an awkward, sidewise motion that

Reds manager Sparky Anderson was hamstrung from the beginning, as two of his top starters, Jim Merritt and Wayne Simpson, came in hurt. Simpson wasn't able to pitch at all in the Series, and Merritt didn't escape the second inning in his only start.

Game 1, in Cincinnati, saw the Reds jump to a 3–0 lead early, but the Orioles tied the game on Boog Powell's two-run homer in the fourth and Elrod Hendricks' solo shot in the fifth. The Reds threatened in the bottom of the sixth but failed to score thanks to a brilliant play by Brooks Robinson and a terrible call by plate umpire Ken Burkhart. Burkhart called Bernie Carbo out at home, even though catcher Hendricks tagged Carbo with his glove while the ball was still in his throwing hand. Robinson homered in the seventh to give Baltimore a 4–3 lead, and that's how it ended.

Baltimore starter Mike Cuellar got knocked out early in game 2, but a quartet of relievers held the Reds after that, and the O's came back to post another one-run victory (6–5). The Series moved to Memorial Stadium for game 3, and the O's were running on all cylinders. Brooks Robinson made three spectacular plays at third, starter Dave McNally hit a grand slam, and Baltimore cruised, 9–3.

Dick Hall (*AP/Wide World Photos*)

On the verge of elimination, the Reds stayed alive thanks to Lee May's three-run homer in the eighth inning of game 4, which gave Cincinnati a 6–5 lead they were able to hold. Cuellar, roughed up in game 2, allowed three runs in the first inning of game 5. Earl Weaver stuck with Cuellar, though, and the left-hander pitched eight shutout innings. Meanwhile, the Oriole hitters ripped a succession of Cincinnati hurlers. The final score was 9–3, and the Orioles were World Champs for the second time in five years.

Postscript: After the World Series, the Hall of Fame asked for and received Brooks Robinson's glove. However, unable to find a suitable replacement, he reclaimed his magical mitt before the 1971 season.

The Ballpark: For the most part, Earl Weaver didn't care if his corner outfielders could run, and this was due, at least in part, to the peculiar characteristics of Memorial Stadium. The concrete walls slanted across the outfield, which meant that balls hit off them ricocheted toward center field. This allowed the Orioles to bunch their outfielders, and it made speed a lesser priority. The ballpark cut triples in the neighborhood of 40 percent, and it was also tough on batting averages and (less so) on home runs. All in all, Memorial Stadium was a pretty good pitcher's park.

Books about the 1970 Orioles: At last count, Frank Robinson has done three books, though none focus specifically on his time with the Orioles of this period. Earl Weaver has co-authored three books, and all of them are quite good. The most relevant for our purposes is *Winning!* (New York: William Morrow & Co, 1972); his other books are *It's What You Learn After You Know It All That Counts: The Autobiography of Earl Weaver* (Garden City, NY: Doubleday, 1982) and the classic *Weaver on Strategy* (New York: Collier Books, 1984). Terry Pluto's biography of Weaver, *The Earl of Baltimore* (Piscataway, NJ: New Century Books, 1982) is excellent. Brooks Robinson came out with a pair of autobiographies in the early 1970s, but neither are particularly interesting. Jim Palmer did a lightweight tome in 1996, mostly about his relationship with Weaver, called *Together We Were Eleven Foot Nine* (Kansas City, MO: Andrews and McNeel, 1995). If only the book were as interesting as its title.

suggests a man feeling under his bed for a lost collar stud. He throws a sneaky fast ball and never, or *almost* never, walks batters." It's true. Hall was a major leaguer for sixteen seasons, a reliever mostly, and he always had great control. Beginning in about 1965, Hall's control went from great to unbelievable. From '65 through '71 (his last season), Hall issued 62 walks in 462 innings. That's impressive.

But wait, it gets better. Of those 62 walks, *39 were intentional.* So in 462 innings, Hall issued 23 non-intentional walks. In case you're not a math whiz, that's one walk every 20 innings. In 1970, Hall issued six walks, and he carefully regulated them: one in April, one in May, one in June, one in July, one in August, one in September.

And finally, my favorite Dick Hall stat. (Drum roll, please.) Hall totaled, in his major league career, 1,259⅔ innings, and he didn't throw his first (and only) wild pitch until late in his last season.

Hall ruined his perfect
record on August 20, 1971,
when he zinged an offering
to the backstop with Steve
Braun batting, allowing
George Mitterwald to
advance to third base.—*Rob*

Stats 'n' Stuff

◆ On June 26 against the
Senators, Frank Robinson hit
bases-loaded homers in both
the fifth and sixth innings.
But he wasn't the only Oriole
who performed well with the
sacks full in 1970. As a team,
the O's batted .303 with an
868 OPS with the bases
loaded. Don Buford, Boog
Powell, and Merv
Rettenmund were
particularly successful.

◆ Lore holds that after
getting beaned by Angels
pitcher Ken Tatum on May
31, Paul Blair was never the
same. Perhaps. But look
what Blair did from August 1
through the end of the
season: .521 slugging
percentage, .377 OBP, .314
batting average, and 10
home runs in 188 at-bats.

◆ People used to say
that Mike Cuellar loved to

We Grow 'em on the Farm

How were the Orioles built? For the most part, the Orioles were a
home-grown club, with most of the best players having been
signed before the institution of the amateur draft in 1965. The most
famous exception, of course, was Frank Robinson, who became an
Oriole thanks to one of the most lopsided, best-remembered trades
in the history of the game.

Or, as Annie Savoy says at the beginning of *Bull Durham,* "Who can
forget Frank Robinson for Milt Pappas, for God's sake?" Actually, it
wasn't just Milt Pappas. On December 9, 1965, the Orioles sent
starter Milt Pappas, reliever Jack Baldschun, and reserve outfielder
Dick Simpson to the Cincinnati Reds and received Frank Robinson in
return. Pappas was a good pitcher for a long time, and Baldschun was
a fine reliever for a few years though, as it turned out, neither pitched
particularly well in Cincinnati.

Neither Baldschun nor Simpson had ever actually played for the
Orioles. Baltimore acquired Simpson a week before the Robinson
trade in exchange for Norm Siebern, and Baldschun was acquired
three days before the trade for Jackie Brandt and Darold Knowles. In
reality, from Baltimore's point of view, the trade was Milt Pappas,
Norm Siebern, Jackie Brandt, and Darold Knowles for Frank Robinson.

In public, Reds GM Bill DeWitt seemed to demonstrate the same
poor grasp of the facts that has plagued baseball men forever, cau-
tioning skeptics, "Don't forget, pitching is the name of the game. The
lack of it, especially in the bullpen, beat us last season." However, it
is also true that Robinson had been involved in some off-the-field in-
cidents that upset Reds management, and it's also true that DeWitt
generally didn't like to keep players after they turned thirty. Orioles
coach Gene Woodling was a bit more prescient, saying, "If we don't
win the pennant with him this year, then we all ought to be fired.
He'll be the best hitter the Orioles ever had." Robinson was indeed
the best hitter the Orioles ever had, and they won not only the pennant in 1966, but the World Series as well, humiliating the Dodgers
in four straight games.

The entire infield of the 1969–71 Orioles was home-grown, although Boog Powell was an Oriole due, quite literally, to fate. In the
spring of 1959, the O's and the Cardinals were both particularly in-

terested in signing Powell. According to then-Baltimore scout Jim Russo, both clubs were willing to offer a bonus in the neighborhood of $75,000, which was a lot of money back then.

Rather than engage in a bidding war, Orioles farm director Jim McLaughlin called his St. Louis counterpart, Walter Shannon, and offered a deal. Why not flip a coin, with the loser dropping out of the Powell sweepstakes? Shannon agreed, and Russo called "tails" for the Orioles. Tails it was, and the O's got Powell for $25,000.

Between them, Powell and Brooks Robinson won two MVP awards and finished in the top five in MVP voting seven times. Robinson, Dave Johnson, and Mark Belanger won a combined twenty-seven Gold Gloves. Fittingly, the infield combined for twenty-seven All-Star berths (home-grown catcher Andy Etchebarren earned a pair of All-Star berths, too). As Tigers manager Mayo Smith once observed, "Trying to hit a ball through the Baltimore infield is like trying to throw hamburgers through a brick wall."

In 1964, the Orioles were after Jim Palmer. The other team in the running was Houston, represented by manager Paul Richards. Richards had served as both manager and general manager of the O's in the 1950s and early 1960s, and in 1964 he did his old club a big favor. Supposedly, in the middle of his presentation to the Palmer family, Richards picked up a putter and started hitting golf balls in the living room. Later, he ordered Jim's younger sister to get him a glass of water. After Richards left, the Baltimore scouts showed up. They offered Palmer a $40,000 bonus, and he signed. This time, the "Wizard of Waxahachie" (as Richards was known) wasn't much of a wizard.

The signing of four-time 20-game winner Dave McNally in 1962 cost Orioles farm director Jim McLaughlin his job. Here's McLaughlin from Kevin Kerrane's book, *Dollar Sign on the Muscle:* "[O]ne of those pitchers, Dave McNally, was the reason I got fired. There were two separate factions in the Baltimore organization. Richards and I each had our own people . . . then I authorized a bonus of eighty thousand for McNally—without Richards' approval—and I was gone."

Palmer and McNally combined for a dozen seasons with 20 or more wins. Palmer won three Cy Young awards. McNally finished second in the Cy Young voting in 1970 and for many years co-held the record for consecutive pitching victories, with 17. These two home-grown pitchers were named to the All-Star team nine times.

pitch in hot weather. His record in April through June in 133 innings was 8-5 with a 4.41 ERA. In July through September and 165 innings, he was 16-3 with a 2.84 ERA. The season ended on October 1, which means that Cuellar essentially won 16 games in three months. And speaking of pitching well in the heat, Dave McNally went 7-0 with a 1.32 ERA in August.

◆ Jim Palmer's strikeout to walk ratio in April was 21 to 24. The rest of the season it was 178 to 76. Palmer missed most of 1967, all of 1968, and a decent part of 1969 with arm injuries. Thus, he may still have had some rust in April.

◆ Cuellar and Dave McNally were nearly impossible to run against in 1970. Here are their opponents' stolen base data:

Pitcher	IP	SB	CS
Cuellar	298	2	5
McNally	296	5	9
Totals	594	7	14

◆ Left-handed pitcher Pete Richert struck out 41

right-handed batters in 109 at-bats.

◆ On August 2, the Orioles beat the Kansas City Royals for the 23d straight time, setting a major league record.

Around the Majors

April 7 After a four-year absence, Major League Baseball returns to Milwaukee, as the Seattle Pilots move to Wisconsin after just one season and are renamed the Milwaukee Brewers. The Brewers lose their first game, 12–0, to the California Angels.

April 13 In their home opener, the Oakland A's use gold-colored bases. The Rules Committee will soon ban this "innovation."

April 16 Cincinnati Reds ace Jim Maloney, who has already pitched three no-hitters in his career, tears his Achilles tendon while running the bases and will never pitch again.

April 22 New York Mets ace Tom Seaver sets a major

In addition to the acquisition of Frank Robinson, the trade for Don Buford was also key to the Orioles' success. Buford came over from the White Sox after the 1967 season in a trade that sent future Hall of Fame shortstop Luis Aparicio to Chicago.

Trading Aparicio opened up a spot for Mark Belanger, a defensive standout like Aparicio but significantly younger. And after Earl Weaver took over as manager at the 1968 All-Star break, one of his first moves was the insertion of Buford into the everyday lineup. Buford had mostly played third and second base in Chicago, but Weaver shifted him to left field. Buford's peak didn't last long, but he was a *very* important player for the Orioles as a leadoff hitter, posting OBPs of .397, .406, and .413 in the three pennant-winning seasons.—Eddie and Rob

Underrated Greatness

Here I am again, writing a piece about a Baltimore Orioles team. Well, despite the fact that I don't really have any ties to the Orioles anymore, I still have ties to the teams I grew up rooting for. I started to get into sports in the late 1960s, when I was about nine years old, which was a little later than most of my friends. The late arrival as a sports fan probably owed much to the fact that both of my parents were born in Europe, didn't come to the United States until their mid-thirties, and weren't really a part of the mainstream American culture. So, not surprisingly, they didn't have any interest in American sports, and it took a while for me to get the bug.

Baltimore had tremendously successful teams in the late 1960s and early 1970s. For example, for the sports year 1970, Baltimore had the champions in what were the two dominant sports at that time. The Orioles were the 1970 World Series champs, winning the series in October, and the Colts were the 1970 NFL champs, winning the Super Bowl in January of 1971. The Orioles, of course, won three straight American League pennants, winning over 100 games each year from 1969 to 1971. The Colts, despite the upset loss to the Jets in Super Bowl III, were very successful. In fact, when they went 8-5-1 in 1969, that was considered a terrible year by Colts fans. When you look at the seasons surrounding that year (11-1-2 in 1967, 13-1 in 1968, 11-2-1 in 1970, and 10-4 in 1971), you can understand why.

The Baltimore Bullets of the NBA were also successful, although they were usually a playoff disappointment.

As we may have mentioned somewhere before, this Orioles team, the first three full years under Earl Weaver, is the only team in major league history to post an SD score of 3.00 or higher for three straight years. The 1936–39 Yankees just missed making it four in a row, but their 1938 SD score was +2.97.

Weaver's first Orioles teams are remembered, certainly, but they are remembered as much for losing to the Mets in the 1969 World Series as they are for being a truly great team. The Orioles nearly led the league in most runs scored and fewest runs allowed in each of these three seasons, finishing second in runs scored to the 1969 Twins (who played in a better hitter's park). For the three seasons in total, the Orioles scored more runs than any other A.L. team on the road and allowed fewer runs than any other A.L. team in road games.

Watching those Weaver teams taught me very early that batting average was overrated, because the O's seldom had an exceptionally high average, but they always scored a lot of runs. I also remember watching that team play, expecting them to win every game, and then waiting breathlessly for the box score the next day in the newspaper.

The 1969 team won 109 games, a total that was not surpassed in a 162-game schedule until 1998, but their longest winning streak was just eight games. One of my best friends, Gary Lazarus, is not as fond of the '69 team as he might be and not just because they lost to the Mets. It's because his favorite player, Brooks Robinson, didn't have one of his best years at the bat. My favorite player was *Frank* Robinson, and Frank had a damn good year after the horror that was 1968. I am now very fortunate to be able to consider Frank Robinson a friend.

Games are not played on paper, but the regular-season performance of the Orioles and Mets can hardly be compared. The 1969 Orioles had an SD score of +3.34; the 1969 Mets had a +1.06 SD score, by far the lowest ever for any 100-plus win team. (The average SD score for a 100-plus win team is +2.72.) The Mets' "projected" record based on their run differential was 92-70; their actual record was 100-62. The fact that the 1970 Mets followed up their championship with an 83-79 mark, and followed that up with another 83-79 record, is not surprising. The club simply wasn't a great collection of

league record, striking out nineteen San Diego Padres, including ten straight to end the game.

June 1 Commissioner Bowie Kuhn reprimands pitcher Jim Bouton for writing his book, *Ball Four.* Thanks in part to the publicity, *Ball Four* becomes the best-selling sports book in history (to that time).

July 14 The National League wins its eighth straight All-Star Game 5–4 in 12 innings, as Cincinnati's Pete Rose crashes into Indians catcher Ray Fosse to score the winning run.

August 23 Roberto Clemente collects five hits in a game for the second straight day, thus becoming the first player in the twentieth century to do so.

September 11 A's lefthander Vida Blue, only twenty-one years old, tosses a one-hit shutout against the Royals just eight days after being called up from the minors. Ten days later, he will no-hit the Twins.

talent. However, anything can happen in a short series. The 1969 World Series was the first one I watched and, at the time, I didn't fully understand the magnitude of the upset.

The 1970 Orioles had almost an identical record to the 1969 Orioles and almost an identical SD score: +3.31. The Reds were actually a lot like the Mets in that they seemed to overachieve that season. Cincinnati won 102 games, but their run differential "predicted" a 91-71 record, and their SD score was just +1.57 (so perhaps their 79-83 record in 1971 should not have been a big surprise).

I think that the Orioles' two-year record of 217-107 in 1969–70 is nothing short of remarkable. They won more than two-thirds of their games for two years. Since the inception of the 162-game schedule, only five other teams have played .667 ball or better for *one* season, let alone two.

What sticks out in my mind about the 1971 season was *rain.* I think the Orioles had something like 20 rainouts, which is why they played only 158 games. Those four "missing" games were just never made up. The 1971 Orioles won their last 11 regular-season games, swept the A's three straight in the ALCS, then won the first two games of the 1971 World Series—a 16-game winning streak, in which they outscored their opponents 105 to 30! Unfortunately, they then lost four of their next five, and you know what four losses means in the World Series. If the same scenario had occurred during the regular season, it would have had a much different meaning. As you may know, the 1971 Orioles featured four 20-game winners: Dave McNally (21-5 in just 30 starts, 2.89 ERA), Pat Dobson (20-8, 2.90), Jim Palmer (20-9, 2.68), and Mike Cuellar (20-9, 3.08). With the five-man rotation now firmly in place, it seems unlikely we will ever see that again. Over the three-season stretch, the Orioles boasted nine 20-game winners (Cuellar and McNally three times each, Palmer twice, and Dobson).

The 1971 Orioles led the league in runs scored by a significant margin despite the missing four games. They were the only Earl Weaver team to lead the league in batting average. They also drew 91 more walks than any other team in the league and 132 more walks than the average A.L. team, despite having no player in the top five in the league. They were fourth in the league in home runs, but had only three fewer home runs than the number two team (and again, remember that they played only 158 games).

From where I'm sitting, what strikes me most about the 1969–71 Orioles is their balance. Their run-scoring prowess has already been documented here, but they were the best offensive team in the league despite not having any player lead the league in on-base or slugging percentage during this period. (They did have at least one player in the top five in both categories in each of the three seasons.) They allowed the fewest runs in the league each season without an ERA champion (granted, with a little help from Memorial Stadium), but they did have at least one pitcher in the top three in ERA in each of those three seasons. Orioles won eleven Gold Gloves from 1969 through 1971. On a historical level, they had three first-ballot Hall of Famers and a Hall of Fame manager. I mean, what else can you do? Well, they might have won just one more World Series. Although the ultimate goal in baseball is to win the World Series, the nature of the game means that the best team doesn't always win. These Orioles were truly one of the very best teams of all time, by any reasonable and objective measure. They are not really considered as such because they were upset in the 1969 World Series and because they blew a 2–0 lead in the 1971 World Series. But the truth is the truth.—Eddie

Oh, Those Bases on Balls

Looking at the great teams, one of the things you see with team after team is a great walks differential; that is, nearly every one of these teams' hitters drew far more walks than their pitchers gave up. The 1970 Orioles are at the head of the class in this particular category. The following table below lists the walks differential for each team in this book, along with its league rank:

Team	Walks Differential	League Rank
1970 Orioles	+248	1st (of 12)
1927 Yankees	+226	1st (of 8)
1975 Reds	+204	1st (of 12)
1998 Yankees	+187	1st (of 14)

Team	Walks Differential	League Rank
1912 Giants	+176	1st (of 8)
1953 Yankees	+156	1st (of 8)
1955 Dodgers	+155	1st (of 8)
1974 Athletics	+138	1st (of 12)
1939 Yankees	+134	1st (of 8)
1986 Mets	+122	1st (of 12)
1942 Cardinals	+78	1st (of 8)
1929 Athletics	+56	4th (of 8)
1961 Yankees	+1	4th (of 10)
1906 Cubs	+2	3d (of 8)
1911 Athletics	−63	7th (of 8)
Average	+124	

We've ranked the teams by differential, and the O's would be atop the list even if we had adjusted for the fact that they played seven more games than did the '27 Yankees. That +248 differential is the third highest of all time. The first highest? In 1971, these same Baltimore Orioles would go +256.—Rob

Weaver before He Was Weaver

Just as Joe McCarthy had his Ten Commandments of Baseball and Connie Mack had his "code of conduct for players," Earl Weaver had his "Laws," which are detailed in his wonderful book (co-written with Terry Pluto), *Weaver On Strategy*.

The Weaver most of us remember is the Weaver of the late 1970s, the Weaver who fought with the umpires and relied on a strong bench and the famous "three-run homer." According to *The Ball Clubs*, Weaver "abhorred bunting."

Not in 1970 he didn't. That season, the Orioles laid down 64 sacrifice bunts, seventh most in the American League. And over Weaver's first three full seasons as manager, 1969–71, the O's . . . well, let's run an illustrative chart:

A.L. Rank and Team	Sacrifice Hits, 1969–71
1. Seattle/Milwaukee	294
2. California	227
2. Oakland	227
4. Baltimore	223
5. Minnesota	208
5. Detroit	208

Surprised to see the Orioles in the No. 4 spot, and only four bunts behind the teams tied for No. 2? We were. Those 223 sacrifices certainly don't square with our image of Weaver as King of the Sacrifice Haters. (The Orioles got a lot of runners on base and, of course, pitchers still hit in the American League back then. If we just consider sacrifice hits by non-pitchers, the O's rank sixth in the league over the three-year span.)

A couple of notes on the top team on this list. The expansion Seattle Pilots moved to Milwaukee in 1970, and Dave Bristol took over as manager. Bristol absolutely loved to bunt, and 222 of those 294 sacrifices in the chart came in '70 and '71.

How much did Weaver change? His best other three-year stretch as manager was from 1978 through 1980, when the O's won 292 games. The Orioles recorded only 125 sacrifice hits in those years, by far the fewest in the American League.—Rob

Winning 20, One at a Time

Over the three years the Orioles won the pennant, they blended (as we have seen) a wonderful combination of hitting, fielding, and pitching. Many fans remember the 1971 Orioles as the only team to feature *four* 20-game winners. As it happens, they weren't the only such team, but they were close. I sat down with *Total Baseball* and entered every team's 20-game winner(s) into a spreadsheet. That allowed me to come up with, among other things, the following chart of teams with three or more 20-game winners from 1920 to 1998:

Team	20-Game Winners
1970 Baltimore Orioles	Cuellar, McNally, Palmer
1971 Baltimore Orioles	Cuellar, Dobson, McNally, Palmer
1920 Chicago White Sox	Cicotte, Faber, Kerr, Williams
1923 Cincinnati Reds	Donohue, Luque, Rixey
1951 Cleveland Indians	Feller, Garcia, Wynn
1952 Cleveland Indians	Garcia, Lemon, Wynn
1956 Cleveland Indians	Lemon, Score, Wynn
1920 New York Giants	Barnes, Nehf, Toney
1973 Oakland Athletics	Blue, Holtzman, Hunter
1931 Philadelphia Athletics	Earnshaw, Grove, Walberg

A few notes on the data:

◆ Baltimore had twenty-one 20-win seasons from pitchers from 1969 through 1982, Weaver's first stint as manager not counting his partial season of 1968.
◆ The Orioles had nine 20-win seasons from 1969 through 1971, the most in any three-season stretch since 1920.
◆ Under Weaver, the Orioles had *more* than one 20-game winner in six different seasons: 1969, 1970, 1971, 1975, 1976, and 1980.
◆ Most of the teams listed in the table are either in this book or they're well known to you. But you might not know much at all about the '23 Cincinnati Reds (we didn't). They finished a strong second to the Giants as Dolf Luque had a great year, leading the league in wins (27), ERA (1.93), and shutouts (6).
◆ From 1920 through 1960, Washington Senators pitchers had ten 20-win seasons. From 1940 though 1960, they had two.
◆ From 1920 through 1949, the Phillies had no 20-game winners.—Eddie

Merv Rettenmund

Atlanta's Merv Rettenmund is among the most respected batting coaches in the game. Rettenmund was a member of the 1969–71 Orioles, playing the outfield and contributing a potent bat. He graciously sat down with me in February 1999 to discuss that team.

Merv was born in Michigan and went to Ball State University in Indiana, where he played baseball and football (running back). He made the Orioles out of spring training in 1968, but was sent back to their Triple-A club at Rochester early in the season. I'll let him pick up the story from there.

Rettenmund: I didn't want to go back to the majors. I was having fun, playing every day and leading off, and eventually I was named Minor League Player of the Year. Baltimore called me up in August, between games of a day/night doubleheader, and I stayed in Rochester for the second game instead of leaving right away.

The 1968 Orioles were a little short of pitching and a little short in other areas. In 1969, Jim Palmer's return and the acquisition of Mike Cuellar really bolstered the pitching staff. Palmer was not expected to contribute in 1969, so having him as much as we did was like getting a number one starter out of the blue.

Q: What first comes to mind when you think about the 1969–71 Orioles?

Rettenmund: Togetherness. Many of the players had been together in the minors, and Weaver had managed many of them in the minors. Players like McNally, Palmer, Etchebarren, Blair, Johnson, and Belanger were products of the Orioles' minor league system. So it was a tight-knit group. The team had continuity and that was very, very important. The players knew how to play, they knew their positions, and they knew they could count on each other.

Q: What was it like playing for Earl Weaver?

Rettenmund: Weaver was brilliant. While it's hard to say that he was well-liked, I respected him and so did everyone else. It was Weaver's club and he ran the show. His moves didn't seem to make sense sometimes, but they almost always seemed to work. He got everyone playing time and his use of batter/pitcher match-up information helped him do that.

Q: What happened in the 1969 World Series?

Rettenmund: You have to tip your hat to the Mets, but to be honest we probably didn't take them as seriously as we should have, especially after we beat Seaver in the first game. Even as the Series went on, we still expected to win, although the events in New

York were hard to believe. Anything can happen in a short series. The loss in the '69 Series was a motivating factor all year in 1970.

Q: What else strikes you about 1970?

Rettenmund: Paul Blair got beaned that year, and that was my opportunity to get some playing time. I think I probably would have been traded if it hadn't been for the beaning.

   We knew we were going to win the ALCS against Minnesota, and they probably knew it, too. We expected to win the World Series, especially since the Reds' pitching staff was a little beat up. It may surprise you to hear this, but Wayne Simpson was the best right-handed pitcher I ever saw. He got hurt mid-season, though, and was out of the Series. I don't think Jim Merritt was 100 percent, either. It turned out to be a lopsided Series and, of course, Brooks Robinson was phenomenal. The only thing that we "worried" about was the fact that the games in Cincinnati were to be played on Astroturf, and we were not used to playing on it. That doesn't sound like a big deal today, but it was then.

Q: Who was the MVP of that Orioles team?

Rettenmund: Frank Robinson, and not just because he was a great player, one of the best who ever played. It was also because of the way he played. If a player was on first, we were very good at getting down to second base and breaking up the double play. That really came from Frank and is an example of how he influenced us.

Q: What do you remember about some of the other players on that team?

Rettenmund: It was the best defensive team I've ever seen, especially the left side of the infield. Mark Belanger was the best defensive shortstop I've ever seen. Boog Powell had unbelievable hands at first base. Brooks Robinson was a leader, but in his way. He had fun every day. In general, we were very confident. We expected to win. We had a great big league club and a tremendous minor league system.

Q: You also played for the 1975 Reds. Which team do you think was better?

Rettenmund: Over a full season, I'd take the Orioles, although I don't know who I'd take in a short series.—Eddie

TEAM STATISTICS

Hitting

	Games by Position	Age	G	AB	R	H	2B	3B	HR	RBI	BB	SO	SB	Avg	OBP	Slug
Boog Powell	1B,145	28	154	526	82	156	28	0	35	114	104	80	1	.297	.412	.549
Dave Johnson	2B,149; SS,2	27	149	530	68	149	27	1	10	53	66	68	2	.281	.360	.392
Mark Belanger	SS,143	26	145	459	53	100	6	5	1	36	52	65	13	.218	.303	.259
Brooks Robinson	3B,156	33	158	608	84	168	31	4	18	94	53	53	1	.276	.335	.429
Frank Robinson	OF,120; 1B,7	34	132	471	88	144	24	1	25	78	69	70	2	.306	.398	.520
Paul Blair	OF,128; 3B,1	26	133	480	79	128	24	2	18	65	56	93	24	.267	.344	.438
Don Buford	OF,130; 2B,3; 3B,3	33	144	504	99	137	15	2	17	66	109	55	16	.272	.406	.411
Ellie Hendricks	C,95	29	106	322	32	78	9	0	12	41	33	44	1	.242	.317	.382
Merv Rettenmund	OF,93	27	106	338	60	109	17	2	18	58	38	59	13	.322	.394	.544
Terry Crowley	OF,27; 1B,23	23	83	152	25	39	5	0	5	20	35	26	2	.257	.394	.388
Andy Etchebarren	C,76	27	78	230	19	56	10	1	4	28	21	41	4	.243	.313	.348
Chico Salmon	SS,33; 2B,12; 3B,11	29	63	172	19	43	4	0	7	22	8	30	2	.250	.287	.395
Curt Motton	OF,21	29	52	84	16	19	3	1	3	19	18	20	1	.226	.369	.393
Bobby Grich	SS,20; 2B,9	21	30	95	11	20	1	3	0	8	9	21	1	.211	.279	.284
Dave May*	OF,9	26	25	31	6	6	0	1	1	6	4	4	0	.194	.286	.355
Clay Dalrymple	C,11	33	13	32	4	7	1	0	1	3	7	4	0	.219	.350	.344
Don Baylor	OF,6	21	8	17	4	4	0	0	0	4	2	3	1	.235	.300	.235
Johnny Oates	C,4	24	5	18	2	5	0	1	0	2	2	0	0	.278	.333	.389
Roger Freed	1B,3; OF,1	24	4	13	0	2	0	0	0	1	3	4	0	.154	.294	.154
Bobby Floyd*	SS,2; 2B,1	26	3	2	0	0	0	0	0	0	0	2	0	.000	.000	.000
Totals		29	162	5,545	**792**	1,424	213	25	179	**748**	**717**	952	84	.257	**.351**	.401

*Played for another team during season. Statistics are those compiled with 1970 Baltimore Orioles only.

Pitching

	Threw	Age	Games	GS	CG	ShO	IP	H	HR	BB	SO	W	L	Pct	Sv	ERA
Jim Palmer	Right	24	39	39	17	5	305	263	21	100	199	20	10	.667	0	2.71
Mike Cuellar	Left	33	40	40	21	4	298	273	34	69	190	24	8	.750	0	3.48
Dave McNally	Left	27	40	40	16	1	296	277	29	78	185	24	9	.727	0	3.22
Jim Hardin	Right	26	36	19	3	2	145	150	13	26	78	6	5	.545	1	3.53
Tom Phoebus	Right	28	27	21	3	0	135	106	11	62	72	5	5	.500	0	3.07
Dick Hall	Right	39	32	0	0	0	61	51	8	6	30	10	5	.667	3	3.08
Marcelino Lopez	Left	26	25	3	0	0	61	47	2	37	49	1	1	.500	0	2.08
Eddie Watt	Right	29	53	0	0	0	55	44	3	29	33	7	7	.500	12	3.25
Pete Richert	Left	30	50	0	0	0	55	36	5	24	66	7	2	.778	13	1.98
Moe Drabowsky*	Right	34	21	0	0	0	33	30	7	15	21	4	2	.667	1	3.78
Dave Leonhard	Right	29	23	0	0	0	28	32	5	18	14	0	0	—	1	5.08
Fred Beene	Right	24	0	0	0	0	6	8	1	5	4	0	0	—	0	6.00
Totals		29	386	162	60	12	1,479	1,317	139	469	941	108	54	.667	31	3.15

*Played for another team during season. Statistics are those compiled with 1970 Baltimore Orioles only.

CHAPTER 15

1974 Oakland A's

So which teams were better, the A's of the early seventies or the Reds of the middle seventies? Since they never played each other in real games, no one will know for sure. More to the point, a tangible examination of each team's accomplishments proves that the A's did achieve more over a longer period of time. When you add it up, two divisional crowns, two league pennants, and two world championships in two years is not as impressive as five divisional crowns, three league pennants, and three World Series victories over five years. The bottom line is this: two seasons do not make a dynasty; five seasons do.

—Bruce Markusen in *Baseball's Last Dynasty: Charlie Finley's Oakland A's*

Record: 90-72, .556 (483d)
Two-Year (1973–74): 184-140, .568
 (350th)
Three-Year (1972–74): 277-202, .578
 (241st)

SD Score: +3.15 (23d)
Two-Year: +5.35 (38th)
Three-Year: +7.98 (20th)
 It's worth noting that if we used 1973–75 rather than 1972–74 data, the A's would fare better in both the two- and three-year measures because they won 98 games in 1975. But we included 1972 because the A's won the World Series that season.

Results:
1972 World Champions
1973 World Champions
1974 World Champions

Days in First Place: 142 of 181;
 clinched on September 27

Longest Winning Streak: 6 games
Longest Losing Streak: 4 games

Against the Contenders: Even though the A's won only 90 games, there really weren't any strong contenders in the American League West. The Texas Rangers finished five games off the pace, but they needed an August surge to get close, and this was after losing 105 games in 1973. The Minnesota Twins (82-80) were the only other West club to finish above .500. The A's were just 8-10 against the Rangers, but took 13 of 18 from the Twins.

Runs Scored: 689 (3d)

The American League was strangely bunched in 1974. The A's finished just seven runs behind the league-leading Red Sox (696) and 27 runs ahead of eighth-spot Cleveland (662).

Runs Allowed: 551 (1st)

Here's where the A's really shone. The Orioles, Oakland's eventual opponent in the ALCS, finished second in this category, and they allowed 612 runs.

Pythagorean Record: 97-65

Manager: Alvin Dark

Dick Williams had managed the A's to World Championships in 1972 and 1973, but after three years of putting up with owner Charlie Finley's bullshit, Williams quit. Finley then hired Alvin Dark. Dark had been successful as manager of the Giants in the '60s, but he'd been away from the game for a few years and didn't know the American League at all. Given the strong personalities that populated Oakland's roster and the great respect most of them had for Dick Williams, you had the makings for a clubhouse revolt.

There were plenty of early-season grumblings, and everything came to a head after the A's lost an eleven-inning game to Boston on June 19. Team captain Sal Bando, frustrated both with Dark's managerial moves and with himself for making the last out, stormed into the A's locker room, kicked a garbage can, and screamed, "That motherfucker couldn't manage a fucking meat market!" What Bando didn't know was that Dark had just walked into the clubhouse. The two patched things up quickly, but *San Francisco Chronicle* sportswriter Glen Dickey was there, too, so the incident made headlines.

The players never really did trust Dark's baseball acumen like they had Williams', but they did come to respect his willingness to admit his mistakes. And twenty-odd years later, Bando admitted, "Once a third of the season was over, Alvin had a firm handle of the club and what guys can do."

Regular Lineup:

Player	Position	ROV	OW%
Bert Campaneris	SS	.277	.615
Billy North	CF	.264	.566
Sal Bando	3B	.292	.667
Reggie Jackson	RF	.339	.785
Joe Rudi	LF	.302	.696
Gene Tenace	1B	.289	.654
Deron Johnson	DH	.201	.287
Ray Fosse	C	.200	.282
Dick Green	2B	.193	.250

Bench: By October, Deron Johnson was long gone, having been sold to the Brewers on June 24. Angel Mangual, once labeled "the next Roberto Clemente," took over the designated-hitter duties for a spell, but he was worthless with the stick. So in early July, the A's summoned from the minors a nineteen-year-old prospect named Claudell Washington. He was in the lineup most of the rest of the season, splitting his time between DH and the outfield. Veteran Jesus Alou performed the same chores all season long. Ted Kubiak backed up Dick Green at second base and also filled in at shortstop and third base.

Scouting the Pitchers: Catfish Hunter (25-12, 2.49) might not have had the best "stuff" on the staff, but he was smart and he had a rubber arm; beginning in 1968, Hunter pitched at least 234 innings in ten straight seasons. His repertoire was all power: fastballs and sliders.

The guy with the real stuff was Vida Blue (17-15, 3.25), who had led the American League with eight shutouts and a 1.82 ERA in 1971, when he was twenty-two years old.

Though he's not remembered much today, Ken Holtzman (19-17, 3.07) was a fine pitcher, a Jewish lefthander who drew the inevitable

Catfish's Stretch Run

Although Oakland was just 29-29 from August 1, 1974, through the end of the season, Catfish Hunter sewed up his only Cy Young award with a remarkable stretch of pitching. In his last 15 starts, he went 11-3 with a 1.77 ERA, which lowered his season ERA from 3.07 to 2.49. He allowed two runs or fewer in 11 of those 15 starts.

Although he was hit hard in game 1 of the 1974 ALCS, allowing six runs in 4⅔ innings in the A's 6–3 loss, he pitched seven scoreless innings and got the win in the game 4 clincher. In the World Series, he got the final out and the save in the 3–2 A's win in game 1 and then started and won game 3, allowing just one run in 7⅓ innings.—*Eddie*

Around the Majors

April 8 In the fourth inning of Atlanta's home opener, Henry Aaron drives an Al Downing fastball over the wall in left field for his 715th home run, thus breaking Babe Ruth's career record.

April 9 With the Padres losing their home opener 9–2, new owner Ray Kroc grabs the public-address microphone and says, "Ladies and gentlemen, I suffer with you. . . . I've never seen such stupid baseball playing in my life."

May 27 Pirates lefthander Ken Brett carries a no-hitter into the ninth inning against the Padres, before settling for a two-hit shutout. In the nightcap of the doubleheader, Brett's two-run, pinch-hit triple gives Pittsburgh an 8–7 victory.

June 4 It's Ten-Cent Beer Night in Cleveland, and the Indians are forced to forfeit their game to the White Sox when, with the score tied 5–5 in the ninth, drunken fans overrun the field.

June 19 Royals righthander Steve Busby no-hits the Brewers, thus becoming the first pitcher in

comparisons to Sandy Koufax. Holtzman even threw two no-hitters while pitching in the National League. And like Koufax, Holtzman depended on a fastball and a curve, though Holtzman's bender was slower than Koufax's.

How Were They Built? The A's, especially the core of the club, were built mostly through the amateur draft. Owner Charlie Finley, who served as his own general manager, did make a pair of astute trades.

In 1971, he sent former number one draft pick Rick Monday to the Cubs for Holtzman. Along with Blue and Hunter, Holtzman gave the A's a wonderful trio of starters, and he won 77 games from 1972 through 1975. In 1972, Finley went to the Cubs again, this time for young center fielder Bill North, who had played poorly in Chicago and was also considered something of an attitude problem. To get North, Finley surrendered Bob Locker, a thirty-four-year-old sinker-ball reliever who had gone 6-1 with a 2.65 ERA that season. So why make the trade? Locker had pitched poorly against Detroit in the ALCS, and Dick Williams had little confidence in him. And in 1971 Reggie Jackson had played center field, a position for which he was not suited. North wasn't much of a hitter, but he could run like the wind and played a great center field.

What Brought Them Down? See separate article, "Death of a Dynasty."

Most Valuable Athletic: Superficially, Reggie Jackson's 1974 campaign doesn't look all that impressive. He didn't score or drive in 100 runs, and he hit "only" 29 home runs, tied for the eighth-best total of his career. Look a little deeper, though, and you find a pretty awesome season. Jackson led the A's in runs, home runs, on-base percentage, and slugging percentage. In fact, Reggie's .514 slugging percentage ranked second in the American League despite the fact that the Oakland Alameda County Coliseum was a great pitcher's park. Jackson also stole twenty-five bases and was caught only five times, for a league-leading 83 percent success rate. Jackson's .785 OW% was outstanding and shows just how valuable he was.

Worst Regular: Dick Green only batted 287 times, but he was the closest thing to a regular second baseman the A's had. And though

Green was regarded as a brilliant defensive player, by 1974 he was pretty much helpless at the plate.

Hall of Famers: Reggie Jackson, Catfish Hunter, and Rollie Fingers.

Our Hall of Famers: Reggie's easy. However, it's quite possible that neither Fingers nor Hunter would be in the Hall had they pitched for lesser teams.

Fingers certainly ranks among the top relief pitchers since 1970. But is his record any better than that of Goose Gossage, a near-contemporary who hasn't gotten much support in the Hall of Fame voting?

Hunter won 20 or more games in five different seasons, but given that his ERAs generally were not outstanding—he led the American League in ERA but once, despite toiling in pitcher-friendly parks—there's little doubt that he benefited from the powerful A's lineup. Hunter finished with 224 victories, low by Hall of Fame standards. His .574 career winning percentage doesn't rank among the top 100 all-time. His tenure as an effective starter lasted only six or eight seasons, low by Hall of Fame standards. He was pretty much washed up by the time he was thirty-two, young by Hall of Fame standards.

So why did Hunter make it so easily, in his third year of eligibility? Well, his five 20-win seasons came consecutively, which means he spent five straight seasons on everyone's minds. Too, he went 9-6 with a 3.27 ERA in postseason games, and that also made an impression on the voters.

The 1974 American League Championship Series: Oakland's opponents in the ALCS were Earl Weaver's Baltimore Orioles, who were eight games off the pace near the end of August but won 28 of their last 34 to edge the Yankees by two lengths. The O's continued their hot streak in the first game of the playoffs, driving Catfish Hunter from the mound in the fifth inning on their way to a 6–3 victory.

The Athletics' Ken Holtzman—whose career postseason record was perhaps even more impressive than Hunter's—put the clamps on Baltimore in game 2, firing a five-hit shutout.

After a day off, the Series resumed in Baltimore, where Vida Blue outdid his teammate Holtzman with a *two-hit* shutout. And Blue needed to be that good because Jim Palmer was pitching nearly as

major league history to throw no-hitters in his first two seasons.

August 20 Angels righty Nolan Ryan strikes out nineteen hitters (in 11 innings) for the second time in three starts.

September 7 Yankees third baseman Graig Nettles loses a single and is ejected when his bat explodes and six rubber balls fly out. Nettles is not suspended, however.

No-Hitting the Dynasty

On July 30, 1973, Texas Rangers righthander Jim Bibby fired a no-hitter in Oakland, beating the A's 6–0 despite issuing six walks. On July 19, 1974, Indians righthander Dick Bosman fired a no-hitter in Cleveland, beating the A's 4–0. (Bosman would have pitched a perfect game but for his own throwing error in the fourth inning.)

It might seem incredibly unlikely that a team would be no-hit in two straight seasons in which it eventually won the World Series. And to be sure, the odds were certainly against the A's or, for that matter, any team being victimized by a no-hitter in consecutive seasons. But the chances of a particular team being victimized by a no-hitter are solely a function of their team batting average. And although the A's of the early 1970s were an excellent offensive team, like some of the other great teams in this book they did *not* generally post high batting averages. In 1973, Oakland topped the American League with 758 runs scored, but their .260 team batting average ranked just sixth in the circuit. In 1974, the A's finished third with 689 runs scored (only seven behind the league-leading Red Sox), but their .247 team batting average ranked eleventh (in a twelve-team league!).

So yes, the odds were against the A's getting no-hit in two straight seasons. But World Champs or no World Champs, it was just about as likely to happen to them as

well for the Orioles. Palmer permitted just four hits and one run, the lone tally coming on Sal Bando's home run in the fourth inning.

Catfish Hunter, so ineffective in the opener, came back with seven shutout innings in game 4. His opponent, Mike Cuellar, pitched 4⅔ hitless innings, but walked nine, including four in a row in the fifth to give the A's a 1–0 lead. Oakland scored again in the seventh, when Bando walked and Reggie Jackson plated him with a double. That second run proved decisive, as Rollie Fingers permitted a run in the ninth before striking out Don Baylor to end the game and clinch Oakland's third straight American League pennant.

The 1974 World Series: The 1974 A's might not have won as many regular-season games as the '72 and '73 editions, but they certainly outperformed their forebears in the World Series. In both '72 and '73, the A's needed seven games to dispatch their N.L. opponents, but in 1974 they took care of the Dodgers in only five (though in fairness to the National Leaguers, those five included four *close* games).

Reggie Jackson accounted for the first run of the Series with a second-inning blast over the wall in left-center, and A's starter Ken Holtzman—who hadn't batted all season long—doubled in the fifth and eventually scored. The Dodgers made it 2–1 in the bottom of that inning, thanks to a couple of Oakland errors, but the A's added an insurance run in the eighth. They needed it because, with two outs in the ninth and nobody on base, Jimmy Wynn homered off Rollie Fingers to make the score 3–2, and Steve Garvey followed with a single. Catfish Hunter hadn't pitched in relief all season, but Alvin Dark summoned him from the bullpen to face Joe Ferguson, who struck out to end the game. It was the second and final save of Hunter's major league career.

Game 2 was a case of role reversal, as this time the A's came out on the short end of a 3–2 stick. Vida Blue pitched well, but couldn't match Don Sutton, who pitched shutout ball until the ninth. Reliever Mike Marshall came in and, after allowing Joe Rudi's two-run single, struck out Gene Tenace, picked off pinch-runner Herb Washington, and struck out Angel Mangual to seal the victory.

After the first two games in Los Angeles, the clubs winged north for three in Oakland. The A's took game 3 in a squeaker, 3–2, thanks to some sloppy Dodger defense early. Bill Buckner and Willie Crawford brought the Dodgers back with solo home runs in the late innings, but Fingers got Bill Russell to bounce into a game-ending double play.

Game 4 would be the only Series contest not decided by a single run. Ken Holtzman gave the A's the lead with a solo homer in the third, but moments later he gave up a pair of runs when Russell drove a triple to right-center field. The Dodgers still owned a 2–1 lead when Oakland batted in the sixth, and the A's exploded for four runs, pinch-hitter Jim Holt's two-run single the big blow. That made the score 5–2, and that's how it ended after ace relievers Marshall and Fingers put the clamps on.

The A's opened game 5 with a pair of early runs, but Don Sutton settled down and the Dodgers tied the game with two of their own in the sixth. Just before the bottom of the seventh, the game was delayed for six minutes by fans throwing debris onto the field. When the game finally resumed, Joe Rudi hit the first pitch he saw into the left-field stands, and the A's had yet another one-run lead.

Fingers came in to pitch the top of the eighth, and Bill Buckner led off with a liner to center field that got past Bill North and rolled to the wall. At that point in his career, Buckner was fast, and he steamed around second base even though you're not supposed to make the first out of an inning at third base. Meanwhile, Reggie Jackson hustled over from right field to retrieve the ball and threw a strike to second baseman Dick Green, who turned and fired to Sal Bando. Two perfect throws, and Buckner was out. Fingers was near perfect from there, and the World Series ended when he retired pinch-hitter Von Joshua on a tapper back to the mound. The A's thus became the first team to win three straight World Series since the Yankees had won their five straight.

The Ballpark: The players called the Oakland Alameda County Coliseum "the Mausoleum," and with good reason. Once described by poet Tom Clark as "a large anonymous-looking bowl of gray concrete grimly typical of 1960s stadium design," the Coliseum was reviled by pretty much everybody that ever played there.

Books about the 1974 Athletics: Bruce Markusen's book, *Baseball's Last Dynasty: Charlie Finley and His A's* (Indianapolis, IN: Masters Press, 1998), is wonderfully researched and comprehensive. If you want to

any other A.L. team. (In 1917 the Chicago White Sox, eventually World Champions, were no-hit on consecutive *days*.) Interestingly, in 1990 the Oakland Athletics—another great team, but another one that didn't hit for a high average—were no-hit by Nolan Ryan, another Texas Rangers righthander.—*Rob* know specifics—when a player went on the disabled list, who was fighting who on which day, that kind of stuff—there is no better source.

The A's might not have drawn particularly well in Oakland, but they were an interesting team and thus the subject of quite a few books at the time. Tom Clark's *Champagne and Baloney* (New York: Harper and Row, 1976) is entertaining, and there are others. Aside from the books about Finley, many of the players did books either during or after their days in Oakland. Finally, Dick Williams (*No More Mr. Nice Guy* [New York: HBJ, 1990]) and Alvin Dark (*When in Doubt, Fire the Manager* [New York: E. P. Dutton, 1980]) both have done autobiographies, and both books have plenty to say about Finley's A's. Surprisingly, Charlie O. Finley, one of the most self-absorbed and controversial figures in the history of sports, never bothered to write a book about himself.

Death of a Dynasty

What brought the A's down? You want the short answer, or the long answer?

The short answer is *Charlie Finley and Peter Seitz.* For the long answer, let's start with Seitz. On the eve of the '74 World Series, the *Chicago Sun-Times* reported that Catfish Hunter and his agent, Jerry Kapstein, had charged Charlie Finley with breach of contract. Hunter was working on a two-year contract, which ran from 1974 through 1975. The contract stipulated that half of Hunter's $100,000 salary would be deferred and paid to the Jefferson Standard Life Insurance Company of Greensboro, North Carolina.

In mid-September, Hunter's lawyers had written to Finley about the payment. Had Finley then made the payment within ten days, everything would have been fine. But he waited until October 4, and by then it was too late. Hunter's contract included a standard clause saying, "The Player may terminate this contract upon written notice to the Club, if the Club shall default in the payments to the Player provided for . . . and if the Club shall fail to remedy such a default within 10 days after the receipt by the Club of written notice of such default." That's lawyer-speak for, "Team, you've got ten days to fix the problem, and if you don't, the player can do whatever he wants."

In fact, Hunter could have declared free agency on September 26, even before the regular season ended. But he didn't want to distract his teammates, so he kept it quiet. On November 19, Finley and the Players' Association both made their cases to arbitrator Peter Seitz. On December 13, Seitz announced that (1) Finley owed Hunter the $50,000 payment (with interest), and (2) Hunter was a free agent, immediately.

Every team in the major leagues wanted Hunter, who eventually narrowed his list of potential teams to five. On December 31, 1974, Hunter signed the richest deal in baseball history: $3.75 million for five years with the New York Yankees. With Hunter gone, second baseman Dick Green announced his retirement. "I'm just not coming back," Green said. "Catfish is the best pitcher in baseball and we won't win without him."

Two things about this. One, Green had also retired, only to un-retire, each of the three previous winters. This time, though, he stayed retired. And two, the A's *did* win without Hunter. They won 98 games in 1975, *eight more than they'd won in 1974.* Phil Garner proved an adequate replacement for Green at second base, while Stan Bahnsen and Dick Bosman helped pick up the slack in the pitching rotation.

But just as the Athletics' failure in the 1914 World Series foreshadowed their destruction, the A's failure in the 1975 American League Championship Series (they were swept in three straight games by the Red Sox) foreshadowed theirs. In the previous few years, salary arbitration had been an option when teams and players could not agree on contracts. However, the Collective Bargaining Agreement had expired after the 1975 season, and with no new agreement in place, arbitration was no longer an option. So Finley simply sent most of his players standard contracts that included 20 percent *cuts* from the year before. The players had a choice between holding out or playing, but if they played without a contract, they could become unconditional free agents at the end of the season because of the most well-known Seitz decision, the Messersmith/McNally case, so that's what most of them did.

Just a few days before the 1976 season started, Finley traded Reggie Jackson, Ken Holtzman, and a minor leaguer to the Baltimore

Orioles for pitcher Mike Torrez, outfielder Don Baylor, and pitcher Paul Mitchell. Finley actually had the gall to announce, "This trade was made because I feel this deal will lead us to another world championship. I feel that Baylor is the equal of Reggie Jackson."

On June 15, with the A's in fifth place, 11 games behind the first-place Kansas City Royals, Finley announced that he'd sold Joe Rudi and Rollie Fingers to the Red Sox for the grand sum of $1 million. A few minutes later, he sold Vida Blue to the Yankees for $1.5 million. But on June 18, before any of those three had played for their new teams, Major League Baseball Commissioner Bowie Kuhn, citing his power to act in "the best interests of baseball," declared the sales null and void. Kuhn was on shaky legal ground, and Finley filed a $10 million lawsuit. In the meantime, Rudi, Fingers, and Blue returned to the A's, but Finley didn't let them play, leaving manager Chuck Tanner (Dark had been fired the previous fall) with a twenty-two-man roster. With no action on the legal front, on June 27 the A's voted 21-0 in favor of striking unless Finley allowed Rudi, Fingers, and Blue to play. Faced with a united front, Finley relented. (In 1977, he lost his lawsuit and, in 1978, the Supreme Court refused to hear an appeal.)

Maybe all that heartache brought the team together, maybe it took Tanner a while to figure out the team, or maybe the talent just played up to its ability, but however you want to explain it, the fact is that after Finley tried to sell his three stars, the A's went 59-43 the rest of the way.

The A's had played 13 games without Rudi, Fingers, and Blue, and they went 8-5 in those 13 games. Of course, 8-5 is not bad, and given that the A's finished the season 2½ games behind Kansas City for the West title, it's unlikely that Rudi, Fingers, and Blue would have made a difference. Yes, it would have been easier to go 11-2 with them than without them, but when Finley tried to make the deals the A's *were* 11 games out.

After the final game of the season, the players threw a champagne party in the clubhouse, as Rudi, Fingers, Tenace, Campaneris, and Bando toasted their upcoming free agency. They couldn't wait to escape, and in 1977 they were all gone. In 1977, after capturing first or second place in eight straight seasons, the A's plummeted to the basement, finishing below even the expansion Seattle Mariners with a 63-98 record. It wasn't 1915 all over again, but it was close.—Rob

Reggie Jackson *(AP/Wide World Photos)*

Reggie

Reggie Jackson was certainly not everyone's cup of tea. He could be arrogant, aloof, obstinate, overly flamboyant, uncoachable . . . well, you get the point. From all of the controversy that surrounded him, it didn't seem as though he was particularly popular with his teammates, and he certainly wasn't popular with all of his managers.

Many GM's, managers, and other baseball executives think that clubhouse chemistry is the most important ingredient in a winning team. To them, a player like Jackson would be a detriment to the team because of the controversy and bad feelings. Well, if Jackson hurt his team's chances of winning, one can only imagine how good his teams would have been if he hadn't been there, right? Do you detect a note of sarcasm? For fifteen consecutive seasons (1968–82) and with four different teams, every one of the teams that Jackson played for had a winning record. Ten of those fifteen teams finished in first place, six of those teams played in the World Series, and five of them won the World Series. I am not for a moment suggesting that Jackson was the only, or even the most important, reason for the successes of his teams, but if he were really a hindrance, then why did those teams keep winning? If Jackson's teams won so much, can his "type" of player really be an obstacle?

For his career, the record of the teams Jackson played for was 1,843-1,494, a .552 winning percentage. Eleven of those teams finished in first place. During the peak of Jackson's career, 1968–80, the record of his teams was 1,215-882, a .579 winning percentage. Eight of those thirteen teams finished first. Five of them won the World Series.

Obviously, the more productive a player is, the more "outside stuff" a team is likely to put up with. So, just how good a player was Reggie Jackson? Okay, he was no defensive whiz. However, some people downplay Jackson's hitting accomplishments because he struck out a lot and didn't have a good batting average. Dear Reader, if you learn nothing else from this book please learn the *fact* that batting average is not the most important offensive number. For his career, Jackson had a real offensive value of .299, and an offensive winning percentage of .661 (when an average ROV is .250 or .260 and an average OW% is .500). He had a .300-plus ROV ten times and a .700-plus OW% eight times. During his peak, 1968–80, Jackson's ROV was .314 and his OW% was .723. His first full season as a below-average offensive player didn't come until 1983, which was his sixteenth full season in the majors. For his career, he averaged 83 runs scored and 91 RBI per 150 games; his peak numbers were 90 runs scored and 97 RBI per 150 games.

Reggie Jackson may not have been an easy guy to like. And yes, I know that people will probably be a little more productive if they like their colleagues. However, the facts are very clear about Jackson. He was an excellent hitter and his teams won. No objective analysis can lead to any other conclusion.—Eddie

Nothing's Perfect

In this book, we repeatedly (and repeatedly) extol the virtues of the SD score. We do this, of course, because SD scores allow us to rate teams from different eras with little bias toward what era they played in. No doubt, some of you are asking why we didn't use winning percentage (or Pythagorean winning percentage) as the key statistical method to rate teams. That's easy: winning percentage is "biased" toward the first part of the century. You don't believe it? Okay, look at the number of teams with a .650-plus winning percentage:

1901–45	Excluding Yankees	1946–98	Excluding Yankees
39	30	13	9

In 45 seasons from 1901 through 1945, 39 teams won at least 65 percent of their games in a season (just 30 if one excludes the Yankees). (No, there's nothing magic about 65 percent. Any other very good winning percentage would give you the same relative result. I used .650 because it yielded a decent number of teams.) In 53 seasons from 1946 through 1998, only 13 teams won at least 65 percent of their games (just nine teams if we exclude the Yankees). How can anyone objectively look at that data and say that winning percentage is the best statistical way to compare teams across eras?

On the other hand, look at the same type of distribution illustrating the number of teams with a 3.00-plus SD score:

1901–45	Excluding Yankees	1946–98	Excluding Yankees
17	11	20	18

An interesting quirk of this data is that the ratio of team seasons at 3.00 or higher to total seasons is *identical* in both periods. All that being said, a potential weakness of the SD score method manifests itself with the 1974 Athletics. The standard deviation of team runs scored in the 1974 American League was not just unusually low; it was the lowest for either runs scored or runs allowed in major league history, at just 24.5. Boston led the league with 696 runs scored; California was last in the twelve-team league at 618. With 689 runs scored, Oakland was third in the league and just about 1 SD better than average, even though they were just 24 runs scored above the league average of 665. Therefore, their fine +3.15 SD score may be as much a function of the weird bunching of the league that year as it is of the A's own performance. Then again, maybe not.

The 1974 result would have been a bit more bothersome if the A's other SD scores from this period hadn't been as good as they are. The A's were +2.63 in 1972, +2.20 in 1973, and +2.37 in 1975, which are all good scores and not really inconsistent with the A's 1974 SD score. Besides, the bulk of their positive 1974 score comes from the runs allowed department: a most impressive 2.16 SD better than average in runs allowed; the standard deviation of runs allowed in the 1974 American League was a more normal 52.7.—Eddie

Finley's Fliers

What Oakland player is responsible for this one-season stat line?

Games	AB	Runs	Hits	RBI	SB	CS	OBP	Slug	Avg
35	0	16	0	0	7	4	—	—	—

It has to be Herb Washington, right? Sorry, the answer is Allan Lewis in 1973, the year before Washington joined the A's. Lewis, nicknamed "The Panamanian Express," was the first overt manifestation of Charlie Finley's fascination with having a full-time pinch-runner on his roster. Lewis' career major league numbers look like this:

Year	G	AB	R	H	RBI	SB	CS	OBP	Slug	Avg
1967	34	6	7	1	0	14	5	.167	.167	.167
1968	26	4	9	1	0	8	4	.400	.250	.250
1969	12	1	2	0	0	0	0	.000	.000	.000
1970	25	8	8	2	1	7	1	.250	.625	.250
1972	24	10	5	2	2	8	3	.200	.300	.200
1973	35	0	16	0	0	7	4	—	—	—
Totals	156	29	47	6	3	44	17	.233	.345	.207

Although the switch-hitting Lewis occasionally played the outfield and got a few at-bats, for all intents and purposes Lewis was a designated runner before anyone had ever heard of Herb Washington. That's an amazing thing, for a non-pitcher to record three RBI in 156 games. (Extra credit if you noticed that, given Lewis' .625 slugging percentage in 1970, one of his two hits that year must have been a home run.)

The rest of the Athletics didn't much care for Finley's pinch-runners. Though Lewis played 35 games in 1973, he didn't come to the plate even once, and his teammates only voted him one-tenth of a World Series share. But say what you will about Allan Lewis, the evidence suggests that he was pretty good at his job. In all honesty, the same cannot be said for Herb "Hurricane" Washington.

Lewis was released during the winter after the 1973 season. Two weeks before the 1974 season opened, Finley signed the twenty-two-year-old Washington, who had never played an inning of professional baseball and, in fact, hadn't played any baseball at all since high school. But Washington, generally described as "a world-class sprinter" (whatever that means), could run. The A's distributed a press release, written by Finley, that declared, "Finley and Dark feel that Washington will be directly responsible for winning 10 games this year."

Washington spent the entire season on the A's roster, appearing in 92 games, stealing 29 bases in 45 attempts, and scoring 29 runs. In essence, the A's won the division, the pennant, and the World Series playing a man short. (Although more extreme, this was somewhat similar to when a team tries to carry a Rule 5 draftee [who must stay in the majors all season or be offered back to the team from which he was drafted] on its 25-man roster all year. For example, in 1985 the Toronto Blue Jays won 99 games and the American League East title with two Rule 5 players on the roster, Manny Lee and Lou Thornton. Lee played in 64 games but had just 43 plate appearances, whereas Thornton played in 56 games and had just 75 plate appearances. The difference here being that Washington never batted or played the field.) Washington got into only two World Series games and was picked off first base in the ninth inning of game 2, the only game the A's lost.

Things really got silly in 1975. On March 28, with Washington still on the roster, Finley acquired minor league outfielder Don Hopkins from the Montreal Expos. Hopkins had zero power and had never played above Class A, but he *had* stolen 49 bases the previous season. What's more, the A's actually announced that Hopkins was on the club solely to run, thus giving the club *two* pinch-runners. On April 28, Finley made it three with the acquisition of Cubs minor leaguer Matt "The Scat" Alexander, yet another fast guy with zero value at the plate and little value in the field.

Happily for Alvin Dark, this state of affairs did not last long. On May 5, the A's requested waivers on Herb Washington for the purposes of giving him his unconditional release. And so ended one of the strangest careers in major league history. Just for kicks, here's a combined stat line for the A's three pinch-runners in 1975:

Games	AB	Runs	Hits	RBI	SB	CS	OBP	Slug	Avg
158	16	45	2	0	40	20	.263	.125	.125

Like Allan Lewis, Matt Alexander was a switch-hitter, and like Lewis he had a surprisingly long major league career, primarily as a pinch-runner, playing for three different teams and in all or part of nine different seasons. With most modern teams carrying twelve or more pitchers, it's essentially impossible to carry a specialist runner these days, at least not until September when the rosters expand. But there's little doubt that a fast runner, assuming he has good baseball instincts (as Matt Alexander did, but Herb Washington did not), can help a team in certain situations.

Many of us are secretly mesmerized by pet ideas that are far outside the mainstream, and there's no doubt that many important inventions have resulted from such unconventional thinking. However, not all of these ideas are truly useful. And not everyone is in a position, as Charlie Finley was, to implement such ideas.—Eddie and Rob

Defending Their Record

Okay, how can we include a team with a 90-72 record, the 1974 A's, among the greatest teams of all time? First off, their SD score was the best among Oakland's division/World Series champions from the 1970s, and ranks twenty-third best of the twentieth century. Second, and in a related point, at 97-65 their Pythagorean record—that is, the record we would have expected, given their runs scored and allowed—was much better than their actual record, which means that it is very likely that the real quality of the team wasn't represented by their record. Here are the Pythagorean records for all five A's division champions:

1971	95-66
1972	97-58
1973	96-66
1974	97-65
1975	97-65

Yes, they are amazingly consistent. As you can see, the best Pythagorean win-loss percentage was actually posted by the 1972 club, and I suppose we could have picked that team for this chapter instead of the 1974 edition. One possible explanation for the 1974 A's less-than-imposing record is that they coasted the last two months. Here are the American League West standings as August dawned:

Team	W	L	Pct	GB
Oakland	61	43	.587	—
Kansas City	51	50	.505	8.5
Texas	53	52	.505	8.5
Chicago	51	51	.500	9.0
Minnesota	50	54	.481	11.0
California	41	64	.390	20.5

The A's were, of course, famously antagonistic toward their owner. Perhaps they had a tough time giving it their best once the pennant seemed well in hand. Although 8½ games with two months to play is certainly not an insurmountable lead, you could probably count the number of teams that have blown such leads on two hands, or maybe two hands and two feet.—Eddie

Everything Old Is New Again

Connie Mack broke up his great Athletics team in 1914, in part because of declining attendance, even though his team was still winning pennants. Charlie Finley broke up his three-time World Series champion Oakland A's because of the birth of free agency, but their attendance was also well below what one would expect for such a successful team.

As hard as it may be to believe, Oakland's attendance was below the league average *every year* that they won their division (1971–75). In 1974, on their way to a third straight World Series title, they were next-to-last in the league in attendance (1970 and 1976 are included for purposes of a "before and after" comparison):

Year	Attendance	Rank	League Average	Relative to League
1970	778,355	9 (of 12)	1,007,095	−22.7%
1971	914,993	7 (of 12)	989,047	−7.5%
1972	921,323	5 (of 12)	953,212	−3.3%
1973	1,000,763	8 (of 12)	1,119,467	−10.6%
1974	845,693	11 (of 12)	1,087,275	−22.2%
1975	1,075,518	6 (of 12)	1,099,119	−2.1%
1976	780,593	11 (of 12)	1,221,484	−36.1%

Yes, they drew better when they were winning championships than when they weren't, but this is not an impressive attendance record. Over the five-year span of division titles, the A's ranked seventh in the American League in attendance, about 9 percent lower than the average.

What about the presence of their neighbors, the San Francisco Giants? That is a factor, of course, but the A's drew very well during their period of success in 1988–90. In both 1989 and 1990, Oakland was second in the league in attendance, comfortably above the league average. (Combined, the two Bay Area teams drew about 4.7 million in 1989 and nearly 4.9 million in 1990.)

The attendance problems might well have something to do with the Oakland Raiders, who were immensely popular in the late 1960s and throughout the 1970s. Perhaps it's no coincidence that when the A's were drawing so well in the late 1980s, the Raiders had taken up (temporary) residency 400 miles to the south, in Los Angeles.

Charlie Finley has never received proper credit for building the 1970s Athletics team. People have focused on his negative traits, and of course they have a lot to focus on. However, it is amazing that people put someone into a category, good or bad, and then everything that is not consistent with their characterization is ignored. Bill James discusses this in his book about the Hall of Fame: "It is my observation . . . that there is some truth in what everybody says, but that they will almost all distort the truth to defend their position. . . . They all say things that they know or should know are not true, but which they feel they must say to defend the extreme positions they have taken." Bill is referring to politicians, but the same point can be made about people in general. Almost no one is all good or all bad, and *no one* is right or wrong all the time. So let's remember that Charlie Finley played a large role in building a great team. However, he also played a large role, the largest, in creating negative publicity about this team. Without question, this made it virtually impossible for the fans to support the team as much as their success warranted.

At the end of the twentieth century, once again there is uncertainty about the future of the Athletics franchise. The team is for sale and much speculation exists that the A's could relocate, perhaps to Sacramento or San Jose. For the A's, everything old is new again.—Eddie

The Swingin' A's

The early 1970s Oakland A's, like the Gashouse Gang Cardinals before them and the Bronx Zoo Yankees after them, were famous for their internecine squabbling. And although a lot of people think you need "harmony in the clubhouse," many fine teams over the years have had anything but harmonious clubhouses.

After the 1973 season, catcher Ray Fosse admitted, "Sure, we had turmoil all year, but it's not really dissension. We kind of blow it up." "We try to stir things up," Fosse went on, "because we think we're a better team when everybody's yelling at each other." But although the psychological effect of clubhouse fighting is certainly open to debate, there's no question that sometimes the *physical* effect is a real problem.

Case in point: June 5, 1974. Visitors' locker room at Tiger Stadium. Reggie Jackson vs. Bill North. As Jackson described the action:

> That evening after I got to the ballpark, I had stripped off my civvies and was sitting by my locker without any clothes on, getting ready to get into my uniform.
>
> In walked Billy and he began to blast me. "You're a fucking jerk, you know that?"

I was surprised by it. He'd been baiting me, but this was heavy talk. "Hey, what's going on?" I asked. I wasn't angry. I figured he was having fun.

"You're a fucking asshole is what you are! You're no fucking good! If you're a superstar, I never saw one."

I started to lose my temper, but I couldn't figure out why the sudden assault. I said to myself, "Hey, hold on, find out what's happening here." And I asked him, "What's eating you?"

He said I was. I told him to just go away and leave me the hell alone. He said he wasn't going anywhere and he wasn't going to get off my back. So I went at him. I don't know why. I lost my temper. . . . I grabbed him and he grabbed me and we wrestled down to the ground and some of the guys grabbed us and pulled us apart.

Vida Blue, with help from Ray Fosse, eventually broke up the fight, though a few minutes later the combatants had to be separated yet again. There are different explanations for the dispute between North and Jackson, who had been good friends just the season before. Now, a quarter-century later, it's pretty much irrelevant. What we do know is that the fight had repercussions beyond those few angry moments in the clubhouse. In the second skirmish between North and Jackson, Reggie suffered a bruised shoulder that reportedly affected his swing. Worse, peacemaker Fosse was seriously injured, as a separated cervical disc and a pinched nerve in his neck landed him in traction in an Oakland hospital. Fosse, the A's starting catcher, was placed on the disabled list, where he would remain for nearly ten weeks.

In Fosse's absence, first baseman Gene Tenace went behind the plate, Deron Johnson went from DH to first base, and Angel Mangual went from the bench to DH. Thus the A's were weakened defensively at two positions (catcher and first base), and offensively at one (DH). And when Tenace suffered his own pinched neck nerve not long afterward, third-string catcher Larry Haney was thrown into the breach.

There was one more potentially damaging fracas before the year was done. Before game 1 of the World Series, Blue Moon Odom approached Rollie Fingers in the clubhouse and started to rib Fingers about his recent marital woes. Earlier, Fingers had warned his teammates to avoid that particular subject, but Odom paid no heed. So Fingers snapped and threw a punch with his right (pitching) hand.

His hand sustained no damage, but Fingers did need five stitches to repair a gash in his scalp suffered when Odom pushed him back into a metal hook inside a locker. Odom wound up twisting his ankle in the process, jeopardizing his availability for the start of the Series.—Rob

TEAM STATISTICS

Hitting

	Games by Position	Age	G	AB	R	H	2B	3B	HR	RBI	BB	SO	SB	Avg	OBP	Slug
Gene Tenace	1B,106; C,79; 2B,3	27	158	484	71	102	17	1	26	73	**110**	105	2	.211	.367	.411
Pat Bourque*	1B,39	27	73	96	6	22	4	0	1	16	15	20	0	.229	.327	.302
Dick Green	2B,100	33	100	287	20	61	8	2	2	22	22	50	2	.213	.269	.275
Sal Bando	3B,141;DH,3	30	146	498	84	121	21	2	22	103	86	79	2	.243	.352	.426
Bert Campaneris	SS,133,DH,1	32	134	527	77	153	18	8	2	41	47	81	34	.290	.347	.366
Joe Rudi	OF,140; 1B,27; DH,2	27	158	593	73	174	**39**	4	22	99	34	92	2	.293	.334	.484
Bill North	OF,138; DH,8	26	149	543	79	141	20	5	4	33	69	86	**54**	.260	.347	.337
Reggie Jackson	OF,127; DH,19	28	148	506	90	146	25	1	29	93	86	105	25	.289	.391	.514
Deron Johnson*	DH,50; 1B,28	35	50	174	16	34	1	2	7	23	11	37	1	.195	.239	.345
Angel Mangual	OF,74; DH,37; 3B,1	27	115	365	37	85	14	4	9	43	17	59	3	.291	.338	.362
Claudell Washington	DH,38; OF,32	19	73	221	16	63	10	5	0	19	13	44	6	.255	.311	.429
Ted Kubiak	2B,71; SS,19; 3B,14	32	99	220	22	46	3	0	0	18	18	15	1	.261	.324	.439
Jesus Alou	DH,41; OF,25	32	96	220	13	59	8	0	2	15	5	9	0	.208	.280	.292
Ray Fosse	C,68; DH,1	27	69	204	20	40	8	3	4	23	11	31	1	.196	.241	.324
Larry Haney	C,73; 3B,3; 1B,2	31	76	121	12	20	4	0	2	3	3	18	1	.165	.185	.248
Dal Maxvill*	2B,30; SS,29; 3B,1	35	60	52	3	10	0	0	0	2	8	10	0	.192	.300	.192
Jim Holt*	1B,17; DH,3	30	30	42	1	6	0	0	0	0	1	9	0	.143	.182	.143
Gaylen Pitts	3B,11; 2B,6; 1B,1	28	18	41	4	10	3	0	0	3	5	4	0	.244	.326	.317
Manny Trillo	2B,21	23	21	33	3	5	0	0	0	2	2	8	0	.152	.222	.152
Phil Garner	3B,19; SS,8; 2B,3	25	30	28	4	5	1	0	0	1	1	5	1	.179	.207	.214
Champ Summers	OF,12; DH,2	28	20	24	2	3	1	0	0	3	1	5	0	.125	.160	.167
Vic Davalillo	OF,6; DH,4	37	17	23	0	4	0	0	0	1	2	2	0	.174	.231	.174
John Donaldson	2B,7; 3B,3	31	10	15	1	2	0	0	0	0	0	0	0	.133	.133	.133
Tim Hosley	C,8; 1B,1	27	11	7	3	2	0	0	0	1	1	2	0	.286	.333	.286
Rich McKinney	2B,3	27	5	7	0	1	0	0	0	0	0	0	0	.143	.143	.143
Herb Washington		22	92	0	29	0	0	0	0	0	0	0	29	—	—	—
Totals		29	162	5,331	689	1,315	205	37	132	637	568	876	**164**	.247	.329	.373

*Played for another team during season. Statistics are those compiled with 1974 Oakland A's only.

Pitching

	Threw	Age	Games	GS	CG	ShO	IP	H	HR	BB	SO	W	L	Pct	Sv	ERA
Catfish Hunter	Right	28	41	41	23	6	318	268	25	46	143	**25**	12	.676	0	**2.49**
Vida Blue	Left	24	40	40	12	1	282	246	17	98	174	17	15	.531	0	3.25
Ken Holtzman	Left	28	39	38	9	3	255	273	14	51	117	19	17	.528	0	3.07
Dave Hamilton	Left	26	29	18	1	1	117	104	10	48	69	7	4	.636	0	3.15
Glenn Abbott	Right	23	19	17	3	0	96	89	4	34	38	5	7	.417	0	3.00
Rollie Fingers	Right	27	**76**	0	0	0	119	104	5	29	95	9	5	.643	18	2.65
Paul Lindblad	Left	32	45	2	0	0	101	85	4	30	46	4	4	.500	6	2.06
Blue Moon Odom	Right	29	34	5	1	0	87	85	4	42	52	1	5	.167	1	3.81
Darold Knowles	Left	32	45	1	0	0	53	61	6	35	18	3	3	.500	3	4.22
Leon Hooten	Right	26	6	0	0	0	8	6	1	4	1	0	0	—	0	3.24
Bill Parsons	Right	25	4	0	0	0	2	1	0	3	2	0	0	—	0	0.00
Totals		28	378	162	49	12	1,440	**1,322**	**90**	**430**	755	90	72	.556	28	**2.95**

CHAPTER 16

They Just Missed the Cut

Some of the teams included in this book were no-brainers, like the 1927 Yankees. Some made the book not because of ultra-high SD scores and/or win-loss records, but because of long-term dominance, which was the case with the 1953 Yankees, who really represent the 1949–53 Yankees if not all of the Stengel-managed Yankees. That being the case, some of you may be asking why a given team (or teams) does not appear. Rest assured, some of these selections were very difficult, and if we are fortunate enough to write another edition of this book, some of the teams might change.

The omission of any 1990s Atlanta Braves team might strike many of you as odd. One can certainly argue that very, very few teams in history have enjoyed that type of long-term, upper-echelon success. Not counting the strike-shortened 1994 season, the Braves finished first in their division every year from 1991 through 1998. The two most important reasons why they did not get their own chapter are their SD scores and their postseason record. Although neither criterion by itself made or broke any team, in combination they were an important factor in selecting teams. Excluding the strike-shortened 1994 season, here are the Braves' SD scores and postseason outcomes:

Year	SD Score	Postseason
1991	+2.08	Lost World Series
1992	+2.72	Lost World Series
1993	+2.39	Lost NLCS
1995	+1.64	Won World Series
1996	+1.49	Lost World Series

Year	SD Score	Postseason
1997	+2.49	Lost NLCS
1998	+2.88	Lost NLCS
1999	+1.91	Lost World Series

The Braves did not achieve a +3.00 SD score in any of these seasons and did not reach +2.00 in three of them. (Their SD score was below +2.00 in 1994 as well.) The parallel is obvious between the 1990s Braves teams and the late 1940s/mid-1950s Dodgers teams who *are* represented in the book. So why the Dodgers and not the Braves? That's a good question. With two and now three rounds of postseason play, it is more difficult to win the ultimate prize than it was during the 1940s and 1950s. Let's look at the last eight seasons of the "Boys of Summer."

Year	SD Score	Postseason
1949	+3.07	Lost World Series
1950	+1.92	—
1951	+2.18	—
1952	+2.33	Lost World Series
1953	+2.80	Lost World Series
1954	+0.70	—
1955	+3.03	Won World Series
1956	+1.95	Lost World Series

Rob and I did not calculate an average SD score for every team for every conceivable period. Let's see . . . the Dodgers' average SD score from 1949 to 1956 was +2.25; the Braves' average from 1991 to 1999, excluding 1994, was +2.20. Including 1994, the Braves average was +2.14. Gee, that's pretty damn close, isn't it? All we can say is that the Dodgers had two teams over +3.00 and one of those won the World Series. (Just for informational purposes, the 1949–53 Yankees had an average SD score of +2.32 and, of course, they won five straight World Series.)

The team the Braves beat in the 1995 World Series, the Cleveland Indians, are another outstanding team that didn't make the cut. That edition, 1995, had the tenth highest SD score of the twentieth century (+3.51). The 1995–96 Indians ranked eighteenth in two-year

SD score. However, when looking at more than those two years, their SD scores (and win-loss records) drop dramatically.

Year	W-L Pct	SD Score
1995	.694	+3.51
1996	.615	+2.24
1997	.534	+0.75
1998	.549	+0.87

Despite only listing SD scores and win-loss records for one, two, and three seasons in the team chapters, we did consider how these teams performed over four and five seasons. The Indians also failed to win the World Series during this era.

As the crow flies, Cleveland and Detroit are no more than 100 miles apart. The Tigers have multiple teams that were great for a period of time too short to earn a chapter. We'll get to the 1968 and 1984 Tigers, "one-year wonders," a little later, but the 1934–35 Tigers were a two-year wonder. They won consecutive American League pennants and a World Series title, had a .600-plus winning percentage each year, and an SD score of +3.00 or higher in each season. However, to borrow a phrase from atomic physics, this Tigers team just didn't reach critical mass:

Year	W-L Pct	Finish	SD Score
1931	.396	7th	−1.49
1932	.503	5th	+0.18
1933	.487	5th	+0.04
1934	.656	1st	+3.02
1935	.616	1st	+3.17
1936	.539	2d	+0.48
1937	.578	2d	+1.03
1938	.545	4th	+0.78

Anyway you slice it, this team was great for two straight seasons but barely good the season before and the season after, not a long enough period of time to merit consideration as a "diamond dynasty," given the criteria that Rob and I decided to use.

In general, teams failed to make the cut because of not being dominant for a long enough period (basically, any team that wasn't very good or great for at least three seasons wasn't considered) or because their SD scores and/or their win-loss records weren't "good" enough. The failure to win the World Series was also a factor in some cases. What follows is a brief discussion of other teams that didn't make it, in no particular order.

1921–24 New York Giants

Although remembered for winning four straight National League pennants (1921–24), this team was actually quite good for six consecutive seasons, 1919–24, posting a .600+ winning percentage in five of those years and SD scores of at least +2.19 in all of them. However, their highest SD score was +2.47 (1921, not among the 100 best of the twentieth century) and their highest winning percentage was .621 (1923, also not in the top 100). In other words, they were consistently very good, but not quite great.

1920–23 New York Yankees

These Yankees weren't good as long as their intracity rivals, but they did post an excellent +3.22 SD score in 1923, their first World Series–winning season. Probably the most important reason we left them out is that they are so close in time to the 1927 Yankees.

1917–19 Chicago White Sox

The team that preceded the Yankees as the perceived powerhouse of the American League, the infamous "Black Sox" team, is surrounded by—probably to the point of being shrouded in—its off-the-field legacy. That they were a good team is clear, and their best season, 1917, was a great season: .649 winning percentage, +3.00 SD score, and World Series championship. However, they didn't have consecutive first-place finishes; in fact, they only won two pennants from 1915 to 1920. The 1919 team that "threw" the World Series lost to a team with a better record and a better SD score. The mythology that is linked with them probably leads many to overrate their real ability.

1912–18 Boston Red Sox

Although this period really represents more than "one" team, primarily due to the debut of Babe Ruth in 1915 and the trade of Tris

Speaker in 1916, 1912–18 was the Red Sox golden age. (If you're a Red Sox fan, that's kind of a sad statement.) This team had no representation among our elite because of their surprisingly poor SD scores. Only in 1912 were they even above +2.00. They were overachievers. Without getting too technical, the relationship between winning percentage and SD score is quite strong, as one might imagine, and one number can be predicted using the other. Take a look at the following table:

Year	SD Score	W-L Pct	Predicted W-L Pct Using SD Score
1912	+2.98	.691	.646
1913	+0.21	.527	.510
1914	+1.22	.595	.560
1915	+1.55	.669	.576
1916	+0.71	.591	.535
1917	+1.14	.592	.556
1918	+1.87	.595	.592

No doubt we will be accused of relying too much on SD scores, but so be it. The strength of the SD score and its seeming ability to rate teams across eras without any temporal bias make it a great tool for a project like this.

1901–03 Pittsburgh Pirates

The primary reason this team was omitted was its timing. That is, this was an era of flux in major league baseball, somewhat like the period before 1892. It is difficult to gauge how good they really were, given the emergence of the American League as a competitor. It is almost always written that the Pirates' incredible 1902 season (103-36 record, +3.62 SD score, 27½-game victory margin) was the result of the fact that they were the only N.L. team to avoid losing any key players to the American League.

In his book *Where They Ain't*, Burt Solomon asserts that it was a deliberate strategy by Ban Johnson, American League president, to leave the Pirates alone and ruin the N.L. pennant races. Neither Rob nor I have ever seen or heard that explanation anywhere else. In any event, the factors surrounding the Pirates' success seem to diminish their accomplishments, ever so slightly. Perhaps on further study and re-flection, if we do another edition in the future, this team could be in-cluded.

1988–90 Oakland Athletics

Jumping from one end of the century to the other, this team very nearly made the book. In the end, we decided on the 1974 Athletics because they were part of a team that had a longer run of success and, of course, more World Series championships. Part of the difference can be seen using SD scores. For a three-year period, the 1988–90 Athletics rank 7th best of the twentieth century; the 1972–74 Ath-letics rank 20th. Looking at a four-year stretch, however, the 1972–75 A's rank 17th, whereas the 1987–90 A's rank 69th. Over a five-year span, the 1971–75 A's rank 18th, whereas the later A's don't crack the top 100.

The 1988–90 team does somewhat resemble the 1969–71 Orioles (three straight dominating seasons, two upset losses in the World Se-ries, a famous manager, etc.) who are in the book, so why the Orioles and not the Athletics? One reason, as we pointed out in the 1970 Ori-oles chapter, is that the 1969–71 Orioles have the *best* three-year SD score of the twentieth century. Their three-year win-loss record ranks 16th best. The 1988–90 Athletics' record ranks 57th best for three seasons. In addition, when looking at four and five seasons, the Ori-oles team of this era has at least one representative in the top *five* for SD score, whereas the Athletics don't crack the top 50.

1976–78 New York Yankees

We have enough Yankees teams in the book already, don't you think? Undoubtedly, given which teams are in and not in the book, Rob and I will be accused of an East Coast bias even though we both live on the West Coast (yes, I was born and raised in the East). Yet, just as undoubtedly, a few rabid Yankee fans will also accuse us of anti-Yankee bias for not including even more Bronx Bombers. The late 1970s Yankees were a very good team, and they did win consecutive World Series after being swept in 1976 by the Big Red Machine. We just felt that their peak wasn't high enough (based primarily on their SD scores, two of which were less than +2.50) and their run wasn't long enough. You can't really stretch their run out to 1980 because then you have to include their less-than-stellar 1979 season.

1960s Los Angeles Dodgers

As further proof that Rob and I have an East Coast bias, the Koufax Dodgers are not in the book. (I am being facetious, of course.) Once again, they were a good team and they were good for a period of years, but they just weren't good enough. Remember, this book is about the absolute best teams of all time and not just about good teams. Take a look:

Year	W-L Pct	Finish	SD Score
1962	.618	2d	+2.86
1963	.611	1st	+1.41
1964	.494	6th	+0.67
1965	.599	1st	+1.38
1966	.586	1st	+1.18

Yes, they almost won four pennants in five years. However, in a historical context, their performance was not overwhelming. Throw in the fact that their best SD score came in a second-place season, and we really didn't feel too badly about leaving these Dodgers out of the book.

1960s St. Louis Cardinals

This is starting to sound like a broken record, so instead of more narrative let me show you the facts:

Year	W-L Pct	Finish	SD Score
1960	.558	3d	+0.38
1961	.519	5th	+0.61
1962	.519	6th	+2.08
1963	.574	2d	+1.31
1964	.574	1st	+0.80
1965	.497	7th	+0.34
1966	.512	6th	−0.35
1967	.627	1st	+2.18
1968	.599	1st	+1.83
1969	.537	4th*	+0.62

*Fourth in Eastern Division; 1969 was first year of division play.

The Cardinals had some great players, but every team with great players isn't necessarily a great team, just as every team that wins consecutive pennants isn't necessarily a great team. Great teams are not an annual phenomenon; their rarity is an indication of their value.

1984 Detroit Tigers

The 1984 Tigers team is probably the best and most out-of-context one-year wonder in history. For that year, they were superb: 104-58 record, +3.65 SD score (sixth best of the twentieth century), and the World Series championship. For the seasons immediately surrounding 1984, they were just another decent team. If we were rating teams solely on the basis of one season, the 1984 Tigers would have easily made the list. Time for another table:

Year	W-L Pct	Finish*	SD Score
1982	.512	4th	+0.99
1983	.568	2d	+1.74
1984	.642	1st	+3.65
1985	.522	3d	+0.52
1986	.537	3d	+1.47

*All rankings in Eastern Division play.

Yes, the Tigers had another good team in 1987, but we can't just ignore 1985 and 1986.

1968 Detroit Tigers

Best known for Denny McLain's 31-win season, Mickey Lolich's three World Series wins, and outfielder Mickey Stanley's playing shortstop in the World Series, the '68 Tigers are part of the Detroit "tradition" for great teams that didn't last. I began following baseball in the winter between the 1968 and 1969 seasons. Every baseball magazine I read picked the Tigers to win the "new" American League Eastern Division in 1969. Alas, how could those prognosticators have known? I think we've had enough tables in this chapter already; suffice it to say that the Tigers' win totals for 1965–71 were 89, 88, 91, 103, 90, 79, and 91; and their SD scores were +1.11, +0.21, +1.47, +3.19, +1.29, −0.93, and +0.67.

1954 Cleveland Indians

The "beauty" of the SD score method manifests itself with the 1954 Cleveland Indians. Despite their gaudy 111-43 record, their +2.22 SD score is good, but not great, and not consistent with their record. The 1954 American League was a strange league, with two very good (but not great) teams, one good team, and a bunch of clunkers. As we probably mention somewhere else in this book, the fourth-place, "first-division" (in name only) Red Sox finished 42 games out of first place. The Indians really fattened up on four of the five also-rans, winning *75 of 88 games* from Boston, Washington, Baltimore, and Philadelphia. This wide dispersion of talent naturally created large standard deviations of runs scored and runs allowed totals. The standard deviation for both was over 100 runs, which was the last of the four times it has happened in the twentieth century.—Eddie

CHAPTER 17

1975 Cincinnati Reds

Comparing teams of different eras is always difficult because strategy and equipment have radically changed over the years. But it is possible to compare to what degree teams have dominated the game in their eras, and no team has ever been more dominating than the 1975–76 Reds.

—Greg Rhodes and John Erardi, *Big Red Dynasty*

Record: 108-54, .667 (tie, 33d)
Two-Year (1975–76): 210-114, .648 (43d)
Three-Year (1974–76): 308-178, .634
   (48th)

SD Score: 3.42 (11th)
Two-Year: 6.05 (11th)
Three-Year: 7.99 (19th)

Results:
1974, second place, National League
   West
1975 World Champions
1976 World Champions

Days in First Place: 122 of 175;
   clinched on September 7

Longest Winning Streak: 10 games
Longest Losing Streak: 6 games

The Pennant Race: In his book, Joe Morgan wrote of 1975, "There wasn't much of a race in the West that season. We got off to a big lead early and coasted the rest of the way." That's not precisely true. When they took the field on May 3, the Reds trailed the first-place Dodgers by four games. But Pete Rose shifted to third base that day (see article, "The Great Eight"), and Cincinnati won six of its next seven games. However, next came a six-game losing streak that left the Reds 5½ games behind the Dodgers. The Reds finally pulled ahead by percentage points on June 2, and they went ahead for good on June 7. From there, they did indeed coast.

Even though the starters were frequently rested in September, the Reds went 18-9 that month and finished with a 20-game lead, the biggest margin in the major leagues since 1906 (when the Cubs finished 20 games ahead of the Giants).

Against the Contenders: For nearly all practical purposes, there were only two N.L. West clubs in the 1970s, as the Reds and Dodgers won six and three titles, respectively (the Giants won in 1971). So at the beginning of each season, Cincinnati and Los Angeles knew there was one team they had to beat. And though the Reds finished 20 games ahead of the second-place Dodgers in '75, L.A. actually won the season series, 10-8.

Runs Scored: 840 (1st)

Runs Allowed: 586 (3d)

Nobody was close to the Reds when it came to scoring, as the runner-up Phillies were 105 runs behind. The Dodgers led the National League in pitching, but of course their ballpark gave them a big edge there. One criticism of the Reds has been that they didn't lead the National League in pitching, in either 1975 or 1976. What those critics fail to consider is the context. Cincinnati's Riverfront Stadium was, at that time, a fun place for the hitters, and it would have been difficult for any team to lead the National League in pitching while playing half its games there.

Pythagorean Record: 107-55

Manager: Sparky Anderson

Regular Lineup:

Player	Position	ROV	OW%
Pete Rose	3B	.314	.725
Ken Griffey	LF	.295	.671
Joe Morgan	2B	.379	.850
Johnny Bench	C	.310	.715
Tony Perez	1B	.289	.654
George Foster	LF	.303	.696
Dave Concepcion	SS	.249	.500
Cesar Geronimo	CF	.254	.522
Gary Nolan	P		

If you take one thing away from the lineup, it should be Joe Morgan's amazing offensive winning percentage, which is on a par with those of Babe Ruth and Lou Gehrig in 1927. He also led the National League in RC/27 and OPS.

Bench: Merv Rettenmund, a key contributor with the Baltimore Orioles when they won their three straight A.L. titles, joined the Reds in 1974 and thus picked up a couple of World Series rings (and checks) in '75 and '76, serving as the club's fourth outfielder. Dan Driessen also played some outfield, but his primary role was second-string first baseman, and he would take over the position in 1977 after Tony Perez was traded to Montreal. Johnny Bench caught only 121 games in 1975, and his backup was Bill Plummer, who totaled only 19 RBI in 65 games. (But on June 5, 1976, he would knock in seven runs against the Cardinals, thanks to an RBI single, a bases-loaded triple, and a three-run homer.) Darrel Chaney and Doug Flynn were utility infielders in almost every sense of the term, as both saw action at second, short, and third.

Scouting the Pitchers: Gary Nolan threw really hard when he first came up in 1967, but a series of injuries robbed him of a few miles an hour on his fastball, and by 1975 he was more of a finesse pitcher, working the corners. Don Gullett depended on a great fastball, but threw the other three main pitches (slider, curve, change-up). Jack Billingham relied on a great sinker and, like Gullett, mixed in the slider, change, and curve. Fred Norman had a fastball, screwball, and curve. He had trouble throwing strikes, but he did have one of the better pickoff moves in the league. Among the relievers, Rawly Eastwick threw high heat, Will McEnaney had a great curve and a moving fastball, and Pedro Borbon and Clay Carroll both relied on sinking fastballs.

Be Sure and Count Your Fingers

In retrospect, it almost doesn't seem possible, and in reality it is rare: acquiring superstar players via trade. Although most of the key members of the Cincinnati's mid-1970s powerhouse came up through the farm system, in 1971 the Reds traded for two players who would win three consecutive MVP awards.

Quite simply, Morgan was the best player in baseball from 1970 through 1976. As you probably know, "Little Joe" was a product of the Houston organization. Considering his ability to get on base and his speed, Morgan was a great fit for the Astros and the Astrodome. But by 1971, the Astros had grown disenchanted with Morgan, and he with them. So on

How Were They Built? Johnny Bench was the first player drafted in the amateur draft to be elected to the Hall of Fame. That says a lot for how the Big Red Machine was built (as well as saying something for the relative brevity of Bench's career). Although some trades played important roles (see sidebar, "Be Sure and Count Your Fingers"), the Cincinnati team that blitzed through the National League in the mid-1970s was primarily home-grown.

Bench was a second-round draft pick, thirty-sixth overall, in the first amateur draft in 1965. Who was Cincinnati's first-round pick that year? Bernie Carbo (who has his own place in Reds lore because his eighth-inning, three-run homer for Boston tied game 6 of the 1975 World Series). Sixteen of the thirty-five players drafted ahead of Bench never made the major leagues. Jim McLaughlin's name comes up again, as he was with the Reds when they drafted Bench. McLaughlin as quoted in *Dollar Sign in the Muscle:* "I was with Cincin-

Johnny Bench (*AP/Wide World Photos*)

nati in 1965, the first year of the draft, and a friend of mine with another club said, 'You better send someone down to Binger, Oklahoma, to look at this kid Bench. We're not gonna draft him, because the general manager's seen another catcher he likes in New England.' . . . [W]e took Bench on the second round. It was kind of a poker game. Nobody else knew much about him; his team hadn't played many games." (Cincinnati drafted another pretty good player, Hal McRae, in 1965, but they traded him to Kansas City in 1972.)

Pete Rose, of course, was a Cincinnati kid signed by the hometown team in 1960. That same year, Tony Perez signed with the Reds. Perez put together an outstanding minor league track record, winning the Pacific Coast League MVP award in 1964. Dave Concepcion was signed by Cincinnati in 1967 out of Venezuela. Ken Griffey, Sr., was a twenty-ninth-round draft pick in 1969. Here are some composite major league numbers for the "home-grown five":

Games	Runs	RBI	Hits	HR	All-Star Games
13,082	6,650	6,151	13,505	1,181	50

All five of these players appeared in more than 2,000 major league games and collected more than 2,000 hits. Granted, all of these numbers were not compiled for Cincinnati, but the bulk of them were. That's an outstanding collection of talent to come from one farm system in a relatively short period. The Reds also evaluated amateur pitchers well, although two of their prize finds, Gary Nolan and Don Gullett, had their careers cut short by injury.

Nolan was Cincinnati's first-round pick, thirteenth overall, in the '66 draft. The very next year, Nolan went 14-8 with a 2.58 ERA and 206 strikeouts in 227 innings for the major league team. However, the consequences of letting a nineteen-year-old pitch that many innings at any level, let alone the big leagues, soon manifest themselves. Nolan missed time in 1968 and 1969 with injuries and later missed most of 1973 and all of 1974. He returned to give Cincinnati two good seasons in 1975 and 1976, but 1977 was the last year of his big league career. Gary Nolan was twenty-nine years old in 1977. He finished his big league career with a 110-70 record (.611 winning percentage) and a 3.08 ERA.

Gullett was the Reds' first-round pick (fourteenth overall) in 1969, the same year they picked Griffey and Rawly Eastwick (third round).

November 29, 1971, Reds general manager Bob Howsam worked a deal with the Astros that netted not only Morgan, but also Ed Armbrister, Jack Billingham, Cesar Geronimo, and Denis Menke. In return, Howsam sent Astros GM Spec Richardson, who made a number of poor trades over the years, three players: Lee May, Tommy Helms, and Jimmy Stewart.

Not only did Howsam get Morgan (whose accomplishments are detailed elsewhere in this chapter), but in Geronimo he got a four-time Gold Glove center fielder and, in Billingham, a pitcher who won 65 games with a 3.52 ERA in his first four seasons in Cincinnati. No offense intended to May, Helms, or Stewart, but it turned out to be an incredibly lopsided trade.

Howsam was a little luckier in getting George Foster from San Francisco in May 1971. Yes, the Reds gave up shortstop Frank Duffy and pitcher Vern Geishert to get Foster. But the Reds were apparently willing to take either Foster or another outfielder named Bernie Williams (no, not *that* Bernie Williams). The Giants wanted Duffy, probably as a defensive caddy for Chris Speier. San Francisco decided to trade Foster, in part, because his military-draft physical report revealed that he'd been rejected for military service because of a high school back injury. Foster didn't blossom right away after going to the Reds. He spent most of 1972 on the bench and most of 1973 in the minors. His emergence in 1975, however, helped Cincinnati distance itself from the competition. He also played well in 1976 and was the National League's MVP in 1977.

The following table sums up the 1971 trades:

The Reds got . . .	The Reds gave up . . .
Joe Morgan	Lee May
George Foster	T. Helms
Jack Billingham	Frank Duffy
Cesar Geronimo	J. Stewart
Denis Menke	V. Geishert
Ed Armbrister	

Like Gary Nolan, Gullett's stay in the minors was brief, as he pitched, and pitched well, for Cincinnati's 1970 N.L. champions. Just a year out of high school, Gullett had a 5-2 record, six saves, a 2.43 ERA, and 76 strikeouts in 78 innings. As they did with Nolan, the Reds worked Gullett hard for his age. He pitched 218 innings in 1971 at the age of twenty. In 1973, Gullett made 30 starts *and* pitched in 15 games in relief. He had a slightly unorthodox delivery that may have made him susceptible to injury, anyway. After pitching 243 innings in 1974, Gullett was never again able to pitch an entire season and he didn't pitch after 1978. He was twenty-seven years old in 1978. Gullett's final major league numbers were great: a 109-50 record (.686 winning percentage) and a 3.11 ERA.

Although the Reds were certainly astute judges of talent, and even given that Gullett left the Reds as a free agent after the 1976 season, their handling of these two pitchers cost Cincinnati even more success. For example, the Reds finished just four games behind the Dodgers in 1974. Even though their starting pitching was good that year, the Reds might have won the division with Nolan in the rotation. Tom Carroll and Roger Nelson combined for 25 starts that year and combined for an 8-7 record with a 3.52 ERA. A healthy Nolan likely would have done better than that.

Ultimately, judging talent is just one factor in a team's success. Knowing how to use that talent is also very important. Bob Howsam and Sparky Anderson did almost everything right from 1970 through 1976, but the Reds might have been even better if they'd been a bit more careful with their young pitchers.

What Brought Them Down? The Reds spent most of 1977 in second place, but it was a distant second place. By the end of April, they were 7½ games behind the Dodgers and never really threatened after that.

Some, if not most of the Reds, trace the demise of the dynasty to December 16, 1976, the day Tony Perez was traded to the Montreal Expos. Perez, they'll tell you, was the spiritual center of the team, and they never really recovered from his departure. Perhaps. It's funny, though, that the departure of Perez didn't seem to affect Cincinnati's hitters much. In 1976, the Reds scored 857 runs, tops in the National League. In 1977, the Reds scored 802 runs, second in the National League.

Why did the Reds trade Perez and reliever Will McEnaney for pitchers Woodie Fryman and Dale Murray? Cincinnati's lineup was loaded with veterans, and Perez was the only one with an understudy (Dan Driessen) waiting in the wings. As Bob Howsam later recalled, "Driessen could give us more speed and he could help us in a way that we weren't going to grow old." And performance-wise, at least, there was virtually no difference between Perez in Montreal (a .283 batting average, 19 homers, 91 RBI, and 815 OPS in 154 games) and Driessen in Cincinnati (a .300 batting average, 17 homers, 91 RBI, and 843 OPS in 151 games).

The pitching (and defense, if you like) suffered far more. Reds pitchers posted a 3.51 ERA in 1976, but a 4.21 mark in 1977. So you can blame the Machine's decline on the Perez trade if you want, but the real problems were a subpar (for them) pitching staff and an outstanding Dodgers club.

There was one last gasp in 1979, as the Reds won the National League flag before getting swept by the Pirates in the National League Championship Series. And in 1981, the Reds—with five players still left over from the '76 club—won more games than any other N.L. club. But they didn't win either half of the strike-split season and thus missed out on a postseason berth. The Reds plummeted to last place in 1982, thus ending an era.

Most Valuable Red: You'd have to say Joe Morgan was the most valuable Red, because he deservedly was named the National League's MVP. Morgan, although not the greatest defensive second baseman who ever lived, worked hard and did win five Gold Gloves. When he wasn't wearing his glove he was an astounding combination of patience, power, and speed.

Worst Regular: Cesar Geronimo was a defensive specialist who didn't hit much. He wasn't a *bad* player, really, but compared to his lineup mates he didn't enjoy a particularly long or productive career.

Hall of Famers: Johnny Bench and Joe Morgan were both elected in their first year of eligibility. Sparky Anderson will presumably be elected as a manager when he becomes eligible in 2000.

I'm not that great a student of baseball trades, but it's hard to imagine a team doing better than the Reds did with two different trades in the same year.—*Eddie*

A Tale of Two Teams

In 1975, the Cincinnati Reds replaced the Oakland A's as baseball's dominant team. In many respects, the two clubs were opposites—old-school conformity replacing "mod" rebelliousness—and this was best epitomized by their on-field appearance.

Infielder Woody Woodward (later the general manager of the Seattle Mariners) joined the Reds in 1968. Woodward wasn't much of a hitter, but he looked neat and orderly in the Cincinnati uniform, and Reds General Manager Bob Howsam made sure a photo of Woodward, with every uniform tuck and fold in place, was displayed in the Reds clubhouse for many years.

When Howsam joined the Reds in 1967, the club's logo for years had been an old-style uniformed figure with a giant, mustachioed baseball head, commemorating the team's legacy as the first openly professional franchise. A year later, the mustache was gone, and baseball man sported a modern Reds uniform.

Whereas the A's *popularized* white baseball shoes, the Reds weren't *allowed* to wear shoes with even a thin white stripe. Whereas the A's were *encouraged* to grow flamboyant mustaches, the Reds were *prohibited* from sporting facial hair of any kind.

It should be noted that for all of the Reds' sartorial conformity on the field, once off the field they dressed as modishly and garishly as all the other stylin' athletes of the early 1970s.—*Rob*

The Nickname

The 1914 Boston Braves have one, but the 1906 Chicago Cubs don't. The 1969 New York Mets have one, but the '86 Mets don't. Neither do the '54 Indians. We're talking

Our Hall of Famers: We've got no argument with Bench or Morgan, both of whom rank among the top two or three players of all time at their respective positions. There's a good chance that two or three other Big Reds will eventually be elected by the Veterans Committee. Tony Perez played forever, and he was a good player for most of his career. However, he was a great player for only a few seasons, and those came before the Reds hit their peak. Dave Concepcion also played forever, and he was a fine defensive shortstop who could hit some, too. There are certainly players in the Hall who weren't as good as Concepcion, but there are also a number of players not in the Hall who were *better* than Concepcion. It's awfully hard to argue for a guy like this.

And what about Pete Rose? Though it's true that Rose is quite often overrated as a player, it's also true that his career numbers merit a spot in Cooperstown. Everyone remembers that Rose was The Hit King and Charlie Hustle, but in his prime he was also a fine all-around player who hit some home runs, drew some walks, and could play wherever you needed him in the field.

The 1975 World Series: The Reds topped the Red Sox in a thrilling, seven-game Series, with Boston actually outscoring Cincinnati, 30–29. For more, see article, "Remembering the Losers."

The Ballpark: Riverfront Stadium was typical of the multi-purpose, carpeted, ashtray stadiums built in the late 1960s and early 1970s. Riverfront's turf was hard, and the ballpark in general was somewhat favorable to the hitters.

Books about the 1975 Reds: There are lots of books about the Big Red Machine. Lots and lots of them. Sparky Anderson has written at least three books, but only *The Main Spark* (Garden City, NY: Doubleday, 1978) is concerned primarily with his days in Cincinnati. Pete Rose has written a number of books, too. His autobiography, *Pete Rose: My Story* (New York: Macmillan, 1989)—told in the third person and penned by Roger Kahn—devotes eighty-odd pages to the Reds. *Joe Morgan: A Life in Baseball* (New York: W. W. Norton, 1993), by Joe Morgan and David Falkner, is probably the most worthwhile of Machinery autobiographies. More recently, Morgan's book *Long Balls, No Strikes* (New York: Crown, 1999) contains an entire chapter comparing the '75 Reds to the '98 Yankees. Dayton sportswriter Ritter Collett's *Men of the Machine* (Dayton, OH: Landfall Press, 1977) offers profiles of all the everyday players and starting pitchers, and Robert Harris "Hub" Walker's *Cincinnati and the Big Red Machine* (Bloomington, IN: Indiana University Press, 1988) is a sort of social history.

The single best book about the 1970s Reds (and one of the better baseball books ever published) is Greg Rhodes and John Erardi's *Big Red Dynasty: How Bob Howsam & Sparky Anderson Built the Big Red Machine* (Cincinnati, OH: Road West, 1997). In fact, some of the best information in this chapter is borrowed from Rhodes and Erardi.

No Competition

Joe Morgan was one of my absolute favorite players. Despite his Hall of Fame selection and his visibility as a broadcaster, I'm not sure people really appreciate how great a player he was. Although I doubt he would talk about his playing days in terms of OPS and RC/27, using these measures helps illustrate how he dominated the National League in the mid-1970s.

The 1975 season best exemplifies Morgan's outstanding run as the best player in baseball. That year, he created 10.52 runs per 27 outs. That figure was not only the best in the National League, but 3.27 runs per 27 outs better than *the second-best player.* Only nineteen times this century has the league-leading player had a margin of 3.00 RC/27 or more over the second-best player, and eleven of those times are claimed by guys named Ruth or Williams. In fact, Morgan was the first player since Ted Williams in 1949 to attain that distinction. (Babe Ruth holds the all-time record, finishing 6.11 RC/27 ahead of Tris Speaker in 1920. Ruth's 16.44 mark that season is the best ever. In 1998, Mark McGwire became the first player since Morgan to post a 3.00-plus RC/27 advantage over the second-best player.) Morgan batted .327 in 1975, stole 67 bases, and led the National League with 132 walks. For all this (and more), Morgan was named National League MVP by the biggest margin in the history of the award.

Morgan was a five-time Gold Glover, he finished in the top five in the league in RC/27 every year from 1972 through 1977, he led the league in that category three straight seasons (1974–76), and he also

about nicknames, of course, and the 1975 Reds have one of the best: The Big Red Machine. According to *Big Red Dynasty,* "[T]he name surfaced in 1969, but its origins are murky. Bob Hunter, a Los Angeles writer, hung the name on the Reds after they outslugged the Phillies, 19–17 [on August 3 of that season]. But Pete Rose claimed he used the name to distinguish the Reds from his red antique Ford (which he called 'the little red machine')." I don't know about you, but I'll go with Hunter's imagination over Rose's gift for self-promotion.—*Rob*

Stats 'n' Stuff

◆ The Reds set a National League record for home victories, with 64.

◆ The Reds stole 168 bases (the most in the National League) while being caught only thirty-six times, for an .824 success rate that was (and still is) the best in major league history.

April 8 Frank Robinson debuts as player-manager for the Indians and hits a home run in his first at-bat. It's Robinson's eighth opening day homer, setting a major league record.

May 2 Astros first baseman Bob Watson scores what is calculated as the one-millionth run in major league history.

June 1 Nolan Ryan throws his fourth no-hitter to beat the Orioles 1–0. Five days later, Ryan will toss a two-hitter at the Brewers, with Henry Aaron's sixth-inning single the first safety for Milwaukee.

June 18 Red Sox rookie Fred Lynn drives in 10 runs with three homers, a triple, and a single as Boston destroys Detroit, 15–1. Lynn will go on to become the first (and only) player to be named Rookie of the Year and MVP in the same season.

August 21 Cubs hurlers Rick Reuschel and Paul

led the league in OPS in 1975 and 1976. Very few players in history have achieved that level of combined offensive and defensive excellence.

Just like Morgan, the Reds dominated the National League in run production in their pennant-winning seasons of 1975 and 1976. The '75 Reds are the last non–Colorado Rockies team to lead their league in runs scored by a margin of 100 or more. Only fifteen teams have done that in the twentieth century, including the Rockies (in '96 and '97). Some of the other teams in this fairly exclusive club are the 1902 Pittsburgh Pirates, the 1927 New York Yankees, the 1936 New York Yankees, and the 1953 Brooklyn Dodgers.

The runs-scored component of the 1975 Reds SD score (+2.36) is the sixth best of the century and is really better than that, as two of the teams ahead of them are the 1996 and 1997 Colorado Rockies. (In those two seasons, '96 and '97, the Rockies scored 1,203 runs at home and just 681 runs on the road.) The 1976 Reds' +2.44 runs-scored component actually ranks one place ahead of the 1975 team. I haven't generated "component" SD scores for multiple seasons, but I doubt many teams, if any, have had a better two-year score than the 1975–76 Reds, not counting the Rockies.

The 1976 Reds led the league in virtually every positive, meaningful offensive category: runs scored, hits, doubles, triples, home runs, walks, stolen bases, stolen-base percentage, batting average, on-base percentage, slugging percentage, and fewest grounded into double plays. Bill James once wrote, "The 1975–76 Reds were probably the most diverse, broad-based offense in the history of baseball." The Reds' offense was outstanding—just like their second baseman.—Eddie

The Great Eight

In the second half of the twentieth century, two lineup changes stand out above all others in terms of their impact on pennant races.

On July 20, 1951, New York Giants manager Leo Durocher shifted outfielder Bobby Thomson to third base, propelling the Giants to a miraculous pennant run capped by Thomson's "Shot Heard Round the World" to beat the Dodgers in a pennant playoff. On May 3, 1975, Cincinnati Reds manager Sparky Anderson shifted left fielder Pete

Rose to third base, propelling the Reds to a runaway victory in the N.L. West and two straight World Series championships.

But let's back up one month. Entering the 1975 season, third base was less the "the hot corner" than "the lame corner" for the Reds. Dan Driessen had tried the position in 1974, but he couldn't really handle the defensive demands. After the season, the Reds tried to trade Tony Perez for a slugging third baseman, but a deal for Yankees star Graig Nettles couldn't be worked out. So when the '75 season opened, light-hitting, good-fielding John Vukovich was nominally the regular at third.

This did not last long. Anderson routinely subbed for Vukovich in the middle of games. On April 16 against the Dodgers, Anderson pinch-hit for Vukovich in the second inning with the bases loaded. Vukovich's parents were in the stands, and (so the story goes, as quoted in *Big Red Dynasty*) he "smashed light bulbs all the way down the runway from the dugout to the clubhouse." Over the next couple of weeks, Vukovich, Darrel Chaney, and Doug Flynn played third, but they didn't do much. Actually, that's being too kind. The Cincinnati third baseman had as bad a month as you could imagine. How bad? Well, through May 2 they'd hit two doubles and knocked in three runs in 24 games. Here are the stats for all Cincy third basemen through May 2, projected through the complete 162-game schedule:

Games	AB	R	H	2B	3B	HR	RBI	BB	SO	OBP	Slug	Avg
162	472	40	67	20	0	0	20	60	74	.241	.186	.143

Nice, huh? And at the close of play that evening, the third-place Reds, with 12 wins and 12 losses, trailed the first-place Dodgers by four games. So even though the third-base situation would have improved by default even if Vukovich had remained in the lineup, Sparky Anderson had to do *something*. So before the May 2 game, Sparky Anderson asked Rose how he felt about playing third base, beginning the next afternoon (an NBC Game of the Week). This would make for some offense at third base and also get the talented George Foster into the lineup, in left field.

Rose had briefly played third base back in 1966. He hadn't been consulted beforehand, though, and his poor attitude and a hitting slump had soon gotten him moved back to his original position (sec-

Reuschel combine to beat the Dodgers, 7–0. It's the first time pitching brothers have collaborated on a shutout.

September 16 Pirates second baseman Rennie Stennett ties the major league record by going 7-for-7 in a nine-inning game. Stennett also scores five runs to help his club trounce the Cubs, 22–0.

ond base). This time, though, Rose worked his ass off at third base. According to Reds broadcaster Marty Brennaman, "[O]nce the decision was made to put him at third base, he was there every day well in advance of all of the rest of the guys. He'd take [coach] Alex Grammas with him or [coach] George Scherger, and take groundball after groundball after groundball. He was the only guy out on the field." That was on game days. On off days, Rose would show up at the ballpark and take some more groundballs. Say what you will about Pete Rose, but the man loved to play the game.

Even with all the practice, Rose was never smooth at third base. But he was at least adequate, which allowed Sparky the luxury of another bat in the lineup. The lineup switch was by no means a magic elixir, not immediately. The Reds beat the Padres on May 3, 7–6, but then they won only six of their next dozen games and fell even further behind the Dodgers. But on May 17, after a Sparky Anderson tirade in the clubhouse, the Reds beat the Expos 5–3 on a Bench home run. That began a stretch that saw the Reds win 40 of their next 50 games, and go from 5½ games *behind* the Dodgers to 12½ games *ahead* of the Dodgers. By the All-Star break, the Western Division pennant race was over.

Cincinnati's most famous lineup, the Great Eight, first was used on July 4 and was, in order, Rose, Griffey, Morgan, Bench, Perez, Foster, Concepcion, and Geronimo. That exact lineup was used only 24 times in the regular season because of injuries, the need to play Driessen, and the Reds' huge September lead. However, Cincinnati went 19-5 in those 24 games, and the Great Eight started all 10 postseason games. In 1975 and 1976 combined, the Great Eight played 87 games together, including regular and postseason games. They went 69-18, for an astounding .793 winning percentage. Was it the greatest starting lineup in history? The line forms here, pal.—Rob

Why 1975?

Invariably, when one of the Big Red Machine teams is considered in the Greatest Team debate, it's the 1976 squad, which not only won 102 regular-season games, but also zipped through the postseason with seven wins and zero losses. The '76 Reds outscored the Phillies and Yankees 41-19 in those seven games; the '75 Reds were actually outscored by the Red Sox in the World Series (29–30), although they dominated the Pirates in the NLCS (19–7). Now's about the time you might be wondering, "So why did they pick 1975?" Well, even though the ultimate goal of a baseball team is to win the World Series, no matter what is at stake, one cannot draw too many conclusions from a single best-of-five and/or a single best-of-seven series.

The 1976 Reds were certainly a match for the 1975 club in terms of run production. The '76 club scored a few more runs (857 to 840) and had a slightly better runs scored SD score (+2.44 to +2.36). As noted somewhere else in this chapter, the 1976 Cincinnati Reds led the National League in virtually every meaningful offensive category. Besides leading in the two categories that best correlate with run production (OBP and slugging), the Reds showed amazing balance. They led in "speed categories" like triples and stolen bases, and they also led in "Babe Ruth categories" like home runs and walks.

However, just as we said when comparing the 1953 and 1955 Dodgers, this is not a book about the greatest hitting teams of all time, but about the greatest *teams* of all time. The 1975 and 1976 Reds were both offensive powerhouses, but the 1975 Reds were better in the pitching/defense phase of the game. Take a look:

	Runs Scored (SD Score)	Runs Allowed (SD Score)	Overall SD Score
1975	840 (+2.36)	586 (+1.06)	+3.42
1976	857 (+2.44)	633 (+0.18)	+2.63

The 1975 Reds were more than one whole standard deviation better than the league average in runs allowed, whereas the 1976 club was barely better than average. Let's also not forget that the 1975 club won six more games than the '76 club (108 to 102). The 1975 team is one of only six to play .667 ball or better in a season since the beginning of divisional play in 1969. In fact, the 1975 club had an amazing 80-33 record (a .708 winning percentage) from June 1 on. Given their better record, their better overall SD score, their better run differential, and the fact that they did win the World Series, picking the 1975 Reds to represent the Big Red Machine seems like the logical choice.—Eddie

Remembering the Losers

Ask twenty casual baseball fans, "Who won the World Series when Carlton Fisk hit the home run?" and I'll bet you half of them will give the wrong answer. If you're reading this book, you already know that the Reds beat the Red Sox. But for a great majority of fans, the '75 Series means Fisk "willing" his long fly ball fair in the twelfth inning of game 6. But wait, we're getting ahead of ourselves.

The Series opened in Fenway Park, and game 1 was scoreless through six innings. Boston exploded for six runs in the seventh, however, and Luis Tiant finished with a five-hit shutout. The next night in game 2, the Red Sox owned a 2–1 lead after eight innings, but the Reds scored a pair of runs after two were out, and Rawly Eastwick retired the Sox in order and earned the victory for Cincinnati.

The Series shifted to the Queen City for game 3, which featured six home runs, the last of them Dwight Evans' two-run shot in the top of the ninth that tied the contest at five runs apiece. Cesar Geronimo led off the bottom of the tenth with a single. Pinch-hitter Ed Armbrister then attempted a sacrifice bunt. He got tangled up with catcher Fisk, who threw wildly into center field. Geronimo ended up on third base, Armbrister at second. The Sox claimed interference, but plate umpire Larry Barnett let the play, forever after known as "The Armbrister Incident," stand as called. One intentional walk and one strikeout later, Joe Morgan drove a ball over center fielder Fred Lynn's head to end the game.

Luis Tiant recorded his second Series victory in game 4, a 5–4 affair. Tiant went the distance, and all five Boston runs came in the fourth, two of them on Dwight Evans' triple to the right-field wall. Lynn saved the game with a brilliant catch of Ken Griffey's drive to deep left in the bottom of the ninth. Had the ball gotten past Lynn, two runs would have scored and the Reds would have won. In game 5, Tony Perez busted an 0-for-15 slump with a pair of home runs, and the Reds took an easy 6–2 victory.

Game 6 was scheduled for two days later, but torrential rains in Boston delayed things for three extra days, further heightening the drama. When the Series finally resumed, Tiant started again for the Red Sox, but he labored and finally left in the eighth, trailing 6–3. All hope seemed lost for the Red Sox. But in the bottom of the eighth with two outs, pinch-hitter (and ex-Red) Bernie Carbo blasted a three-run homer into the center-field bleachers, and the game was tied. Boston had a chance to win in the ninth, as they loaded the bases with just one out. Fred Lynn lifted a short, foul fly to George Foster in left field, and Denny Doyle was nailed at the plate trying to tag up from third base (against his coach's advice), thus ending the threat. In the top of the eleventh, with one out and Griffey on first base, Morgan drove a long fly to right field. Actually, it would have been to the right-field bullpen for a home run, except Dwight Evans made a spectacular leaping grab. As a bonus, the Sox easily doubled up Griffey, thus ending *that* threat.

So it was still 6–6 when Fisk led off the bottom of the twelfth, four hours after game 6 had started. Fisk lifted Pat Darcy's second pitch high down the left-field line. The ball was hooking all the while, and Fisk edged slowly toward first base, swinging his arms and exhorting the ball to stay fair. And stay fair it did, caroming off the foul pole for a game-winning homer. This, of course, is the famous moment of the 1975 World Series, but Fisk's blast didn't win the Series, and Boston didn't win the Series.

The Red Sox went ahead early in game 7 (just as they would eleven years later), scoring three runs in the third, two of those coming on bases-loaded walks. However, relievers Jack Billingham, Clay Carroll, and Will McEnaney held Boston scoreless after that. In the sixth, Tony Perez made the score 3–2 with his third homer of the Series. One inning later, Pete Rose's RBI single tied the game. Cincinnati finally went ahead in the ninth, 4–3, when Morgan's bloop single to center plated Griffey. McEnaney retired the Red Sox in order in the bottom of the inning, and the Reds were World Champs for the first time since 1940.—Rob

Captain Hook

The 1970s Reds are best remembered by their nickname, "The Big Red Machine." Several players also had colorful nicknames—Charlie Hustle, Doggie, Little Joe—but manager George Anderson outdid them all, answering to *two* aliases, "Sparky" and "Captain Hook." Anderson earned the second moniker through his famous impatience for his starting pitchers and a corresponding reliance on his bullpen. But did Anderson deserve his nickname? And, if so, was it because of his pitching staff or because he was, by his very nature, "Captain Hook"?

Anderson was certainly not the first successful manager to rely on his bullpen rather than his starting pitching. Hank Bauer led the 1966 Orioles to the World Series title with a staff that completed only 23 games (ninth in the ten-team American League), but led the league in saves and finished fourth in ERA. A year later, the 1967 World Series was the first to feature opponents (the Cardinals and the Red Sox) that both finished the season with more saves than complete games. That foreshadowed a trend that has continued unabated; today, saves outnumber complete games by about four to one.

Sparky, though, was the standard-bearer for this trend, disregarding the complete game almost completely. In both 1972 and 1975, the Reds won the pennant while finishing last in the league in complete games, something that had not happened since Connie Mack's Philadelphia Athletics won the 1913 A.L. crown. Connie Mack was no "Captain Hook," however: the A's completed 77 games in 1913, compared to the Reds' 25 in 1972 and 22 in 1975.

Anderson used his bullpen more frequently than almost any other successful manager. From 1970 through 1978, Cincinnati finished first in the National League in saves five times, second twice, and third once. Only once during Anderson's nine years in Cincinnati did a team with a better ERA have more relief appearances than the Reds, and thirteen times during this span Cincinnati relievers finished in the top five in appearances in the National League. So the nickname "Captain Hook" certainly fit Anderson. But did it reflect his pitching philosophy, or his pitching *staff?*

Well, the pitchers he inherited certainly were not accustomed to finishing games. Cincinnati finished last in the National League in complete games in both 1967 and 1968 and next to last in 1969 (when the staff completed only 23 games, then an all-time franchise low).

Although Anderson had no proven workhorses, he did keep a tighter rein on his starters than most managers might. Jack Billingham, who was known to grouse about Sparky's quick hook, is a good example. Billingham completed a career-high 16 games for the Reds in 1973, but then Anderson allowed him to finish only 21 of 119 starts from 1974 through 1977. The next year, Billingham went the distance in 10 games for the Tigers. But Anderson knew how to put away the hook with a proven finisher. When Tom Seaver came to the Reds during the 1977 season, Sparky let him complete 14 of his 20 starts, though he had finished only five of 13 games with the Mets.

If you want proof that Anderson's quick hook was simply a product of his Cincinnati staff, look no further than his tenure as manager of the Detroit Tigers, 1980 through 1995, when the Captain apparently lost his hook on his way to the Motor City. The Tigers finished last in the league in complete games in 1979, but after Anderson took charge, Detroit finished in the top four in complete games each of the next four years and placed lower than fifth only five times in Anderson's sixteen seasons. Having a pitcher like Jack Morris will do that to a guy.

Like every great manager, Anderson adapted to his team's strengths. Because the Reds generally had outstanding relievers and starters with relatively little stamina, Anderson became known as "Captain Hook," but it could have been different. Without that stellar bullpen, Anderson might instead have been associated with the Big Red Machine's explosive offense, in which case we'd be regaling our kids with tales of "Captain Crunch."—Steve Schulman

TEAM STATISTICS

Hitting

	Games by Position	Age	G	AB	R	H	2B	3B	HR	RBI	BB	SO	SB	Avg	OBP	Slug
Tony Perez	1B,132	33	137	511	74	144	28	3	20	109	54	101	1	.282	.350	.466
Joe Morgan	2B,142	31	146	498	107	163	27	6	17	94	132	52	67	.327	.466	.508
Dave Concepcion	SS,130; 3B, 6	27	140	507	62	139	23	1	5	49	39	51	33	.274	.326	.353
Pete Rose	3B,137; OF,35	34	162	662	112	210	47	4	7	74	89	50	0	.317	.406	.432
Ken Griffey, Sr.	OF,119	25	132	463	95	141	15	9	4	46	67	67	16	.305	.391	.402
Cesar Geronimo	OF,148	27	148	501	69	129	25	5	6	53	48	97	13	.257	.327	.363
George Foster	OF,125; 1B,1	26	134	463	71	139	24	4	23	78	40	73	2	.300	.356	.518
Johnny Bench	C,121; OF,19; 1B,9	27	142	530	83	150	39	1	28 .	110	65	108	11	.283	.359	.519
Dan Driessen	1B,41; OF,29	23	88	210	38	59	8	1	7	38	35	30	10	.281	.386	.429
Merv Rettenmund	OF,61; 3B,1	32	93	188	24	45	6	1	2	19	35	22	5	.239	.356	.314
Darrel Chaney	SS,34; 2B,23; 3B,13	27	71	160	18	35	6	0	2	26	14	38	3	.219	.280	.294
Bill Plummer	C,63	28	65	159	17	29	7	0	1	19	24	28	1	.182	.291	.245
Doug Flynn	3B,40; 2B,30; SS,17	24	89	127	17	34	7	0	1	20	11	13	3	.268	.324	.346
Terry Crowley	1B,4; OF,4	28	66	71	8	19	6	0	1	11	7	6	0	.268	.333	.394
Ed Armbrister	OF,19	26	59	65	9	12	1	0	0	2	5	19	3	.185	.254	.200
John Vukovich	3B,31	27	31	38	4	8	3	0	0	2	4	5	0	.211	.286	.289
Don Werner	C,7	22	7	8	0	1	0	0	0	0	0	0	0	.125	.222	.125
Totals		28	162	5,581	840	1,515	278	37	124	779	691	916	168	.271	.360	.401

Pitching

	Threw	Age	Games	GS	CG	ShO	IP	H	HR	BB	SO	W	L	Pct	Sv	ERA
Gary Nolan	Right	27	32	32	5	1	211	202	18	29	74	15	9	.625	0	3.16
Jack Billingham	Right	32	33	32	5	0	208	222	22	76	79	15	10	.600	0	4.11
Fred Norman	Left	32	34	26	2	0	188	163	23	84	119	12	4	.750	0	3.73
Don Gullett	Left	24	22	22	8	3	160	127	11	56	98	15	4	.789	0	2.42
Pat Darcy	Right	25	27	22	1	0	131	134	4	59	46	11	5	.688	1	3.58
Clay Kirby	Right	27	26	19	1	0	111	113	13	54	48	10	6	.625	0	4.72
Pedro Borbon	Right	28	67	0	0	0	125	145	6	21	29	9	5	.643	5	2.95
Clay Carroll	Right	34	56	2	0	0	96	93	2	32	44	7	5	.583	7	2.62
Will McEnaney	Left	23	70	0	0	0	91	92	6	23	48	5	2	.714	15	2.47
Rawly Eastwick	Right	24	58	0	0	0	90	77	6	25	61	5	3	.625	22	2.60
Tom Carroll	Right	22	12	7	0	0	47	52	1	26	14	4	1	.800	0	4.98
Tom Hall*	Left	27	2	0	0	0	2	2	0	2	3	0	0	—	0	0.00
Totals		28	439	162	22	8	1,459	1,422	112	487	663	**108**	**54**	**.667**	**50**	3.37

*Played for another team during season. Statistics are those compiled with 1975 Cincinnati Reds only.

CHAPTER 18

1986 New York Mets

When did the Mets win? Whenever and wherever they took the field. They won at home and on the road with almost equal ease. They beat left-handers and right-handers at almost the same rate. They won on grass as easily as on turf, and on turf as easily as on grass. They won day games as often as at night. . . . They were, in short, a great ballclub, and a beautiful demonstration of what talent can do when assembled with planning and guided by intelligence.

—Bill James in *The Bill James Baseball Abstract 1987*

Record: 108-54, .667 (tie, 33d)
Two-Year (1986–87): 200-124, .617
   (97th)
Three-Year (1986–88): 300-184, .620
   (72d) (74th)

SD Score: 3.62 (7th)
Two-Year: 5.89 (14th)
Three-Year: 9.28 (5th)

Results:
1986 World Champions
1987, second place, National League East
1988 National League East Champions

Days in First Place: 170 of 182;
   clinched on September 17

Longest Winning Streak: 11 games
Longest Losing Streak: 4 games

Against the Contenders: In both 1985 and 1987, the Mets finished second, three games behind St. Louis. However, in '86 the Cards were hardly contenders, finishing 28½ games behind the Mets. As you'd expect, New York dominated the season series, taking 12 of 18 games. The Phillies surprised everyone by finishing second (albeit 21½ games out), and the Phils played well against the Mets, winning 10 of 18 games.

Runs Scored: 783 (1st)

Runs Allowed: 578 (2d)

The Houston Astros allowed slightly fewer runs (569) than the Mets, but one must remember that the Astros were a fine team themselves and the Astrodome at that time was one of the friendliest parks for pitchers ever (though it actually played as a hitter's park in '86).

Pythagorean Record: 103-59

The Mets won 108 games, five more than "expected" given their runs scored and allowed, which is a substantial difference. Relatively few teams win five more games than the Pythagorean method would predict. The Astros, who won the West, were also +5, and the Mets and Astros were the only N.L. clubs to exceed expectations by more than four wins. Of course, most teams with great records *do* outperform their Pythagorean expectations. That's how they get great records.

Manager: Davey Johnson

Davey Johnson played second base for Earl Weaver for five years, and it was fitting that Weaver's managerial career ended right around the same time Johnson's began.

Regular Lineup:

Player	Position	ROV	OW%
Lenny Dykstra	CF	.312	.716
Wally Backman	2B	.288	.644
Keith Hernandez	1B	.322	.741
Gary Carter	C	.273	.590

Player	Position	ROV	OW%
Darryl Strawberry	RF	.309	.708
Ray Knight	3B	.278	.611
Mookie Wilson	LF	.288	.645
Rafael Santana	SS	.190	.232
Dwight Gooden	P		

A brilliant lineup. Except for Rafael Santana, every regular finished with an offensive winning percentage close to or better than .600.

Bench: As much as any great team you'll find, the Mets relied on a deep, talented bench. Kevin Mitchell didn't have a regular position but played 108 games (including 24 at shortstop in a supreme testament to Davey Johnson's imagination). Tim Teufel platooned at second base with Wally Backman (a switch-hitter who couldn't hit lefties at all). Howard Johnson, cast off by Sparky Anderson in Detroit, hit 10 home runs and slugged .445 while playing part-time. Danny Heep served as the club's fifth outfielder, and George Foster hit 13 homers before drawing his release in early August.

Scouting the Pitchers: At his best, Dwight Gooden (17-6, 2.84) pitched like a right-handed Sandy Koufax in that his mid-90s fastball and a sharp curve were all he needed to befuddle N.L. hitters. Sid Fernandez (16-6, 3.52) didn't throw terribly hard, but he posted the highest strikeout rate on the staff (even higher than Gooden's), thanks to an amazingly deceptive delivery. Ron Darling (15-6, 2.81) had all the pitches, starting with a good fastball that he complemented with an excellent forkball, an outstanding curveball, and a change-up and slider. Bob Ojeda (18-5, 2.57) was the staff junkballer, as his fastball topped out at about 87 miles an hour. He fooled guys with a great change-up, a solid curve, and even the occasional screwball, and he finished with a better ERA than his stronger-armed teammates.

How Were They Built? See separate article, "Every Which Way."

What Brought Them Down? In the spring of 1989, I (Rob) wrote a memo to Bill James (then my employer), suggesting that the Mets were due for great and continued success in the coming seasons. After all, they were coming off a 100-win season, Strawberry was just entering his prime years, Gregg Jefferies looked like he might become the best player of the coming decade, and Davey Johnson was running the show. But more than all that, what really impressed me was the Mets' pitching, specifically its quality and youth. Here are the career N.L. stats, through the '88 season, for the projected 1989 rotation:

Pitcher	Age	W-L (Pct)	ERA
Dwight Gooden	24	91-35 (.722)	2.62
David Cone	26	25-9 (.735)	2.85
Ron Darling	28	73-41 (.640)	3.36
Sid Fernandez	26	55-40 (.579)	3.33
Bob Ojeda	31	31-23 (.574)	2.83
Totals		**275-148 (.650)**	**3.01**

In short, it was a deep, young rotation with a history of great success. And there were a couple of future All-Star closers in the bullpen in Randy Myers and Rick Aguilera.

Make no mistake, the Mets didn't exactly collapse in '89. Gooden hurt his shoulder and started only 17 games. Ojeda and Darling were just okay. Nevertheless, the Mets posted a 3.29 ERA, second best in the National League. The hitters were nearly as good, scoring 683 runs, third most in the league. The Mets just weren't quite good enough, finishing 87-75, six games behind the flukey Cubs.

In 1990 they were runners-up yet again, winding up four lengths behind the East-winning Pirates, at 91-71. That made seven straight seasons in which the Mets finished either first or second. Unfortunately for their place in popular history, those seven seasons included five seconds and two firsts. If it had been the other way around, well, we would remember the Mets more than we do, wouldn't we?

Big deal, right? As Eddie likes to say, if my aunt had balls she'd be my uncle. Anyway, the real collapse didn't come until 1991, when the Mets finished fifth and posted their first sub-.500 record (77-84) since 1983. Strawberry was gone, Gooden was quite mortal, Jefferies never really panned out, and Davey Johnson had been fired in '90 after the club got off to a relatively slow start. It would not be until 1997 that the Mets would contend for the postseason again.

Hearn for Cone

The Mets' backup catcher in 1986 was a twenty-five-year-old rookie named Ed Hearn. Hearn, a .287 hitter in eight minor league seasons, hit .265 with decent power for the Mets.

Just a few days before the '87 season started, the Mets sent Hearn, along with pitchers Rick Anderson and Goose Gozzo, to the Kansas City Royals. In exchange, the Mets received minor league catcher Chris Jelic . . . and David Cone. Cone went 20-3 for the Mets in 1988 and, at this writing, stands a decent chance of eventually getting into the Hall of Fame. The other four guys in the trade did, almost literally, nothing in the major leagues. Kansas City's general manager, John Schuerholz, would eventually meet with great success in Atlanta. But this time, he got fleeced by Frank Cashen in the most lopsided trade of the decade.—*Rob*

Stats 'n' Stuff

◆ Bob Ojeda, who began 1986 as the fifth starter and is probably the least-remembered member of the Met rotation, topped the staff in wins (18), winning percentage (.783), and ERA (2.57). The season before, Ojeda had gone 9-11 for the Red Sox.

◆ Roger McDowell finished the season 14-9, despite not making a single start all season (he also led the Mets with 22 saves). No pitcher has recorded as many relief decisions (23) since.

◆ Owing to Davey Johnson's fondness for his bench, you won't find many Mets atop the N.L. stats in 1986. Keith Hernandez paced the loop with 94 walks, and with a .413 on-base percentage, he finished just behind league leader Tim Raines.

◆ The top four pitchers in N.L. winning percentage were Mets.

Most Valuable Met: Hernandez or Strawberry? Or Carter? Hard to pick among these, but we'll go with Hernandez. He posted a higher OPS than Strawberry and, of course, he was the top defensive first baseman in the National League, if not the major leagues. Carter actually finished third in the MVP voting, just ahead of Hernandez.

Worst Regular: By most accounts, Rafael Santana was a fine defensive shortstop. The problem was that he wasn't much of a hitter. Actually, that's being too kind. Santana was to hitting what Ronald Reagan was to details. Santana drew 36 walks in 1986, which looks pretty good until you pull out your STATS All-Time Major League Handbook and discover that a dozen of those walks were intentional (and we can probably assume that another dozen or so were semi-intentional), issued because the pitcher was due up next. The funny thing is, Santana was always a terrible hitter—lifetime 602 OPS, just a little better than his distant successor, Rey Ordonez—but in 1986 (541 OPS) he was *really* terrible. A typical Santana season, bad as it was, might have meant another win or two for the Mets.

Hall of Famers: At this writing, none. Zippo. What's more, it might stay that way for quite some time. And if twelve years ago you'd told intelligent baseball fans the '86 Mets wouldn't wind up with anyone in the Hall of Fame, they'd have thought you were nuts. Why? Because in 1986 two of the world's best baseball players were Dwight Gooden and Darryl Strawberry. At the end of that season, Gooden was twenty-one years old and his career record in the majors was 58-19. Fifty-eight wins and nineteen losses. His career ERA was 2.38. Strawberry was twenty-four and already could boast 108 home runs off major league pitchers. As we all know, a devastating combination of personal problems and injuries sidetracked both Gooden and Strawberry, and we'll always be left to wonder what might have been. If there is any justice in this world, Davey Johnson will one day be elected.

Our Hall of Famers: See separate article, "Two for Cooperstown."

The 1986 National League Championship Series: The Mets topped the Houston Astros in six games. See separate article, "The Greatest League Championship Series Ever Played?"

The 1986 World Series: The Mets beat the Boston Red Sox in seven games, outscoring the Sox 32–27. See separate article, "Blaming Billy Buck."

The Ballpark: Shea Stadium, home to the Mets since 1964, consistently played as one of the best pitcher's parks in the league, which makes the '86 club's league-leading offense look all the more impressive. The dimensions were fairly short, but there was lots of foul territory and visibility for the hitters was awful, making Shea a great place for power pitchers.

Books about the 1986 Mets: Only two Mets players came out with books immediately after the 1986 season. There would likely have been more, but both Keith Hernandez (*If at First . . .* [New York: McGraw-Hill, 1986]) and Davey Johnson (*Bats* [New York: G. P. Putnam's Sons, 1986]) released books just *before* the season. Those books, of course, do include plenty of material on players who were still with the Mets in '86. The two guys who did "write" books after the season were Gary Carter (*A Dream Season* [San Diego: HBJ, 1987]) and Lenny Dykstra (*Nails* [Garden City, NY: Doubleday, 1987]), and Dykstra's book is quite possibly the biggest waste of paper since Gutenberg.

If you're looking for a tad more literary value, try Mike Sowell's *One Pitch Away* (New York: Macmillan, 1995), subtitled "The Players' Stories of the 1986 League Championships and World Series." Sowell's book includes the ALCS as well as the stirring N.L. playoffs, but aside from accounts of all the postseason games, you'll find chapters devoted to Gary Carter, Ray Knight, and Mookie Wilson. Jerry Izenberg's *The Greatest Game Ever Played* (New York: Henry Holt, 1987) is all about game 6 of the 1986 NLCS.

The Greatest League Championship Series Ever Played?

At this writing, the 1986 NLCS between the Mets and the Houston Astros remains perhaps the most dramatic of all league champi-

Around the Majors

April 29 Red Sox pitcher Roger Clemens strikes out twenty Seattle Mariners to set a major league record. Clemens will finish the season with a 24-4 record and a 2.48 ERA, and he will win his first Cy Young award.

May 14 California Angels slugger Reggie Jackson hits his 537th home run, moving him past Mickey Mantle and into sixth on the all-time list.

June 16 Rangers knuckleball pitcher Charlie Hough pitches a one-hitter against the Angels, but loses 2–1 when California scores both their runs in the ninth inning.

June 27 Giants second baseman Robby Thompson is thrown out trying to steal four times, setting a new major league record.

August 25 A's third baseman Mark McGwire hits his first home run, a 450-foot moon shot off Tigers pitcher Walt Terrell.

September 14 San Francisco's Bob Brenly, a catcher by trade, is pressed into service at third base and commits four errors in one inning. He atones with two home runs, one of them a game winner in the bottom of the ninth.

September 25 Houston's Mike Scott throws a no-hitter against the Giants, thus clinching the N.L. West title for the Astros.

October 12 In game 5 of the American League Championship Series, the Boston Red Sox mount one of the more improbable comebacks in postseason history, scoring three runs in the ninth inning and two more in the eleventh to beat the Angels, 7–6.

onship series, at least since they went to the best-of-seven format in 1985. This remains true, even though the series only lasted six games.

Game 1 matched Dwight Gooden against eventual Cy Young winner Mike Scott, and Scott allowed just five hits and one walk, while striking out fourteen, to beat the Mets, 1–0. The Mets grabbed game 2 behind Bob Ojeda, 5–1.

In New York for game 3, the Mets trailed 5–4 when they came to bat in the ninth. Wally Backman led off with a drag bunt down the first-base line, and he avoided Glenn Davis' tag with a sweeping slide. Astros manager Hal Lanier argued that Backman was out of the baseline, but umpire Dutch Rennert disagreed. After Backman went to second on a passed ball, pinch-hitter Danny Heep flied out. That brought up Lenny Dykstra. Dykstra had homered only eight times all season, but he drove Dave Smith's second pitch, a forkball, over the right-field wall for a two-run, game-winning home run. According to Dykstra, "The last time I hit a home run in the bottom of the ninth inning to win a game was in Strat-O-Matic."

Game 4 was another Mike Scott Show. This time he struck out only five Mets, but he also limited them to three hits and cruised to a 3–1 victory. Houston's runs came on Alan Ashby's two-run homer in the second and Dickie Thon's solo shot in the fifth. So far, Scott had pitched eighteen innings and allowed one run. The Mets complained, to anyone who would listen, that Scott's famous split-finger fastball was actually an illegal scuffball. Whatever the case, the fact was that they couldn't hit Scott, and they desperately wanted to avoid facing him in a decisive game 7.

Game 5, postponed for a day by rain, matched two of the game's top power pitchers, Gooden and Nolan Ryan (Ryan had lost game 2). Gooden allowed just one run in ten innings, Ryan allowed one in nine, and it was still 1–1 after eleven frames. It probably shouldn't have been, though. In the second inning, first-base umpire Fred Brocklander missed a call at first, which prevented an Astro run from scoring on what Brocklander called a double play. Anyway, in the bottom of the twelfth, Gary Carter broke out of a 1-for-21 slump with a line shot up the middle that scored Backman with the winning run.

It was back to Houston for game 6, and the Astros grabbed a 3–0 lead in the first inning against Bob Ojeda (who settled down and lasted five innings). Amazingly, it was still 3–0 after eight frames, with Astro starter Bob Knepper working on a two-hitter. But Dykstra led off the ninth with a triple and scored on Mookie Wilson's single. Moments later, Keith Hernandez doubled in Wilson. That brought on closer Smith, who promptly walked Carter and Strawberry, thus loading the bases. Ray Knight followed with a sacrifice fly, and the game was tied. The score remained three-all until the fourteenth. The Mets went ahead on Backman's run-scoring single, but the Astros re-tied the contest when Billy Hatcher drove a Jesse Orosco delivery off the screen attached to the left-field fair pole. So with the score 4–4, Strawberry led off the sixteenth with a pop-fly double to short center. That started a three-run rally, assisted by a pair of wild pitches from Houston reliever Jeff Calhoun.

A three-run lead in extra innings is generally pretty safe, but of course this wasn't your typical ballgame. With one out in the bottom of the sixteenth, pinch-hitter Davey Lopes walked, and he advanced to second on Bill Doran's single. Hatcher singled, too, plating Lopes. One out later, Davis singled in Doran, and it was 6–5. But Jesse Orosco, finishing up his third inning and obviously tired, threw six straight breaking balls to strike out Kevin Bass, and the Mets were World Series–bound. Credit for the victory belonged to, as much as anyone, Met relievers Rick Aguilera and Roger McDowell, who combined for eight consecutive scoreless innings (six through thirteen), allowing just two hits and zero walks.

It was the longest game in postseason history—sixteen innings, 4 hours and 42 minutes—and had the result been different, you would not be reading this particular chapter.

Before we leave this subject, a sort of mini-controversy arose from Glenn Davis' at-bat in the sixteenth, which resulted in an RBI single. As it happens, that base hit was considered as something of a victory by the Mets. Davis, as you might remember, was one of the N.L.'s top power hitters in the mid-1980s. Had he played in an easier ballpark, he might well have hit 40-odd home runs a few times. Anyway, with Davis in a position to win the game with a three-run homer, Hernandez and Carter converged on the pitcher's mound. According to Carter, Hernandez said, "Whatever you do, Gary, don't let Jesse throw Davis a fastball." But according to Hernandez, he told Carter, "If you call for one more fastball, we're going to fight right here, in front of everybody." To this day, I suspect, both are sticking to their original stories. I also suspect that the truth lies somewhere in the middle.—Rob

Two for Cooperstown

I'm sure there is someone, somewhere, who will make a Hall of Fame case for Dwight Gooden and/or Darryl Strawberry. But we're not that someone. No, in our minds, the two best Hall of Fame candidates among the 1986 New York Mets are catcher Gary Carter and first baseman Keith Hernandez. Hernandez became eligible for the Hall in 1996 and drew scant support from the Baseball Writers Association of America, garnering 24 votes with 353 needed for election. We'll talk about Hernandez later on.

Carter was first eligible for consideration by the BBWAA in 1998 and didn't fare nearly as well as we expected. True, the voters have been getting awfully picky in recent years, but Carter's credentials . . . well, let's get into them.

In *Total Baseball*, Gary Carter ranks ninety-fourth all-time in total player rating (TPR). Now, that ranking is obviously excellent, but there are a number of players higher on the list who have yet to be admitted to the Hall. You have to remember, though, that career TPR does something of a disservice to catchers because the careers of top catchers generally don't last as long as, say, the careers of top first basemen. Yes, Bob Boone and Jim Sundberg and Carlton Fisk all played into their forties, but this is a recent phenomenon. Most people consider Johnny Bench the greatest catcher ever, but he was an everyday backstop for only eleven seasons. Next-greatest? Probably Yogi Berra, who caught 100-plus games in only ten seasons. I could go on. Anyway, here are the top ten catchers through 1998, ranked by career TPR:

Catcher	TPR
Gabby Hartnett	40.1
Yogi Berra	36.2
Bill Dickey	35.4
Mickey Cochrane	31.4
Gary Carter	29.6
Buck Ewing	29.5
Mike Piazza	29.5
Johnny Bench	24.3
Carlton Fisk	24.0
Roy Campanella	21.6

Of the men on the list above, only Carter, Piazza, and Fisk are not in the Hall of Fame (and Piazza's not eligible yet). So the list includes seven Hall of Famers. There are eleven catchers in the Hall, the other four being Roger Bresnahan (19.7), Rick Ferrell (10.1), Ernie Lombardi (17.3), and Ray Schalk (6.5). Ferrell and Schalk are in for somewhat mysterious, though not nefarious, reasons. Lombardi was a great hitter with the mobility of a crippled slug.

Carter's career hitting stats—his 777 OPS, for example—might not look all that impressive, but we have to remember that 777 wasn't bad for a catcher in the 1970s and early 1980s. Furthermore, Carter played nearly his entire career in two pitcher's parks, Stadia Olympique and Shea. Oh, and one of his other seasons came in *the* pitcher's park, Dodger Stadium.

We do, of course, have to consider defense as well. Carter came up with the Expos at the tail end of 1974, and he then spent the next two seasons splitting time between catcher and the outfield. Now, this might lead one to think that Carter was a poor catcher, but I haven't been able to find any evidence that this was true.

When Dick Williams, who was no fool, took over as manager of the Expos in 1977, one of the first things he did was install Carter behind the plate. In 1980, Carter won his first of three straight Gold Gloves. By the mid-1980s, various knee problems hindered Carter's throwing, but he remained a solid signal-caller and was one of the National League's best at blocking the plate.

So Carter was one of the better-hitting catchers ever, he was no slouch with the glove, and he played forever. What does that leave? Not much, and we think Carter's combination of offensive prowess, defensive skills, and durability are enough to qualify him for Cooperstown. Now we just have to convince the BBWAA. As the late, great Jim Murray once wrote, "Gary Carter is the type of guy who, if he saved a child from drowning, the mother would look at him and say, 'Where's his hat?'"

Keith Hernandez clearly isn't a Hall of Famer if you focus only on his batting stats. Although Hernandez finished his career with a .296 batting average and a healthy .388 on-base percentage, his career .436 slugging percentage is paltry for a first baseman. He never hit more than 18 home runs in a season, and he knocked in 100 runs just once. That was in 1979, when he drove in 105, led the league with 116 runs scored, and shared the National League MVP award with Willie

Stargell. There simply isn't any way to interpret Hernandez's batting stats as those of a Hall of Famer, not when slugging first basemen like Gil Hodges and Tony Perez are still on the outside looking in.

But his glove . . . O, his glove. Beginning in 1978, his second season as an everyday player, Hernandez won eleven straight Gold Gloves at first base. Only four other non-pitchers—Brooks Robinson (sixteen), Ozzie Smith (thirteen), Roberto Clemente (twelve), and Johnny Bench (ten)—won at least ten straight Gold Gloves, and it's safe to say that those guys deserved most of their awards. As did Hernandez, who was wondrous with the mitt. I never saw Vic Power or Wes Parker play, but Hernandez is the best I've seen, and his stats matched his appearance and his reputation.

In the end, though, we can't really advocate the election of Hernandez, for two reasons. One, there are already a bunch of first basemen in the Hall, first basemen who were better hitters than Hernandez, and the almost-certain eventual enshrinements of Hodges and Perez will only add to the congestion. Two, so much of Hernandez' argument is predicated on his glove work and, to this point, we simply haven't developed tools that allow us to define, with any real precision, the defensive value of first basemen.

Better him than Mattingly, though.—Rob

Blaming Billy Buck

Davey Johnson's Mets won only one World Series, which of course hurts their standing in the court of popular opinion. Making it even worse is how they won that one World Series. For, as we all know, the Mets didn't *win* the 1986 World Series so much as Bill Buckner *lost* it.

In case you've forgotten, here's a brief synopsis of game 6. The Boston Red Sox, having twice beaten Dwight Gooden, entered game 6 needing just one victory to clinch their first World Championship since 1918. Boston grabbed a 3–2 lead in the seventh, and it would have been 4–2, but Jim Rice was nailed at the plate by Mookie Wilson to end the inning. That non-run made a huge difference, as the Mets tied the game in the bottom of the eighth and, after a scoreless ninth, the contest moved to extra frames.

Dave Henderson, hero of the ALCS, led off the top of the tenth with a blast into the left-field stands. Later on, the Sox added an insurance run, or at least what looked like an insurance run, when Marty Barrett's two-out single plated Wade Boggs, who had doubled.

In the bottom of the tenth, with the Sox leading 6–4, Wally Backman and Keith Hernandez flied out, leaving the Sox just one out away from the championship. Just then, a Mets employee accidentally hit a wrong button, and for a few seconds Shea Stadium's giant Diamond Vision screen congratulated the Red Sox on winning the World Series. But Gary Carter singled, and so did Kevin Mitchell. That brought up Ray Knight, who fell behind Boston reliever Calvin Schiraldi, 0-and-2. One strike away. Schiraldi made a good pitch to Knight, who blooped it into center field. Carter scored and Mitchell raced to third. Six to five, Sox.

Bob Stanley came in to pitch to Mookie Wilson, who fouled off pitch after pitch. Finally, Stanley threw an inside fastball past Wilson. Unfortunately, Wilson didn't swing at the ball, and Rich Gedman didn't catch it, either. Mitchell scored the tying run and Knight advanced to second on what was ruled a wild pitch, but could have been a passed ball. Mookie fouled off two more pitches, then sent a limp little grounder down the line, an easy play for first baseman Bill Buckner, sore knees or no sore knees. The ball skipped a few times while Buckner was bending over to field the ball, the likes of which he had stopped thousands of times in the course of a nineteen-year professional career. Long story short, the baseball went under his glove and through his legs, and Ray Knight trotted home with the winning run. Ergo, Bill Buckner lost the 1986 World Series. Ergo, the Mets were just bystanders.

However, there are some things people forget. First, when the ball rolled between Buckner's legs, the game was already tied. Even had Buckner made the play cleanly, the contest would have moved to the eleventh inning, where the odds would have slightly favored the Mets, given that they were the better team, they were at home, and they had a better bullpen.

Second, Red Sox manager John McNamara committed a classic blunder by not replacing the gimpy Buckner with defensive specialist Dave Stapleton. McNamara had been making that move all October, but at the moment of truth he let his heart win a debate with his head.

Revisionism

In his 1999 autobiography, *Heat*, Dwight Gooden (or his collaborator, Bob Klapisch) wrote, "The club traded Hubie [Brooks] in 1985, then got rid of [George] Foster, who was leading the team in home runs in 1986, because he said the Mets made certain decisions based on race. The statements caused such a commotion, everyone got hurt. George was out of a job, and we lost our most productive hitter at the time." I probably shouldn't be, but I'm always a little surprised when such blatant errors find their way into print, especially now that we're in the Computer Age (or the Gates Dynasty, if you prefer).

Foster played his last game for the Mets on August 6, 1986, at which time he had 254 plate appearances. Among the ten Mets with at least 200 plate appearances at that point, Foster ranked *ninth*, with a 718 OPS (.289 on-base, .429 slugging). He ranked seventh among the regulars in slugging percentage and ninth in on-base percentage.

Danny Heep doesn't make the list of ten regulars because he falls just short of the 200 plate appearances cutoff I've used, but Heep—who was competing with Foster for playing time—had a 774 OPS at the time of Foster's release.

Finally, Foster was *not* leading the team in home runs. With 13, he trailed Gary Carter (18) and Darryl Strawberry (16). We all make errors when we write books, but this one's a whopper.—*Rob (with thanks to Tom Ruane for the data)*

Boys Will Be Boys . . .

◆ In July, Tim Teufel, Rick Aguilera, Ron Darling, and Bob Ojeda were out on the town in Houston. Teufel left a bar carrying a half-full cup of beer, and a pair of off-duty cops told him to go back inside. A little scrap ensued, and Teufel wound up with a swollen, bloody face and spent the night in jail.

Third, *it was only game 6*. The Red Sox still had another chance and, in fact, they owned a 3–0 lead after 5½ innings of game 7. But starter Bruce Hurst allowed three runs in the bottom of the sixth, and then in the seventh Schiraldi got hammered for the second time in as many games. And that was all she wrote.

Yes, Bill Buckner deserves his share of the blame. But a bunch of his teammates didn't help much, and the New York Mets were indeed more than just innocent bystanders.—Rob

The Swingin' Mets

The Mets were involved in four serious brawls during the 1986 season, and the last of them resulted in one of those situations that lends baseball much of its color. (By the way, have you ever wondered why baseball's the only sport where fights are called "brawls"?)

◆ **May 27 versus Dodgers.** In the bottom of the sixth, George Foster walloped a long grand slam off Tom Niedenfuer, who had been struggling since the National League Championship Series the previous autumn. The next hitter was Ray Knight, and Niedenfuer plunked Knight in the hip. Knight charged the mound and got in a couple of good shots before he and Niedenfuer were separated. Believe it or not, neither Niedenfuer nor Knight was ejected from the game.

◆ **June 6 versus Pirates.** Rick Rhoden was pitching for Pittsburgh, and the word was that Rhoden liked to scuff the baseball with sandpaper, which of course was (and is) illegal. The Mets beat the Pirates 17 out of 18 in 1986 (and this would be their only loss). With Gary Carter at the plate, first-base coach Bill Robinson, who had played with Rhoden, yelled at Carter to have the baseball checked. Plate umpire Billy Williams looked at the ball and gave Rhoden a new one. After the inning, when Robinson and Rhoden passed each other on the way to their respective dugouts, Robinson muttered, "Quit cheatin'. We know you do." Rhoden told Robinson to screw himself, Robinson took a poke at Rhoden, the benches emptied, and there was much brawling and rassling in the land.

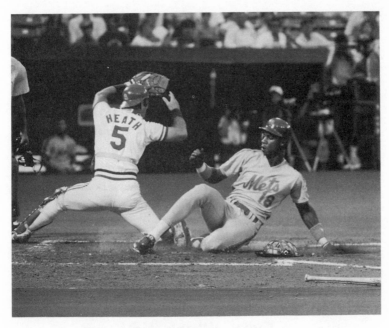

Darryl Strawberry (*AP/Wide World Photos*)

◆ **July 11 versus Braves.** Gary Carter hit a three-run homer off David Palmer in the first inning. Strawberry, up next, paid for Carter's blast with a fastball off his hip. Straw charged the mound, and a typical baseball fracas ensued. Just as on May 27, both of the main antagonists were allowed to remain in the game. When Carter came up again in the second inning, he hit a grand slam. Somehow, further fisticuffs were averted.

◆ **July 22 versus Reds.** In the tenth inning, Cincinnati's Eric Davis came in to run for player-manager Pete Rose, who had singled. Davis stole second base, and then he stole third. When Davis popped up from his slide, he shouldered Ray Knight, and the two exchanged words. Knight punched Davis in the jaw, and you can guess what happened after that. Eventually, Knight and Davis were both kicked out of the game, and so was Kevin Mitchell. That left the Mets without a third baseman, as Howard Johnson had already replaced Rafael Santana at shortstop. So Gary Carter was dispatched to the hot corner for only the second time in his career. (He played well, too, and even served as the pivot man on a 3-5-4 double play.)

That play was far from the game's defensive highlight.

◆ In game 6 of the World Series, a particular game situation compelled Davey Johnson to remove Darryl Strawberry after the eighth inning. Strawberry didn't take part in the postgame celebrations and complained to reporters about being "snatched" from the Series. In the pregame introductions before game 7, Strawberry alone took his place on the baseline without shaking hands with those who had been announced before him so that he wouldn't have to press the flesh with Davey.

◆ On the plane flight back to New York after the Mets beat the Astros in the NLCS, the players and their wives threw a little party. According to United Airlines, which billed the Mets for $7,500 in damages, the party resulted in ripped upholstery, damaged seats, and a beer-soaked airplane.—*Rob*

Mitchell's ejection not only cost the Mets their third-string third baseman, but also their right fielder, as Mitchell had replaced Strawberry earlier in the contest. Here's what happened next. Davey Johnson sent relief pitcher Jesse Orosco to right field and brought Roger McDowell in to pitch. For the rest of the game (try to stay with me), Orosco and McDowell took turns pitching. If a right-handed hitter was up, Orosco played the outfield and McDowell pitched. If a lefty was up, Orosco pitched and McDowell trooped out to the garden. They played left or right, depending on where Johnson thought they'd do the least damage, with Mookie Wilson playing the other spot. It was strange but it worked. Orosco caught a fly ball, the pair combined for five shutout innings, and Howard Johnson won the game with a three-run homer in the bottom of the fourteenth.—Rob

Every Which Way

The '86 Mets were anything but a homegrown club. Of the eight regulars listed earlier, only Dykstra, Backman, Strawberry, and Santana were originally signed by the Mets. True, that's four of eight. But of the other four, three—Hernandez, Carter, and Knight—ranked among the team's biggest stars. And then there's the rotation. Gooden, of course, was a product of the Mets' farm system. But Bob Ojeda came in a trade from the Red Sox, Ron Darling came in a trade from the Rangers, and Sid Fernandez came over from the Dodgers. Let's look at what the Mets gave up for those three starters, along with the four regulars mentioned earlier.

Player	Date Acquired	Team Traded From	Player(s) Traded For
Keith Hernandez	6/15/83	Cardinals	Neil Allen, Rick Ownbey
Gary Carter	12/10/84	Expos	Hubie Brooks, Mike Fitzgerald, Herm Winningham, Floyd Youmans

Player	Date Acquired	Team Traded From	Player(s) Traded For
Ray Knight	8/28/84	Astros	Gerald Young, Manny Lee, Mitch Cook
Rafael Santana	1/17/84	Free Agent	
Bob Ojeda	11/13/85	Red Sox	Calvin Schiraldi, Wes Gardner, John Christensen, LaSchelle Tarver
Ron Darling	4/1/82	Rangers	Lee Mazzilli
Sid Fernandez	12/8/83	Dodgers	Carlos Diaz, Bob Bailor

It certainly doesn't take any analytical genius to see a pattern here. All the guys on the left contributed to New York's fantastic season, whereas most of the guys on the right never contributed to, well, much of anything. Schiraldi did pitch well for the Red Sox in '86, at least until the postseason when he got hammered, but he was never worth much after that. Hubie Brooks played wonderfully for Montreal in 1986, but he was limited by injuries to 80 games. The rest of his career, he was an out machine.

Hernandez came to the Mets so cheaply because he had a drug problem, or at least he was using, and Whitey Herzog simply didn't want him in St. Louis any longer. I've no idea if Hernandez rode the straight and narrow as a Met, but if he was impaired or a bad influence, you certainly can't tell it from the stats or the club's record.

The best deals were probably the ones that brought the Mets Ron Darling and Sid Fernandez. Darling was the Rangers' first-round pick (ninth overall) in the 1981 June draft. He pitched fairly well (4-2, 4.44 ERA) in his first professional action, which came in the Class AA Texas League. Just before the 1982 season began, the Rangers, in a move typical of their mostly unsuccessful history, traded the twenty-one-year-old Darling and twenty-three-year-old Walt Terrell to the Mets, who had only to surrender hometown idol Lee Mazzilli.

A lot of organizations probably wouldn't have had the balls to trade a guy like Mazzilli, who was only twenty-seven years old, a New York native, and really good-looking. But Mets general manager

Frank Cashen knew what he was doing. Mazzilli was a good player in the late 1970s, but he suffered through an awful 1981 campaign, and the Mets were lucky to get anything at all for him. A year later, the Mets traded Terrell to Detroit for Howard Johnson, who's not in the chart above but was a solid contributor in '86 and soon became one of the better players in the National League.

The Sid Fernandez deal was similarly lopsided. Fernandez spent the first three years of his pro career zipping through the Dodger farm system, tossing a pair of no-hitters in a seven-week span, and racking up a 32-11 record. He pitched brilliantly for Class AA San Antonio in 1983 and finished the season in Los Angeles. That December, though, the Dodgers traded Fernandez and a decent middle-infield prospect named Ross Jones to the Mets. In return, the Dodgers got Carlos Diaz and Bob Bailor. Diaz was a middle reliever who enjoyed a couple of pretty good years, and Bailor was a past-his-prime utility player. Of the four players in the trade, only Fernandez played in the majors after 1987.

Let me repeat, the man responsible for all these moves was general manager Frank Cashen. Cashen's strength was that he was rarely satisfied with what he had. The Mets came oh-so-close in 1985, but did Cashen rest? No, he traded for Gary Carter. The Mets won the World Series in 1986, but did Cashen rest? No, he traded for Kevin McReynolds, who turned a weakness (left field) into a strength. Okay, not a huge strength, but McReynolds in left and Mookie/Lenny in center was better than Mookie in left and Lenny in center. (One might argue that the Mets would have been better off with Kevin Mitchell—who went to San Diego for McReynolds—in left field, but at least Cashen wasn't afraid to make a move.)—Rob

Davey Dangerfield

I tellya, I don't get no respect . . .

In 1983, the New York Mets went 68-94 and finished last in the N.L. East, 22 games out of first place. In 1986, the New York Mets went 108-54 and won the N.L. East by 21 1/2 games, plus they won the World Series. In 1989, the Mets went 87-75, good enough for a second-place finish and six games out of first. In 1992, the Mets went

72-90 for fifth place and 24 games out of first. Dave Johnson's first full year as Mets manager was 1984; his last was 1989 (he was dismissed in May 1990). The 1986 Mets were one of only four post–World War II teams to have a 40-plus win increase in a three-season span. The 1993 Mets were one of only nine post–World War II teams to have a 30-plus win decrease in a three-season span; their record was 59-103.

I know that I am not the only one who has written this about Dave Johnson, about how incongruous it seems that such a successful manager has such a hard time holding on to his job. As I write this, Johnson has managed ten full seasons in the major leagues, and his team finished first or second all ten seasons. All three of the teams he managed made postseason appearances. What am I missing?

I've heard all of the talk that club discipline tends to fall apart after Johnson has managed a team for a few years and that he can be tough to work with, aloof, and condescending. As for the first point, Johnson got to manage the Orioles for only two seasons, during which time they were 186-138, a .574 winning percentage. The two seasons before Johnson got the job, the Orioles posted a .523 winning percentage. And the O's virtually collapsed the season after he left. Johnson managed the Reds for only two full seasons, during which time they played .585 ball, compared to the .506 winning percentage they compiled in the two seasons *before* Johnson and the .485 in the two seasons *after* Johnson.

Back to Johnson and his Metropolitans. The Mets posted three 90-plus-win seasons in Johnson's first three seasons as the manager (1984–86) after having only one 90-plus-win season (1969) in their previous *history*. (It's at least a little ironic that Johnson was on the 1969 Orioles team that was upset by the Mets in the World Series, and he even made the last out in the last game.) The Mets' winning percentage during Johnson's first three seasons was .609; in the three seasons before Johnson took over, it was .407.

To me, the only reason why Johnson gets so little respect despite his accomplishments is that he is not, by most accounts, someone who tries to stroke people. It's too bad that people can't separate what a person is from what he can do.—Eddie

TEAM STATISTICS

Hitting

	Games by Position	Age	G	AB	R	H	2B	3B	HR	RBI	BB	SO	SB	Avg	OBP	Slug
Keith Hernandez	1B,149	32	149	551	94	171	34	1	13	83	94	69	2	.310	.413	.446
Wally Backman	2B,113	26	124	387	67	124	18	2	1	27	36	32	13	.320	.376	.385
Rafael Santana	SS,137; 2B,1	28	139	394	38	86	11	0	1	28	36	43	0	.218	.285	.254
Ray Knight	3B,132; 1B,1	33	137	486	51	145	24	2	11	76	40	63	2	.298	.351	.424
Darryl Strawberry	OF,131	24	136	475	76	123	27	5	27	93	72	141	28	.259	.358	.507
Len Dykstra	OF,139	23	147	431	77	127	27	7	8	45	58	55	31	.295	.377	.445
Mookie Wilson	OF,114	30	123	381	61	110	17	5	9	45	32	72	25	.289	.345	.430
Gary Carter	C,122; 1B,9; OF,4; 3B,1	32	132	490	81	125	14	2	24	105	62	63	1	.255	.337	.439
Kevin Mitchell	OF,68; SS,24; 3B,7; 1B,2	24	108	328	51	91	22	2	12	43	33	61	3	.277	.344	.466
Tim Teufel	2B,84; 1B,3; 3B,1	27	93	279	35	69	20	1	4	31	32	42	1	.247	.324	.369
Howard Johnson	3B,45; SS,34; OF,1	25	88	220	30	54	14	0	10	39	31	64	8	.245	.341	.445
Danny Heep	OF,56	28	86	195	24	55	8	2	5	33	30	31	1	.282	.379	.421
George Foster*	OF,62	37	72	233	28	53	6	1	13	38	21	53	1	.227	.289	.429
Ed Hearn	C,45	25	49	136	16	36	5	0	4	10	12	19	0	.265	.322	.390
Lee Mazzilli*	OF,10; 1B,8	31	39	58	10	16	3	0	2	7	12	11	1	.276	.417	.431
Kevin Elster	SS,19	21	19	30	3	5	1	0	0	0	3	8	0	.167	.242	.200
Stan Jefferson	OF,7	23	14	24	6	5	1	0	1	3	2	8	0	.208	.296	.375
Dave Magadan	1B,9	23	10	18	3	8	0	0	0	3	3	1	0	.444	.524	.444
John Gibbons	C,8	24	8	19	4	9	4	0	1	1	3	5	0	.474	.545	.842
Barry Lyons	C,3	26	6	9	1	0	0	0	0	2	1	2	0	.000	.100	.000
Tim Corcoran	1B,1	33	6	7	1	0	0	0	0	0	2	0	0	.000	.222	.000
Totals		28	162	5,558	783	1,462	261	31	148	730	631	968	118	.263	.347	.401

*Played for another team during season. Statistics are those compiled with 1986 New York Mets only.

Pitching

	Threw	Age	Games	GS	CG	ShO	IP	H	HR	BB	SO	W	L	Pct	Sv	ERA
Dwight Gooden	Right	21	33	33	12	2	250	197	17	80	200	17	6	.739	0	2.84
Ron Darling	Right	25	34	34	4	2	237	203	21	81	184	15	6	.714	0	2.81
Bobby Ojeda	Left	28	32	30	7	2	217	185	15	52	148	18	5	**.783**	0	2.57
Sid Fernandez	Left	23	32	31	2	1	204	161	13	91	200	16	6	.727	1	3.52
Rick Aguilera	Right	24	28	20	2	0	142	145	15	36	104	10	7	.588	0	3.88
Roger McDowell	Right	25	75	0	0	0	128	107	4	42	65	14	9	.609	22	3.02
Jesse Orosco	Left	29	58	0	0	0	81	64	6	35	62	8	6	.571	21	2.33
Doug Sisk	Right	28	41	0	0	0	71	77	0	31	31	4	2	.667	1	3.06
Rick Anderson	Right	29	15	5	0	0	50	45	3	11	21	2	1	.667	1	2.72
Bruce Berenyi	Right	31	14	7	0	0	40	47	5	22	30	2	2	.500	0	6.35
Randy Niemann	Left	30	31	1	0	0	36	44	2	12	18	2	3	.400	0	3.79
Randy Myers	Left	23	10	0	0	0	11	11	1	9	13	0	0	—	0	4.22
John Mitchell	Right	20	4	1	0	0	10	10	1	4	2	0	1	.000	0	3.60
Terry Leach	Right	32	6	0	0	0	7	6	0	3	4	0	0	—	0	2.70
Ed Lynch*	Right	30	1	0	0	0	2	2	0	0	1	0	0	—	0	0.00
Totals		26	414	162	27	11	**1,484**	1,304	**103**	509	1,083	**108**	**54**	**.667**	46	**3.11**

*Played for another team during season. Statistics are those compiled with 1986 New York Mets only.

CHAPTER 19

1998 New York Yankees

All my life I've hated them. Growing up in an American League city in the 1950s, it was impossible not to hate the Yankees, unless you were an egregious front runner. The Detroit kids I knew who liked the Yankees were the same kids who wore preknotted ties to school, had perfect parts in their hair, and were really good at making dioramas. They liked General Motors and, for all I know, the IRS.

And now I'm one of them. To make matters worse, this superb, balanced, record-setting, stunningly appealing team is not only wearing the loathed pinstripes; it's wearing pinstripes supplied by George Steinbrenner, for heaven's sake. Somehow this man—this bully, this human plague—has got far enough out of the way to allow the assembly of as close to perfect a baseball team as anyone under 70 has seen.

—Daniel Okrent in *Time,* July 27, 1998

Record: 114-48, .704 (8th)
Two-Year (1997–98): 210-114, .648 (43d)
Three-Year (1997–99): 308-178, .634
   (48th)

SD Score: +3.88 (1st)
Two-Year: +6.70 (1st)
Three-Year: +9.41 (3d)

Results:
1997 American League Wildcard
1998 World Champions
1999 World Champions

Days in First Place: 161 of 180;
   clinched on September 9

Longest Winning Streak: 10 games
Longest Losing Streak: 4 games

The Pennant Race: There was no pennant race. By the end of May, the Yankees boasted a 7½-game lead over the second-place Red Sox, and they never were threatened.

Against the Contenders: Yeah, right.

Runs Scored: 965 (1st)

Runs Allowed: 656 (1st)

In case you missed it above, those 965 runs scored and 656 runs allowed resulted in a +3.88 SD score, which is the highest this century.

Pythagorean Record: 108-54

The Yankees out-performed expectations by six games, a healthy figure. As we've noted elsewhere in this book, however, nearly all teams that win an extraordinary number of games out-perform Pythagoras.

Manager: Joe Torre

Regular Lineup:

Player	Position	ROV	OW%
Chuck Knoblauch	2B	.284	.535
Derek Jeter	SS	.320	.653
Paul O'Neill	RF	.312	.629
Bernie Williams	CF	.343	.714
Tino Martinez	1B	.300	.591
Darryl Strawberry	DH	.306	.613
Scott Brosius	3B	.305	.608
Jorge Posada	C	.284	.536
Chad Curtis	LF	.270	.485

The 1998 Yankees really had a balanced lineup. See the article, "Who Needs Superstars?"

Left field remained a question mark for most of the season, but that was nothing new for the Yankees. Chad Curtis started 76 games in left field, the most for any Yankee since Mel Hall (99) in 1992. Cur-

Roy Hobbs or Joe Hardy?

Roy Hobbs was The Natural. Joe Hardy sold his soul to the devil in exchange for supernatural baseball skills. Both of them came from nowhere, just like Shane Spencer. Okay, maybe not nowhere. Shane Spencer came from Columbus, home of New York's Class AAA farm club. Twenty-six years old in 1998, Spencer had been kicking around in the Yankees' farm system for eight years, never playing well enough to be regarded as a real prospect or poorly enough to get released.

In 1997, Spencer hit 30 home runs with Columbus. He also could manage only a .241 batting average, but 30 home runs will get you noticed. By August 17, 1998, Spencer had been summoned from Columbus to New York three times . . . and sent from New York back to Columbus three times, seeing very little action in each of his visits to Gotham (though he did go 5-for-5 with two doubles and two

tis played particularly well early in the season (and was rewarded with a three-year contract extension on July 14), but he slumped badly in the second half (.216 batting average, 631 OPS), and Tim Raines, Shane Spencer, and Ricky Ledee all took their turns in left field, too. Otherwise, the Yankees got great production from every position.

In *The New Yorker*, Roger Angell wrote, "In this era of the tape-measured four-hundred-and-fifty-foot home-run blast, the Bronx Bombers have gone cerebral. They play the slowest game in the majors, over three hours, on average—almost a pictorial stat, illustrating the grave attention that their batters, top to bottom, give to the pitch and the situation, and to the fate of the base runner."

Bench: The Yankee bench was not particularly productive, but this was partly due to an injury that cost DH Chili Davis most of the season. Joe Girardi played almost as much behind the plate as Posada, and nonproductive Luis Sojo manned shortstop when Jeter was out for two weeks in June.

Scouting the Pitchers: Perhaps the most creative American-born pitcher of his era, David Cone (20-7, 3.55) seemed to just make things up as he went along. As *The New York Post*'s Tom Keegan wrote, Cone "mixes a 92-MPH fastball with a diving splitter, a nasty slider, and two curveballs with different speeds and breaks. He throws all of his pitches from varied arm angles." Cone's sidearm curve to right-handed hitters was known around the American League as "Laredo," because it came from so far south.

Portly David Wells (18-4, 3.49), who threw a perfect game on May 17, featured a solid fastball and a hard curve, and he threw strikes. Lots of strikes. Wells walked only 29 hitters in 214 innings. Possessor of one of baseball's best pickoff moves, Andy Pettitte (16-11, 4.24) relied on his cut fastball and his change-up. Cuba's Orlando "El Duque" Hernandez (12-4, 3.13) and Japan's Hideki Irabu (13-9, 4.06) provided the international flavor to the rotation. Hernandez used a funky delivery and a physics-defying slider. At his best, Irabu's fastball-splitter combination gave hitters fits.

How Were They Built? It's easy to say the Yankees bought a World Championship, given George Steinbrenner's deep pockets and the club's $75 million payroll. However, it's important to remember that a number of key players were products of the Yankee farm system. This list includes Bernie Williams, Derek Jeter, Jorge Posada, Andy Pettitte, and Mariano Rivera. A number of others—Hideki Irabu, Tino Martinez, David Cone—came to the organization by trades in which the Yankees surrendered some of the solid talent developed in the system. The money—thank you, cable television—didn't hurt, either. Orlando Hernandez defected from Cuba in late 1997, and after a fierce bidding war among various major league teams, he signed a four-year, $6.6 million contract with the Yankees.

What Brought Them Down? At this writing, nothing's brought them down or appears likely to. One might predict that Steinbrenner's arrogance will eventually bring about their demise, but in recent years The Boss has taken a less active role in management, to the benefit of the franchise. Entering the 1999 season, the Yankee farm system was loaded with fine prospects and, of course, there's always plenty of cash on hand.

Most Valuable Yankee: Tough, tough call. Bernie Williams and Derek Jeter both played key defensive positions with aplomb, and both ranked among the league's best hitters at their position. However, both also spent a few weeks on the disabled list. Paul O'Neill turned in a typical New York season, for him, and thus ranked among the American League's top right fielders.

Then you've got the pitchers. Toronto's Roger Clemens, who would join the Yankees for the '99 campaign, won the 1998 Cy Young award, but in a lot of seasons the Yanks would have boasted three strong candidates in David Cone, David Wells, and Mariano Rivera.

We'll take Jeter because he played in 21 more games than Williams. (The MVP voters agreed, by the way, tabbing Jeter for third place and Williams for seventh.)

Worst Regular: Chad Curtis started 121 games and was the only Yankee regular with a sub-.500 offensive winning percentage.

Hall of Famers: Obviously, none of the 1998 Yankees are eligible for the Hall of Fame yet, and they won't be for some time. Joe Torre has decent qualifications as a player, but is no longer eligible. However,

homers against Kansas City on August 7).

Finally, on August 31 Spencer was brought to New York to stay, and he enjoyed one of the great Septembers. Spencer played only 14 games that month, but in those 14 games he hit eight home runs and collected 21 RBI. What's more, 12 of those RBI came on three hits. Three grand slams, to be precise. Though it took him only a month, Spencer was only the seventh Yankee to hit at least three grand slams in a season, and he joined some pretty exclusive company: Don Mattingly, Tommy Henrich, Lou Gehrig, Joe DiMaggio, Babe Ruth, and Mike Stanley (which one of those is not like the others?).

Spencer continued his heavy hitting in the Division Series against the Rangers, cranking a solo homer in game 2 and a three-run blast in game 3. He slumped in the ALCS, however, and played in only one of the World Series games.

Shane Spencer wasn't a great player. But he was great for a few weeks, and if you're going to be great for a few weeks, New York is the place to do it.—*Rob*

Stats 'n' Stuff

◆ By winning 20 games, David Cone set a record for longest stretch between 20-victory seasons. He last accomplished the feat in 1988, when he went 20-3 for the Mets.

◆ The Yankees held a lead in 48 straight games, a major league record.

◆ Bernie Williams became the first player to win a batting title, a Gold Glove, and a World Series in the same season.

◆ The Yankees opened their season with a trip to the West Coast. They lost their first three games, then split their next two. In two of those four losses, they'd been blown out, so at the close of play on April 6, the Yankees were 1-4 and had been outscored 36-15. On April 7, they beat the Mariners 13–7, beginning an eight-game winning streak and a four-week stretch that would see the Yankees go 22-2.

his two World Championships (at this writing) might be enough to get him elected as a manager.

Our Hall of Famers: Derek Jeter and Bernie Williams obviously possess Hall of Fame–type abilities, but both still have a way to go. It was common, to the point of annoying, to hear broadcasters say things like, "As great as the Yankees are, it's amazing that there's not one sure Hall of Famer on the roster." We have to respond with a hearty "Huh?" In '98, Tim Raines was a Yankee. Frankly, any broadcaster who doesn't think Raines is a Hall of Famer should turn in his microphone, and any baseball writer who doesn't think Raines is a Hall of Famer should turn in his laptop computer.

In the 1999 edition of *Total Baseball*, Raines ranks 21st all-time with a 52.6 total player rating. It probably goes without saying, but the twenty players ahead of Raines are all in the Hall (except for Rickey Henderson and Barry Bonds, who of course aren't eligible yet). But maybe you don't trust Pete Palmer's methods, and you just can't believe that Raines is the 21st most valuable non-pitcher in major league history. So let's suppose that, instead, Raines is the 42d most valuable non-pitcher ever. Well, of the top 41, only two eligible players—Bobby Grich and Bill Dahlen—are not in the Hall, and both of them should be. The other top candidate is David Cone, who continued to establish his credentials in 1999, when he threw a perfect game. Through the 1999 season, Cone's 180-102 career record falls a bit short of Cooperstown's normal standards, but his winning percentage (.638) will likely get him in, assuming he can tack on another 30 or 40 victories.

The 1998 Division Championship Series: The Texas Rangers went just 2-6 against the Yankees in the regular season, but they did average 6.6 runs in those eight games, so they and their fans held at least a glimmer of hope. Whatever. The Rangers scored the grand total of one run in three games, on 13 base hits. The Yankees swept the series, 2–0, 3–1, and 4–0.

The 1998 American League Championship Series: Jaret Wright, masterful against the Yankees in the 1997 ALCS, started the opener for Cleveland in 1998. Wright couldn't escape the first inning, and the Yankees cruised to a 7–2 triumph behind David Wells.

After eleven innings of game 2, the score was still 1–1. In the top of the twelfth, Cleveland pinch-runner Enrique Wilson was on first base when Travis Fryman attempted a sacrifice bunt down the first-base line. Tino Martinez pounced on the ball and fired to Chuck Knoblauch covering first base. However, the ball hit Fryman in the back and bounced 20 feet away. Knoblauch didn't go after the ball, electing instead to argue with plate umpire Ted Hendry, and Wilson scored all the way from first. Kenny Lofton added a two-run single moments later, and Indians closer Mike Jackson retired the Yankees in order in the bottom of the twelfth to seal Cleveland's 4–1 victory.

The "Fryman-Knoblauch Incident" was reminiscent of a similar play in game 4 of the 1969 World Series involving J. C. Martin and Elrod Hendricks, except this time the umpire got the call right. Unless one interprets the rules extremely liberally, Fryman had every right to run where he ran. One thing no one remembers is that even if Knoblauch had gone after the ball immediately, the Indians would likely have had runners on first and third with nobody out and, thus, would likely have taken the lead anyway. If you want to blame someone for the loss, don't blame Knoblauch or Hendry, even though both might have erred in judgment. Blame Tino Martinez, whose poor throw precipitated the brouhaha.

Cleveland's Bartolo Colon beat New York with a four-hitter in game 3, and suddenly the Yankees were looking something less than invincible. Orlando "El Duque" Hernandez, a recent defector from Cuba, evened the series at two games apiece, holding the Indians to three hits and zero runs over seven innings of game 4. Thus, with normalcy returned, New York breezed by Cleveland, taking games 5 and 6 by 5–3 and 9–5 scores, respectively.

The 1998 World Series: The Yankees faced off against the San Diego Padres, and the Yanks were heavily favored. History was on their side, that's for sure. The Yankees won 16 more regular-season games (114) than the Padres (98). Before 1998, five World Series had matched opponents with differences of 15, 16, or 17 regular-season victories. The favorites—three of whom are in this book—won all five of those World Series, winning 20 games and losing only three in the process.

If there was a decisive moment in the 1998 World Series, it came in the seventh inning of game 1. Entering that inning, the Padres

◆ Tim Raines was one of the last two players in the major leagues to wear a batting helmet with no earflap (Gary Gaetti was the other). Raines was in the majors before 1983, and thus he had the right to forgo the earflap.

◆ The Yankees totaled 207 home runs, the highest ever for a team without a single player with 30 or more homers.

Around the Majors

March 31 Two expansion teams, the N.L.'s Arizona Diamondbacks and the A.L.'s Tampa Bay Devil Rays, play their first games. Both teams lose at home.

April 7 For the first time in the twentieth century, a team has switched from one major league to another, and today the National League returns to Milwaukee as the Brewers play their first home game as members of the National League after twenty-nine seasons in the

American League (including their one year in Seattle).

May 6 In his fifth major league start, Cubs rookie righthander Kerry Wood tosses a one-hitter against the Astros, setting the N.L. strikeout record and tying the major league record with 20 strikeouts.

May 28 Barry Bonds is issued a bases-loaded intentional walk, the first such walk since 1944 (Bill Nicholson). The move, ordered by Diamondbacks (and ex-Yankees) manager Buck Showalter, "works," as the next Giants batter (catcher Brent Mayne) lines out to end the game.

September 8 St. Louis Cardinals first baseman Mark McGwire hits his 62d home run off Cubs pitcher Steve Trachsel, thus breaking the record Roger Maris set in 1961. McGwire will finish the season with an unfathomable 70 home runs, and Cubs right fielder Sammy Sosa is right behind with 66.

September 20 Baltimore Orioles third baseman Cal

boasted a 5–2 lead thanks to a pair of home runs from Greg Vaughn and one from Tony Gwynn, and they had ace Kevin Brown on the mound. However, Brown had been struck on the shin by a Chili Davis line drive in the second inning, and he finally exited in the bottom of the seventh after permitting a single and a walk. Donne Wall, excellent during the regular season, promptly gave up a game-tying homer to Knoblauch, the first batter he faced. After Derek Jeter singled, lefty Mark Langston came in to face Paul O'Neill, who flied out. Two outs, a man on first, a tie game . . . the Padres were still very much alive. But Langston wild-pitched Jeter to second base, and Bruce Bochy ordered an intentional walk for Bernie Williams. Then came a walk to Chili Davis, unintentional and loading the bases for Tino Martinez, who carried a long history of postseason futility into the Series.

With the count 2-and-2 on Martinez, Langston fired a fastball down the middle, at or just below knee level. Langston thought he had the strikeout, but plate umpire Richie Garcia thought it was low. Martinez drove Langston's next pitch over the right-field wall for a grand slam. That made the score 9–5, it ended 9–6, and the Series was essentially over.

Battling flu symptoms, Padres starter Andy Ashby didn't escape the third inning of game 2, and the Yankees cruised to a 9–3 laugher behind seven strong innings from El Duque.

The Series shifted to San Diego for game 3, and at least half of the 64,667 fans at Qualcomm Stadium left the park scratching their heads at Bruce Bochy's late-game strategy.

Padres closer Trevor Hoffman was the N.L.'s top relief pitcher in 1998, but he rarely entered games before the ninth inning. With the Padres nursing a 3–2 lead in the top of the eighth, however, Bochy summoned Hoffman from the bullpen. Moments later, Scott Brosius blasted a Hoffman fastball over the centerfield wall for a three-run homer.

Down 5–4 in the ninth, the Padres rallied with two outs. First Carlos Hernandez singled, and pinch-hitter Mark Sweeney did the same. That put the potential tying run on second base, leaving a perfect situation for John Vander Wal, San Diego's top pinch-hitter. Unfortunately, Bochy had inexplicably already used Vander Wal to pinch-run for Hernandez. That left Andy Sheets to hit, and he struck out to end the game.

Most of the bounces had been going New York's way, and nothing changed in game 4. The Yankees scored once in the sixth and twice in the eighth, both rallies assisted by infield singles, whereas the Padres had ten baserunners but couldn't score at all. The final score was 3–0, and the Yankees had fittingly capped their amazing season with the first World Series sweep since 1990.

The Ballpark: Yankee Stadium circa 1998 was significantly different than it had been in 1961. The House That Ruth Built was substantially rebuilt in 1974 and 1975 (during which time the Yankees shared Shea Stadium with the Mets). The "new" Yankee Stadium featured more symmetrical dimensions, and the infamous "Death Valley" in deepest left-center field was shortened from 457 feet to 430. Meanwhile, the distances down the lines were lengthened from around 300 feet to approximately 310.

The fences were moved again in 1985 and 1988, resulting in a ballpark not much different from others around the league (though left-center field was still somewhat deeper than right-center). Even with the general trend toward moving the fences in, Yankee Stadium remained a pitcher's park in 1998, relative to the rest of the league, and it was toughest for right-handed-hitting power hitters.

Yankees owner George Steinbrenner, eager for a new ballpark, loved to complain about the aging Stadium and the neighborhood around it. On April 13, Steinbrenner's prayers were answered when a 500-pound concrete and steel beam fell from beneath the Stadium's upper deck into seats below. Fortunately, this happened hours before that evening's scheduled game, which was postponed. With the ballpark temporarily closed to the public, another game was postponed, but on April 15 the Yankees hosted the Anaheim Angels at Shea Stadium. That evening, the Mets hosted the Cubs, thus marking the only time in the twentieth century that four major league teams played in one stadium on the same day.

Books about the 1998 Yankees: A couple of quickie paperbacks were published within two weeks of the Yankees clinching the World Series, both about as good as you'd expect. Joe Torre did a book after the 1996 season, *Chasing the Dream* (New York: Bantam, 1997), which is not as good as you'd hope from a man who'd been in professional baseball for nearly thirty-seven years.

Ripken ends his consecutive-games streak at 2,632, the all-time professional record.

September 28 In a one-game playoff, the Chicago Cubs beat the San Francisco Giants, 5–3, thus earning the N.L.'s wildcard postseason berth.

The Pinstripe Legacy

Love 'em or hate 'em, there can be no denying the New York Yankees' place in baseball history. They are obviously the dominant franchise in the history of the game, and perhaps in the history of team sports. The Yankees' 1998 World Series title was their twenty-fourth and came in their thirty-fifth World Series appearance. Think about that. The World Series began in 1903 and has been played every year since then except 1904 and 1994, which means there have been 94 World Series (through 1998). One team, playing in a sport that now has thirty teams and which has had at least sixteen teams for every season with a World Series, has won more than one-quarter of all of the championships. The Yankees have won as many World Series titles as the next *three* most franchises combined (nine each for the Athletics and Cardinals, six for the Dodgers). This book is about the greatest baseball teams of all time, but this chapter seems like the appropriate place to talk about the greatest franchise of all time.

When the American League began play as a major league in 1901, it had no New York franchise. As recounted elsewhere in the book, the Baltimore franchise was moved to New York for the 1903 season and was originally known as the Highlanders. The club took the nickname "Yankees" in 1913, but for the most part remained unsuccessful until the arrival of Babe Ruth in 1920. As Robert Creamer points out in *Babe: The Legend Comes to Life*, "The moribund [Baltimore] Orioles followed him [John McGraw] to New York . . . the franchise becoming the New York Highlanders, who in time were renamed the New York Yankees, who were made famous by Baltimore's Ruth. How beautifully circuitous is history."

The Yankees made their first World Series appearance in 1921. Beginning with that season and ending with the Yankees' last of their five straight World Series trips in 1964—a span of forty-four years—the Yankees won the American League pennant almost twice as many times as *the rest of the teams in the league combined*, winning twenty-nine of those forty-four pennants. In the sixteen years from 1949 through 1964, the Yankees won fourteen pennants and nine World Series. Here's Sandy Koufax talking about the 1963 World Series, from his excellent autobiography (written with Ed Linn), "[I]n 1963 the Yankees were still *the Yankees*. There are those who still feel that a World Series is something less than a World Series if the Yankees aren't in

"*I dreamed the Yankees lost in Game Seven.*"

it. . . . There is the feeling, as I have already said, that an occasional wildcat World Series may be played somewhere else, but the official World Series is played in Yankee Stadium."

In 1999, the Yankees were once again World Champs. Many of today's fans attribute their success simply to the fact that they have more resources than any other team. If one looks objectively around the current baseball landscape, one can see that there are other teams with high levels of resources who are not as successful as the Yankees. In today's baseball, it's very easy to spend a lot of money, but much more difficult to spend it wisely. Consistent with the tradition of the franchise, the current Yankees are wisely utilizing their vast resources. The Babe and Colonel Ruppert wouldn't want it any other way.—Eddie

A Scout's Eye View

Ken Bracey, Padres' Special Assistant to the GM, got a first-hand look at the 1998 Yankees. He was assigned to scout the Yankees in advance of a potential World Series matchup between the two clubs, a matchup that wound up happening. Bracey, a scout since 1968, is one of the most respected evaluators in the business. Except for a four-year stint with Milwaukee, he has worked for the Padres ever since their admission into the National League in 1969.

Q: How do the 1998 Yankees stack up compared to other teams you have seen?

Bracey: This year's [1998] Yankees team is, overall, the best I've seen since I started scouting. The reason I say that is the overall depth of their twenty-five-man roster—position players and starting pitchers.

Q: Many in the media portrayed the Yankees as a great team, but without any great players or superstars. Do you agree?

Bracey: I think that Derek Jeter and Bernie Williams are superstars, by today's standards, because they are as good at their positions as anybody else in the game.

Q: Who do you think are some of the other important players on the Yankees?

Bracey: Chuck Knoblauch was a great addition, because he was a stabilizer. Even though he didn't have a great year, his experience and ability in the middle of the infield was very important. Paul O'Neill is important because of his intensity, which rubs off on his teammates. In general, the Yankees seem to have a lot of smart players who get the most out of their ability and who play hard. They are selfless and seem to feed off each other.

Q: How did you assess the Padres' chances of beating the Yankees?

Bracey: If we had any chance of beating them, we had to win the first game. The first-game wins against Houston and Atlanta were so important to our winning those [1998 postseason] series. Quite honestly, I didn't think we'd win [the World Series], especially with games 6 and 7 in New York. I think it was the Yankees' year; it's hard to imagine any team that lost just 48 games all year losing the World Series.—Eddie

The Straw:
What Might Have Been

What kind of career totals does this player have?

Age	Major League Season	Games	AB	R	H	HR	RBI
24	4th	136	475	76	123	27	93
36	16th	101	295	44	73	24	57

Well, these numbers look like they came from a player who was good at an early age and who retained his power as he got older. It is certainly not unusual for a player who shows real ability at an early age to remain productive, albeit in diminishing playing time, into his mid-thirties. Of course, these two seasons are part of Darryl Strawberry's career (1986 and 1998).

It is not my intention to get involved in the debate about substance abuse and its causes and treatments. I am not a doctor or psychologist. What I want to do is simply estimate what all of Strawberry's lost years, resulting from the drug use plus various injuries, have done to his career totals.

After his productive first year with the Dodgers in 1991, Strawberry saw limited time for the next six seasons. In a crude attempt to guess what he might have done, I used a weighted average of 1989–91 as his projected season for 1992. Except for 1994 (which screws everything up, thanks to the player strike), I then decreased his playing time in a linear fashion using his 1998 season as the other end; in other words, I wanted the decline in the number of games played and at-bats to be equal from the 1992 projection to the 1998 actual. In the projected seasons, I kept the projected rates of performance, such as the home runs to at-bats ratio, more or less equal to the 1992 rates, although I did project a slight yearly decline in batting average and runs scored per at-bat. I know that a player's career does not progress in a straight downhill line; however, for the group of six seasons as a whole, this projection seems reasonable. I'll shut up now and show you the projected versus the actual numbers:

Darryl and Eric

The lives of Darryl Strawberry and Eric Davis are, in many ways, amazingly similar. They were both born in Los Angeles two and a half months apart in 1962. They were both two-sport stars in high school (basketball and baseball), though they did not go to the same school, as many believe (Strawberry went to Crenshaw, Davis went to Fremont). Darryl and Eric were both blessed with tremendous athletic ability, the chief baseball manifestations of which were bat speed, running speed, and great arms.

Both made their big league debuts in May: Strawberry in 1983, Davis in 1984. Both had many good seasons, but both were dogged by criticisms that they weren't as good as they could be. Strawberry and Davis both had more than their share of injuries and illnesses. They both experienced a decline phase in their career, only to come back with at least one more productive season (both in

1998). Of course, Davis has had two comebacks: one from a decline that ended with him retiring for an entire season and the other from colon cancer. In fact, they both have had colon cancer.

People who believe in spirits and transmigration of the soul might say that Strawberry and Davis are really the same person. I don't know about that, but their lives have had a similarity that borders on the eerie. Neither will ever be in the Hall of Fame, but both had that kind of ability.—*Eddie*

	Projected						Actual					
Year	G	AB	R	H	HR	RBI	G	AB	R	H	HR	RBI
1992	142	512	85	135	31	98	43	156	20	37	5	25
1993	135	473	77	123	29	91	32	100	12	14	5	12
1994	88	300	48	77	18	57	29	92	13	22	4	17
1995	121	397	63	102	24	76	32	87	15	24	3	13
1996	115	365	57	93	22	70	63	202	35	53	11	36
1997	108	330	50	83	20	63	11	29	1	3	0	2

If the games played totals seem low for the projection, remember that Strawberry was never an iron man, even in his youth. He never played as many as 160 games in a season and topped 150 games only three times.

Through the 1998 season, Strawberry's actual career totals were 888 runs scored, 1,385 hits, 332 home runs, and 994 RBI. Plugging in the projected numbers from 1992–97, those totals become 1,172 runs scored, 1,845 hits, 448 home runs, and 1,344 RBI. These estimates could be seen as conservative, because if Strawberry had been able to maintain a level of just 140 games a season, the combination of the extra playing time and the surge in home runs and run production that really started in 1994 could have meant even better career numbers. Of course, we'll never really know how Darryl Strawberry's career *would* have turned out. Predicting human behavior in any endeavor, even baseball, is tricky business. Nevertheless, it seems clear that Strawberry's difficulties significantly changed what might have been.—Eddie

Teaching the Youngsters

As if Joe McCarthy were still around, the modern-day Yankees get it. They understand that as much for hitters as for pitchers, success revolves around command of the strike zone. (McCarthy actually had more patience with wild pitchers than he did with "wild" hitters.) In fact, the 1998 Yankees might have been the first team in history to attain a certain amount of fame for taking pitches.

The funny thing, though, is that people seem to miss the best thing about plate discipline. In *Sports Illustrated's 1999 Baseball Preview*, writer L. Jon Wertheim wrote an article titled "Picky, Picky, Picky!" It was, as you might guess, a feature on the Yankees' collective plate discipline in 1998. Yet Wertheim, in discussing the effects of New York's pickiness, focused on how starting pitchers get fatigued earlier in games, and how taking pitches forces the pitcher to show his entire repertoire of pitches.

That's all well and good, yet somehow Wertheim ignored the single most important advantage of taking pitches, which is that taking pitches results in walks, walks result in baserunners, *and baserunners result in runs.* The Yankees ranked just fourth (albeit a close fourth) in the American League in slugging percentage, yet they led the American League in runs scored. Why? Because their .364 on-base percentage was tops in the league, seven points better than that of Texas. And why did the Yankees lead the league in OBP? Because they led the league in baserunners. And why did the Yankees lead the league in baserunners? Because they finished second in hits and *first* in walks. Runs are primarily a function of baserunners. If you ignore the benefit of taking pitches as they relate to walks and runs, you're ignoring a fundamental precept of the game.

The 1998 Yankees were simply carrying on with a proud pinstriped tradition. The dynasty of sixty years earlier was similarly dominant in the Department of Bases on Balls. The Yankees drew 700-plus walks in 1936, 1937, 1938, *and* 1939, while not even one other major league team of the time managed to collect 700 in a season. The Yankees averaged 715 walks per season over that same four-season stretch; the rest of the American League averaged 584 walks per season.

Plate discipline was a huge factor in the success of the 1938 Yankees, and it was a huge factor in the success, sixty years later, of the 1998 Yankees. And the success of the big league Yankees in this area doesn't come from out of the sky. In their minor league system, hitters are taught to be as selective as possible and to look for their pitch to hit. The performance of the Yankees' four full-season minor league clubs in 1995 is fairly typical:

Team	Class	Walks	(Rank)	League Avg	OBP	(Rank)	League OBP
Columbus	AAA	456	3 (of 10)	447	.337	2 (of 10)	.329
Norwich	AA	559	2 (of 10)	512	.343	2 (of 10)	.333
Tampa	A+	557	1 (of 14)	455	.336	3 (of 14)	.326
Greensboro	A	525	3 (of 14)	483	.330	6 (of 14)	.322

As you can see, all of these teams were above their league average in walks and on-base percentage, and most were significantly better than average. Furthermore, from 1991 through 1998, twenty-five of the Yankees' thirty-four full-season minor league affiliates were above the league average in walks and thirteen finished first or second in the league; twenty-six finished above the league average in on-base percentage and ten were first or second.

Mark Newman, the Yankees' vice-president in charge of scouting and player development, spoke with us about the Yankees' minor league hitting program in July 1999. Newman, one of the brightest minds in the game, has been with the Yankees since 1989. "Teaching plate discipline has been a priority for a long time here, since the late 1980s," Newman said. "We teach our young hitters that you're never any better than the pitch you swing at. That belief is the foundation of our hitting program, and we consider it more important than physical hitting mechanics or strength and conditioning, although those aspects are important. From the minute a player enters our minor league system, he is taught this approach." Newman also said that the 1998 big league Yankees were almost the perfect living embodiment of the Yankees' overall baseball program.

With so much history and study to teach us, it is almost sickening to see so many big league hitters who have no idea of the strike zone, and don't seem to care. Too many hitting instructors simply tell their charges, "Be aggressive, don't leave the bat on your shoulder," without any meaningful dialogue about the mental approach needed to be a successful hitter. Overly passive hitters are seldom effective, but hitters who are too aggressive usually end up with short careers. Joe McCarthy knew it, Branch Rickey knew it, and the modern Yankees know it, too.—Eddie and Rob

Who Needs Superstars?

One of the "criticisms" of the 1998 Yankees is that they didn't have any superstars. For example, from the 1999 edition of *The Sports Encyclopedia: Baseball:* "New York was not a team of superstars. Instead, they won with a roster that was unusually solid and deep." Well, I don't know that I agree that they had no superstars. Derek Jeter, al-

Bernie Williams (*AP/Wide World Photos*)

though perhaps not yet having the longevity to have that word attached to his name, will be one of the dominant players in baseball for a long time, barring unforeseen circumstances such as serious injury.

Nevertheless, the 1998 Yankees did feature an unusually balanced lineup. Can we measure that? (You were afraid I would ask that question.) Well, in this book we rely heavily on standard deviation to measure the dispersion or scattering of a set of numbers. Can we do the same with the productivity of the players in a lineup? Not really, but (you knew there'd be a but) without getting too technical, if one is going to take the standard deviation of some number that's a proportion or a percentage, such as slugging percentage or batting average, then the sample sizes of the observations are supposed to be equal in size. However, that didn't stop me from looking at the starting lineups of our fifteen teams in an attempt to measure their balance. I figured if I just used the regulars, the differences among them in outs made or plate appearances wouldn't be so great as to totally ruin the analysis.

There won't be any long technical charts or formulas, but based on my less than technically correct methods, the 1998 Yankees did indeed employ an unusually balanced lineup. The standard deviation of the real offensive values (ROV) in their starting lineup was the lowest of the fifteen teams. The coefficient of variation of ROV (the standard deviation divided by the mean) was also the lowest. The same is also true for offensive winning percentage (OW%). The 1998 Yankees starting lineup had the lowest standard deviation of OW% and the lowest coefficient of variation. Ah c'mon, let me show you a little chart:

1998	Average ROV	Standard Deviation of ROV	Coefficient of Variation of ROV	Average OW%	Standard Deviation of OW%	Coefficient of Variation of OW%
Yankees	.303	.020	6.7%	.597	.065	10.9%

The average ROV for the 1998 Yankees' starting lineup was .303. The standard deviation of the ROVs was .020 (remember that making such a calculation is a technical no-no). The average OW% was .597, and the standard deviation was .065.

The two teams in the book with the highest standard deviation of ROV in their starting lineups were also Yankees teams, 1927 and 1961, at .058, or nearly three times as large as the 1998 Yankees. The team with the highest standard deviation of OW% was the 1974 Athletics, at .175, which again is much larger than that of the 1998 Yankees (.065). They also had the highest coefficient of variation at 29.5% (1998 Yankees, 10.9%). The 1961 Yankees had the highest coefficient of variation of ROV, at 19.8% (1998 Yankees, 6.7%). If I haven't lost you, you might have a better picture of just how balanced the 1998 Yankees were. If I have lost you, then you'll just have to take my word for it.—Eddie

TEAM STATISTICS

Hitting

	Games by Position	Age	G	AB	R	H	2B	3B	HR	RBI	BB	SO	SB	Avg	OBP	Slug
Tino Martinez	1B,142	30	142	531	92	149	33	1	28	123	61	83	2	.281	.355	.505
Chuck Knoblauch	2B,149	29	150	603	117	160	25	4	17	64	76	70	31	.265	.361	.405
Derek Jeter	SS,148	24	149	626	**127**	203	25	8	19	84	57	119	30	.324	.384	.481
Scott Brosius	3B,150; 1B,3; OF,1	31	152	530	86	159	34	0	19	98	52	97	11	.300	.371	.472
Paul O'Neill	OF,150	35	152	602	95	191	40	2	24	116	57	103	15	.317	.372	.510
Bernie Williams	OF,123; DH,5	29	129	499	101	169	30	5	26	97	74	81	15	**.339**	.422	.575
Chad Curtis	OF,148	29	151	456	79	111	21	1	10	56	75	80	21	.243	.355	.360
Jorge Posada	C,99; DH,6	26	111	358	56	96	23	0	17	63	47	92	0	.268	.350	.475
Darryl Strawberry	DH,81; OF,16	36	101	295	44	73	11	2	24	57	46	90	8	.247	.354	.542
Tim Raines	DH,56; OF,47	38	109	321	53	93	13	1	5	47	55	49	8	.290	.395	.383
Joe Girardi	C,78	33	78	254	31	70	11	4	3	31	14	38	2	.276	.317	.386
Luis Sojo	SS,20; 1B,19; 2B,8	32	54	147	16	34	3	1	0	14	4	15	1	.231	.250	.265
Chili Davis	DH,34	38	35	103	11	30	7	0	3	9	14	18	0	.291	.373	.447
Ricky Ledee	OF,42	24	42	79	13	19	5	2	1	12	7	29	3	.241	.299	.392
Homer Bush	2B,24; DH,13; 3B,3	25	45	71	17	27	3	0	1	5	5	19	6	.380	.421	.465
Shane Spencer	OF,22; DH,4; 1B,1	26	27	67	18	25	6	0	10	27	5	12	0	.373	.411	.910
Dale Sveum	1B,21; 3B,6; DH,3	34	30	58	6	9	0	0	0	3	4	16	0	.155	.203	.155
Mike Lowell	3B,7; DH,1	24	8	15	1	4	0	0	0	0	0	1	0	.267	.267	.267
Mike Figga	C,1	27	1	4	1	1	0	0	0	0	0	1	0	.250	.250	.250
Totals		30	162	5,643	**965**	1,625	290	31	207	**907**	**653**	1,025	153	.288	**.364**	.460

Pitching

	Threw	Age	Games	GS	CG	ShO	IP	H	HR	BB	SO	W	L	Pct	Sv	ERA
Andy Pettitte	Left	26	33	32	5	0	216	226	20	87	146	16	11	.593	0	4.24
David Wells	Left	35	30	30	8	5	214	195	29	29	163	18	4	**.818**	0	3.49
David Cone	Right	35	31	31	3	0	208	186	20	59	209	**20**	7	.741	0	3.55
Hideki Irabu	Right	29	29	28	2	1	173	148	27	76	126	13	9	.591	0	4.06
Orlando Hernandez	Right	28	21	21	3	1	141	113	11	52	131	12	4	.750	0	3.13
Ramiro Mendoza	Right	26	41	14	1	1	130	131	9	30	56	10	2	.833	1	3.25
Mike Stanton	Left	31	67	0	0	0	79	71	13	26	69	4	1	.800	6	5.47
Mariano Rivera	Right	28	54	0	0	0	61	48	3	17	36	3	0	1.000	36	1.91
Darren Holmes	Right	32	34	0	0	0	51	53	4	14	31	0	3	.000	2	3.33
Mike Buddie	Right	27	24	2	0	0	42	46	5	13	20	4	1	.800	0	5.62
Jeff Nelson	Right	31	45	0	0	0	40	44	1	22	35	5	3	.625	3	3.79
Graeme Lloyd	Left	31	50	0	0	0	38	26	3	6	20	3	0	1.000	0	1.67
Willie Banks*	Right	29	9	0	0	0	14	20	4	12	8	1	1	.500	0	10.05
Ryan Bradley	Right	22	5	1	0	0	13	12	2	9	13	2	1	.667	0	5.68
Joe Borowski	Right	27	8	0	0	0	10	11	0	4	7	1	0	1.000	0	6.52
Jim Bruske*	Right	33	3	1	0	0	9	9	2	1	3	1	0	1.000	0	3.00
Jay Tessmer	Right	26	7	0	0	0	9	4	1	4	6	1	0	1.000	0	3.12
Mike Jerzembeck	Right	26	3	2	0	0	6	9	2	4	1	0	1	.000	0	12.79
Todd Erdos	Right	24	2	0	0	0	2	5	0	1	0	0	0	—	0	9.00
Totals		30	496	162	**22**	11	1,457	**1,357**	156	466	1,080	**114**	**48**	**.704**	48	**3.82**

*Played for another team during season. Statistics are those compiled with 1998 New York Yankees only.

CHAPTER 20

And the Winner Is . . .

Rob: All right, it's time for the toughest chore of all, comparing these teams to each other and ranking them. Taking them in chronological order, we'll start with the 1906 Cubs. We all know that they lost the World Series, but they bounced back to win the Series in each of the next two seasons, and their one-, two-, *and* three-year winning percentages are the best all-time. So I'm not bothered by the World Series loss. What does bother me are those SD scores, which are fantastic but rank "only" tenth all-time over the three years, 1906–08. Another thing that bothers me is that the Cubs only had one legitimate Hall of Famer (Three Finger Brown).

Eddie: The SD scores don't bother me as much because they rank sixth for two years and

seventh over five years (1906–10), but I see your point. The only thing that really bothers me about this team is its era, the deadball era. I really believe that baseball before 1920 was very different from the post-1920 game. Other than that, I see no flaws except the same one all pre-1947 teams had. I think this Cubs team was clearly the best of the dead-ball era.

Rob: Yeah, and just so everybody knows, pre-1947 means pre–Jackie Robinson. It's something to consider, but if we really decided to hold that against anybody, then we wouldn't have bothered with almost half the teams in the book. You touched on something big here, which is that the Cubs were *awesome* for five years, winning four pennants and fin-

Rob's Rankings

15. *1953 New York Yankees*
How much are five straight World Series worth? In my book, fifteenth place in the rankings.

14. *1955 Brooklyn Dodgers*
One of my favorite teams, but their performance doesn't match their reputation.

13. *1912 New York Giants*
A great team, even if they went 0-3 in their World Series.

12. *1974 Oakland A's*
Had they won three straight World Series *and* averaged 95 wins per season, they'd rank three or four spots higher.

11. *1911 Philadelphia Athletics*
I'm not sure if they deserve to be even this high, but the A's did dominate the American League for about five years running.

ishing a strong second in the other year. Also, I think that with Wildfire Schulte, Harry Steinfeldt, and Frank Chance, the Cubs would have fared pretty well with a more lively ball.

Eddie: If ability and longevity are related for individual players, then it's only logical that they be related for teams as well. The fact that the same team, with relatively few changes, could dominate a league for five years speaks very well as to the true quality of the team.

The next team is the 1911 Athletics. Obviously, all of the reservations I have about the 1906 Cubs in terms of their era also apply to the 1911 A's. In addition, although they were clearly a great team, in this company their SD scores are a little short. Looking at periods from one to five seasons, only their three-year SD score ranks in the top ten. I guess I'm also holding the reasons for the breakup of this team against it, even though I know that's not fair.

Rob: Well, I don't hold the breakup against them because they were awesome over a five-year stretch, and I still think Connie Mack could have kept the club together if he'd wanted to. Would they have competed with the Red Sox for A.L. hegemony? Probably not, because his pitchers were old. Still, with Eddie Collins and Frank Baker they'd have been a quality team.

Next, we have the 1912 Giants. This club has received very little attention as a "dynasty" because it never won a World Series, losing three straight from 1911 through 1913. Do you think the Giants of this era relied too much on aggressive baserunning? As you know, the Giants stole 347 bases in 1911, 319 in 1912, and 296 in 1913, leading the National League all three seasons. But in the three World Series, they made a lot of outs on the bases, combining for 21 steals but 24 caught.

Eddie: It's one thing to be very aggressive against poor teams, but against good or great teams you're probably just going to run yourself out of a lot of productive innings. The 1912 Giants appeal to me because of John McGraw, and it would have felt strange not to have a McGraw-managed team in the book.

We both think that the 1911–13 Giants reached a higher peak

than the 1921–24 Giants, although the run of the earlier Giants was relatively short. To be honest, they may not be better than some of the teams we left out.

Rob: I can't argue with that, though it seems like we had a good reason when we did it. Can you remind me what that reason was and then introduce the next team?

Eddie: I think we focused a little too much on 1912, which was a damn good year (.682 win-loss percentage, +3.32 SD score) except for the World Series loss, and that was hardly a blowout.

The next team is still *the one* according to almost everyone who has written about the greatest baseball teams of all time, the 1927 New York Yankees. Even the phrase *1927 Yankees* still seems to possess some magical, mystical quality. I think that for performance in one season, the 1927 Yankees were the best team of all time. They had the fourth-highest SD score, behind two teams from expansion years and a dead-ball era team. They led their league wire to wire, won 110 games in a 154-game schedule, and swept the World Series. Contrary to their "Murderers Row" reputation, they were an extremely balanced team. In Ruth and Gehrig, they had the greatest one-two batting punch in history. They weren't perfect, as I'm sure Rob will point out, and I'm not saying that their run (1926–28) is the best of all time.

Rob: Well, let me play devil's advocate for a moment. I'm not the first to notice this, but the '27 Yankees did not exactly feature a balanced lineup. There were holes in their lineup, at least offensively, at three positions: catcher, shortstop, and third base. I mean, the '75 Reds these guys weren't. I can't help but wonder what would have happened if Ruth or Gehrig had broken an ankle or something.

Obviously, the '27 Yanks benefited hugely from having two of the all-time greatest players having two of the all-time greatest seasons. I'm not saying that they should be downgraded because of this, but it was something of a happy coincidence. The only weakness is the lack of consistency in the lineup, but Ruth and Gehrig can make up for a lot of weaknesses.

Eddie's Rankings

15. *1912 New York Giants*
Very good team, but no World Series titles, a relatively short period of excellence, and a dead-ball era team.

14. *1955 Brooklyn Dodgers*
In all of my efforts to objectively measure performance among these teams, this team came in last. The World Series title and the more modern context pushed them out of the cellar.

13. *1911 Philadelphia Athletics*
In this company, their short-term SD scores weren't good, and they were a dead-ball era team.

12. *1929 Philadelphia Athletics*
Their win-loss records were out of context with their basic performance.

11. *1942 St.Louis Cardinals*
I do discount their accomplishments because of the war. Their short-term SD scores (one- and two-year) were near the bottom of the group.

10. *1961 New York Yankees*
They're overrated because of the home runs, but they were still great.

9. *1942 St. Louis Cardinals*
Yes, the war might have "helped" the Cardinals, but I'm just so impressed with their consistency and, as I probably wrote earlier, they'd have been great no matter what.

8. *1986 New York Mets*
Great players, great manager, but didn't play as well in October as they might have.

7. *1929 Philadelphia Athletics*
SD scores or no SD scores, this team won a lot of games *and* two World Series.

6. *1927 New York Yankees*
I'm not sure I'd even say they were the best for one year, but you have to like a team that has great pitching *and* two of the greatest hitters of all time.

Eddie: Well, yes, the 1927 Yankees did have some weak spots in the lineup, but ultimately it's what the team does as a whole that counts. The core of a great team is great players and, in Ruth, the '27 Yankees had the greatest player of all time while Gehrig was probably the best first baseman. A relative lack of injuries usually plays a factor in a team having an excellent season.

I think the '27 Yanks don't get enough credit for how good their pitching and defense were. The runs allowed component of their SD score (+1.84) was almost identical to the runs scored component (+1.85). They allowed 109 fewer runs than the next best team and 163 fewer than the league average. As we pointed out, they had the league's first, second, and third finishers in ERA. It's the balance of the team that impresses me the most.

Rob: Well, you know that chicks dig the long ball, and so do sportswriters. But yeah, the Yankees did have great pitching in 1927 and, yeah, that's forgotten too often.

Next up, the 1929 Philadelphia Athletics. You have to love the lineup, with three top-notch Hall of Famers, or four on the days Lefty Grove pitched. You can argue that Jimmie Foxx is the second-greatest first baseman ever (after Gehrig), Mickey Cochrane is the second-greatest catcher ever (after Bench), and I *have* argued that Lefty Grove is the greatest left-handed pitcher, or maybe even the greatest *any*-handed pitcher.

The single most interesting thing about the 1929–31 A's, I think, is how far they outperformed Pythagorean expectations. As we've noted, based on their runs scored and allowed, we would expect them to have won 290 games. They actually won 313, and that's a huge difference. Do we give them credit for the 290, the 313, or do we somehow split the difference?

Eddie: History tells us that a team's run differential is probably a better measure of its quality than its record. In the A's case, however, one of the factors that might explain at least part of the difference is Lefty Grove. In addition to being the ace starter, he was the team's "closer." In 1929–31, Grove pitched in 34 games in relief, finishing 32 of those, with 18 saves and 9 relief wins. If Connie Mack had not used Grove in relief at all, the A's would probably have lost more of those close games than their Pythagorean "surplus" suggests they won.

Rob: It's also worth mentioning (again) that the Athletics played wonderfully in 1928, winning 98 games and finishing only 2½ behind the Yankees. So essentially, three games is all that separated the A's from winning four straight pennants, and I wonder how differently we would view them if they'd done that?

Eddie: That's a good point, and yet the '28 club may have "underachieved" in terms of their win-loss record relative to their other numbers, so maybe all of these things do even out over time.

Well, the next team is one that kept looking more impressive the more research we did, the 1939 New York Yankees. Of course, they were the last of McCarthy's "four-straighters" and they simply were an amazing team. Besides playing in the monochrome era, do you think they have any weaknesses?

Rob: Well, as we noted in their chapter, the '39 team featured one of the worst first basemen in the league, in Babe Dahlgren. And Gehrig, already sick in '38, wasn't so great that season, either. Aside from that, it's hard to find anything wrong with this club. They probably weren't deep in the infield, but because everybody played every day (and played well), it didn't become an issue. The pitching staff featured two Hall of Fame starters, and Johnny Murphy was the league's top relief pitcher.

I worried some that the Yankees didn't have any competition, but looking at the American League in the late 1930s, you find some pretty decent teams. The Tigers had two future Hall of Famers in their lineup (Hank Greenberg and Charlie Gehringer), and solid pitching with Tommy Bridges and Schoolboy Rowe. The Red Sox and the Indians were competitive. Yes, the Browns and the Athletics were both terrible, but the rest of the league was decent enough.

I'd like to mention again my favorite single fact about the Yankees of this period. From 1936 through 1939, they led the American League in *most* runs scored and *fewest* runs allowed *all four seasons.* This is simply an awesome accomplishment, unmatched by any other team in the history of the game.

10. *1986 New York Mets*
Great long-term (three-, four-, and five-year) SD scores, but no consecutive first-place finishes.

9. *1953 New York Yankees*
Their SD scores are lower than the 1961 Yankees, but five World Series in a row is five World Series in a row.

8. *1961 New York Yankees*
I may have them a little too high. Their SD scores rank near the bottom of the group, but five straight pennants (1960–64) is impressive.

7. *1974 Oakland A's*
Better SD scores than their win-loss records would suggest; five straight division titles and three straight World Series titles.

6. *1975 Cincinnati Reds*
This high ranking is partly attributable to all of the former players who told me they were the best team they ever saw.

5. *1906 Chicago Cubs*

Yes, baseball in 1906 was different. But these guys were the best at it.

4. *1975 Cincinnati Reds*

Wonderful blend of speed and power, perhaps the greatest lineup ever. If only they'd had an ace pitcher.

3. *1998 New York Yankees*

In five years, they might jump ahead of the Orioles, but I'm not quite ready yet.

2. *1970 Baltimore Orioles*

I love their consistency, as they won 109, 108, and 101 games from '69 through '71. Best three-year SD score ever.

1. *1939 New York Yankees*

One year, two years, three years, four years . . . no matter where you draw the line, they're wall-to-wall brilliant.

Eddie: When one considers that a team leading its league in runs scored and runs allowed in the same season has only happened twenty or twenty-five times total, then what the 1936–39 Yankees did really is awesome.

As to not having any competition, except for war years there are always plenty of other good players in a major league. I think it just looks like they didn't have any competition because they were so much better than everyone else.

Rob: Agreed, and again it's worth pointing out that the Yankees finished two games out of first place in 1940, then won three straight pennants from 1941 through 1943, all by large margins. In other words, with two or three more breaks in 1940, this team could have won *eight straight* American League pennants. And if they'd done that, there would be no question about the greatest dynasty in baseball history.

Whether you did it on purpose or not, your aside about the "war years" leads us to our next team, the 1942 St. Louis Cardinals. They were late entries in the greatest team derby, in part because my Redbird-loving family would have given me big-time grief if there weren't a single St. Louis team in the book. But the more I look at the '42 Cardinals, the more I like them: Hall of Famers in left and right field, outstanding defense up the middle, a great manager, and they responded with a brilliant stretch run in the face of fierce competition.

Eddie: Yeah, and if Jeff Heath hadn't had such an out-of-context rotten year in 1940, then the Cleveland Crybabies—I'm sorry, the Cleveland Indians—would have won the pennant. On a more serious note, your point about the Yankees is right on the money and really speaks to the quality of the team.

I think the 1942 Cardinals may be the first team about which we have a fairly large difference of opinion. They had a very good team, but they were lucky in terms of who got called to military service. They only lost Musial for one season; Mort Cooper and Whitey Kurowski were 4-F (physically unable to serve), so they didn't serve; and Walker Cooper and Marty Marion also had ailments that kept them from serving. So, although the 1942–44 Cardinals have great records and SD scores, they were favored by chance. In the National League, only Cincinnati lost fewer player-seasons to WWII than St. Louis did.

Rob: I can't argue with your facts, but remember that the Cardinals finished only three games out of first place in 1945, and then in 1946—with almost all the real major leaguers discharged from the service—the Cardinals won yet another pennant, and then dispatched the Red Sox in the World Series. I sincerely believe that, war or no war, the Cardinals would have been the best team in the National League in the mid-1940s. And for what it's worth (not much) if Branch Rickey hadn't left the club, they would have dominated the entire decade.

Eddie: We'll have to agree to disagree about the Cardinals.

Another team that might lead to some debate is the 1953 Yankees. Some of you might be saying, "What debate? They won five straight world championships." True, but in a historical context, the regular-season performance of those teams was not off the charts. The reason they're *in* the book is out of respect for all the World Series titles.

Rob: You want to expand on that a little? I know that they didn't generally win all that many games or finish with big leads at the end of the season. Can you refresh our memories regarding the SD scores?

Eddie: Sure thing. The standard of excellence for SD scores is +3.00 or higher for a single season, a mark reached by thirty-seven teams from 1901 to 1998. The highest SD score for any of Stengel's "five-timers" was +2.72, in 1953. The 1949 club didn't even reach +2.00 (+1.91).

Now, I can hear some of you out there saying, "More nerds who don't know baseball, focusing on everything except what's important." Well, if this team had won three pennants and two World Series in those five years and everything else had been exactly the same, we wouldn't have put them in the book. We are trying to pick and rank the greatest teams of all time. In doing that, one needs methods to evaluate teams across eras, and the SD score seems to have little or no time bias. That's why we rely on it so

5. *1906 Chicago Cubs*
   If era were not a consideration, I would have ranked them higher.

4. *1998 New York Yankees*
   Maybe I'm suffering from lack of perspective, but they had the best one-year and two-year SD scores in history and won three World Series titles in four years, when it took many more wins to do it than was the case for most of baseball history.

3. *1970 Baltimore Orioles*
   The best three-year SD score in history and, in the context of their day, one of the best three-year win-loss records.

2. *1927 New York Yankees*
   I still think it's the best single season by any team in history.

1. *1939 New York Yankees*
   Simply too dominant across the board to rank anywhere else.

much. I hope it makes sense to those of you reading. By the way, the aggregate win-loss percentage for those teams with an SD score of +3.00 or higher is .654, the equivalent of a 106-56 record.

Rob: Well, it all makes sense to me. I do have two questions for you. One, how good might the Yankees have been if DiMaggio and Mantle had ever played a full season together? And two, what was the Yankees' SD score in 1954, when they won 103 games—the most of any of Stengel's teams—but finished eight games behind Cleveland?

Eddie: Wow, 1939 DiMaggio and 1956 Mantle in the same outfield. Do you think the Mick would have been happy not playing center field?

The 1954 Yankees' SD score was +2.28; again, not close to the magic 3.00. In Chapter 16, we talk about how skewed the American League was in 1954. The Indians' SD score that year was +2.22 (lower than the Yanks'), 111 wins or not.

Rob: All right, let's move on to the Yankees' traditional antagonists, the Brooklyn Dodgers, yet another team with SD scores that don't quite match their reputation. A lot of people, I think, believe that the "Boys of Summer" Dodgers were actually better than the Yankees in the early to mid-1950s, at least until October. What would you say to that?

Eddie: I would say no. The Brooklyn Dodgers from 1949 through 1956 were obviously a terrific team, given that they were able to contend almost every year for eight years. Actually, going back to 1946, they contended almost every year for eleven years. However, they weren't as consistent as the Bronx Bombers. (Hey, if the Yankees move to Manhattan, will they still be the Bombers?)

The Dodgers' SD scores from this era are good, except for their down year of 1954, but they're not great. It's true that they did crack the magic +3.00 barrier twice (1949 and 1956), but they also have scores just under and just over +2.00. For much of the 1950s, the Cubs and Pirates were punching bags, so the fact that the Dodgers were able to spend most of this period with better than a .600 winning percentage is a little less impressive.

Rob: Let's go over the weaknesses. One thing that hurts them is the lack of more than two quality starters, Newcombe and Erskine. And how good would the Dodgers have been in '52 and '53 if Newcombe hadn't been in the army? (That's not an excuse, because the Yankees did just fine when Whitey Ford was in the service.) And the Dodgers never had a truly productive left fielder in this period. Everybody remembers Andy Pafko, but he was only in Brooklyn for a season and a half, and his best years had been earlier, with the Cubs. (Oh, and if the Yanks move to Manhattan, they'll be the "Maulers.")

Eddie: It's also true that Campanella had only one "Campanella season" after 1953 because of the hand injury. And it's still more true that it's the sum of the parts that counts. The 1961 Yankees had a lot of home run parts, but it's my contention that their place among the super teams in history is overblown. Their run differential and SD score are nothing special in this company. They had good pitching and a lot of power, but with all their power they didn't lead the league in runs scored or runs scored in road games. Their pitchers got *a lot* of help from Yankee Stadium.

Rob: If the '61 Yankees are one of the more overrated teams, then the 1970 Baltimore Orioles are probably one of the most underrated teams of all time. Like the Yankees, they benefited from expansion-thinned competition, but the Orioles posted gaudy records in three seasons, not one.

Eddie: Well, I'm probably not that objective about this team because it's the team I was raised on, but I agree that because of their two World Series losses, this team is underrated by history. Nevertheless, they have the *best* three-year SD score in history and the most wins over three seasons by any A.L. team in history. Frank Robinson, fourth on the all-time home run list and the only player to be named MVP in both leagues, played for them. Brooks Robinson, who won sixteen Gold Gloves, and Jim Palmer, who had eight 20-win seasons out of nine, played for them. Anyway, I'd better stop, but I think they were a truly great team whose only knock is that their run really lasted for just three seasons.

Rob: This is probably a good time to discuss expansion. Namely, should expansion color our evaluation of SD scores? Clearly, the Orioles' amazing record from 1969 through 1971 (318-164) was related to the fact that two new teams joined the American League in '69. But the way I understand it, expansion shouldn't affect SD scores. Am I right?

Eddie: Well, I haven't really studied the expansion issue in depth, but if expansion increases the dispersion of team ability in a given season or seasons, then the standard deviation of winning percentage, runs scored, and runs allowed should increase with it, meaning that SD score should not be that affected. However, and for whatever it's worth, two of the top three single-season SD scores of all time were compiled in expansion seasons.

Rob: That's what I thought. Doesn't it seem unlikely that the two highest SD scores would come out of expansion seasons by coincidence? I just wonder if we're missing something, and I'm not smart enough to figure out what it is.

As for the Orioles, you have to like their personnel. Jim Palmer, Frank and Brooks Robinson, American League MVP Boog Powell . . . whatta team!

Eddie: The effect of expansion on SD scores would have to be studied more, because two out of three is hardly a big sample. For example, only four of the thirty-seven SD scores of +3.00 or higher were in expansion seasons.

Rob: Well, let's see, four out of thirty-seven is about 11 percent. There have been six expansion seasons out of the approximately ninety-five seasons we considered for this book, and six out of ninety-five is about 6 percent. So it still seems to me that something weird might be happening in those expansion seasons. I'm not saying something weird *is* happening, just that it might. If I'm deciding between two apparently equal teams and one of them comes from an expansion year, I'll probably take the other.

Eddie: Not so fast, my friend. Only eight of the top 100 SD scores are from expansion seasons. I'm inclined to think that it's only a minor factor at most. Gotta have significant samples to draw conclusions.

Rob: Hey, that makes me feel better.

On to the 1974 Oakland A's, who like the '42 Cardinals were a late entry in the book. I wasn't fond of this team, but the more you read about them, the more you respect them. That they were able to do what they did, given the instability in the front office (such as it was), was a real feat.

Eddie: The 1974 A's are the anti-chemistry team. They didn't like each other and they hated their owner, but they finished first five years in a row and won three straight World Series. Given their "ordinary" win-loss records, their SD scores are surprisingly good. They're a big reason I get suspicious about someone when they talk about chemistry and the *huge* role it plays in a successful team.

Rob: Well, they fought a lot, but I wouldn't say they didn't like each other. They *did* hate their owner, and perhaps that common bond drew the A's together and actually improved their "chemistry." This was clearly a wonderful team, and their SD scores were excellent even going back to 1971, when they went 101-60 for their best record of the century. Of course, nobody talks about Oakland's records or their SD scores. They talk about the World Series, but I just can't see rating the A's above the O's simply because they won a few more games in October. Sure, maybe the A's coasted with their big leads late in the season, but why didn't any of the other great teams do the same?

Eddie: People over-dramatize the postseason. Was the pebble that caused the ball to bounce up and hit Tony Kubek on the throat in the seventh game of the 1960 World Series a sign of greatness or intestinal fortitude on the part of the Pirates? Was Willie McCovey's line drive that went straight to Bobby Richardson to end the 1962 World Series a sign of Giant weakness, or were the Yankees just lucky?

I do think that there was a lot of tension among players on those A's teams. They wouldn't have had so many clubhouse fights, otherwise. One team that didn't have clubhouse problems was the

1975 Reds. This team had a very high peak performance, although they weren't great for as long as most people think. I can't tell you how many ex-players told me that the 1975–76 Reds were the best team they ever saw.

Rob: In 1998, the Reds were the team most often mentioned when people compared the Yankees to the all-time greatest teams, but I suspect this is partly because so many figures from that team are still in the public consciousness, from Joe Morgan and Pete Rose to Johnny Bench and Sparky Anderson. Top to bottom, the '75 Reds lineup just might be the best ever. Not in terms of single-season production, perhaps, but in overall quality. Nearly all eight of the regulars enjoyed long, productive careers.

Eddie: One of the things we wanted to do for the book, but didn't, was to measure how many major league games were played, in total, by the various lineups and rosters in the book. I'd be surprised if the 1975 Reds didn't come out on top, at least for their position players. By the way, of all of the teams in the book, the 1975 Reds' starting lineup had the highest aggregate offensive winning percentage.

Rob: Well, do you want to talk about their pitching, or should I?

Eddie: Their pitching wasn't as bad as most people remember—they were third in the league in ERA while playing half their games in a hitter's park—but they certainly didn't have any dominant starters. Gullett was very good when he could pitch, but he only made 22 starts. Their bullpen got a lot of work: McEnaney, Eastwick, Borbon, and Clay Carroll appeared in 251 games and pitched 402 innings, and the Reds easily led the league in saves.

Rob: The outstanding attribute of the '75 Reds was, I think, their amazing combination of power, walks, and speed. It strikes me that, in this respect, they resembled the early-1950s Dodgers as much as anybody. This is, perhaps, not surprising when you learn that Reds general manager Bob Howsam revered Branch Rickey.

Eddie: Of course, Howsam is far from the only baseball person who revered Rickey. The Reds probably had the most multi-faceted offense in baseball history.

Rob: Yeah, and I think that counts for something because it suggests that they'd have been successful no matter when they played.

Our next team is the 1986 New York Mets, which might surprise some people given that the Mets only reached one World Series in the three-year span. Every other team in the book played in at least two World Series, and most played in three.

Eddie: The 1986 Mets are clearly a team that we considered because of their SD scores, which were excellent, particularly in the long term. For example, the 1985–88 Mets' four-year SD score is the third-best of the twentieth century. It is true that their post-season resumé is a little short given the company they're keeping in this book.

Rob: That's an amazing thing, don't you think, that the team with the third-best four-year SD score would have only reached the post-season twice in those four years? Maybe it's worth noting that in 1985 the Mets won 98 games but finished three behind St. Louis in the N.L. East and in 1987 they won 92 games and again finished three behind the Cardinals. Both years, if they'd have been in the other division, their record would have been good enough for a title.

Eddie: Yes, but in a sport with such a long history, things will happen that seem a bit incongruous and yet are simply random. If I remember correctly, too, Darryl Strawberry hurt his thumb and missed about 50 games in 1985, during which time the Mets didn't have a great record. The Mets were 70-38 in the games Strawberry started and 28-26 when he didn't start. The Mets finished three games behind the Cardinals. You can't count on luck, but you have to have at least a little bit to be successful.

Rob: Yeah, but sometimes you also need a good bench (and I mean the guys who don't normally play every day, not the Cincinnati catcher). As a Royals fan, I'm sure glad the Mets didn't win their division in 1985 because I think they probably would have made K.C. look bad in a World Series matchup.

Eddie: Point well taken, but some regulars can't be replaced no matter how good the bench is. Your point about a potential Mets-Royals World Series in 1985 makes another good point. The fact that Strawberry missed 50 games in 1985 doesn't affect the Mets' long-term SD scores very much, if at all, and yet it may have cost them a World Series title and changed the way baseball history views that team. Without trying to get too esoteric, so much of what happens in baseball is just random deviation from an unobservable mean; it's just that human beings almost always have to try to attach a cause to what they view as an effect, when many times there is no real cause.

Speaking of World Series heartbreaks, our most recent team prevented me, at least for now (as a member of the Padres' organization), from getting the big World Series ring. Of course, it's the 1998 New York Yankees. They have the distinction of having the best one-year *and* two-year SD scores in history, along with the A.L. record for the most wins in a season. Are we going to have a hard time with them because we may lack historical perspective?

Rob: Yeah, the lack of historical perspective does make it hard. Although many fans will rush to judgment and say, "Of *course* Cal Ripken is the greatest shortstop ever" or "Of *course* the 1998 Yankees are the greatest team ever," I like to wait awhile and let things percolate. However, we don't have that luxury with this team. It's impressive, that two-year SD score, especially when you remember that the third year, 1999, saw the Yankees win yet another World Series. One thing about that, though: do you think we should take into account the relative instability of this team over the long term? I mean, only two pitchers were in the rotation all three seasons, and only four of the nine regular position players were the same. I know that this is simply a sign of the times, but the relative instability of modern rosters makes it tougher to get a read on a team's true quality.

Eddie: An astute observation about the roster flux, but I don't know that there's anything we can do about it. However, the two best

Subscribe & Save

Politics / News Analysis / Entertainment / Health & Medicine

Save **91%** off the cover price

☐ 1 year (52 issues) for $29.95   ☐ 2 years (104 issues) for $44.95

↙ BEST DEAL!

Name _____
(please print)

Address _____ Apt. _____

City _____ State _____ Zip _____

E-mail address _____

☐ Payment enclosed.   ☐ Bill me later.   TDE6241

FREE GIFT when you order online! (with paid order)

Order at: time.com/freegift or call 1-866-345-2114

16ITDIAC

players on the 1998 team, Jeter and Williams, were there all three years. In fact, by my count sixteen players played on all three teams. Pettitte and Cone were in the rotations. Joe Girardi didn't "start" in 1999, but he did play a lot, and four of the other position-playing regulars (Martinez, Jeter, Williams, O'Neill) were the same on all three teams. Mariano Rivera closed for all three.

Rob: Yes, and, in a sense, the club's success over the three seasons is a testament to their front office, especially general managers Bob Watson and Brian Cashman. It's one thing to have the money and another thing to spend it wisely.

Eddie: If excellence in a single season were our primary criterion for ranking the best baseball teams of all time, then I would almost certainly pick the 1927 Yankees as the best. They dominated their league from start to finish, excelling in all areas of performance. The '27 Yankees are one of just a very few teams to have a .700-plus winning percentage. Their +3.69 SD score is outstanding, the fourth best of the twentieth century. Although they are perceived as a team whose hitting was their dominant characteristic, in fact they were very balanced. The runs scored and runs allowed components of their SD score were virtually identical: runs scored, +1.85; runs allowed, +1.84. They are the only team in history to have both scores equal or exceed +1.75. Of course, they won the World Series in a four-game sweep, although two of the games were close.

For many reasons, however, Rob and I decided that a single season's performance would not be the most important reason for picking these teams. That decision is the reason we didn't consider the 1984 Tigers, for example, who were truly outstanding in that year, but that year was out of context with their seasons before and/or after. Even though the 1926 and 1928 Yankees were fine teams that won the pennant, even though I have tremendous respect and affection for the Orioles teams of 1969–71, and while acknowledging other teams such as the 1949–53 Yankees and the 1971–75 A's, the best performance by a team in a group of contiguous seasons (sounds like a category for the Academy Awards) was the 1936–39 Yankees. They led the league in runs scored and fewest runs allowed for four straight seasons, a feat unmatched by any other team. Their four-year record is outstanding; their four-year SD score is the best of all time, by far. They easily won four consecutive World Series. Despite the loss of Lou Gehrig, the 1939 Yankees were the best of the 1936–39 Yankees teams. So, by virtue of being the "best of the best" in addition to other qualifications, such as having the best run differential of the twentieth century, an SD score that ranks in the top ten of all time, and a .700-plus winning percentage, I am picking the 1939 Yankees as the best team of all time.

Rob: As am I. See the sidebars for our complete rankings, and I should point out that we didn't look at each other's lists until both were completed.

Standard Deviation Scores

The Top 50 One-Year SD Scores of the Twentieth Century

1.	1998 New York Yankees	+3.88	15.	1912 New York Giants	+3.32
2.	1906 Chicago Cubs	+3.73	16.	1970 Baltimore Orioles	+3.31
3.	1962 San Francisco Giants	+3.70	17.	1937 New York Yankees	+3.22
4.	1927 New York Yankees	+3.69	18.	1923 New York Yankees	+3.22
5.	1917 New York Giants	+3.68	19.	1971 Baltimore Orioles	+3.21
6.	1984 Detroit Tigers	+3.65	20.	1968 Detroit Tigers	+3.19
7.	1986 New York Mets	+3.62	21.	1935 Detroit Tigers	+3.17
8.	1902 Pittsburgh Pirates	+3.62	22.	1911 Philadelphia Athletics	+3.15
9.	1939 New York Yankees	+3.52	23.	1974 Oakland Athletics	+3.15
10.	1995 Cleveland Indians	+3.51	24.	1936 New York Yankees	+3.12
11.	1975 Cincinnati Reds	+3.42	25.	1974 Los Angeles Dodgers	+3.10
12.	1988 New York Mets	+3.39	26.	1905 Chicago White Sox	+3.10
13.	1990 Oakland Athletics	+3.35	27.	1998 Houston Astros	+3.08
14.	1969 Baltimore Orioles	+3.34	28.	1949 Brooklyn Dodgers	+3.07

29. 1947 New York Yankees	+3.05	40. 1961 New York Yankees	+2.97
30. 1944 St. Louis Cardinals	+3.05	41. 1938 New York Yankees	+2.97
31. 1985 St. Louis Cardinals	+3.05	42. 1942 St. Louis Cardinals	+2.94
32. 1914 Philadelphia Athletics	+3.05	43. 1915 Philadelphia Phillies	+2.91
33. 1955 Brooklyn Dodgers	+3.03	44. 1904 New York Giants	+2.91
34. 1942 New York Yankees	+3.02	45. 1988 Oakland Athletics	+2.90
35. 1934 Detroit Tigers	+3.02	46. 1985 New York Yankees	+2.90
36. 1978 Los Angeles Dodgers	+3.01	47. 1928 Philadelphia Athletics	+2.89
37. 1917 Chicago White Sox	+3.00	48. 1918 Chicago Cubs	+2.89
38. 1912 Boston Red Sox	+2.98	49. 1903 Boston Pilgrims	+2.88
39. 1929 Philadelphia Athletics	+2.97	50. 1998 Atlanta Braves	+2.88

The Top 50 Two-Year SD Scores of the Twentieth Century

1. 1997–98 New York Yankees	+6.70	26. 1974–75 Oakland Athletics	+5.51
2. 1969–70 Baltimore Orioles	+6.64	27. 1942–43 New York Yankees	+5.49
3. 1998–99 New York Yankees	+6.59	28. 1977–78 Los Angeles Dodgers	+5.48
4. 1970–71 Baltimore Orioles	+6.52	29. 1989–90 Oakland Athletics	+5.47
5. 1938–39 New York Yankees	+6.48	30. 1983–84 Detroit Tigers	+5.39
6. 1936–37 New York Yankees	+6.35	31. 1960–61 New York Yankees	+5.39
7. 1906–07 Chicago Cubs	+6.29	32. 1976–77 Philadelphia Phillies	+5.37
8. 1927–28 New York Yankees	+6.20	33. 1997–98 Atlanta Braves	+5.37
9. 1934–35 Detroit Tigers	+6.19	34. 1911–12 New York Giants	+5.37
10. 1937–38 New York Yankees	+6.19	35. 1913–14 Philadelphia Athletics	+5.36
11. 1975–76 Cincinnati Reds	+6.05	36. 1974–75 Cincinnati Reds	+5.36
12. 1961–62 San Francisco Giants	+5.91	37. 1973–74 Oakland Athletics	+5.35
13. 1986–87 New York Mets	+5.89	38. 1961–62 New York Yankees	+5.34
14. 1928–29 Philadelphia Athletics	+5.86	39. 1904–05 New York Giants	+5.33
15. 1943–44 St. Louis Cardinals	+5.84	40. 1988–89 New York Mets	+5.32
16. 1912–13 New York Giants	+5.81	41. 1909–10 Chicago Cubs	+5.27
17. 1910–11 Philadelphia Athletics	+5.77	42. 1926–27 New York Yankees	+5.26
18. 1902–03 Pittsburgh Pirates	+5.76	43. 1957–58 New York Yankees	+5.25
19. 1995–96 Cleveland Indians	+5.75	44. 1952–53 New York Yankees	+5.22
20. 1985–86 New York Mets	+5.75	45. 1947–48 New York Yankees	+5.22
21. 1942–43 St. Louis Cardinals	+5.73	46. 1923–24 New York Yankees	+5.19
22. 1941–42 New York Yankees	+5.70	47. 1971–72 Pittsburgh Pirates	+5.18
23. 1987–88 New York Mets	+5.66	48. 1941–42 Brooklyn Dodgers	+5.16
24. 1905–06 Chicago Cubs	+5.65	49. 1909–10 Philadelphia Athletics	+5.14
25. 1916–17 New York Giants	+5.56	50. 1952–53 Brooklyn Dodgers	+5.13

The Top 50 Three-Year SD Scores of the Twentieth Century

1.	1969–71 Baltimore Orioles	+9.86	26.	1960–62 New York Yankees	+7.76
2.	1937–39 New York Yankees	+9.70	27.	1976–78 Philadelphia Phillies	+7.75
3.	1997–99 New York Yankees	+9.41	28.	1973–75 Oakland Athletics	+7.72
4.	1936–38 New York Yankees	+9.31	29.	1943–45 St. Louis Cardinals	+7.71
5.	1986–88 New York Mets	+9.28	30.	1951–53 New York Yankees	+7.68
6.	1942–44 St. Louis Cardinals	+8.78	31.	1996–98 New York Yankees	+7.67
7.	1988–90 Oakland Athletics	+8.37	32.	1944–46 St. Louis Cardinals	+7.66
8.	1935–37 New York Yankees	+8.35	33.	1971–73 Baltimore Orioles	+7.60
9.	1909–11 Philadelphia Athletics	+8.28	34.	1987–89 New York Mets	+7.59
10.	1905–07 Chicago Cubs	+8.21	35.	1956–58 New York Yankees	+7.58
11.	1906–08 Chicago Cubs	+8.20	36.	1974–75 Cincinnati Reds	+7.55
12.	1941–43 New York Yankees	+8.17	37.	1973–74 Oakland Athletics	+7.50
13.	1901–03 Pittsburgh Pirates	+8.16	38.	1961–62 New York Yankees	+7.49
14.	1968–70 Baltimore Orioles	+8.12	39.	1912–14 New York Giants	+7.48
15.	1970–72 Baltimore Orioles	+8.11	40.	1903–05 New York Giants	+7.43
16.	1938–40 New York Yankees	+8.07	41.	1976–78 New York Yankees	+7.39
17.	1988–90 New York Mets	+8.05	42.	1921–23 New York Yankees	+7.31
18.	1985–87 New York Mets	+8.02	43.	1951–53 Brooklyn Dodgers	+7.31
19.	1974–76 Cincinnati Reds	+7.99	44.	1910–12 New York Giants	+7.30
20.	1972–74 Oakland Athletics	+7.98	45.	1940–42 New York Yankees	+7.29
21.	1928–30 Philadelphia Athletics	+7.86	46.	1910–12 Philadelphia Athletics	+7.28
22.	1911–13 New York Giants	+7.85	47.	1997–99 Atlanta Braves	+7.28
23.	1939–41 New York Yankees	+7.78	48.	1934–36 New York Yankees	+7.28
24.	1926–28 New York Yankees	+7.77	49.	1917–19 New York Giants	+7.27
25.	1961–63 New York Yankees	+7.77	50.	1922–24 New York Giants	+7.26

The Top 50 Four-Year SD Scores of the Twentieth Century

1.	1936–39 New York Yankees	+12.83	9.	1939–42 New York Yankees	+10.81
2.	1969–72 Baltimore Orioles	+11.45	10.	1938–41 New York Yankees	+10.75
3.	1985–88 New York Mets	+11.41	11.	1942–45 St. Louis Cardinals	+10.65
4.	1968–71 Baltimore Orioles	+11.33	12.	1906–09 Chicago Cubs	+10.61
5.	1935–38 New York Yankees	+11.31	13.	1941–44 St. Louis Cardinals	+10.60
6.	1937–40 New York Yankees	+11.29	14.	1934–37 New York Yankees	+10.50
7.	1986–89 New York Mets	+11.21	15.	1943–46 St. Louis Cardinals	+10.44
8.	1970–73 Baltimore Orioles	+10.90	16.	1996–99 New York Yankees	+10.38

17. 1972–75 Oakland Athletics	+10.34	34. 1944–47 St. Louis Cardinals	+9.66
18. 1987–90 New York Mets	+10.32	35. 1910–13 Philadelphia Athletics	+9.60
19. 1960–63 New York Yankees	+10.19	36. 1955–58 New York Yankees	+9.55
20. 1905–08 Chicago Cubs	+10.12	37. 1911–14 New York Giants	+9.53
21. 1928–31 Philadelphia Athletics	+10.12	38. 1920–23 New York Giants	+9.50
22. 1911–14 Philadelphia Athletics	+10.03	39. 1949–52 Brooklyn Dodgers	+9.49
23. 1951–54 New York Yankees	+9.96	40. 1952–55 New York Yankees	+9.47
24. 1971–74 Oakland Athletics	+9.91	41. 1921–24 New York Yankees	+9.46
25. 1920–23 New York Yankees	+9.86	42. 1917–20 New York Giants	+9.46
26. 1973–76 Cincinnati Reds	+9.83	43. 1973–76 Oakland Athletics	+9.30
27. 1909–12 Philadelphia Athletics	+9.80	44. 1953–56 New York Yankees	+9.29
28. 1910–13 New York Giants	+9.78	45. 1919–22 New York Giants	+9.27
29. 1940–43 New York Yankees	+9.76	46. 1972–75 Cincinnati Reds	+9.27
30. 1907–10 Chicago Cubs	+9.74	47. 1950–53 Brooklyn Dodgers	+9.23
31. 1921–24 New York Giants	+9.73	48. 1974–77 Cincinnati Reds	+9.18
32. 1961–64 New York Yankees	+9.72	49. 1941–44 New York Yankees	+9.17
33. 1950–53 New York Yankees	+9.69	50. 1929–32 Philadelphia Athletics	+9.16

The Top 50 Five-Year SD Scores of the Twentieth Century

1. 1935–39 New York Yankees	+14.83	18. 1971–75 Oakland Athletics	+12.28
2. 1936–40 New York Yankees	+14.42	19. 1967–71 Baltimore Orioles	+12.27
3. 1969–73 Baltimore Orioles	+14.24	20. 1960–64 New York Yankees	+12.14
4. 1937–41 New York Yankees	+13.97	21. 1909–13 Philadelphia Athletics	+12.12
5. 1986–90 New York Mets	+13.94	22. 1928–32 Philadelphia Athletics	+12.05
6. 1938–42 New York Yankees	+13.77	23. 1933–37 New York Yankees	+12.05
7. 1906–10 Chicago Cubs	+13.47	24. 1950–54 New York Yankees	+11.97
8. 1934–38 New York Yankees	+13.47	25. 1917–21 New York Giants	+11.93
9. 1942–46 St. Louis Cardinals	+13.39	26. 1972–76 Oakland Athletics	+11.93
10. 1985–89 New York Mets	+13.34	27. 1951–55 New York Yankees	+11.93
11. 1939–43 New York Yankees	+13.28	28. 1920–24 New York Giants	+11.92
12. 1968–72 Baltimore Orioles	+12.93	29. 1972–76 Cincinnati Reds	+11.90
13. 1910–14 Philadelphia Athletics	+12.65	30. 1953–57 New York Yankees	+11.85
14. 1905–09 Chicago Cubs	+12.53	31. 1954–58 New York Yankees	+11.83
15. 1941–45 St. Louis Cardinals	+12.47	32. 1920–24 New York Yankees	+11.83
16. 1943–47 St. Louis Cardinals	+12.44	33. 1952–56 New York Yankees	+11.80
17. 1949–53 Brooklyn Dodgers	+12.29	34. 1919–23 New York Giants	+11.74

35. 1970–74 Baltimore Orioles	+11.67	43. 1995–99 New York Yankees	+11.27
36. 1949–53 New York Yankees	+11.59	44. 1932–36 New York Yankees	+11.27
37. 1947–51 New York Yankees	+11.58	45. 1944–48 St. Louis Cardinals	+11.21
38. 1966–70 Baltimore Orioles	+11.48	46. 1927–31 Philadelphia Athletics	+11.21
39. 1910–14 New York Giants	+11.46	47. 1974–78 Los Angeles Dodgers	+11.19
40. 1957–61 New York Yankees	+11.36	48. 1958–62 New York Yankees	+11.18
41. 1907–11 Chicago Cubs	+11.34	49. 1946–50 New York Yankees	+11.15
42. 1916–20 New York Giants	+11.34	50. 1940–44 St. Louis Cardinals	+11.13

The Bottom 50 One-Year SD Scores of the Twentieth Century

1. 1962 New York Mets	−5.91	26. 1945 Philadelphia Phillies	−3.43
2. 1916 Philadelphia Athletics	−4.39	27. 1963 Washington Senators	−3.43
3. 1919 Philadelphia Athletics	−4.35	28. 1973 San Diego Padres	−3.41
4. 1943 Philadelphia Athletics	−4.31	29. 1921 Philadelphia Phillies	−3.40
5. 1938 Philadelphia Phillies	−4.02	30. 1925 Boston Red Sox	−3.39
6. 1939 Philadelphia Phillies	−4.01	31. 1954 Pittsburgh Pirates	−3.39
7. 1963 New York Mets	−3.99	32. 1909 Washington Senators	−3.39
8. 1952 Pittsburgh Pirates	−3.99	33. 1969 San Diego Padres	−3.38
9. 1961 Philadelphia Phillies	−3.95	34. 1978 Seattle Mariners	−3.37
10. 1996 Detroit Tigers	−3.83	35. 1906 Boston Pilgrims	−3.35
11. 1904 Washington Senators	−3.82	36. 1955 Pittsburgh Pirates	−3.31
12. 1903 Washington Senators	−3.79	37. 1965 New York Mets	−3.30
13. 1974 Detroit Tigers	−3.78	38. 1910 St. Louis Browns	−3.29
14. 1988 Baltimore Orioles	−3.75	39. 1973 Texas Rangers	−3.27
15. 1974 San Diego Padres	−3.74	40. 1942 Philadelphia Phillies	−3.25
16. 1979 Oakland Athletics	−3.71	41. 1979 Toronto Blue Jays	−3.23
17. 1908 New York Highlanders	−3.68	42. 1971 Cleveland Indians	−3.23
18. 1941 Philadelphia Phillies	−3.66	43. 1987 Cleveland Indians	−3.21
19. 1951 St. Louis Browns	−3.64	44. 1990 New York Yankees	−3.20
20. 1989 Detroit Tigers	−3.58	45. 1934 Cincinnati Reds	−3.20
21. 1988 Atlanta Braves	−3.58	46. 1937 St. Louis Browns	−3.18
22. 1903 St. Louis Cardinals	−3.57	47. 1924 Boston Braves	−3.13
23. 1962 Chicago Cubs	−3.53	48. 1932 Boston Red Sox	−3.12
24. 1913 St. Louis Cardinals	−3.51	49. 1977 Seattle Mariners	−3.10
25. 1975 Detroit Tigers	−3.46	50. 1918 Philadelphia Athletics	−3.08

The Bottom 50 Two-Year SD Scores of the Twentieth Century

1. 1962–63 New York Mets	−9.90		26. 1964–65 New York Mets	−6.14
2. 1938–39 Philadelphia Phillies	−8.04		27. 1978–79 Toronto Blue Jays	−5.98
3. 1903–04 Washington Senators	−7.61		28. 1978–79 Oakland Athletics	−5.88
4. 1918–19 Philadelphia Athletics	−7.43		29. 1972–73 San Diego Padres	−5.86
5. 1919–20 Philadelphia Athletics	−7.38		30. 1945–46 Philadelphia Phillies	−5.86
6. 1915–16 Philadelphia Athletics	−7.38		31. 1950–51 St. Louis Browns	−5.86
7. 1974–75 Detroit Tigers	−7.24		32. 1907–08 St. Louis Cardinals	−5.79
8. 1973–74 San Diego Padres	−7.15		33. 1988–89 Atlanta Braves	−5.73
9. 1939–40 Philadelphia Phillies	−7.05		34. 1902–03 St. Louis Cardinals	−5.72
10. 1941–42 Philadelphia Phillies	−6.91		35. 1920–21 Philadelphia Phillies	−5.70
11. 1942–43 Philadelphia Athletics	−6.89		36. 1921–22 Philadelphia Phillies	−5.65
12. 1952–53 Pittsburgh Pirates	−6.85		37. 1977–78 Atlanta Braves	−5.64
13. 1963–64 New York Mets	−6.84		38. 1954–55 Kansas City Athletics	−5.59
14. 1940–41 Philadelphia Phillies	−6.70		39. 1957–58 Washington Senators	−5.58
15. 1954–55 Pittsburgh Pirates	−6.70		40. 1933–34 Cincinnati Reds	−5.57
16. 1995–96 Detroit Tigers	−6.66		41. 1911–12 St. Louis Browns	−5.57
17. 1916–17 Philadelphia Athletics	−6.65		42. 1920–21 Philadelphia Athletics	−5.56
18. 1960–61 Philadelphia Phillies	−6.55		43. 1965–66 New York Mets	−5.56
19. 1977–78 Seattle Mariners	−6.47		44. 1912–13 St. Louis Cardinals	−5.55
20. 1925–26 Boston Red Sox	−6.45		45. 1926–27 Boston Red Sox	−5.55
21. 1951–52 Pittsburgh Pirates	−6.36		46. 1937–38 Philadelphia Phillies	−5.55
22. 1910–11 St. Louis Browns	−6.28		47. 1936–37 St. Louis Browns	−5.54
23. 1972–73 Texas Rangers	−6.25		48. 1937–38 St. Louis Browns	−5.54
24. 1953–54 Pittsburgh Pirates	−6.25		49. 1923–24 Boston Braves	−5.53
25. 1987–88 Baltimore Orioles	−6.16		50. 1951–52 St. Louis Browns	−5.53

The Bottom 50 Three-Year SD Scores of the Twentieth Century

1. 1962–64 New York Mets	−12.75		9. 1916–18 Philadelphia Athletics	−9.73
2. 1938–40 Philadelphia Phillies	−11.08		10. 1917–19 Philadelphia Athletics	−9.70
3. 1939–41 Philadelphia Phillies	−10.71		11. 1915–17 Philadelphia Athletics	−9.64
4. 1918–20 Philadelphia Athletics	−10.47		12. 1972–74 San Diego Padres	−9.60
5. 1952–54 Pittsburgh Pirates	−10.23		13. 1953–55 Pittsburgh Pirates	−9.56
6. 1963–65 New York Mets	−10.13		14. 1937–39 Philadelphia Phillies	−9.56
7. 1940–42 Philadelphia Phillies	−9.95		15. 1959–61 Philadelphia Phillies	−9.23
8. 1919–21 Philadelphia Athletics	−9.92		16. 1951–53 Pittsburgh Pirates	−9.22

17.	1974–76 Detroit Tigers	−9.08		34.	1921–23 Philadelphia Phillies	−8.05
18.	1925–27 Boston Red Sox	−8.94		35.	1926–28 Philadelphia Phillies	−8.02
19.	1973–75 San Diego Padres	−8.93		36.	1973–75 Detroit Tigers	−7.98
20.	1950–52 Pittsburgh Pirates	−8.91		37.	1920–22 Philadelphia Phillies	−7.94
21.	1910–12 St. Louis Browns	−8.86		38.	1960–62 Chicago Cubs	−7.93
22.	1903–05 Washington Senators	−8.77		39.	1977–79 Seattle Mariners	−7.90
23.	1977–79 Toronto Blue Jays	−8.76		40.	1936–38 St. Louis Browns	−7.89
24.	1941–43 Philadelphia Athletics	−8.58		41.	1904–06 Boston Beaneaters	−7.89
25.	1964–66 New York Mets	−8.40		42.	1978–80 Toronto Blue Jays	−7.89
26.	1902–04 Washington Senators	−8.39		43.	1935–37 St. Louis Browns	−7.89
27.	1941–43 Philadelphia Phillies	−8.34		44.	1909–11 St. Louis Browns	−7.87
28.	1965–67 New York Mets	−8.28		45.	1937–39 St. Louis Browns	−7.87
29.	1922–24 Boston Braves	−8.25		46.	1943–45 Philadelphia Athletics	−7.85
30.	1956–58 Washington Senators	−8.24		47.	1988–90 Atlanta Braves	−7.78
31.	1949–51 St. Louis Browns	−8.19		48.	1919–21 Philadelphia Phillies	−7.76
32.	1951–53 St. Louis Browns	−8.11		49.	1950–52 St. Louis Browns	−7.74
33.	1971–73 Texas Rangers	−8.05		50.	1954–56 Kansas City Athletics	−7.74

The Bottom 50 Four-Year SD Scores of the Twentieth Century

1.	1962–65 New York Mets	−16.04		19.	1971–74 San Diego Padres	−11.05
2.	1938–41 Philadelphia Phillies	−14.74		20.	1940–43 Philadelphia Athletics	−11.03
3.	1916–19 Philadelphia Athletics	−14.08		21.	1958–61 Philadelphia Phillies	−10.80
4.	1939–42 Philadelphia Phillies	−13.96		22.	1903–06 Washington Senators	−10.72
5.	1952–55 Pittsburgh Pirates	−13.54		23.	1923–26 Boston Red Sox	−10.69
6.	1918–21 Philadelphia Athletics	−13.00		24.	1977–80 Toronto Blue Jays	−10.67
7.	1917–20 Philadelphia Athletics	−12.73		25.	1977–80 Seattle Mariners	−10.55
8.	1915–18 Philadelphia Athletics	−12.73		26.	1909–12 St. Louis Browns	−10.46
9.	1951–54 Pittsburgh Pirates	−12.61		27.	1942–45 Philadelphia Athletics	−10.43
10.	1937–40 Philadelphia Phillies	−12.60		28.	1953–56 Pittsburgh Pirates	−10.41
11.	1963–66 New York Mets	−12.40		29.	1920–23 Philadelphia Phillies	−10.35
12.	1950–53 Pittsburgh Pirates	−11.77		30.	1950–53 St. Louis Browns	−10.33
13.	1919–22 Philadelphia Athletics	−11.54		31.	1910–13 St. Louis Browns	−10.29
14.	1972–75 San Diego Padres	−11.38		32.	1935–38 St. Louis Browns	−10.24
15.	1940–43 Philadelphia Phillies	−11.38		33.	1955–58 Washington Senators	−10.23
16.	1936–39 Philadelphia Phillies	−11.37		34.	1936–39 St. Louis Browns	−10.22
17.	1964–67 New York Mets	−11.12		35.	1949–52 Pittsburgh Pirates	−10.19
18.	1925–28 Boston Red Sox	−11.08		36.	1959–62 Philadelphia Phillies	−10.15

37.	1924–27 Boston Red Sox	−10.11		
38.	1949–52 St. Louis Browns	−10.08		
39.	1973–76 San Diego Padres	−10.06		
40.	1948–51 St. Louis Browns	−10.04		
41.	1919–22 Philadelphia Phillies	−10.01		
42.	1921–24 Philadelphia Phillies	−9.96		
43.	1904–07 Boston Beaneaters	−9.95		

44.	1951–54 Baltimore Orioles	−9.90
45.	1954–57 Kansas City Athletics	−9.90
46.	1943–46 Philadelphia Athletics	−9.87
47.	1941–44 Philadelphia Phillies	−9.86
48.	1936–39 Philadelphia Athletics	−9.84
49.	1973–76 Detroit Tigers	−9.82
50.	1901–04 Washington Senators	−9.73

The Bottom 50 Five-Year SD Scores of the Twentieth Century

1.	1962–66 New York Mets	−18.30		26.	1922–26 Boston Red Sox	−12.78
2.	1938–42 Philadelphia Phillies	−17.98		27.	1949–53 St. Louis Browns	−12.66
3.	1916–20 Philadelphia Athletics	−17.12		28.	1935–39 St. Louis Browns	−12.57
4.	1915–19 Philadelphia Athletics	−17.08		29.	1972–76 San Diego Padres	−12.51
5.	1937–41 Philadelphia Phillies	−16.26		30.	1969–73 San Diego Padres	−12.48
6.	1951–55 Pittsburgh Pirates	−15.92		31.	1942–46 Philadelphia Athletics	−12.45
7.	1939–43 Philadelphia Phillies	−15.39		32.	1919–23 Philadelphia Phillies	−12.41
8.	1917–21 Philadelphia Athletics	−15.26		33.	1951–55 Baltimore Orioles	−12.32
9.	1950–54 Pittsburgh Pirates	−15.16		34.	1936–40 Philadelphia Athletics	−12.29
10.	1963–67 New York Mets	−15.12		35.	1920–24 Philadelphia Phillies	−12.26
11.	1918–22 Philadelphia Athletics	−14.62		36.	1924–28 Boston Red Sox	−12.26
12.	1936–40 Philadelphia Phillies	−14.41		37.	1953–57 Pittsburgh Pirates	−12.17
13.	1952–56 Pittsburgh Pirates	−14.39		38.	1941–45 Philadelphia Athletics	−12.12
14.	1939–43 Philadelphia Athletics	−13.53		39.	1950–54 Baltimore Orioles	−12.12
15.	1903–07 Washington Senators	−13.40		40.	1942–46 Philadelphia Phillies	−12.06
16.	1935–39 Philadelphia Phillies	−13.33		41.	1948–52 St. Louis Browns	−11.93
17.	1941–45 Philadelphia Phillies	−13.29		42.	1909–13 St. Louis Browns	−11.89
18.	1923–27 Boston Red Sox	−13.19		43.	1973–77 San Diego Padres	−11.88
19.	1949–53 Pittsburgh Pirates	−13.05		44.	1938–42 Philadelphia Athletics	−11.85
20.	1940–44 Philadelphia Phillies	−12.90		45.	1985–89 Atlanta Braves	−11.74
21.	1925–29 Boston Red Sox	−12.89		46.	1934–38 St. Louis Browns	−11.74
22.	1970–74 San Diego Padres	−12.84		47.	1935–39 Philadelphia Athletics	−11.72
23.	1919–23 Philadelphia Athletics	−12.84		48.	1958–62 Philadelphia Phillies	−11.72
24.	1971–75 San Diego Padres	−12.83		49.	1955–59 Washington Senators	−11.67
25.	1947–51 St. Louis Browns	−12.79		50.	1940–44 Philadelphia Athletics	−11.62